THE PROGRESSES, PAGEANTS, AND
ENTERTAINMENTS OF QUEEN ELIZABETH I

The Progresses, Pageants, and Entertainments of Queen Elizabeth I

Edited by
JAYNE ELISABETH ARCHER
ELIZABETH GOLDRING
and
SARAH KNIGHT

OXFORD
UNIVERSITY PRESS

OXFORD
UNIVERSITY PRESS

Great Clarendon Street, Oxford OX2 6DP

Oxford University Press is a department of the University of Oxford.
It furthers the University's objective of excellence in research, scholarship,
and education by publishing worldwide in

Oxford New York

Auckland Cape Town Dar es Salaam Hong Kong Karachi
Kuala Lumpur Madrid Melbourne Mexico City Nairobi
New Delhi Shanghai Taipei Toronto

With offices in

Argentina Austria Brazil Chile Czech Republic France Greece
Guatemala Hungary Italy Japan Poland Portugal Singapore
South Korea Switzerland Thailand Turkey Ukraine Vietnam

Oxford is a registered trade mark of Oxford University Press
in the UK and in certain other countries

Published in the United States
by Oxford University Press Inc., New York

British Library Cataloguing in Publication Data

Data available

Library of Congress Cataloging in Publication Data

Data available

Typeset by Laserwords Private Ltd., Chennai, India
Printed in Great Britain
on acid-free paper by
Biddles Ltd., King's Lynn, Norfolk

ISBN 978–0–19–929157–1

1 3 5 7 9 10 8 6 4 2

Preface and Acknowledgements

This volume of essays has grown out of work undertaken on the University of Warwick's John Nichols Research Project, for which a new edition of Nichols's seminal *Progresses and Public Processions of Queen Elizabeth* (London, 1788–1823) is being prepared for publication by Oxford University Press. Seven of the essays in this collection were first presented as papers at the Elizabethan Progresses Conference, held at the Shakespeare Centre in Stratford-upon-Avon in April 2004, and organized under the auspices of the Nichols Project and Warwick's AHRB (now AHRC) Centre for the Study of Renaissance Elites and Court Cultures. The Conference received generous support from the British Academy and the University of Warwick's Humanities Research Centre.

Our deepest thanks are due to Dr Elizabeth Clarke, Director of the Nichols Project; to Professors Julian Gardner and Steve Hindle, successive Directors of the AHRC Centre for the Study of Renaissance Elites and Court Cultures; to Professor Michael Whitby, Pro-Vice-Chancellor of the University of Warwick; and to the members of the Steering Committee of the Nichols Project, in particular Professor Bernard Capp, Dr H. Neville Davies, Mr Julian Pooley, and Dr Sarah Ross. We would like to express our sincere gratitude to Dr Margaret Shewring and Professor J. R. Mulryne, former Directors of the Nichols Project and of the AHRC Centre, respectively. The Nichols Project was conceived and initiated by Dr Shewring and Professor Mulryne; without their scholarly expertise, commitment, and vision, this publication would not have been possible. We would also like to thank the Arts and Humanities Research Council for its generous financial support of the Nichols Project. Finally, we are indebted to Andrew McNeillie, Val Shelley, Tom Perridge, Christine Rode, and Elizabeth Robottom of Oxford University Press for their unfailing patience and support in bringing this volume to completion and to Lawrence Green for compiling the index.

J.E.A., E.G., and S.K.

Contents

III. PRIVATE RECEPTIONS FOR QUEEN ELIZABETH I

IV. AFTERLIFE: CAROLINE AND ANTIQUARIAN
PERSPECTIVES

Notes on Contributors

Dr Jayne Archer is lecturer in Medieval and Renaissance Literature in the Department of English, University of Wales (Aberystwyth). She is an Associate Fellow of the Centre for the Study of the Renaissance, University of Warwick, where she spent four years as AHRC postdoctoral Research Fellow on the John Nichols Project. She is General Editor of *Court and Culture in the Reign of Queen Elizabeth I: A New Edition of John Nichols's Progresses* (OUP, forthcoming), and has published articles on Elizabethan and Jacobean masques, early modern women's receipt books, and alchemy in early modern literature. She is currently working on a book-length study of the relationship between housewifery and natural philosophy in early modern England.

David M. Bergeron, Professor of English, University of Kansas, has published extensively on civic pageantry. His well-known book *English Civic Pageantry 1558–1642* has been republished in a revised edition (Arizona State University Press, 2003). His most recent book, *Textual Patronage in English Drama, 1570–1640* (Ashgate, 2006), focuses on epistles dedicatory and addresses to readers in dramatic texts. He has published widely on Shakespeare, Renaissance drama, and the Stuart royal family, including *King James and Letters of Homoerotic Desire* (University of Iowa Press, 1999) and *Practicing Renaissance Scholarship* (Duquesne University Press, 2000).

Mary Hill Cole is Professor of History at Mary Baldwin College, Virginia. She is the author of *The Portable Queen: Elizabeth I and the Politics of Ceremony* (University of Massachusetts Press, 1999), a study of the Elizabethan progresses. She has published essays in the collections *Ceremony and Text in the Renaissance* (University of Delaware Press; Associated University Presses, 1996) and *Elizabeth I: Always her Own Free Woman* (Ashgate, 2003). Her article 'Maternal Memory: Elizabeth Tudor's Anne Boleyn' was recently published in *Explorations in Renaissance Culture* (Summer 2004). She is currently engaged in research for a book on women in Tudor England.

Professor Patrick Collinson read History at Cambridge and carried out doctoral research in London which was the basis of *The Elizabethan Puritan Movement* (Cape, 1967). He held lectureships in the University of Khartoum and King's College, London; and chairs in the universities of Sydney, Kent at Canterbury, Sheffield, and Cambridge, where he was Regius Professor of Modern History. He is a Fellow of Trinity College, Cambridge. He has delivered the Ford Lectures in Oxford (published as *The Religion of Protestants* (Clarendon Press, 1982)) and the Birkbeck Lectures in Cambridge. He is a Fellow of the British Academy. His new book will be *From Cranmer to Sancroft*, a collection of essays on religion in post-Reformation England.

Peter Davidson is Chalmers Regius Professor of English in the University of Aberdeen and Chair of the Aberdeen Centre for Early Modern Studies. His most recent publications are *Early Modern Women Poets* (OUP, 2001), edited in collaboration with Jane Stevenson, and *The Idea of North* (Reaktion, 2005).

Dr Elizabeth Goldring is a Research Fellow in the University of Warwick's Centre for the Study of the Renaissance and an Associate Fellow of Warwick's History of Art Department. She is a General Editor of *Court and Culture in the Reign of Queen Elizabeth I: A New Edition of John Nichols's Progresses* (OUP, forthcoming), for which she has edited several entertainment texts, including those pertaining to the 1575 Kenilworth festivities. Previous publications include (co-editor) *Court Festivals of the European Renaissance: Art, Politics and Performance* (Ashgate, 2002) and (Associate General Editor) *Europa Triumphans: Court and Civic Festivals in Early Modern Europe* (Ashgate, 2004). In 2006 she served as Consultant to English Heritage for the exhibition 'Queen and Castle: Robert Dudley's Kenilworth'. Current projects include a book-length study of the Sidney–Leicester circle's patronage of the arts.

Dr Felicity Heal is a lecturer in the Faculty of History, University of Oxford, and a Fellow of Jesus College. She has published extensively in various historical fields, including sixteenth-century English society and the Reformation. She has written books on the Tudor bishops, hospitality in early modern England, and, with Clive Holmes, on the gentry of England and Wales. Her latest volume is *Reformation in Britain and Ireland* (OUP, 2003), and more recently she has written on the English Reformers and Early Church History. Her current research is on gift exchange in early modern Britain.

Dr Elizabeth Heale teaches in the School of English and American Literature at Reading University. She is a member of the University's Early Modern Research Centre where she helps to run an interdisciplinary MA which first stimulated her work on the Cowdray entertainment. Her publications have included *The Faerie Queene: A Reader's Guide* (Cambridge University Press, 1987) and *Wyatt, Surrey and Early Tudor Poetry* (Longman, 1998). Her most recent book is *Autobiography and Authorship in Renaissance Verse* (Palgrave Macmillan, 2004). Other research interests include verse miscellanies in the early and mid-Tudor periods and Renaissance adventurers.

Gabriel Heaton completed his doctorate at the University of Cambridge in 2003. From 2003 to 2005 he was a Research Fellow on the John Nichols Project at the University of Warwick. He is an Associate General Editor of *Court and Culture in the Reign of Queen Elizabeth I: A New Edition of John Nichols's Progresses* (OUP, forthcoming) and has contributed essays to *The Review of English Studies* (2003), *Huntington Library Quarterly*, and *Queen Elizabeth I and the Culture of Writing* (The British Library, 2006). He is currently working on a book provisionally entitled *Reading and Writing Court Entertainments: From George Gascoigne to Ben Jonson* (OUP, forthcoming). He now works as a manuscript specialist in the Department of Printed Books and Manuscripts at Sotheby's.

Dr Siobhan Keenan is a senior lecturer in English Literature at De Montfort University, Leicester. She has published a number of essays on theatre history and Renaissance drama, and is the author of *Travelling Players in Shakespeare's England* (Palgrave Macmillan, 2002), which was short-listed for the Theatre Society Book Prize 2002. Her current research projects include studies of a seventeenth-century woman's manuscript miscellany and a Caroline closet drama. She has research interests in Shakespeare, Renaissance drama and poetry, early modern women's writing, and theatre history.

Dr Sarah Knight is lecturer in Shakespeare and Renaissance Literature at the University of Leicester. She has published essays on early seventeenth-century satire and on academic print culture in Elizabethan and Jacobean England, and has translated and co-edited Leon Battista Alberti's *Momus* for the I Tatti Renaissance Library (Harvard University Press, 2003). Dr Knight is Associate General Editor of *Court and Culture in the Reign of Queen Elizabeth I* (OUP, forthcoming), and as Section Editor has edited and translated material relating to the University of Oxford. She is currently working on a study of satire and learning in early modern England.

James Knowles is Professor of English at Keele University. He has edited Jonson's *Entertainments* and selected *Masques* for the forthcoming Cambridge University Press *Complete Works of Ben Jonson*. He co-curated an exhibition, 'Royalist Refugees', on William and Margaret Cavendish in exile, for the Rubenshuis in Antwerp, which opened in September 2006, and is editing a book on Cavendish's patronage, provisionally titled *Prince of the Northern Quarter*.

Hester Lees-Jeffries took her first degrees in New Zealand before coming to Cambridge as a UK Commonwealth Scholar in 1999; she completed her doctoral thesis on fountains in Renaissance literature in 2002. Formerly a Research Fellow at Magdalene College, Cambridge, she is now a college lecturer and Fellow of St Catharine's College, Cambridge, where she is finishing her book *England's Helicon: Fountains in Early Modern Literature and Culture* (OUP, forthcoming). She has published on the *Hypnerotomachia Poliphili*, the *Roman de la Rose*, and works by Sidney, Spenser, and Jonson, and has worked on the new Cambridge editions of the works of John Webster and Ben Jonson. Her next project is about Shakespeare and memory.

C. E. McGee is a professor in the English Department of St Jerome's University, at the University of Waterloo, Canada, where he teaches courses in Renaissance English Drama, Shakespeare in Performance, and Editing Literary Texts. He has edited several texts of early modern English entertainments, including, most recently, *The World Tossed at Tennis* for the Oxford Middleton and *The Presentment of Mr Bushell's Rock* in *Medieval and Renaissance Drama in England* (2003). He is currently working in collaboration with others on the *Records of Early English Drama: Wiltshire* and the *New Variorum Shakespeare Othello*.

Julian Pooley is an archivist at Surrey History Centre, Woking, and Honorary Visiting Fellow of the Centre for English Local History at the University of Leicester. He is preparing an analytical guide to the archive of the Nichols family of printers and antiquaries between the time of John Nichols (1745–1826) and the death of his grandson John Gough Nichols in 1873. His recent publications have included an article (written with Robin Myers) on the Nichols family for the *New Oxford DNB*, and studies of the importance of John Nichols in the literary and antiquarian networks of the late eighteenth century for the *New Rambler* (2003/4) and *Surrey Archaeological Collections*.

Jane Stevenson is Reader in the School of Divinity, History, and Philosophy, University of Aberdeen. Her most recent publications include *Early Modern Women Poets* (OUP, 2001), a novel *The Empress of the Last Days* (Cape, 2003), and *Women Latin Poets: Language, Gender, and Authority from Antiquity to the Eighteenth Century* (OUP, 2005).

List of Illustrations

List of Maps

1

Elizabetha Triumphans

Jayne Elisabeth Archer and Sarah Knight

THE RIDDLE OF THE PROGRESSES

So deare a darling is *Elizabeth*,
Renowned Queene of this renowned land,
Renowned land, because a fruitfull soile:
Renowned land through people of the same:
And thrise renown'd by this her Virgin Queene,[1]

At the opening of *Elizabetha Triumphans* (1588), James Aske invokes the vital and fraught interconnectedness of the bodies of the English Queen, her subjects, and her land. Although he writes in celebration of a naval victory, the Armada, it is telling that Aske begins (and will, indeed, end) his poem with an evocation of the monarch's 'two bodies', and with an affirmation of the embeddedness of both within the 'fruitfull soile', the matter of England.[2] What is remarkable about Aske's poem is how very typical it is of Elizabethan rhetoric by and for the Queen. No other English (or British) monarch has been so closely identified with the land. Nowhere, perhaps, is that identification more powerful than in the Elizabethan progresses—the ritual dance in which the Queen *performed* the mystical relationship between her 'Virgin' body and the fertile matter of England.

The progresses have long fascinated and puzzled historians of Elizabethan England. Like the riddle of Sphinx, the Elizabethan progresses seem to demand—and defy—interpretation. The monumental works of John Nichols

---

The authors would like to thank Elizabeth Goldring, Faith Eales, and Gabriel Heaton for their generous advice and help.

[1] James Aske, *Elizabetha Triumphans* (London: by Thomas Orwin for Thomas Gubbin and Thomas Newman, 1588), 1.

[2] On the monarch's 'two bodies', see Ernst H. Kantorowicz, *The King's Two Bodies: A Study in Medieval Political Theology* (Princeton: Princeton University Press, 1957), and Marie Axton, *The Queen's Two Bodies: Drama and the Elizabethan Succession* (London: Royal Historical Society, 1977).

and E. K. Chambers have enabled generations of nineteenth-, twentieth-, and now twenty-first-century scholars to navigate their own journeys through the vastness and complexities of the topography and timescale of the Elizabethan progresses.[3] Historians and literary historians have used Elizabethan entertainment texts to examine the symbolism used by courtiers and by Elizabeth herself, and to find in them evidence of a dialogue—part critical, part complimentary—between subjects and monarch.[4] This work has been supplemented by studies of particular progresses, pageants, and entertainments, and by the editing of entertainment texts, most notably Jean Wilson's *Entertainments for Elizabeth* (1980) and in the ongoing work of Records of Early English Drama.[5]

But still the riddle of the Elizabethan progresses remains. Explanations and excuses have been offered: the Queen's love of travel and her quest for fresh hunting grounds; an effort to escape the accumulated filth and disease of a large court during the long, hot summer months; and, perhaps, an attempt to offload the expenses of the court onto civic and private hosts. But such hypotheses seem more like contexts rather than pretexts—and certainly not reasons—for Elizabeth's erratic peregrinations. Ugly facts get in the way of these beautiful hypotheses: for long periods of her reign, Elizabeth did not go on summer progress; large areas of England were never visited by her;[6] and the progresses

---

[3] *The Progresses and Public Processions of Queen Elizabeth*, ed. John Nichols, 2nd edn., 3 vols. (London: John Nichols, 1823); E. K. Chambers, *The Elizabethan Stage*, 4 vols. (Oxford: Clarendon Press, 1923).

[4] Philippa Berry, *Of Chastity and Power: Elizabethan Literature and the Unmarried Queen* (London: Routledge, 1989), esp. pp. 92–110; Mary Hill Cole, *The Portable Queen: Elizabeth I and the Politics of Ceremony* (Amherst: University of Massachusetts Press, 1999); William Leahy, *Elizabethan Triumphal Processions* (Aldershot: Ashgate, 2004); Matthew Woodcock, *Fairy in 'The Faerie Queene': Renaissance Elf-Fashioning and Elizabethan Myth-Making* (Aldershot: Ashgate, 2004).

[5] Jean Wilson, *Entertainments for Elizabeth* (Woodbridge: Brewer, 1980). For examples of recent work on specific entertainments, see Curtis Breight, 'Caressing the Great: Viscount Montague's Entertainment of Elizabeth at Cowdray, 1591', *Sussex Archaeological Collections*, 127 (1989), 147–66, and 'Realpolitik and Elizabethan Ceremony: The Earl of Hertford's Entertainment of Elizabeth at Elvetham, 1591', *Renaissance Quarterly*, 45 (1992), 20–48; Marion Colthorpe, 'The Disputed Date of the Theobalds Entertainment, 1591', *REED Newsletter*, 19.2 (1994), 19, and 'Entertainments of Elizabeth at Theobalds in the Early 1590s', *REED Newsletter*, 12.2 (1987), 1–9; Patricia Howard, 'Time in Entertainments for Queen Elizabeth I: 1590–1602', *University of Toronto Quarterly*, 65.3 (Summer 1996), 467–81; Michael Leslie, ' "Something nasty in the wilderness": Entertaining Queen Elizabeth on her Progresses', *Medieval and Renaissance Drama in England*, 10 (1998), 47–72. Modern editions of progress entertainments include Marion Colthorpe, 'The Theobalds Entertainment for Queen Elizabeth I in 1591, with a Transcript of the Gardener's Speech', *REED Newsletter*, 12.1 (1987), 2–9, and 'An Entertainment for Queen Elizabeth I at Wimbledon in 1599', *REED Newsletter*, 10.1 (1985), 1–2; John Lyly, *Queen Elizabeth's Entertainment at Mitcham*, ed. Leslie Hotson (New Haven: Yale University Press, 1953); *The Lady of May* (1578), in *Miscellaneous Prose of Sir Philip Sidney*, ed. Katherine Duncan-Jones and Jan Van Dorsten (Oxford: Clarendon Press, 1973); Robert Langham, *A Letter*, ed. R. J. P. Kuin (Leiden: Brill, 1983).

[6] The possible reasons for these omissions—threats of opposition and revolt in the north, heightened by the presence of Mary Stuart in the 1560s; fears of foreign invasion in the 1580s; and the perennial problems of bad weather, plague, and ill health—are discussed by Mary Hill Cole and Patrick Collinson in this volume: Cole, 'Monarchy in Motion: An Overview of Elizabethan

were—as Burghley and Walsingham frequently lamented—costly to the royal household and detrimental to the conduct of government.[7] Perhaps most satisfyingly, the progresses have been interpreted as an exercise in a thoroughly postmodern, feminocentric form of statecraft. In *The Portable Queen*, Mary Hill Cole argues that Elizabeth's apparent caprice—deciding to stay on, leave early, change direction on a whim—enabled her to be the still centre of her turning world:

> For Elizabeth, going on progress reiterated her central position in the country and in the court. The constant disruption of court life inherent in her progresses generated a climate of chaos . . . whose effect was to keep the queen at the center of everyone's attention, as courtiers and hosts focused on welcoming, entertaining, and petitioning her. Elizabeth's travels inconvenienced every member of the court and hurt her treasury, but as queen she found power in the turmoil of an itinerant court and in a ceremonial dialogue with her subjects.[8]

In Cole's analysis, the 'portable' court is not an early modern mobile panopticon. Rather, it enables Elizabeth to exploit the uncertainties and caprices afforded by the stereotypes of her sex and by life on the road. Thus, Elizabeth becomes a kind of 'dancing queen', who plays off against one another her subjects, hosts, members of the court, the royal household, and the Privy Counsellors.

The essays in this volume reflect current and future directions in research on the Elizabethan progresses. In differing ways, these essays reflect upon the progresses, entertainments, and pageants of Queen Elizabeth I as negotiations in power and meaning—a ceremonial dance in and through which hosts (civic and private), subjects, Queen, and Privy Counsellors compete to represent and advance their interests. The book is interdisciplinary, including work in history, literary history, drama and performance, art history, and antiquarian studies. It is divided into four broad, overlapping sections: patterns, themes, and contexts of the Elizabethan progresses; civic and academic receptions; private receptions; and the 'afterlife' of the Elizabethan progresses, as they were reinvented by subsequent generations.

In her overview of the Elizabethan progresses, Mary Hill Cole gives us some purchase on the scope and nature of this otherwise sprawling, unwieldy phenomenon. Drawing on extant records in regional archives, Cole shows that they afforded an unique opportunity for cities and towns to petition the Queen for grants, licences, charters, and privileges. Felicity Heal looks in detail at the ritual

Progresses', pp. 43–5; Patrick Collinson, 'Pulling the Strings: Religion and Politics in the Progress of 1578', p. 122 n. 1.

[7] On these points, see Cole, *Portable Queen*, 19–25, 58–61. For example, regarding the geographical extent of the progresses, Cole (pp. 23–5) notes that Elizabeth traversed a relatively small area, a 'diamond' extending as far as Stafford (in the north), Norwich (in the east), Southampton (in the south), and Bristol (in the west).

[8] Ibid. 4–5.

of gift-giving—an essential component of a royal visit—by which hosts sought
to entangle the Queen within a relationship of mutual obligations. Despite their
objections to the expense and disruption caused by the sometimes lengthy and
chaotic summer progresses, Privy Counsellors could exploit these journeys into
the regions in order to further their own policies and interests. Patrick Collinson's
account of the 1578 progress through East Anglia is assembled, in part, from the
correspondence of William Cecil, Robert Dudley, Earl of Leicester, and Francis
Walsingham among others. David Bergeron considers the Norwich festivities
of 1578—the 'highlight' of the East Anglian progress—from a very different
perspective. Examining Thomas Churchyard's published account of the entertainments devised for that visit, Bergeron points to the development of a sharply
defined authorial 'I' who is less concerned with recreating the royal visit as it was
experienced by Queen and subjects than with promoting his own distinct voice
and creative genius. Examining the ways in which towns and cities transformed
the forms, devices, and props of traditional pageants and entertainments, C. E.
McGee shows how local, provincial identities could be sharpened by a royal
visit. In Hester Lees-Jeffries's contribution to this volume, the city in question is
London. Lees-Jeffries turns to the first entertainment to be performed before the
newly crowned Queen Elizabeth, and, in particular, the pageant *Veritas Temporis
Filia* (1559). Here, the cityscape, infused with history and memory, becomes part
of the imaginary world of the entertainment text, and the Queen—as on so many
subsequent occasions—is required to play her part and listen to the advice of her
people. Institutions also used the Queen's visits to offer polite counsel. Siobhan
Keenan looks at Elizabeth's progresses to the English universities—Cambridge
in 1564; Oxford in 1566 and 1592—in order to identify the political advice
proffered in the plays, orations, and debates performed before the Queen. (We
will return to Elizabeth's visits to Oxford later in this Introduction.) Elizabeth
Heale examines Lord Montague's use of the Queen's visit to Cowdray in 1591 to
assert his loyalty because—and not in spite—of his Catholicism, and to question
recent legislation against recusancy. Elizabeth Goldring considers Robert Dudley,
Earl of Leicester's use of portraiture and maps, displayed in his picture gallery as
part of the 1575 Kenilworth festivities, to promote visually his desire to advance
his interests—personal, political, and religious. For Leicester, print seems to have
offered another mechanism through which he could disseminate this agenda to
a wider audience. But private hosts could also promote themselves by generating
and circulating manuscript accounts of the hospitality they lavished upon the
Queen. In his analysis of the extant accounts of the Harefield entertainment of
1602, Gabriel Heaton shows how the Egerton family participated in the dissemination of accounts of this event, but also points to ways in which the appetite for
such accounts generated 'unofficial' versions, some of which could run counter
to the host's particular agenda. Self-presentation is also at the heart of the entertainment that is the focus of the essay by Peter Davidson and Jane Stevenson.
Davidson and Stevenson read the Bisham entertainment of 1592 in the context

of Elizabeth, Lady Russell's lifelong programme of self-promotion, which took in funeral inscriptions, Latin verse, and the commissioning of funerary monuments. Such a varied career leads Davidson and Stevenson to advance the idea of Lady Russell as a 'deviser' of the Bisham entertainment—a term which remains sensitive to the nature of the contribution of women patrons such as Lady Russell, but which also recognizes the heterogeneous character of progress entertainments.

In the concluding section, James Knowles and Julian Pooley look to the continuing influence of the Elizabethan progresses, as they were transformed by subsequent generations as part of very different political and intellectual programmes. James Knowles reads the entertainment at Welbeck Abbey in 1633—devised by Ben Jonson for William Cavendish, Earl of Newcastle—in the light of the 1575 Kenilworth festivities, arguing that by identifying himself with the Earl of Leicester, Cavendish invoked Caroline nostalgia for all things Elizabethan in order to criticize and instruct the government, court, and kingship of Charles I. Finally, Julian Pooley examines the intellectual concerns and editorial practices that governed the composition of John Nichols's *Progresses and Public Processions of Queen Elizabeth*, the collection of Elizabethan entertainment texts and related—sometimes curiously *unrelated*—material that was published in two editions and seven volumes between 1788 and 1823. Nichols's *Progresses* is the antiquarian filter through which we still map the movements of Queen Elizabeth. It is to the nascent antiquarianism of Elizabethan writers that we will now turn, in order to re-examine the progresses as a performance of royal chorography.

THE LIBRARY OF QUEEN ELIZABETH

In 1586, the year in which the first Latin edition of his *Britannia* was published, William Camden participated in the formation of the Society of Antiquaries.[9] For the next eighteen years, the Society met to discuss the topography, customs, and institutions of England. In 1602, three of its members presented a petition to Queen Elizabeth, requesting 'the Erecting of a Library and an Academy for the Study of Antiquities and History':

1. The scope of this petition, is to preserve divers old books concerning the matter of history of this realm, original charters, and monuments, in a library to be erected in some convenient place of the hospital of the Savoy, St. Johns, or elsewhere.

---

[9] Other founding members of the Society of Antiquaries included Sir Robert Cotton, Archbishop Matthew Parker, and John Stow. On the Elizabethan Society of Antiquaries, see: Joan Evans, *A History of the Society of Antiquaries* (Oxford: Oxford University Press, 1956); Linda Van Norden, 'The Elizabethan College of Antiquaries' (unpublished doctoral dissertation, University of California at Los Angeles, 1946). On antiquarianism in early modern England and Britain, see Graham Parry, *The Triumphs of Time: English Antiquaries of the Seventeenth Century* (Oxford: Oxford University Press, 1995), esp. 'William Camden' (pp. 22–48), and on the Society of Antiquaries (pp. 43–5); Stuart Piggott, *Ancient Britons and the Antiquarian Imagination: Ideas from the Renaissance to the Regency* (London: Thames and Hudson, 1989).

2. Secondly, for the better information of all noblemen and gentlemen studious of antiquity, whereby they may be enabled to do unto her majesty and the realm, such service as shall be requisite for their place.
3. This library to be intituled *the library of Queen Elizabeth*, and the same to be well furnished with divers ancient books and rare monuments of antiquity, which otherwise may perish; and that at the costs and charges of divers gentlemen which will be willing thereunto.[10]

Perhaps in emulation of the library of John Dee at Mortlake—an archive mined by Martin Frobisher, Ambrose and Robert Dudley (earls of Warwick and Leicester respectively), Sir Philip Sidney, Sir Francis Walsingham, and by Dee himself in their efforts to establish the antiquity, authority, and scope of the nascent 'British Empire'—the Elizabethan Antiquaries, in this petition, acknowledge the relationship between textuality and topography in 'the matter of the history of this realm'.[11] The 'monuments' of England, they assert, are equally textual remains and topographical features.

Texts, land, and history come together in chorography. As Richard Helgerson and others have observed, the 'chorographical enterprise' was at the forefront of the Elizabethan imagination.[12] The subtitle for Camden's *Britannia* (1586) announced 'Florentissimorum regnorum, Angliæ, Scotiæ, Hiberniæ, et insularum adiacentium ex intima antiquitate chorographica descriptio.'[13] In his *Mathematicall Præface* (1570), John Dee, who busied himself with maps of North America, Asia, and the Arctic, dismissed 'Chorographie' as 'an underling or twig of Antiquitie'.[14] But, as Helgerson argues, the Elizabethan mapping of England—its regions and counties—simultaneously expressed and facilitated an important and irrevocable transformation in the intellectual and political discourses within and through which the relationships between subject, monarch, and nation could be conceptualized and realized:

Maps let them [i.e. Englishmen] see in a way never before possible the country—both county and nation—to which they belonged and at the same time showed royal authority—or at least its insignia—to be a merely ornamental adjunct to that country.

---

[10] The petition is printed in *A collection of curious discourses written by eminent antiquaries upon several heads in our English antiquities*, ed. Thomas Hearne, 2 vols. (London, 1771), ii. 324–6.

[11] On the Dee library and its visitors, see *The Diaries of John Dee*, ed. Edward Fenton (Charlbury: Day Books, 1998); *John Dee's Library Catalogue*, ed. Julian Roberts and Andrew G. Watson (London: Bibliographic Society, 1990); William S. Sherman, *John Dee and the Politics of Reading and Writing in the English Renaissance* (Amherst: University of Massachusetts Press, 1995), 29–52.

[12] Richard Helgerson, 'The Land Speaks', in *Forms of Nationhood: Elizabethan Writing of England* (Chicago: University of Chicago Press, 1992), 107–47; Howard Marchitello, 'Political Maps: The Production of Cartography and Chorography in Early Modern England', in Margaret J. M. Ezell and Katherine O'Brien O'Keeffe (eds.), *Cultural Artifacts and the Production of Meaning: The Page, the Image, and the Body* (Ann Arbor: University of Michigan Press, 1994), 13–40.

[13] *Britannia siue Florentissimorum regnorum, Angliæ, Scotiæ, Hiberniæ, et insularum adiacentium ex intima antiquitate chorographica descriptio* (London: Eliot's Court Press, 1586).

[14] Dee, 'Mathematicall Præface', in Euclid, *The Elements of Geometrie*, ed. Henry Billingsley (London: John Day, 1570), 19.

Maps thus opened a conceptual gap between the land and its ruler, a gap that would eventually span battlefields.[15]

The summer progresses enabled the Queen and her subjects to participate in a particular kind of chorographical project, in which the bodies of land and monarch were 'mapped', and both were impregnated (made 'fertile', to use Aske's term) with the myths, motifs, and imagery that are remembered—albeit imperfectly and partially—within the extant entertainment texts. Furthermore, the Queen's movement through her land invited her subjects to reflect critically and creatively upon the relationship between the body of the monarch and the body of her land—a topic that would be of particular significance during the succession crisis of the 1590s and the Union debate of the early 1600s—and to explore the resulting 'conceptual gap between the land and its ruler'.

The land through which Elizabeth progressed was mapped land—land infused with antiquity and mythology. Writing of *Veritas Temporis Filia* in her contribution to the present volume, Hester Lees-Jeffries observes that the London through which Elizabeth progressed was not 'an empty stage or a blank page, but a palimpsestic conglomeration of landscape and monuments inscribed and re-inscribed with the "texts" of historical association, communal memory and accumulated civic pride and idealism'.[16] With the omission of the word 'civic', the same could be said for the towns, cities, and houses that provided the fixed points of Elizabeth's progresses. One of the most powerful images of the emerging 'conceptual gap' identified by Helgerson is the 'Ditchley' portrait of Queen Elizabeth I, executed by Marcus Gheeraerts the Younger. In this painting, the Queen teeters—almost hovers—on pointed, dancing toes, over the land. The southern coast and counties of England are visible; the Midlands and northern counties stretch back under the shadow of her skirts. Importantly, this is mapped land: the various counties are differentiated by use of pastel shades; rivers are clearly visible. Gheeraerts's chorographical painting simultaneously acknowledges the mystical relationship between the body of the monarch and her land, and participates in the process by which that relationship would be unravelled.

As Elizabeth Goldring notes in her essay in the present volume, Gheeraerts's painting was almost certainly commissioned by Sir Henry Lee as a visual accompaniment for the entertainments staged during the Queen's visit to his Oxfordshire residences, Woodstock and Ditchley, 20–1 September 1592.[17] The Ditchley portrait has been used by Peter Stallybrass in his powerful evocation of the Elizabethan state as a *hortus conclusus*:

The [Elizabethan] state, like the virgin, was a *hortus conclusus*, an enclosed garden walled off from enemies. In the Ditchley portrait, Elizabeth I is portrayed standing upon a map

---

[15] Helgerson, *Forms of Nationhood*, 114.

[16] Hester Lees-Jeffries, 'Location as Metaphor in Queen Elizabeth's Coronation Entry (1559): *Veritas Temporis Filia*', p. 66.

[17] Elizabeth Goldring, 'Portraiture, Patronage, and the Progresses: Robert Dudley, Earl of Leicester, and the Kenilworth Festivities of 1575', pp. 186–8 and n. 68.

Figure 1.1. *Queen Elizabeth I* (the 'Ditchley' Portrait), by Marcus Gheeraerts the Younger. *c.*1592. Oil on canvas. 241.3 × 152.4 cm. (The National Portrait Gallery, London)

of England. As she ushers in the golden age, she is the imperial virgin, symbolizing, at the same time as she is symbolized by, the *hortus conclusus* of the state . . . But not only was Elizabeth the maker of that 'paradeice' or 'gardein'; her enclosed body was that paradise (a word derived from the Persian *pairidaeza*, meaning a royal enclosure) projected onto a religious plane, her body was the garden of the Song of Songs, which was interpreted both as the body of the Virgin and as the body of a Church that John King portrayed as 'a several, peculiar, enclosed piece of ground,' a *hortus conclusus* that 'lithe within a hedge or fense,' separated off from '*the grape of Sodome* or *cluster of Gomorrhe*.'[18]

Images of the English state as an enclosed garden recur throughout Elizabethan literature, and the progress entertainments in particular. However, in the Ditchley portrait, as in the accompanying entertainments, the land—provincial, local, private—is consistently shown to resist such enclosure and containment within the body of the Queen, and instead is suggestive of a more ambiguous lack of distinctive boundaries *within* the state.[19] Towards the end of the Ditchley entertainments, Lee—who, in the persona of 'Loricus', has been miraculously restored from a death-like trance—bequeaths his land to the Queen:

Item. I bequethe (to your Highnes) THE WHOLE MANNOR OF LOUE, & the appurtenaunces thereunto belonging:

(viz.) Woodes of hie attemptes,
        Groues of humble seruice,
        Meddowes of greene thoughtes,
        Pastures of feeding fancies,
        Arrable Lande of large promisses,
        Riuers of ebbing & flowing fauors [20]

What at first appears a selfless act is, in fact, an affirmation of the relationship between Lee and his land. In Lee's ideal courtiership, the land is personified. Without regional landowners such as Lee, it is suggested, England will cease to serve and be fruitful for the Queen. The references to 'greene thoughtes', 'feeding fancies', and 'large promisses'—set alongside the deliberately, pointedly ambiguous 'ebbing & flowing fauors' in the final line quoted here—constitute a surprisingly direct attack on the Queen for her neglect of loyal servants such as Lee. As in the Ditchley painting, Elizabeth is represented in an ambiguous position with respect to her land: she stands over and alongside it, but the two will not be reconciled until she acknowledges and rewards the subjects who mediate between her and the land.

This ambiguity was dramatized most poignantly in Elizabeth's final great summer progress, 31 July–2 August 1602, culminating in the entertainments at Harefield, near Uxbridge in Middlesex. As the Antiquaries submitted their

[18] Peter Stallybrass, 'Patriarchal Territories: The Body Enclosed', in Margaret Ferguson, Maureen Quilligan, and Nancy Vickers (eds.), *Rewriting the Renaissance: The Discourse of Sexual Difference in Early Modern Europe* (Chicago: University of Chicago Press, 1986), 123–42.

[19] On this point, see Philippa Berry and Jayne Elisabeth Archer, 'Reinventing the Matter of Britain: Undermining the State in Jacobean Masques', in David J. Baker and Willy Maley (eds.), *British Identities and English Renaissance Literature* (Cambridge: Cambridge University Press, 2002), 119–32.

[20] *Kenilworth Illustrated*, ed. William Staunton and William Hamper (Chiswick: C. Whittingham, 1821), 98.

petition for the '*library of Queen Elizabeth*', Elizabeth and her hosts were busy creating texts with which to remember and renegotiate the relationship between the ageing Queen, her subjects, and their land. As the Queen enters the grounds of Sir Thomas Egerton, Lord Keeper, the estate is transformed into a giant theatre. Time and place come together and are briefly suspended for the duration of Elizabeth's stay—quite literally, in the following dialogue, between 'Time' and 'Place', performed on the first day of the entertainment:

TIME: Tis' true my winges arre clipte indeede: and yt is her hande that hathe Clipped them: my glasse runnes not indeede, yt hathe beene stopte a longe time: yt can never runne as longe as I waite vpon this mistris, I am her time, and time were verie vngratefull yf yt shoulde not euer stande still to serue preserue cherishe & delighte her, that is the glorie of her time, and makes the time happie whearein she liues,

PLACE: And dothe shee not make *Place* happie as well as *Time*? What if shee make thee a continuall holydaye, shee makes mee a perpetuall sanctuarie? dothe not the presence of a Prince make a Cottage a Courte? and the presence of the gods make euerie place heauen? But alas, my litlenes is not capable of that happienes which her great grace woulde imparte vnto me. But were I as large as theire hartes that arre my owners, I shoulde bee the fairest pallace in the worlde: and were I agreeable to the wishes of theire hartes, I should in somme measure resemble her sacred self, and bee in the outwarde fronte exceedinge faire, and in the inwarde furniture exceedinge riche.[21]

'I am her time', and her time is 'a continuall holydaye'. However, 'Place' is not quite so obliging. His (or her) question—'dothe not the presence of a Prince make a Cottage a Courte?'—is answered in the negative: the 'litlenes' of 'Place' defies the best efforts of the Queen to transform him into an elsewhere. Instead, the 'Place' of this progress visit is stubbornly, defiantly local and parochial—the Egertons ('my owners') retain control of this particular piece of England. This polite insistence upon the Queen as a *visitor* to the Egerton estate is reiterated in another of the dialogues. While Elizabeth, still on horseback, shelters from the rain under a tree, a bailiff and dairymaid squabble over who should guide the royal entourage to their lodgings:

BAILIFF: why how now Ioane are yow heere, godes my life, what make yow heere, gaddinge and gazinge after this manner, you come to buy gape seede doe yow; wherefore come yow abroade now I faith can yow tell.

DAIRYMAID: I come abroade to welcome these strangers.

BAILIFF: strangers; how know yow there would come strangers.

DAIRYMAID: All this night I could not sleepe dreaming of greene rushes, and yesternight the chatting of the pyes, and the chirkinge of the frisketts, did foretell as much, and besides that; all this day my lefte ear glowed, and that to me (let them all say what they wil) is all waies a signe of strangers, if it be in the sommer: marye if it be in the winter, its a signe of Anger; but what make yow in this company I pray yow.

²¹ Warwickshire County Record Office, CR 136/B2455.

BAILIFF: I make the way for these strangers, which the way maker himselfe could not doe; for it is a way was neuer past before: Besides the Mistress of this faire company, though she know the way to all mens harts, yet she knowes the way but to few mens howses, except she loue them very well I can tell yow, and therefore I my selfe without any comission, haue taken vpon me to conduct them to the house.[22]

The humour here is gentle, but pointed. The Queen and her courtiers are greeted as 'strangers'. The Queen is a 'stranger' in her own land: she may know the way to men's hearts, but the conventions of hospitality mean that she must wait—in the rain, if need be—to be escorted through Egerton's lands to her rooms. As the peripatetic court settled briefly in the grounds of a private host such as Egerton, his or her household *became* the court—the centre of the nation's focus—and the court *became* the household. However fleetingly, the centre *became* the margins, the regional, and the local; the host became the playwright—or, to use the term advanced by Peter Davidson and Jane Stevenson in their contribution to this volume, the *deviser*—who provided the stage, scenes, and stories in which his or her Queen must perform.

VIDEO ET TACEO

'Video et taceo': I see and am silent. Despite the undoubted physical risks opened up by travelling, the progresses enabled Elizabeth to perform her motto by allowing her to see and to be seen, whilst remaining inscrutable and largely silent. Writing amidst the progress of summer 1568, the Spanish Ambassador, Diego Guzmán, was struck by the Queen's eagerness to make her body visible to her subjects. Guzmán remarks at how the people flock to see her, how she courts their admiration, riding in a carriage that is open on all sides, sometimes stopping where the crowd seems thickest in order to stand and thank her subjects.[23] The account of the Queen's progress to Warwick in 1572 confirmed this strategy: the recorder notes that 'euery part & side of the Coache [was] openyd that all her subiectes present might behold her. Which most gladly they desired.'[24] Indeed, extant records of civic receptions and private entertainments place great emphasis upon being able to see, follow, and describe the body of the Queen—to map and mark the traces of her every movement across the land. The account of Elizabeth's reception at Worcester, 13–20 August 1575, is detailed and solemn, recording clothes worn, gifts given and received, and the Queen's every gesture, from accepting the Mayor's mace to kneeling in church. With her words so sparing, particular significance is accorded to the Queen's facial expressions: she

---

[22] Yorkshire County Record Office (Northallerton), ZAZ 1286/8282-9.

[23] *Calendar of Letters and State Papers, Relating to English Affairs, Preserved Principally in the Archives of Simancas*, ii: *Elizabeth. 1568*–1579, ed. Martin A. S. Hume (London: HMSO, 1894), 50–1.

[24] Warwickshire County Record Office, CR 1618/WA19/6.

listens to the opening oration, by the Recorder, William Bell, with a 'pryncelie' and 'cherfull countenance'; and she greets the Latin oration of the schoolboy Christopher Fletcher with 'verry Attentyve eare' and 'good likyng'.[25]

In contrast, these receptions offer surprisingly few records of the Queen's speeches and impromptu comments. Sir Robert Naunton (1563–1635), writing in his memoirs, first published in 1641, complimented Elizabeth for taking time to address the people during her travels, when she conferred 'the ejaculations of her prayers upon the people'.[26] However, the extant records testify to the Queen's strategic use of equivocation and silence. Whilst the progresses provided opportunities to civic and private hosts to petition the Queen in person, they also enabled her to avoid other, more pressing suits. During the spring progress of 1589, Gilbert Talbot, 6th Earl of Shrewsbury, wrote that he hoped his 'dilligent Attendance' on the Queen while she was at Sir Francis Walsingham's house in Surrey would procure him a 'gratious Answere' on her return, 'for whylste she is there nothinge may be moved to her but matter of delighte & to content her which is the only cause of her goynge thither'.[27] Amidst the advice, compliments, and petitions lavished upon the Queen in the entertainments and pageants devised for her, the extant narratives repeatedly portray a Queen who is sparing, and, above all, controlled, in her words and actions.[28] At Bristol, on 15 August 1574, Elizabeth is reputed to have given thanks for 'preseruing me in this longe and dangerus Iorneye' in the form of a prayer, which is preserved in a contemporary manuscript.[29] In Warwick, 1572, she reassures Edward Aglionby, who has just delivered the town's oration in her honour, that she is more afraid of him than he of her.[30] 'I know [I] made the Queenes highnesse smyle and laugh withall', boasts Thomas Churchyard of one of his devices in the Norwich pageants of 1578.[31] But more often, as at Warwick in 1572, the Queen's words are confined to little more than a slight variation upon the anodyne formula, 'I most hartely thank you all my good peeple'.[32]

The progresses thus form a complement to the rhetorical technique of equivocation that, as Mary Thomas Crane has observed, was characteristic of

[25] Worcestershire County Record Office, County Hall Branch (X496, B[ulk]A[ccession] 9360/A-14), fos. 9–10.
[26] Robert Naunton, *Fragmenta Regalia, or, Observations on the late Queen Elizabeth, her times and favorits* (London: [n. pub.], 1641), 9.
[27] Lambeth Palace Library, London, MS 3200, fo. 9.
[28] On Elizabeth's use of specific modes of speech for particular audiences, see Sara Mendelson, 'Popular Perceptions of Elizabeth', in Carole Levin, Jo Eldridge Carney, and Debra Barrett-Graves (eds.), *Elizabeth I: Always her Own Free Woman* (Aldershot: Ashgate, 2003), 192–213. Mendelson observes that 'when addressing a mass audience, Elizabeth preferred a more spontaneous style that was closer to female modes of discourse' (p. 205).
[29] British Library, London, Lansdowne MS 115, fo. 108.
[30] Warwickshire County Record Office, CR 1618/WA19/6.
[31] Thomas Churchyard, *A discourse of the Queenes Maiesties entertainement in Suffolk and Norffolk with a description of many things then presently seene* (London: Henrie Bynneman, 1578), sig. cij[v].
[32] Warwickshire County Record Office, CR 1618/WA19/6.

Elizabeth's political speeches.[33] Only, it seems, when her host was a university, when her body was strangely distanced from the 'matter' of England, and only when the lingua franca was Latin, did Elizabeth feel it appropriate—and, perhaps, safe—to be heard. In relation to her behaviour during the university visits and to how some university authors represented her, Elizabeth's motto of silent vigilance might be recast as the more actively engaged 'video, lego, audio, *dico*': I see, I read, I listen, I *speak*. The Queen saw many plays during these visits, read manuscript poems and narratives presented to her, heard many speeches, but perhaps most unusually, the narratives of university visits present a Queen who speaks frequently, most often either in sarcastic English asides or in formal, adept Latin orations. Accounts of the visit Elizabeth made to the University of Oxford in 1566 offer an atypical representation of the Queen as chatty interlocutor in a Latin dialogue, critic of contemporary religious factions, provider of emergency medical relief when a wall fell on college theatre-goers, and orator of formal Latin speeches delivered to an academic congregation. The eyewitness narratives, written from various authorial positions, informed by age, status, and institutional affiliation, suggest how members of the University may have perceived Elizabeth, how they consequently depicted her, and how the Queen conducted herself on this particular progress visit. Speeches and entertainments offered on other progress visits singled out different attributes of the Queen, such as her matrimonial status, the military and naval strength of her forces, and, perhaps most frequently, her function as a unifying civic symbol. On the three visits to the English universities Elizabeth undertook during her reign (Cambridge in 1564; Oxford in 1566 and 1592), local scholars unsurprisingly exalted instead her learning, on which the Queen had prided herself from the earliest years of her reign. Wendy Wall has discussed how authors of spectacles performed during the Elizabethan progresses 'inscribed a particular dynamic between sovereign and body politic'.[34] We might consider how the narrators of Elizabeth's visits to Oxford in 1566 sketched out the dynamic between the Queen and the world of institutional scholarship. This visit produced several detailed reflections on Elizabeth's week-long sojourn in the University city, written in English and Latin, issuing from very different standpoints.

If the University panegyricists continually praised Elizabeth's learning, they also showcased their own, and bombarded the Queen with words in various material and linguistic media. When she arrived at Christ Church on 31 August, 'poems of all kinds had been devised to adorn the doors', and a laudatory couplet painted on the doors—the first of many she would have encountered—welcomed her: 'May you live long, O Queen, splendour of the British people, | And may you continue to bestow the benefits of peace, as you

[33] Mary Thomas Crane, ' "Video et Taceo": Elizabeth I and the Rhetoric of Counsel', *Studies in English Literature, 1500–1900*, 28.1 (Winter 1988), 1–15.

[34] Wendy Wall, *The Imprint of Gender: Authorship and Publication in the English Renaissance* (London: Cornell University Press, 1993), 112.

do now.'[35] On 3 September, entering the church of St Mary's, Elizabeth saw 'dyvers sheetes of verses in Lattyn, Greeke, & Ebrewe sett vppon the doores & walles'.[36] As a compliment to Elizabeth's learning, Oxford scholars praised her in the classical and biblical languages as well as in the more patriotic vernacular. Elizabeth returned the compliment, in her oration delivered in Latin.[37] On leaving St Mary's two days later, the Queen was ambushed with a book of Greek poetry composed by George Etheridge, formerly Regius Professor of Greek, which apparently celebrated the virtues of Henry VIII rather than her own.[38] The formal collections of poetry and the 'diverse verses' adorning college walls show how carefully and comprehensively Oxford scholars packaged their erudition and then offered it to the Queen.[39] We might characterize the words presented by the University to the Queen in handwritten and painted, as well as in spoken form, as not only a *rhetorical* exchange of praise. Ros King has referred to the 1566 visit as an 'extensive piece of total theatre',[40] and we might factor into this theatrical experience the spectacle of words Elizabeth encountered in so many forms during her visit to Oxford, which constituted part of the performance of learning offered to her by the University scholars. As well as a spectacle of scholarship, moreover, these erudite verses adorning the walls offered a material vision of the University as yet another kind of 'fruitfull soile', to invoke again James Aske's phrase, displaying, through highly visible media, the 'fertile' intellectual endeavour and literary creativity with which Oxford sought to impress the Queen.

Panegyric poems and speeches offer a rosy perspective on Elizabeth's visit to the University, but the eyewitness narratives provide a fuller view of how the progress visit unfolded. Two accounts in particular stand out: the Corpus Christi student Miles Windsor's 'Receavinge of the Quenes Maiestie into Oxford', a lively diary-style English narrative, and the *Collegiorum Scholarumque Publicarum Academiae Oxoniensis Topographica Delineatio* ('Topographical Delineation of the Colleges and Public Schools of the University of Oxford'), a Latin dialogue

---

[35] Nicholas Robinson, 'Of the Actes done at Oxford when the Quenes Majestie was there' (Folger Shakespeare Library, Washington, DC, MS V.a.176, fo. 155ᵛ): 'Fores istas architectura insignes ornabant hinc inde Carmina omnis generis: etiam in superiori harum parte pingebantur versus isti: Viue diu splendor gentis | Regina Britanniæ, | Et quæ das, pacis commoda perge dare.'

[36] Miles Windsor, 'The receavinge of the Quenes Maiestie into Oxford' (Corpus Christi College, Oxford, MS 257) [henceforth 'Receavinge'], fo. 109ʳ.

[37] For a valuable reading of Elizabeth I's 1566 oration to the University of Oxford and her rhetorical self-fashioning, see Linda Shenk, 'Turning Learned Authority into Royal Supremacy', in Levin et al. (eds.), *Elizabeth I*, 78–96 (pp. 84–7).

[38] 'Receavinge', fo. 111ᵛ: 'This daye vppon the Comminge owte of her Maiestie to Sᵗ Maryes Master Etheridge sometyme Greeke Reader to the vniversitie presented a booke of greeke verses contayninge the noble acts of her Graces Father.'

[39] Richard Stephens, 'A Brief Rehearsall of all suche thinges as were doonne in the Vniversitie of Oxforde', fo. 167ᵛ. For an example of the 1566 panegyric literature, see British Library, London, Royal MS 12A XI.VII, fos. 1ᵛ–27ᵛ, a collection of poems and orations.

[40] *The Works of Richard Edwards: Politics, Poetry, and Performances in Sixteenth-Century England*, ed. Ros King (Manchester: Manchester University Press, 2001), 63.

adorned with gratulatory verse and prose in Hebrew, written by Thomas Neale, Regius Professor of Hebrew.[41] Other accounts survive: Nicholas Robinson, for instance, a Cambridge graduate who became Bishop of Bangor in 1566, produced a Latin prose account that provides copious details of sermons preached during the visit.[42] John Bereblock, an Exeter College Fellow and accomplished draughtsman who provided the drawings for Neale's *Topographica Delineatio*, produced a Latin prose narrative particularly valuable for details of theatrical entertainments performed.[43] But we will concentrate for the moment on Windsor and Neale, whose markedly different narratives offer particularly interesting perspectives on the 1566 visit.

Miles Windsor wrote a fair copy of his narrative alongside his draft, leading us to assume that he wished others to read his account.[44] We know that the 'Receavinge' was read over half a century later by the Oxford antiquary Brian Twyne, because he transcribed it in 1636.[45] Indeed, antiquarian activity at Oxford during the late sixteenth century, conducted by scholars such as Windsor (who published a *Academiarum . . . Catalogus & Enumeratio Breuis* ('Short Catalogue and Recapitulation of Universities') in 1590,[46] and his descendants Twyne and Anthony Wood during the following century, maps interestingly onto the work of the fledgling Society of Antiquaries in London during the same period. Windsor's account was also read by a contemporary of Windsor's at Corpus Christi, Richard Stephens, who wrote a 'Brief Rehearsall' of the visit drawing frequently from Windsor.[47] Windsor's work proved influential for his Oxford contemporaries,

---

[41] Thomas Neale (b. *c*.1519, d. in or after 1590) became a Fellow of New College in 1540, and was made Regius Professor of Hebrew in 1559. For further biographical information, see Louise Durning, 'Introduction', *Queen Elizabeth's Book of Oxford*, ed. Durning (Oxford: Bodleian Library, 2006). The authors would like to thank Dr Durning for generously sharing her work prior to publication.

[42] Nicholas Robinson (*c*.1530–1585) also produced an account of Elizabeth's 1564 visit to Cambridge. See J. Gwynfor Jones, 'Robinson, Nicholas (*c*.1530–1585)', *Oxford Dictionary of National Biography* (Oxford: Oxford University Press, 2004) (www.oxforddnb.com/view/article/23860, accessed 25 Feb. 2006).

[43] John Bereblock (*fl.* 1557–1572) graduated BA from St John's College, Oxford, in 1561, was elected to a fellowship in 1561, and moved to Exeter College. See Durning, 'Introduction', *Queen Elizabeth's Book of Oxford*.

[44] Miles Windsor's narrative is preserved in the archives of Corpus Christi College, Oxford, as MS 257 (fair copy on fos. 104–14; draft on fos. 115–23). See John R. Elliott Jr., 'Queen Elizabeth at Oxford: New Light on the Royal Plays of 1566', *English Literary Renaissance* 18 (1988), 218–29; *Records of Early English Drama: Oxford*, ed. John R. Elliott et al., 2 vols. (Toronto: University of Toronto Press/British Library, 2004), i. 126–35; ii. 696–7.

[45] Twyne's transcription (Bodleian Library, Oxford, MS Twyne 17) was the version Anthony Wood and subsequently John Nichols used: see *The Life and Times of Anthony Wood . . . described by himself*, ed. Andrew Clark, 5 vols. (Oxford: Oxford Historical Society, 1891-5), iv (1895), 212–14.

[46] The full title of Windsor's history of universities is *Academiarum quae aliquando fuere et hodie in Europa, catalogus & enumeratio breuis* (London: Georgius Bishop & Radalphus Newberie, 1590). The account of the 'venerable city-state of Oxford' ('Oxoniensis ciuitas augusta', p. 28) can be found on pp. 28–50.

[47] Stephens's account appears in the same manuscript as Nicholas Robinson's (see n. 42, above). See *REED: Oxford*, ed. Elliott, ii. 697.

but was probably not intended for royal scrutiny. Neale, on the other hand, 'offered [his] book to the Queen's Majesty', in Robinson's phrase.[48] Windsor also informs us that on 2 September, just as George Etheridge would do with his Greek verse three days later, 'Mr Neale Ebrewe Reader gaue vnto the Quenes Maiestie a booke of all the prophets owte of Ebrew. | & a little booke of vearses contayninge the description of everie Colledge in Lattyn vearses.'[49] Windsor and Neale's accounts differ not only in linguistic medium, and institutional status of the writer, then, but also possess a very different 'official' status.

The 'Receavinge', although by no means disrespectful towards Elizabeth, seems often to foreground rather the Queen's enjoyment of the occasion than the University's veneration of its monarch. Windsor seems eager to represent Elizabeth as an engaged participant in the festivities, rather than as a remote personification of royal dignity, noting, for instance, that Elizabeth received the scholars' shouts of 'Vivat Regina' 'verie thankfullie with a ioyefull countenance', and listened to the divinity debates with a 'verye attent eare'.[50] He also includes several examples of the Queen's speech and behaviour—particularly her caustic, impromptu witticisms—that provide valuable insight into Elizabeth's personality. An encounter Windsor describes between the Queen and Lawrence Humphrey, radical Protestant head of Magdalen, is particularly telling. To Humphrey, presumably wearing his full Doctor of Divinity costume, Windsor's Elizabeth says, 'me thinkes this gowne & habite becommethe you verie well & I mervayle that you ar so straighte laced in this poynte but I come not nowe to chyde'.[51] The Queen's cutting allusion here was to the vestment controversy raging at Oxford during the 1560s, whereby Protestants such as Humphrey remonstrated against wearing the surplice and other clerical garb mandated by the royal injunctions.[52] The fact that Elizabeth spoke so freely on an official occasion about such a controversial topic, during the formal welcome to the University at Christ Church, even while acknowledging that the situation demands a different rhetorical register ('I come not nowe to chyde'), is extraordinary. Anthony Wood, the seventeenth-century historian of the University, who relied heavily upon Brian Twyne's transcript of Windsor's narrative for his own account of the 1566 visit, clearly felt that any mention of this aspect of Elizabeth's conduct would be incongruous in his history of Oxford, and so he omits the exact details of the incident. Wood even moves the

---

[48] Nicholas Robinson, 'Of the Actes done at Oxford', fo. 160^v: 'Hunc librum obtulit Regiæ Maiestati'.

[49] Windsor, 'Receavinge', fo. 108^r. The 'booke of all the prophets owte of Ebrew' was Neale's translation of Rabbi David Kimhi's commentaries on the minor prophets (see British Library, London, Royal MS 2 D. XXI, the manuscript to which he affixed a dedicatory preface to the Queen).

[50] Windsor, 'Receavinge', fos. 106^v; 111^r.   [51] Ibid. fo. 106^r.

[52] For further details of the vestment controversy, see Patrick Collinson, *Elizabethan Puritan Movement* (Oxford: Clarendon Press, 1990), 68–83, and C. M. Dent, *Protestant Reformers in Elizabethan Oxford* (Oxford: Oxford University Press, 1983), 34–40.

action to a footnote, stating only that 'The queen reflects upon Dr. Humphrey for his preciseness', and consequently offering a very different impression of the encounter from that Windsor records.[53]

Similarly, other more contemporary narrators of the 1566 visit chose to omit another incident that Windsor preserves. On 2 September, the Queen, courtiers, and scholars gathered to watch the first part of Richard Edwards's *Palamon and Arcite*. At the beginning of the performance, in Windsor's stark phrase, 'theare was by mischaunce of a wall fallinge downe, 3 slayne'.[54] The Queen's immediate response was to send 'forthe presentlye Mr Vicechamberlayne & her owne surgions to helpe them'. But despite the tragedy, *Palamon and Arcite* continues, featuring 'actors [who] notwithstanding so well perfourmed their partes that the Quene laughed afterwardes hartelie'. Significantly, other 1566 accounts omit the Queen's laughter, which Ros King has rightly characterized as part of the 'unsympathetic dialogue' Windsor includes.[55] Robinson, by contrast, states only that 'the play was not interrupted, but continued until midnight'.[56] Stephens emphasizes Elizabeth's sympathy, noting that the Queen 'was very sorie for that missehappe'.[57] Making no specific mention of Elizabeth's behaviour, and describing only a general response and mood, Bereblock records that after the accident, 'everyone returned to the plays, more wary now because of the danger that others had faced'.[58] By including the detail of Elizabeth laughing 'hartelie' shortly after a tragic incident, Windsor gives us a fuller than usual picture of the Queen's behaviour during the progress visit, portraying a reaction that might appear callous, and choosing not to excise the monarch's potentially problematic response from his account.

Thomas Neale's commemoration of the 1566 visit is markedly different from Windsor's realistic, keenly observed account, nor does Neale follow the composers of panegyric and the writers of gratulatory speeches. The *Topographica Delineatio* is a fiction, an imaginary conversation between Elizabeth and Leicester that took place mid-progress, en route to Oxford from the palace of Woodstock, one of Leicester's residences. Neale's Leicester describes to the Queen, as she was 'about to depart from Woodstock',[59] the history and architectural characteristics of the Oxford colleges and other University buildings. Elizabeth interrupts Leicester's account often, sometimes courteously, sometimes imperiously, to ask for more information about the institution. At the start of the dialogue, Leicester asks the

[53] Anthony Wood, *History and Antiquities of the University of Oxford*, ed. John Gutch, 2 vols. (Oxford: printed for the editor, 1792–6), ii (1796), 156 n. 3.

[54] Windsor, 'Receavinge', fo. 108ᵛ.   [55] *Works of Richard Edwards*, ed. King, 79.

[56] Robinson, 'Of the Actes', fo. 159ʳ: 'Verumtamen non fuit intermissum spectaculum, sed ad medio nocte prorogatum.'

[57] Stephens, 'Brief Rehearsall', fo. 168ᵛ.

[58] Bereblock, *Commentarii*, 20: 'Ad spectacula itaque omnes alieno iam periculo cautiores revertuntur.'

[59] Neale, *Topographica Delineatio*, fo. ivᵛ, 'Woodstochio discessuram.'

Queen 'Are you going to leave your home?'[60] Elizabeth replies that she is not travelling far, but is going to a place where 'that entire city is [her] home.'[61] Leicester then asks where she means, since 'the entire site of the kingdom' belongs to her,[62] and Elizabeth responds with an acute characterization of the way her progresses functioned. 'Since I have many homes, and many houses', she asks, 'why should I not frequently change my house?'[63] By putting such a rationale for her peripatetic lifestyle into the Queen's mouth, Neale achieves something relatively rare in progress narratives: Elizabeth, his fictional creation, reflects on the purpose of the progress visit. All of the houses (and towns, cities, and institutions) the Queen visits to some extent belong to her, so why should she not travel among them as she pleases?

Pressed further by Leicester, Elizabeth states her destination: 'I am going towards Oxford,' she says, 'I seek the house | Dedicated to the Muses, accompanied by my own Muses.'[64] The University, Neale suggests, is at the same time one of many houses the Queen might visit throughout her kingdom, and a particularly special house 'dedicated to the Muses'—that is, to learning and to creativity. Many progress hosts announced the particular significance of their town, city, or stately home, but perhaps no other destination put such pressure on the Queen to perform and to some extent *prove* her dedication to the Muses. Of course Elizabeth was expected to show her dedication intellectually, by formulating accomplished speeches in Latin and attending a taxing sequence of formal disputes and academic plays, but Neale also makes a plea for her to prove her commitment financially, by endowing academic buildings in particular. Neale, as did other scholars writing in honour of the 1566 visit, refers back to the munificence of Henry VIII, who endowed Christ Church, or Mary, who had built the Public Schools.[65] The *Topographica Delineatio* is prefixed by a poem in Latin, which praises Elizabeth's 'financial generosity' while invoking that of her 'distinguished father'.[66] Consequently, by the end of the dialogue, a clear message has emerged: the University of Oxford is illustrious, but needs royal funding in order to maintain and consolidate its status. Neale's account is both imaginary and rooted in contemporary actuality. In some ways, the *Topographica Delineatio* is far more fanciful than Windsor's 'Receavinge', and because of its fictional form might appear to offer scholars of the Elizabethan progresses fewer insights into the Queen's actual conduct. At the same time, though, Neale's narrative is revealing in its wish to persuade the intended reader to undertake a

---

[60] Neale, *Topographica Delineatio*, fo. 4ʳ: 'Siccine . . . domo pergis abire tua?'

[61] Ibid.: 'mea est vrbs ea tota domus'.

[62] Ibid.: 'tota | Nam regni sedes est domus ista tua'.

[63] Ibid.: 'Quum sint ergò domus mihi plures, pluraque tecta, | Quid ni mutarem tecta subinde mea?'

[64] Ibid.: 'Oxoniam versùs pergo, Musisque dicata | Tecta peto, Musis concomitata meis.'

[65] See, for example, Edward Lily's Latin poem, a prosopopœia of the University addressed to Elizabeth that praises Henry VIII and Mary (BL, Royal MS 12A XI.VII, fos. 21ᵛ–22ʳ).

[66] Neale, *Topographica Delineatio*, fo. iiᵛ: 'nummis, Elisabetha, tuis'; 'pater . . . tuus inclytus'.

particular course of action, conveying too a sense of urgency as an early modern scholar's uncannily familiar plea for government funding.

Royal visits to the universities offer a picture of civic order, as Siobhan Keenan argues elsewhere in this book, referring in particular to the entertainments presented to Elizabeth at Cambridge and Oxford during the 1560s.[67] The 1566 accounts certainly emphasize this order and social hierarchy, detailing how the scholars lined the Oxford streets in proper academic rank, how decorous speeches and sermons were duly delivered, and plays befitting the supposed tastes of a humanist monarch were duly performed, adding up to an impression of a mostly smooth-running and well-organized progress visit. However, Windsor and Neale's narratives shade more finely the aspects of the visit other accounts depicted without qualification or ambivalence, offering a less conventional but much more richly detailed view of Elizabeth's week in Oxford. In his 'Receavinge', Windsor gives us sharp and colourful insight into the Queen's behaviour, and similarly, despite the conventions of the dialogue form and the customary reverence of the manuscript presented to a royal recipient, Neale's *Topographica Delineatio* does not serve merely as panegyric or as inkhorn travelogue. Through their depiction of Elizabeth's visit to 'the house dedicated to the Muses', both Windsor and Neale offer compelling perspectives on Elizabeth's progress visits, and meditate in particular on the significance of such visits for the academic microcosm. In their accounts, Oxford becomes a location of particular significance for Elizabeth's personal reign.

THE LIBRARY OF QUEEN ELIZABETH REVISITED

The memory of the Elizabethan progresses, and of the late Queen's very personal relationship with her land, was invoked in Michael Drayton's antiquarian and chorographical poem *Poly-olbion* (1612).[68] The illustrated frontispiece seems to celebrate the Jacobean Union, with the seated female figure of 'Great Britain'—identified as '*Albion*' in the corresponding verse, itself surrounded with John Selden's antiquarian annotations—holding a mace and cornucopia, resembling 'Power' and 'Plenty' respectively:

> Through a *Triumphant Arch*, see *Albion* plas't,
> In *Happy* site, in *Neptunes* armes embras't,
> In *Power* and *Plenty*, on her *Cleeuy* Throne
> Circled with *Natures Ghirlands*, being alone
> Stil'd *th'Oceans Island*.

[67] See Keenan, 'Spectator and Spectacle', 86–103.
[68] Michael Drayton, *Poly-olbion* (London: M. Lownes, I. Browne, I. Helme, and I. Busbie, 1612). *Poly-olbion* was published in two parts, with the second part appearing in 1622. Only the first part (1612) contained John Selden's annotations.

Figure 1.2. Illustrated frontispiece, Michael Drayton's *Poly-olbion* [part 1], ed. John Selden (London: M. Lownes, I. Browne, I. Helme, and I. Busbie, 1612). (By permission of the British Library, London, shelfmark C.116.g.2)

Resembling a figure from Samuel Daniel's *Tethys Festival* (1610),[69] this goddess forms the coastline of England, Scotland, and Wales; behind and around her, we can see the sea. The goddess is swathed in a map of Britain. Instead of place names, the map-cum-dress includes pictures of topographical features: hills, rivers, trees, forests, houses, towns, and cities—features that are personified in Drayton's 'Chorographicall' poem.[70] In the Ditchley portrait and James Aske's *Elizabetha Triumphans*, the Queen stood goddess-like and all-powerful over her land; here, the land is her own sovereign power—she needs no other monarch. Drayton's 'Great Britain' is alive; she no longer waits for the vivifying presence of Queen Elizabeth to give her being and meaning. Between the Ditchley portrait and *Poly-olbion*, royal power has been decentered.[71] The mystical significances associated with the chaste body of the virgin queen, who once had the power to stand outside of place and time, has been reclaimed by the land, and on behalf of (certain of her) subjects. In death, the Queen's 'two bodies' are finally resolved and united: the 'body natural' folds back into the 'body politic'. It is an irony not lost on Hamlet, who, with typical gimlet-eyed awareness of the interconnected cycles of life and death, taunts Claudius with the prospect of one final royal progress:

A man may fish with the worm that hath eat of a king, and eat of the fish that hath fed of that worm. . . . a king may go a progress through the guts of a beggar.[72]

The irony would not have been lost on Queen Elizabeth, either, who perhaps embarked on her great summer progress of 1602 knowing that it would be her last.[73]

The Antiquaries' 1602 petition was unsuccessful. Elizabeth died in April 1603, and James quickly closed the Society, suspecting its members of harbouring political, quasi-republican motives.[74] A little under two hundred years later, in 1789, Richard Gough, antiquary and editor (of Camden's *Britannia*, among other titles), proposed a different '*library of Queen Elizabeth*': the collection and

[69] Samuel Daniel, *Tethys Festival*, in *The order and solemnitie of the creation of the High and mightie Prince Henrie . . . Whereunto is annexed the royall maske, presented by the Queene and her ladies, on Wednesday at night following* (London: [by William Stansby] for John Budge, 1610). In this masque, Queen Anna portrayed Tethys, 'Qveene of the Ocean', and her ladies represented 'thirteene Nymphs of seuerall Riuers' (sig. E2ʳ).

[70] Drayton, *Poly-olbion*, unsigned preliminary leaf, 'To the High and Mightie, *Henrie, Prince of Wales.*'

[71] On this point, see Andrew Hadfield, 'Spenser, Drayton, and the Question of Britain', *Review of English Studies*, 51 (2004), 592–9.

[72] William Shakespeare, *Hamlet* (1600/1), ed. Harold Jenkins (London: Methuen (The Arden Shakespeare), 1982), IV. iii. 26–7, 29–30.

[73] For a reading of *Hamlet* in the context of the 1602 progress, see Steven Mullaney, 'Mourning and Misogyny: *Hamlet* and the Final Progress of Elizabeth I', *Shakespeare Quarterly*, 45.2 (1994), 139–58.

[74] See Parry, *The Triumphs of Time*, 44.

publication of documents relating to the reign of Queen Elizabeth I.[75] It is
fitting that John Nichols, printer to the Antiquaries—resurrected in the early
eighteenth century as the Society of Antiquaries of London—should return
to the age which witnessed the genesis of this Society.[76] The result of the
collaboration between Gough, Nichols, and their fellow Antiquarians was the
Progresses and Public Processions of Queen Elizabeth, published in two editions
between 1788 and 1823.[77] The *Progresses* is indeed a kind of '*library of Queen
Elizabeth*', for although the progress entertainments are the focus of Nichols's
endeavour, his work is, in fact, an attempt to create a day-by-day itinerary
of the Queen's every motion, remembered in the texts—letters, petitions,
accounts, inventories, poems, parish records, memoirs, speeches, tracts, and gift
rolls—created by, for, about, and because of her movements.[78] Then, and now,
as the constituent parts and regions which comprise Britain, Great Britain, the
British Isles, and the United Kingdom refine their relationships with one another
and with continental Europe, it is necessary to excavate 'the matter of history
of this realm' in order to re-examine the present. Then, and now, the processes
of mapping, traversing, writing, and remembering the land are political acts,
involving ideas of nationhood, ideology, and who has the right to 'own' their
land.

As Mary Hill Cole, Felicity Heal, C. E. McGee, and James Knowles note
in their essays in the present volume, other monarchs embarked on regular
progresses about the realm, and some—notably King James I, who made the
journey through northern England and Scotland in 1617—went further in their
travels, but the idea of the Elizabethan progresses has lingered for centuries.[79] It is,

[75] R. H. Sweet, 'Gough, Richard (1735–1809)', *Oxford Dictionary of National Biography* (Oxford: Oxford University Press, Sept. 2004), online edn., Oct. 2005 (www.oxforddnb.com/view/article/11141, accessed 8 Mar. 2006). Gough's translation of Camden's *Britannia* was published by Thomas Payne and John Nichols in two editions, in 1789 and 1806.

[76] Meetings began in 1707, and in 1717 the Society was formally reconstituted, receiving a charter from King George III in 1751. On antiquarianism in the eighteenth century, see Rosemary Sweet, *Antiquaries: The Discovery of the Past in Eighteenth-Century Britain* (London: Hambledon and London, 2004), and Julian Pooley's essay in the present volume.

[77] *The Progresses and Public Processions of Queen Elizabeth. Among which are interspersed other solemnities, public expenditures, and remarkable events during the reign of that illustrious princess. Now first printed from original MSS. Of the times; or collected from scarce pamphlets, &c. Illustrated with historical notes.* The first edition of the *Progresses* was published in four volumes between 1788 and 1821. A second edition, with substantial revisions, appeared in three volumes in 1823. On the publishing history of the *Progresses* and preparations for a 'third' edition, see Julian Pooley's essay in the present edition. A new, old-spelling edition of the early modern materials in Nichols's *Progresses* is being prepared for publication as *Court and Culture in the Reign of Queen Elizabeth I: A New Edition of John Nichols's Progresses*, ed. Jayne Archer, Elizabeth Clarke, and Elizabeth Goldring (OUP, forthcoming).

[78] Marion Colthorpe is currently compiling a complete itinerary of Queen Elizabeth's life.

[79] On the Jacobean progresses, see *The Progresses, Processions, and Magnificent Festivities of King James the First, his Royal Consorts and Family, etc.*, ed. John Nichols and John Bowyer Nichols, 4 vols. (London: J. B. Nichols, 1828). A four-volume edition, *Records of Early Drama: Scotland*, is currently being prepared by John J. McGavin and Eila Williamson under the auspices of REED (Records of Early English Drama).

perhaps, precisely because of the geographical limitations of Elizabeth's progresses, and because they were performed at the very moment when 'Englishness' was enfolded within 'Britishness', that they remain an insistent and potent symbol of Englishness. In Naunton's *Fragments*, Nichols's *Progresses*, and even in Aske's *Elizabetha Triumphans*, we can discern the nostalgic yearnings for an England, and, specifically, a unity—between ruler and ruled, monarch and land—that never was, and so can never be forgotten.

PART I

THE ELIZABETHAN PROGRESSES

Patterns, Themes, and Contexts

2

Monarchy in Motion:
An Overview of Elizabethan Progresses

Mary Hill Cole

Thanks to John Nichols, whose work lies at the heart of this collection of essays, our approach to progresses has developed in almost as many directions as he provided documents. In its variety of sources, its perspectives, and especially in its digressions, Nichols's *The Progresses and Public Processions of Queen Elizabeth* (1788–1823) embodies the multi-layered, competing voices of the people who participated in Elizabethan progresses. As Nichols understood, the progresses taxed the energies and purses of all involved, but they also provided an assortment of political, social, and ceremonial benefits to the participants. The frequency of the Queen's progresses (twenty-three during her forty-four-year reign) demonstrated that Elizabeth put the rewards of travel above the difficulties of moving and receiving her court.[1] Furthermore, the Queen's progresses, considered in aggregate, emphasized the personal nature of Elizabethan queenship. By subsidizing the expensive progresses, the usually frugal Queen underscored them as a priority of her monarchy. Their value to her existed both in their content, the interactive discourse of the Queen and her subjects, and in their process, the instability of travel inherent in the organization of hosts and royal household. Moving the court dislocated the government and royal household, which fostered a productive confusion that enabled the Queen to avoid decisions, delay meetings, and retreat from unwanted visitors. The dislocation occurred because the Queen wanted to travel, and her wishes dominated the daily life of court and government in a visible, tangible way during the weeks of a summer

[1] Mary Hill Cole, *The Portable Queen: Elizabeth I and the Politics of Ceremony* (Amherst: University of Massachusetts Press, 1999), 206. The Elizabethan Progresses Conference in Stratford-upon-Avon, April 2004, that generated this collection of essays flourished under the accomplished guidance of Elizabeth Clarke and Jayne Archer. I also would like to thank Jayne Archer, Elizabeth Goldring, and Sarah Knight for their valuable suggestions and skilful editing from which this essay benefited. For their creative and varied support, I am indebted to Judy Cohen, Ken Fincham, Gary Gibbs, Alisha Heimbuch, Eric Jones, Arthur Kinney, Judy Klein, Russ McDonald, Glyn Redworth, my interdisciplinary colleagues at Mary Baldwin College, and especially Ralph Cohen, who generously offered advice and read drafts of this chapter. For permission to draw from *The Portable Queen*, I would like to thank Arthur Kinney and the University of Massachusetts Press.

progress. Against this background, the Queen was a steady, yet mobile, centre in the turbulent, itinerant court; Elizabeth imitated the sun that moved through the universe with planets and solar system in tow. As all eyes focused on the royal centre, the image that embodied the government and nation was that of a woman whose female monarchy was a theological and social oddity. Countering that anomaly, her identity and appearance harked back to those of her father, Henry VIII, and evoked an impression of dynastic stability and royal popularity. By creating chaos, by altering the patterns of royal access, and by highlighting gender amidst convention, the progresses offered Elizabeth a way to rule and to thrive.

In valuing the political assistance of progresses even as she reinterpreted aspects of royal travel to suit her own needs, Elizabeth followed in the tradition of her Tudor ancestors. Monarchs moved their courts to reach clean houses and fresh supplies, avoid plague, and explore regions new to them, but the personal nature of sovereignty underscored the significance of viewing, meeting, or entertaining the monarch. In the aftermath of winning the crown in battle and needing to claim the obedience of Yorkist strongholds, Henry VII visited the recalcitrant areas of northern England in 1486 and 1487 in progresses that combined military action with civic pageantry of capitulation and loyalty.[2] He regularly travelled in central England, but not to Ireland and only once to Wales, and he made frequent visits to Richmond, Woodstock, and Canterbury. Both Henry VII and Henry VIII often lodged in monasteries along their route, and, unlike Elizabeth, they travelled with a reduced number of household members on their summer progresses. Henry VIII loved to hunt and shaped his itinerary to do so as often as possible. He recognized the important social glue that such occasions provided, and under the public gaze on his progresses, he contributed venison from his hunts to local people, enjoyed the spectacles at his civic entries, heard complaints from subjects, and basked in the company of his noblemen, and occasionally that of his wives and children.[3]

The brevity of their reigns, illness, and personal inclination meant few progresses were embarked on by Edward VI and Mary I. Hunting and public display did not compel young Edward to travel, as he typically moved among royal houses near London, and his sole lengthy progress was in 1552 to Portsmouth. Mary's only real progress was her wedding march with Philip II from Winchester

---

[2] Lorraine Attreed, 'The Politics of Welcome: Ceremonies and Constitutional Development in Later Medieval English Towns', in Barbara A. Hanawalt and Kathryn Reyerson (eds.), *City and Spectacle in Medieval Europe* (Minneapolis: University of Minnesota Press, 1994), 220–3; Sydney Anglo, *Spectacle, Pageantry, and Early Tudor Policy* (Oxford: Clarendon Press, 1969), 22–8; John C. Meagher, 'The First Progress of Henry VII', *Renaissance Drama*, NS 1 (1968), 45–73 (p. 47).

[3] Neil Samman, 'The Progresses of Henry VIII, 1509–1529', in Diarmaid MacCulloch (ed.), *The Reign of Henry VIII: Politics, Policy, and Piety* (London: Macmillan, 1995), 60–9; Fiona Kisby, 'Kingship and the Royal Itinerary: A Study of the Peripatetic Household of the Early Tudor Kings, 1485–1547', *Court Historian*, 4.1 (1999), 30–6; Simon Thurley, *The Royal Palaces of Tudor England* (New Haven: Yale University Press, 1993), 68–70; Gladys Temperley, *Henry VII* (Westport, Conn.: Greenwood Press, 1914; repr. 1971), 411–19; S. J. Gunn, *Early Tudor Government 1485–1558* (London: Macmillan, 1995), 63, 196–7.

to London, but the couple experienced little hospitality from local hosts because they stayed in their own royal residences along the way.[4] In general, Edward and Mary wanted their courts' festivities, with the exception of their coronations and London entries, to celebrate the holiday season surrounding Christmas.[5] Her two immediate predecessors left Elizabeth less of a tradition of sustained, ceremonially rich progresses than did her father and grandfather.[6]

The blend of hospitality, ceremonial dialogue, and royal agency expressed in Elizabethan progresses distinguished them from some western European spectacles, especially those staged in France. Royal entries into European cities had a more lavish exuberance, greater frequency, and heavier reliance on classical references than those in sixteenth-century England.[7] The French entries and entertainments emphasized the monarch's dominance over—and separation from—the court and people. During spectacles, the sovereign typically did not speak to the crowd or act in the show; instead, he or she listened to speeches, received gifts, and observed. The nobles did not stage overly elaborate shows for the king or other visiting dignitary because such ostentation from a subject might appear, in royal eyes, to assert an unwelcome rivalry and ambition. Over time, the shows themselves left the public sphere for the more private, enclosed, spaces at court.[8] In contrast, Elizabeth's experience of lodging with her subjects, participating in public shows, exchanging speeches with civic officials, and displaying herself to the citizenry provided another perspective on the nature of monarchy in the Renaissance. The Elizabethan progresses had at their heart a focus on dialogue and access that embodied the spontaneous, at times risky, dynamic of her personal monarchy.

PREPARATIONS FOR A PROGRESS

That the progresses occurred despite organizational obstacles served to heighten the achievement of all who arranged them. Every progress could collapse in

---

[4] David Loades, *Intrigue and Treason: The Tudor Court 1547–1558* (London: Longman, 2004), 94–7, 165–7.

[5] Anglo, *Spectacle*, 340; Anglo notes the unusual festival activity of the Lord of Misrule at Edward's court during the Christmas season (p. 301).

[6] Samman, 'The Progresses of Henry VIII', points out that 'Whilst Henry VIII's progresses lacked the sophistication and elaborate devices of Elizabeth I, nevertheless the progress performed a similar role under both monarchs' (p. 73).

[7] Sydney Anglo, 'Image-Making: The Means and the Limitations', in John Guy (ed.), *The Tudor Monarchy* (London: Arnold, 1997), 16–42 (p. 24); R. J. Knecht, 'Court Festivals as Political Spectacle: The Example of Sixteenth-Century France', in J. R. Mulryne, Helen Watanabe-O'Kelly, and Margaret Shewring (eds.), *Europa Triumphans: Court and Civic Festivals in Early Modern Europe*, 2 vols. (Aldershot: Ashgate, 2004) i. 19–31 (p. 22); Roy Strong, *Art and Power: Renaissance Festivals 1450–1650* (Berkeley and Los Angeles: UCLA Press, 1984), 42, 76.

[8] Knecht, 'Court Festivals', 24–7. Mark Greengrass, in 'Henri III, Festival Culture and the Rhetoric of Royalty,' in Mulryne et al. (eds.), *Europa Triumphans*, i. 112–13, argues that 'like all princes in civic festival culture (the most notable exception was Queen Elizabeth I), he [Henri III] was rendered mute and passive, a public figurehead to whom everything was done, everything was said'.

mid-itinerary with the news of a plague outbreak near the Queen: such fears
about contagion forced Elizabeth to redesign her travels to Cambridge in 1564,
Hampshire in 1569, Worcester in 1575, and Kent in 1577.[9] Plans for progresses
were also vulnerable to foreign affairs that might reshape domestic concerns and
cancel the journey, as happened in 1562, with the proposed meeting in York of
Elizabeth and Mary Stuart.[10] At such times, the organizational effort in preparing
for a progress was for naught, and, worse, required redoing as the court moved
elsewhere.

Equally beyond the control of Elizabeth and her court were the bad weather
and accidents that could mar the carefully planned occasion. Sometimes, it was
an act of God, as in 1572 in Warwick, where because of 'the weather having bene
very fowle [a] long tyme before', Elizabeth took a different route into the town,
leaving the uninformed burgesses to scramble from one muddy site of welcome to
another, so 'to attend her Hieghnes at the uttermost confynes of their Libertye'.[11]
Sometimes, the issue was not an act of nature but more a misdeed of man.
In 1572, errant fireworks used in a mock battle for the Queen's entertainment
in Warwick accidentally torched nearby houses: 'Whether by negligence or
otherwise, it happned that a ball of fyre fell on a house', and fireballs 'did so
flye quiet over the Castell, and into the myds of the Towne, falling downe,
some on houses, some in courts and baksides, and some in the streate . . . to the
great perill, or else great feare, of the inhabitants'.[12] One of the worst accidents
occurred during the 1566 visit to Oxford, when the stage for a play at Christ
Church collapsed, killing three men.[13] While Elizabeth did what she could to
make amends on such occasions, offering money in Warwick and doctors in
Oxford, the possibility of disaster made each progress an adventure in hospitality.

For hosts anticipating a royal visit, the greatest difficulty lay in planning. The
royal retinue sometimes appeared days earlier or later than hosts expected, or, for
reasons of contagion or foreign developments, never came at all. Once the Queen
and her household did arrive, hosts then had to grapple with the logistics of
lodging, provisioning, and entertaining up to two hundred people. To guide his
preparations for the Queen's visit to his house at Kew, Sir John Puckering listed
some seventeen tasks, beginning with the 'manner of receyvinge bothe without
the house and within', and concluding with his concern that 'Greate care to

[9] *Calendar of Letters and State Papers . . . in the Archives of Simancas, 1558–67*, ed. Martin A. S.
Hume (London: HMSO, 1892), 373; British Library, London [BL], Harleian MS 6992, fo. 15; *The
Progresses and Public Processions of Queen Elizabeth*, ed. John Nichols, 2nd edn., 3 vols. (London:
John Nichols, 1823), ii. 60–2. E. K. Chambers, *The Elizabethan Stage*, 4 vols. (Oxford: Clarendon
Press, 1923), iv. 75–116, offers a 'Court Calendar' of Elizabeth's itineraries. Concerning an outbreak
of plague in 1577, Burghley wrote to the Earl of Shrewsbury, 'The Queen's Majesty stays her
determination of any progress, doubting lest this sickness might increase further' (Edmund Lodge,
Illustrations of British History, 2nd edn. 3 vols. (London: G. Nicol, 1838), ii. 87).
[10] *CSP . . . Simancas, 1558–67*, ed. Hume, 254; J. E. Neale, *Queen Elizabeth I* (London:
Jonathan Cape, 1934; repr. 1957), 115–16.
[11] *Progresses*, ed. Nichols, 2nd edn., i. 310, quoting the 'Black Book' of Warwick.
[12] Ibid. 319–20, quoting the 'Black Book' of Warwick.   [13] Ibid. 210, quoting Wood's MS.

be had, and conference with the Gentlemen Ushers, how her Majestie would be lodged for her best ease and likinge, far from heate or noyse of any office near her lodging, and how her bed-chamber maye be kept free from anye noyse near it.'[14] Some ambitious hosts, such as William Cecil, Christopher Hatton, Robert Dudley, Thomas Gresham, and Edward Seymour, erected new houses or redesigned existing ones, but the majority of hosts used tents and temporary structures for extra shelter, and prepared their houses for the Queen by airing, cleaning, and repairing.[15] Although the royal household sent harbingers to assist in these arrangements, hosts bore the ultimate responsibility for completing the projects. For special provisions, hosts canvassed local markets to supplement the large quantities brought by the Queen herself. They also needed to have a gift for Elizabeth, such as clothing or jewels, and for others in the retinue, lesser remembrances, such as food or coin.[16] Hosts often arranged an entertainment for the Queen, a public display rich with opportunities for socially or politically ambitious hosts willing to plan and spend.

When towns received a royal visit, the corporation had obligations of hospitality similar to those of individual hosts. In preparing for the Queen's arrival, civic officials focused on sprucing up appearances. The townspeople repainted and regilded the royal coats of arms on town gates and guildhall; they purchased new gowns of office for civic leaders and new civic regalia; they arranged pageants, orations, bell-ringers, and musicians; and they whitewashed houses, repaired public buildings, cleaned streets, spread reeds, covered dunghills, removed trash, and herded hogs into pens. The town of Lichfield even paid five shillings to William Hollcroft 'for kepynge Madde Richard when her Matie was here'.[17] Towns customarily gave Elizabeth money in a silver cup or silk purse and food, gloves, or coin to members of the retinue.[18] In this way, the expense and work involved to receive the court occupied the civic community well in advance of the Queen's arrival.

[14] Ibid. iii. 252–3, quoting BL, Harleian MS 6850, fo. 90.
[15] See James M. Sutton, *Materializing Space at an Early Modern Prodigy House: The Cecils at Theobalds, 1564–1607* (Aldershot: Ashgate, 2004), and Pauline Croft (ed.), *Patronage, Culture and Power: The Early Cecils* (New Haven: Yale University Press, 2002); *Memoirs of the Life and Times of Sir Christopher Hatton*, ed. Harris Nicolas (London: n.p., 1847), 124–5, 325, 334; John William Burgon, *The Life and Times of Sir Thomas Gresham*, 2 vols. (New York: Burt Franklin, 1964), ii. 447; Ian Dunlop, *Palaces & Progresses of Elizabeth I* (London: Jonathan Cape, 1962), 120; Curt Breight, 'Realpolitik and Elizabethan Ceremony: The Earl of Hertford's Entertainment of Elizabeth at Elvetham, 1591', *Renaissance Quarterly*, 45 (1992), 20–48; and G. W. Bernard, 'Architecture and Politics in Tudor England', in *Power and Politics in Tudor England* (Aldershot: Ashgate, 2000), 175–90.
[16] For examples of gifts from hosts, see *Progresses*, ed. Nichols, 2nd edn., ii. 132; iii. 68, 83, 429, 441–2, 499, 568.
[17] Ibid. i. 529, quoting Mr Sharp of Coventry, Account of City of Lichfield.
[18] Cole, *Portable Queen*, 101–2; Bodleian Library, Oxford, Rawlinson MS B 146, fo. 116. On occasion, the Queen 'regifted' by offering to someone else a present originally given to her. During her 1573 visit to Sandwich, the town presented the Queen with a cup of gold that, six years later, she offered to the Frenchman Jean de Simier, who was serving in the retinue of the duc d'Alençon. See Philippa Glanville, *Silver in Tudor and Early Stuart England* (London: Victoria and Albert Museum, 1990), 28. I appreciate the insights on the common practice of regifting shared by Jane

In two aspects of a royal visit, namely accommodations and financing, towns had options not available to individual hosts. Because the Queen stayed in private residences in or close to the town, her civic hosts usually had little to do with the Queen's lodgings and provisions. When Elizabeth stayed at Sir Roger Manwood's house in Sandwich, at Sir John Young's 'Great House' in Bristol, and at Ambrose Dudley's castle in Warwick, these hosts saved the towns that expense of hospitality.[19] Towns also could spread the cost of a royal visit among the citizenry, who, as corporate hosts, invested and shared in the success of the occasion. Taking advantage of their local elites, towns generally financed a royal visit with a fiscal hierarchy parallel to the social one that governed the corporation. In Gloucester, the chamberlain began by collecting all unpaid fines and then turned to a special tax on the burgesses and on the trading companies, which contributed on a sliding scale with the tailors assessed at £4, down to the weavers at 11s.[20] In Worcester, the aldermen each contributed 40s., and each councillor 20s., towards the Queen's entertainment in 1575.[21] More unusual was the method used by the corporation of Ipswich of levying a general tax to pay for the Queen's visit in 1561. Assessors named by the town council met in the moot hall, determined the amounts owed by burgesses and householders, and enforced the tax with the penalty of disfranchisement.[22] The special circumstance that influenced the corporation of Leicester's financial strategy was the changing schedule of the Queen. The Leicester council assessed citizens using a scale similar to those in Worcester and Coventry, but it would only collect the money two weeks in advance of the Queen's presumed arrival—time enough to plan the ceremonies and tidy the town, but a guard against wasted effort if she did not come.[23]

While hosts faced the challenge of preparing for a royal visit that easily might be derailed, the Queen's own household and government faced their own set of difficulties on the road, with the natural result that no one in the retinue enjoyed the progresses quite as much as Elizabeth herself. Government officials,

Lawson, who is currently editing the New Year gift rolls of Elizabeth I to be published in the British Academy Records of Social and Economic History series.

[19] Thomas Dorman, 'Visits of Two Queens to Sandwich', *Archaeologia Cantiana: Transactions of the Kent Archaeological Society*, 16 (1886), 58–61; 'Transactions at Bristol', *Transactions of the Bristol and Gloucestershire Archaeological Society*, 15 (1980), 1–44 (p. 37).

[20] C. H. Dancey, 'Silver Plate and Insignia of the City of Gloucester', *Transactions of the Bristol and Gloucestershire Archaeological Society*, 30 (1907), 91–122 (p. 107).

[21] *Progresses*, ed. Nichols, 2nd edn., i. 550–1, quoting the accounts of Christopher Dyghton, Bailiff of Worcester.

[22] BL, Add. MS 25334, i, fo. 65; *East Anglian Miscellany*, 7 (1913), 18–19; Nathaniel Bacon, *The Annalls of Ipswiche*, ed. William H. Richardson (Ipswich: S. H. Cowell, 1884), 254–60. When Robert Barker refused to pay his assessment on time, the council deprived him of his status as freeman and spent the next two years trying to collect (Bacon, *Annalls of Ipswiche*, 252–63; P. W. Hasler, *The History of Parliament: The House of Commons, 1558–1603*, 3 vols. (London: HMSO, 1981), i. 248, 394–5).

[23] *Progresses*, ed. Nichols, 2nd edn., i. 417, quoting Leicester Town Records.

while away from London, had to keep the political machinery running, and courtiers had to abandon estates and families and use the slow exchange of letters to make domestic decisions and share news. As the travelling court relied on special posts to convey letters throughout the country, the business of governing continued. On progress, the Queen issued proclamations, corresponded with foreign ambassadors, signed commissions, regularly convened the Privy Council, and kept close to, among others, her Lord Treasurer, Principal Secretary, and Lord Chamberlain. But such constant activity, in the opinion of many, did not yield efficiency. William Tresham deferred his business at court because the Queen 'was in progresse, a tyme very unfitt for negotiation', and critics such as Francis Walsingham bemoaned the wasteful attendance on progress, when 'we are altogether given to banquettinge'.[24] Immediate decisions also could be difficult to wrest from the travelling Queen. In 1592, with 'the coort benge so farr from hence', Sir Thomas Shirley ordered his troops mustered against the Spanish to go to Southampton, a course of action that he hoped Lord Burghley and the Queen would approve after the fact.[25] Sir Simon Musgrave feared not receiving royal instructions regarding defences in Berwick and Newcastle 'because the Quenes matie was goinge in progresse' in 1593.[26] At Winchester in 1572, Sir Thomas Smith complained to Burghley that 'I do well perceive hir highnes is disposed to signe no thyng except your ldship be here.'[27] Progresses thus complicated the business of governing, frustrating courtiers but apparently satisfying a Queen comfortable with procrastination.

The mundane aspects of travel, such as food, beds, and transport, posed the hardest challenge to members of the royal household on whose efforts the Queen's and court's comfort depended. After the Lord Chamberlain drew up the itinerary for the upcoming progress, an advance team of harbingers, who were ushers and grooms of the Queen's chamber, prepared houses for the Queen's arrival.[28] At her own royal residences, her harbingers unlocked and aired the house, then proceeded to check everything from beds to charcoal before determining sleeping arrangements. At privately owned estates, they guided the hosts in organizing accommodations by issuing tickets that indicated whether travellers had rooms in the main house and grounds or were lodged 'outside' the court in nearby inns and private homes.

Feeding the travellers was another organizational and financial challenge. The Queen's household below stairs, with its officers and scores of servants, consisted of departments organized to provide room and board for those at court,

[24] The National Archives, London [NA], SP 12/282/94. For this and other of Walsingham's complaints, see NA, SP 12/109/10; NA, SP 12/45/80; BL, Harleian MS 6992, no. 8, fo. 15; NA, SP 12/105/30.

[25] NA, SP 12/243/7.

[26] NA, SP 15/32/141; Hasler, *The History of Parliament: Commons*, ii. 296.

[27] BL, Harleian MS 6991, no. 7, fo. 15.

[28] BL, Harleian MS 1641, fos. 12–13; BL, Harleian MS 1642, fos. 12–14; BL, Harleian MS 1644, fos. 66–72; NA, LS 13/279/9; Dunlop, *Palaces & Progresses*, 122.

whether on progress or not. The bakehouse, cellar, buttery, spicery, acatery, poultry, scullery, woodyard, and cart takers had the charge of purchasing and transporting provisions. Preparation occurred in the kitchen, boiling house, scalding house, baking house, and pastry, and distribution fell to the larder, pantry, chandlery, confectionary, and laundry. The servants to accomplish those tasks, along with their equipment, joined the caravan of courtiers snaking through the countryside in up to 250 horse-drawn carts, while the Queen rode on horseback or in elaborate open coaches.[29] Because of the expense to the crown, household officers strove to limit the cost of their hospitality even as they fulfilled their obligation to provide it. Guiding their efforts in the doomed battle against waste were household regulations codified during the late fifteenth and sixteenth centuries. The 'Bouche of Court' and the 'Book of the Diet' listed the name or position of people in the court who could claim room and board at the Queen's expense, and they specified, according to status, the number and type of portions.[30] But no one could control the comings and goings at such a vibrant court, nor could theoretical limits on permissible dishes deter hungry attendants. Courtiers flouted the rules also by consuming extra dishes in their private rooms, instead of more frugally sharing them at a common table. Despite genuine, if sporadic, efforts to reform the household, the waste of food and money grew.[31] Sheltering, feeding, and moving the retinue posed a continual challenge and rising expense to the Queen's household.

Gathering supplies for the itinerant court was the difficult job of purveyors, men with a royal licence to purchase food in local markets or from local farmers at a compulsory discount. They also had the authority to commandeer, for a limited time, carts and horses.[32] Purveyors were widely unpopular because some took illegal advantage of sellers and communities: they undervalued the cost

[29] NA, LS 13/168/368–71; Bodleian, Rawlinson MS, B 146, fo. 116; BL, Lansdowne MS 59, no. 25; Allegra Woodworth, 'Purveyance for the Royal Household in the Reign of Queen Elizabeth', *Transactions of the American Philosophical Society*, 35 (1945), 1–89 (pp. 7–8); *Progresses*, ed. Nichols, 2nd edn., i. 269; A. P. Newton, 'Tudor Reforms in the Royal Household', in R. W. Seton-Watson (ed.), *Tudor Studies Presented to A. F. Pollard* (New York: Russell & Russell, 1924), 251–2. According to Harrison's estimate, 'when the Queen's Majesty doth remove from any one place to another, there are usually four hundred cartwares [teams], which amount to the sum of 2,400 horses, appointed out of the countries adjoining, whereby her carriage is conveyed safely unto the appointed place' (William Harrison, *The Description of England*, ed. Georges Edelen (Ithaca, NY: Cornell University Press, 1968), 307). Julian Munby has analysed the construction, costs, and use of royal coaches in 'Queen Elizabeth's Coaches: The Wardrobe on Wheels', *Antiquaries Journal*, 83 (2003), 311–67.

[30] According to Allegra Woodworth in her detailed analysis of the Queen's household, these two books are no longer extant (Woodworth, 'Purveyance', 12 n. 4). Woodworth studied remnants of their contents in the surviving Records of the Board of Greencloth (NA, LS 13/168–9), household reports to Burghley (BL, Lansdowne MS 16, nos. 54, 21, 61–7; BL, Harleian MS 589, nos. 29–30), and the Household Book 43 Eliz in *Household Ordinances*, 281–93. (Woodworth, 'Purveyance', 12 (nn. 3–4), 13 (n. 10), 17 (n. 54), 84 (n. 2).)

[31] For details of the expenses and of the attempts to curtail them, see Cole, *Portable Queen*, 52–61.

[32] Woodworth, 'Purveyance', 471–3; NA, LS 13/179/11.

of provisions, instead of money they gave receipts to be redeemed, and they resold food intended for the court and pocketed the profit. Such embezzling and extortion made purveyors frequent defendants in the legal courts, where the guilty drew sentences of fines, time in the pillory, or even hanging.[33] Some farmers and merchants must have had conflicting responses, therefore, to the news that the Queen intended a progress near their village. To diffuse local anger that might extend to the court itself, and to curb rising prices, in 1589 Elizabeth finally yielded to parliamentary calls for reform as a way of protecting the popularity she sought to cultivate through progresses.[34]

At its heart, then, the challenge of travel for the royal household was a financial one, because the Queen spent more on food, supplies, and accommodation when on progress than when she remained in the London area. While it is hard to get a complete picture of expenses and payments, we can examine areas of cost to the Queen and look at contemporary assessments of the situation. Her greatest expenditures went towards transportation; purveyance of horses, carts, and food; servants' fees and wages; special posts; accommodation; and maintenance of royal palaces. For the 1561 progress into Essex and Suffolk, Thomas Weldon, cofferer of the household, kept a tally of the Queen's expenses at each of the places she stayed during the seventy-six-day trip. The court's expenses varied from £83 to £146 per day, with a total cost of £8,540.[35] These sums attracted the attention of Lord Treasurer Burghley, who, eager to save royal funds, analysed the progresses of 1573 and 1576 in search of cost-cutting opportunities. To the familiar advice of adhering to the set itinerary and to the rules of the Diet, he added the specific extra household charges that accrued due to progresses: the bakehouse spent one penny more for each loaf of bread, for example, and, in order to transport beer, ale, and wine, the buttery and cellar spent £294 more than 'if her majtie remeyined at her standing [houses] within xx myles of London'. He estimated that the 1573 progress in nearby Kent and Sussex cost the Queen an extra £1,018. The seven-week progress of 1576 through Essex, Hertfordshire, Buckinghamshire, and Surrey cost more. As Burghley advised, 'If her matie hade not so long continenewed her prograce, her matie chardgis had not bene as much as it was by two Thousand pounds', a genuine saving in a household budget that he tried to limit to £40,000 annually.[36]

[33] *The Diary of Henry Machyn*, ed. John Gough Nichols (London: Camden Society, 1848), 189; *Calendar of Assize Records: Essex Indictments Elizabeth I*, ed. J. S. Cockburn (London: HMSO, 1978), nos. 389, 892, 1402, 1403, 2154; *Calendar of Assize Records: Kent Indictments Elizabeth I*, ed. J. S. Cockburn (London: HMSO, 1979), no. 1483; *Calendar of Assize Records: Hertfordshire Indictments Elizabeth I*, ed. J. S. Cockburn (London: HMSO, 1975), no. 400.

[34] J. E. Neale, *Elizabeth and her Parliaments*, 2 vols. (London: Jonathan Cape, 1953–7), ii (1957), 208–15; Woodworth, 'Purveyance', 22–5, 37–8.

[35] BL, Cotton MS, Vespasian C, 14, ii, no. 205, fos. 188–96; Hasler, *The History of Parliament: Commons*, iii. 593.

[36] BL, Lansdowne MS 16, no. 51, fos. 106–9; BL, Lansdowne MS 21, no. 67; BL, Harleian MS 589, nos. 31 and 32, fos. 185–6; Woodworth, 'Purveyance', 58–9.

These figures, perhaps, explained why household officers never considered using progresses to decrease royal expenses. Despite her reputation for parsimony, Elizabeth used her own household funds to support her summer progresses. Torn between her desires to govern frugally and to travel widely, Elizabeth chose the progresses, and by her actions she made clear her view that such travel brought benefits.

THE ROLE OF HOSTS

Against what rewards, then, did her hosts and the Queen balance the many difficulties inherent in the progresses? For the hosts, their reward was having access to the Queen and asserting an enhanced status in their locality. Individual and civic hosts valued a royal visit for the opportunity of displaying, through appropriate hospitality, their place within the community and for the possibility of using their access to Elizabeth for personal benefit at some point. Hosts of the travelling court found that even a brief overnight visit gave them the opportunity to discuss private matters with the Queen and burnish their relationships with her for future reward. Whether at that time she heard or ignored any request, or whether the seed of the petition would yield fruit later, the occasion of a royal visit presented possibilities to which few hosts would be immune.[37] Petitioners also hoped to intercept the travelling Queen to lay their requests before her. Gilbert Talbot, the Countess of Derby, and Valentine Lee, for example, sought private favours from Elizabeth, and they eagerly used the opportunities for royal access inherent in the progresses.[38] The verbal, private nature of such communication meant that there were relatively few written accounts of such requests. Indeed, the private nature of this direct contact with Elizabeth, as she used their houses, dined with them, and shared accommodation, was precisely what gave hosts a special access to power that inspired and underscored their hospitality.

This belief in the benefits of hospitality revealed itself in the hosts' careful preparations, their manoeuvring to entertain the Queen, and their disappointment at missing her. In 1577, Thomas Sackville, Lord Buckhurst, disdaining the quality of local foods, imported provisions from Flanders, and speedily renovated

---

[37] Felicity Heal notes in this collection that Elizabeth was even less likely to listen to direct petitions from individual hosts, and entertainment on progress was only one part of a process of seeking royal favour ('Giving and Receiving on Royal Progress', 46–61). But Elizabeth's lack of response did not necessarily negate hosts' asking or manoeuvring indirectly for later results. While Elizabeth might have ignored or rejected the request, her hosts would not have squandered such a special opportunity. Civic petitions did sometimes succeed.

[38] Talbot sought 'a gracious answer in my suit' (Lodge, *Illustrations*, ii. 368); the Countess of Derby sought a return to the Queen's favour (*Memoirs of Hatton*, ed. Nicolas, 346); from the Queen, Valentine Lee sought an order for financial support from her husband Thomas, then in Ireland (*HMC Calendar of the Manuscripts of the Most Hon. the Marquis of Salisbury*, 25 vols. (London: HMSO, 1888–1976), x (1904), 301).

his house, which he hoped 'do not mislike her; that is my cheif care: the rest shalbe performed with that good hart as I am sure yt wilbe accepted'.[39] A similar desire to extend appropriate, yet impressive, hospitality led Sir Thomas Gresham to surprise the Queen at Osterley with a new courtyard wall, erected overnight, in response to her suggestion of the 'handsome' potential of such an addition.[40] But building did not guarantee a royal visit, as Sir Christopher Hatton found after he erected Holdenby in Northamptonshire as a 'shrine to the Queen': although Hatton entertained her in London, she never saw his country house.[41] Henry Percy, Earl of Northumberland, unsuccessfully angled to have Elizabeth stay with him at Petworth on her 1591 progress through Sussex, and Lady Margaret Norris was miffed when Elizabeth bypassed Rycote.[42] The frustration of an absent host unable to welcome the Queen could equal that of a willing host with no royal guest. Sir Thomas Smith was distraught that Elizabeth lodged in his Berkshire house, Ankerwick, while he was serving as her ambassador in France in 1565. While 'he heartily wished to be among' her retinue, Smith wrote to Robert Dudley that her happiness there 'recompenseth all' and that he hoped to entertain her himself in the future.[43] After inviting the Queen to stay with him in 1597 at Ruckholt in Essex, Sir Michael Hickes worried about his wife's gift for Elizabeth and about his small house, which 'had noe convenient place to entertaine sum of hir Maties necessary servants', and in welcoming the Queen, he found that 'I had use neither of speech nor memory.'[44] A few years later during the progress of 1601 into Berkshire, Sir John Popham offered his hospitality to the court at his nearby house, Littlecot. Inviting Sir Robert Cecil and others to stay with him, Popham graciously desired them to 'make the best of what they shall find here, and to take all in good part; otherwise I fear me I shall be utterly ashamed'.[45] The nexus of ideas of hospitality, reputation, and self-interest during progresses provided a fertile environment for display and self-fashioning.

Civic leaders took advantage of the public nature of a royal visit to embed a request for aid within their welcoming pageantry that became a ceremonial dialogue. The people of Folkestone wanted Elizabeth to visit them in 1573, 'in the hope of securing the aid of the crown for their failing haven', and used an escort of fifty trained men and a petition delivered by the Mayor to make their

---

[39] *Original Letters Illustrative of English History*, ed. Henry Ellis, 2nd edn., 3 vols. (London: Harding, Triphook, and Lepard, 1824), ii. 271.

[40] Burgon, *Life of Gresham*, ii. 447; Dunlop, *Palaces & Progresses*, 120.

[41] *Memoirs of Hatton*, ed. Nicolas, 124–6, 155, 334.

[42] Gordon R. Batho, 'The Finances of an Elizabethan Nobleman: Henry Percy, Ninth Earl of Northumberland (1564–1632)', *Economic History Review*, NS, 9 (1957), 433–50 (p. 448); Hasler, *The History of Parliament: Commons*, iii. 203; *Memoirs of Hatton*, ed. Nicolas, 269.

[43] Mary Dewar, *Sir Thomas Smith: A Tudor Intellectual in Office* (London: Athlone Press, 1964), 88–117; John Strype, *The Life of the Learned Sir Thomas Smith* (New York: Burt Franklin Reprints, 1974), 88; Hasler, *The History of Parliament: Commons*, iii. 400.

[44] Ellis, *Original Letters*, ii. 275–6; Alan G. R. Smith, *Servant of the Cecils: The Life of Sir Michael Hickes, 1543–1612* (London: Jonathan Cape, 1977), 108.

[45] *HMC . . . Salisbury*, ii (1888), 361.

appeal.[46] That same year, the citizens of Sandwich, before asking for aid to repair their harbour, orchestrated a welcome for Elizabeth that underlined through ceremony both their need and their merit. After receiving a gift and hearing a minister's oration, Elizabeth watched a spinning demonstration, enjoyed a banquet, and then viewed a mock battle in which armed combatants stormed a fort. When Mayor John Gilbert presented the petition to restore the harbour, the citizens of Sandwich had already conveyed to the Queen a message of their civic status, their industry, and their martial valour.[47] During her visit to Bristol in 1574, the citizens treated Elizabeth to another mock battle, this time between the allegorical opponents War and Peace, to press for the harmonious foreign relations that would foster better trade for their declining harbour. She heard a civic orator assert: 'Our Traed doth stand on sivill lief, and thear our glory lies; And not on strief, the ruen of staets, a storm that all destroys.' When the three-day battle ended in a victory for Peace, sanctioned by the Queen, the civic message was complete.[48] During the long progress of 1575, Elizabeth heard similar petitions for economic aid from the town of Worcester, which sought protection of its guilds, its cloth trade, and the return of the 'old Corts' to town. She later granted some of these requests, based in part on her interactions with the Worcester citizenry, whom she liked 'as well of them as I have liked of any people in all my progresse time, ye in all my life', a sentiment and rhetorical flourish often extended to other civic hosts.[49]

Elizabeth's frequent role as economic patron changed, on rare occasions, into the role of Queen as judicial arbiter. Prior to her arrival in Cambridge in 1564, the Queen settled a dispute between the corporation and university over the power to license the number of alehouses, which temporarily expanded and contracted to accommodate the liquid needs of the travelling court. She upheld the University's right to control alehouses within its liberties and ordered the Mayor not to 'intermeddle' in those affairs again.[50] Her visit to Coventry in

[46] Canon Jenkins, 'On the Municipal Records of Folkestone', *Archaeologia Cantiana: Transactions of the Kent Archaeological Society*, 10 (1876), lxix–lxxxv, cxiii; *Progresses*, ed. Nichols, 2nd edn., i. 336.

[47] *Progresses*, ed. Nichols, 2nd edn., i. 337–9, quoting Boys's *History of Sandwich*, 691–5.

[48] David M. Bergeron, *English Civic Pageantry 1558–1642* (London: Edward Arnold, 1971; repr. Tempe-Arizona State Medieval and Renaissance Studies, 2003), 28–30, 46; David Harris Sacks, 'Celebrating Authority in Bristol, 1475–1640', in Susan Zimmerman and Ronald F. E. Weissman (eds.), *Urban Life in the Renaissance* (Newark: University of Delaware Press, 1989), 187–223; Thomas Churchyard's entertainment in *Progresses*, ed. Nichols, 2nd edn., i. 395–405.

[49] NA, SP 12/105/56; *Progresses*, ed. Nichols, 2nd edn., i. 545–8, quoting from the Chamber Order Book at Worcester.

[50] NA, SP 12/34/57. The additional alehouses created more economic activity in the community during the Queen's visits. Strictly regulated to ensure proper measurements, quality, and price, as well as to prohibit gaming and prostitution, these alehouses reflected the economic turmoil, positive and negative, that the court's presence created in local markets (NA, LS 13/168/31–34, 53–5; *Calendar of Assize Records: Surrey Indictments Elizabeth I*, ed. J. S. Cockburn (London: HMSO, 1980), nos. 3052, 3053). For example, while Greenwich farmers sold their grain at higher prices during progresses, the bakers who relied on it for their livelihood protested that 'by reasone now of

1566 gave the citizens a platform from which to solicit royal judgements on several civic grievances. As John Throckmorton, the vigilant town Recorder, explained in his official speech of welcome, 'sinister, underhand, unjust means' had deprived the town of income intended to support a school established by Henry VIII in 1545, and as the Queen stood on the site of the decayed school, the citizens asked for her help. According to observers, Elizabeth was 'extremely incensed' at the injustice they described and gave them some money towards the school, although full restoration of funds did not happen until a parliamentary Act in 1583.[51] The Queen also intervened in a dispute between 'sour' preachers opposed to the town's Hock Tuesday play and the citizens determined to stage it.[52] In both her 1566 and 1575 visits, she insisted on a performance of the play, in which women took up arms in defence of their country and physically triumphed over Danish invaders.

The essence of hospitality during the progresses, whether in towns, cities, or in manor houses, was the shared sense of propriety that guided hosts in offering their best and the Queen in accepting it. Elizabeth frequently linked the success of her visits to the generosity and welcoming spirit of her hosts. She thanked Coventry citizens for their purse of £100 by remarking that 'I have but few such' gifts.[53] From Warwick citizens, she accepted a purse of £20, filled also with 'their good wills', even though she professed herself 'unwilling to tak any thing of you, because I knowe that a myte of their haunds is as much as a thowsand pounds of some others'.[54] And at Cambridge, 'altogether against her expectation', she 'was so received, that, she thought, she could not be better'.[55] Tudor hospitality varied according to the social stature of the host. The flamboyant gesture from a courtier or close confidant thus differed from the display by a host of lesser means who aimed to impress the visiting Queen.[56] In this spirit of hospitality, the hosts did all they could, relative to their means, to please and impress the Queen; in turn, Elizabeth measured her reception and shaped her response to it

her highnes continuance there', the cost of making bread rose and thus they needed economic aid (NA, SP 12/189/129).

[51] *Progresses*, ed. Nichols, 2nd edn., i. 195; *Victoria County History: Warwickshire*, ed. William Page, 8 vols. (Oxford: Oxford University Press, 1964–69), ii (1908), 324; *Coventry: Its History & Antiquities*, comp. Benjamin Poole (London: J. R. Smith, 1870), 89, 245–51. For a discussion of the dating of the 1566 visit, see Cole, *Portable Queen*, 245 n. 45.

[52] *Records of Early English Drama: Coventry*, ed. R. W. Ingram (Toronto: University of Toronto Press, 1981), 215, 272–6, 583–4; *Progresses*, ed. Nichols, 2nd edn., i. 446–56; Bergeron, *English Civic Pageantry*, 33.

[53] Coventry Record Office, Annals of the City of Coventry, 1348–1684, MS D, 68; *Progresses*, ed. Nichols, 2nd edn., i. 192.

[54] *Progresses*, ed. Nichols, 2nd edn., i. 315, quoting from the 'Black Book' of Warwick.

[55] Francis Peck, *Desiderata Curiosa*, 2 vols. (London: n.p., 1732), ii, bk. 7, 34; John Stow, *Annales, or, a generall chronicle of England* (London: John Beale, Bernard Alsop, Thomas Fawcett, and Augustine Mathewes, 1632), 657; Cambridge University Library [CUL], Baker MS 24, 252–8, and Baker MS 29, 367; BL, Add. MS 5845, fo. 226.

[56] Felicity Heal, *Hospitality in Early Modern England* (Oxford: Clarendon Press, 1990), 26–7, 389–92.

through the filter of her hosts' abilities and expressions of loyalty. Or, as William Cecil defined the experience, Elizabeth should 'see my good will in my service, and all other . . . fynd no lack of good chere'.[57]

Even though many hosts, therefore, willingly entertained the Queen because doing so could bring them the rewards of royal contact without necessarily emptying their coffers, the expense of a royal visit rose during the Queen's later years. Sir William Petre entertained the Queen for four days at Ingatestone in 1561, at a cost of £136, and on the same progress, she stayed with the Earl of Oxford at Hedingham for six days, which cost him £273.[58] However, rising expectations and a competitive opulence during the famous progresses of the 1570s led to higher costs for some hosts that continued to the end of her reign. Sir Nicholas Bacon spent £577 when Elizabeth visited him at Gorhambury in 1577; Lord North entertained the Queen for three days at Kirtling in 1578, which cost him £762; and in 1602 for a four-day visit to Harefield, Sir Thomas Egerton expended close to £2,000.[59] While the Queen continued to assume substantial costs of her progresses, the customs associated with royal visits grew more expensive to hosts.

THE QUEEN'S AGENDA AND ITS LIMITATIONS

From the Queen's perspective, the rewards of progresses extended beyond the pleasures of new vistas, fresh accommodations, camaraderie, and entertainment. The visits fostered a dialogue between sovereign and subjects and reflected the power of her presence—and, on occasion, the power of her absence—that focused attention on important matters of religion, diplomacy, and defence. As sovereign and supreme governor of the Church, Elizabeth pursued her goal of fostering religious conformity among Protestants and Catholics through her choice of destination. Because the public nature of the progresses gave the Queen a natural occasion to speak on religious matters, Elizabeth used her presence to cultivate unity and loyalty. During her 1561 visit to Ipswich, the Queen observed that 'in Cathedrals and Colleges there were so many wives, and widows and children seen', a situation that she tried to rectify by an immediate injunction banning females from clerical lodgings.[60] A few years later, her visits to the two

[57] BL, Cotton MS, Titus B, 13, fo. 173.

[58] F. G. Emmison, *Tudor Secretary: Sir William Petre at Court and Home* (London: Longmans, Green, 1961), 237–45.

[59] Thomas Birch, *Memoirs of the Reign of Queen Elizabeth*, 2 vols. (London: A Millar, 1754), i. 12; *Progresses*, ed. Nichols, 2nd edn., ii. 236–8, quoting from the 'Book of Household Charges . . . of Lord North'; *The Egerton Papers*, ed. J. Payne Collier (London: J. B. Nichols, 1840), 340–57; Paul Johnson, *Elizabeth I: A Study in Power and Intellect* (London: Weidenfeld and Nicolson, 1974), 229.

[60] *Progresses*, ed. Nichols, 2nd edn., i. 96. For the Ipswich quote, Nichols is paraphrasing Strype, *Life of Parker*, 106. For a compelling analysis of Elizabeth's attitude toward married clergy, see Brett Usher, 'Queen Elizabeth and Mrs Bishop', in Susan Doran and Thomas S. Freeman (eds.), *The Myth of Elizabeth* (London: Palgrave Macmillan, 2003), 200–20.

universities had similarly stressed religious conformity. Preparing for the Queen's arrival in Cambridge in 1564, Chancellor William Cecil called for order and uniformity among the scholars 'in apparel & religion', and later, getting what he asked for, he 'reioysed to see theym in so comely aparell'.[61] Religious conformity regarding vestments also concerned the Chancellor of Oxford, Robert Dudley, who supervised the University's readiness to entertain Elizabeth in 1566. On her return to Oxford decades later, in 1592, the Queen continued the theme of conformity, admonishing the scholars to worship 'not according to the opinion of the world, not according to far-fetched, fine-spun theories, but as the Divine Law commands, and as our law preaches'.[62] The confluence of message, speaker, and settings epitomized the value of such public occasions to the itinerant Queen.

In the areas of diplomacy and defence, Elizabeth found progresses helpful in conducting negotiations and presenting herself as England's defender. Sometimes she travelled in the company of foreign ambassadors, who used the opportunity to discuss marriage proposals, while Elizabeth used the display of progress entertainments and public dialogues to impress them with her political authority and popularity. But moving her court also allowed the Queen to practise the fine art of absence and avoid foreign messengers, who, lacking information about the court's location, waited in frustration for her to reappear.[63] In another expression of diplomacy on her visits to fortified towns and cities, harbours, and ships, Elizabeth crafted for herself the military role of protector that she did not, or could not, enact on the battlefield. On visits to such places as Rochester, Sandwich, Deptford, Bristol, Portsmouth, and Southampton, the Queen embraced the martial images created by cannon, guns, fireworks, ships, and staged battles.[64] These displays of military readiness united the Queen with her subjects as joint defenders of England, and they were ceremonies that Elizabeth would welcome for their power to mitigate any lingering doubts about security under a female monarch.

---

[61] Peck, *Desiderata Curiosa*, ii, bk. 7, 23–9; CUL, Ff. 5.14, fos. 88–94.

[62] Stow, *Annales*, 660; *Elizabethan Oxford*, ed. Charles Plummer (Oxford: Oxford Historical Society, 1887), 200; Frederick S. Boas, *University Drama in the Tudor Age* (Oxford: Clarendon Press, 1914; repr. New York, 1966), 89–108; *Progresses*, ed. Nichols, 2nd edn., i. 206–47; George P. Rice, *The Public Speaking of Queen Elizabeth* (New York: Columbia University Press, 1951), 99; CUL, Patrick Papers, no. 34, fos. 5–9, and CUL, Baker MS 36, fos. 446–8. For an analysis of the changing rhetoric and tone in the Queen's speeches at the two universities, see Linda Shenk, 'Turning Learned Authority into Royal Supremacy: Elizabeth I's Learned Persona and her University Orations', in Carole Levin, Jo Eldridge Carney, and Debra Barrett-Graves (eds.), *Elizabeth I: Always her Own Free Woman* (Aldershot: Ashgate, 2003), 78–96.

[63] In an enterprising move of their own, Londoners took advantage of the Queen's absence on progress to engage in unregulated construction. According to a letter from the Privy Council to the justices of the peace of Middlesex, 'in this tyme of vacation and absence of her Majestie in Progresse', disobedient people were erecting new and remodelling old buildings in London, 'taking the oportunity of the tyme as they thinke in the absence of the Court and of the Justices of the Peace for that countie, being for the most parte at their houses in the country' (*Acts of the Privy Council of England: New Series . . . 1591*, ed. J. R. Dasent (London: HMSO, 1890), 422).

[64] Cole, *Portable Queen*, 100, 157–63.

But while her progresses reasserted the nature of her personal monarchy, they also suggested the political limitations of her queenship, particularly in regard to her own safety and reputation. Elizabeth's desire to interact with her subjects gave hundreds of hosts access to Queen and court; her cultivation of her popularity, however, ran into the awkward reality that progresses increased her vulnerability. In view of the assassinations of European rulers and the papal attack on Elizabeth's sovereignty, English officials legitimately worried about crowds and vagrants approaching the travelling court. Royal proclamations, such as that of 5 August 1601, targeted vagrants who sought to profit from access to the court: 'Whereas the Queens moste excellente matie is determined verie shortlie to make her remove from Grenwich unto her castle of Windsore, and soe from there to goe in progresse', all masterless men, boys, vagabonds, rogues, and unauthorized women had twelve hours to leave the court.[65] According to a 1593 memorandum, Burghley wanted household officials during progresses to survey all inhabitants within two miles of the court; anyone without a special warrant or those not enrolled in the porter's book would face imprisonment.[66] The intrinsic difficulty of policing a peripatetic, fluctuating court meant that these efforts had minimal success.

Despite attempts to preserve order within and control access to the court, progresses offered an opportune occasion to harm the Queen, as a malcontent noted, 'for she taketh no care of her going'. For two assassins, Elizabeth's progress into Wiltshire in 1592 seemed an 'opportunietie fitt for this practise . . . the benefitt therof be not over slipped'.[67] The next year Robert Parsons and Gilbert Laton conspired to murder the Queen 'and sheweth howe yt might be performed—her matie being in the progress—and to be executed with a wyer . . . or with a poyniard'.[68] Obviously, both attempts were foiled, but they stand as important examples of how the Queen's programme of progresses could reveal her subjects' venom as well as their esteem.

Such unpredictable responses to Elizabeth's presence and image reflected how communications between subjects and Queen could shift during progresses. While Elizabeth could attract public attention, she could not always control it, and rumours flourished in the wake of the travelling court. The attentiveness and proximity to the Queen of Robert Dudley, partly from his duties as Master of the Horse, led to scandalmongering about the real purpose of Elizabeth's frequent progresses. In Ipswich, a citizen claimed that Elizabeth 'looked like one lately come out of childbed'; about her progress in 1564, 'Some say she is pregnant and is going away to lie in.' Another rumour asserted that 'Lord Robert hath had fyve children by the Quene, and she never goethe in progresse but to be delivered.'[69]

---

[65] NA, LS 13/168/40, 14. See also NA, LS 13/168/5–10, 15–22; Birch, *Memoirs*, i. 149–51, 59.

[66] NA, SP 12/247/98. [67] NA, SP 12/247/61; SP 12/113/173.

[68] NA, SP 12/244/112.

[69] Carole Levin, '*The Heart and Stomach of a King': Elizabeth I and the Politics of Sex and Power* (Philadelphia: University of Pennsylvania Press, 1994), 81; NA, SP 12/148/157.

Such rumours present an unsurprising slander of a Queen who loved travel, men, and power.

PATTERNS OF ELIZABETHAN PROGRESSES

The patterns of her progresses mirrored Elizabeth's priorities as Queen, her relations with courtiers and citizens, and contemporary ideas about hospitality. In arranging her progresses for the summer and autumn, July to September, Elizabeth avoided outbreaks of plague in London and sought the salubrious country air at a time when the business of parliament, not in session, required nothing from her and when hay for the horses was abundant. By favouring special courtiers with long visits of one to two weeks, the Queen through her presence endorsed for them a privileged status; by spending only one or two nights with more typical hosts, she made her visit manageable for them in terms of preparation, entertainment, and expense. Through her visits to about four hundred hosts, the Queen entered the houses and lives of people whose support was important to her sovereignty. Privy Counsellors, justices of the peace, sheriffs, and members of parliament entertained her, as did smaller groups of bishops, women, and Catholics.[70] She targeted important regional towns, the two universities, and cathedral towns.

But against this background, certain geographical and chronological patterns suggest constraints on the Queen's travel and, by extension, on her monarchy. Elizabeth never left England, much less the island, and she set foot in only half of the English counties. The Queen never visited the south-west, nor did she risk travelling in the predominantly Catholic northern regions of England. What parts of England she did see lay within a polygon roughly bounded in the north by Lincolnshire and Staffordshire, in the west by Bristol, and in the south and east by Kent and Norfolk. While her longest progresses took her 150 miles from London, most of the time she travelled within forty or fifty miles of London. The Queen always stayed, therefore, within the relatively populous, wealthy, protected areas of her kingdom.

Thus, Elizabeth did not use progresses to pacify troubled regions; instead, her progresses took her into secure areas where her presence validated her authority and social stability where they already existed. Within England, the rugged terrain, rough roads, and sparse population of the north and west did not, for her purposes, make travel there alluring. In addition, the problematic presence of Mary Stuart in northern England from 1568 to 1587 remained a barrier to any travel there that Elizabeth might consider. Determined not to see the Scottish cousin who insisted on meeting her, Elizabeth kept her distance and avoided even the appearance of

---

[70] See Lucy Wooding, *Rethinking Catholicism in Reformation England* (Oxford: Clarendon Press, 2000), 195–6; Cole, 'Religious Conformity and the Progresses of Elizabeth I', in Levin et al. (eds.), *Elizabeth I*, 63–77.

proximity. Elizabeth remained within the English heartland, therefore, perhaps because it was the safer, easier, and more successful course of action.

A chronological survey also reveals how, throughout her reign, Elizabeth's progresses mirrored her personal and political fortunes. As a new Queen restructuring her Church, government, and foreign policy, Elizabeth kept her first progresses, in 1559 and 1560, brief and close to London, as she stayed with trusted friends in Kent, Surrey, and Hampshire. Her longer progress into Suffolk in 1561 inaugurated a more expansive itinerary, one that continued in 1564 and 1566, when the increasingly confident and experienced Queen visited the universities, Northamptonshire, Coventry, and Kenilworth. But the Northern Rising of 1569 restricted her movements to the London area and Hampshire, and during the next two years the Queen travelled quietly in the region between Oxfordshire and Essex. Then, between 1572 and 1578, Elizabeth embarked on the richly ceremonial, lengthy progresses to Warwick, Gloucestershire, Bristol, Wiltshire, Stafford, Worcester, Canterbury, and Norwich that, in their pageantry and exuberance, embodied the celebrated bond between subjects and Queen. In the turmoil of the 1580s, however, with the crises generated by Mary Stuart and the war with Spain, Elizabeth made no progress, remaining instead with close friends in the London area or in her own safe houses along the Thames.[71] But with the defeat of the Armada in 1588, Elizabeth resumed her travels in ways reminiscent of those she had undertaken a generation earlier: for two months in 1591, she wandered through Sussex into Hampshire, south to Portsmouth and Southampton; and the next year in 1592, she had an equally long journey west through Buckinghamshire, Gloucestershire, and Oxfordshire. But as old friends died and economic problems grew, the ageing Queen travelled in areas closer to London on the few progresses remaining before her death.

By the late 1590s, under the onslaught of dashed expectations of favour, rising costs of entertainment, and anticipation of a new monarch, among some hosts the spirit of hospitality towards the Queen characteristic of Elizabeth's early reign was shrinking. In 1600, Thomas Arundell was 'unwilling to have Warder [Castle] named in a progress time'; and host Sir William Clark, according to a member of the retinue in 1602, 'nether gives mete nor monny to any of the progressers; the house her ma. hathe at commandement and his grasse the gards horses eate, he shafes and this is all'.[72] Sir Henry Lee refused to welcome the Queen in 1600, complaining to Robert Cecil, 'my estate without my undoing cannot bear it, my continuance in her Court has been long, my charge great, my land sold and debts not small: how this will agree with the entertaining of such a Prince your wisdome can best judge'. Lee would have entertained her 'as oft beforetime, if my fortune answered my desire, or part of her Highness' many

---

[71] The one exception was her brief journey in February 1582 through Kent to escort her rejected suitor, the duc d'Alençon, to his transport at Dover (Chambers, *Elizabethan Stage*, iv. 98–9).
[72] *HMC . . . Salisbury*, x (1904), 283; NA, SP 12/284/97.

promises performed'.[73] While these reluctant hosts were unusual in the larger picture of four decades of hospitality, their actions paint a poignant image of declining influence in the waning years of Elizabeth's monarchy.

Seen as a whole, and in the context of their cost and inefficiency, Elizabeth's progresses appear more than a royal hobby: they indicate an expression of her personal statecraft. The court moved or stayed according to her word. Even as hundreds of people participated in the progresses, the Queen happily flourished at the centre of the turbulence that she orchestrated. The attendant ceremonies and entertainments of her travels focused on the presence among her subjects of their Tudor Queen, the daughter of Henry VIII. Paradoxically, through that presence, Elizabeth's very movement kept the idea of the stability of her queenly rule before the changing panoply of her people. By going on progress with all the expense and difficulty, the Queen dodged decisions, delayed commitments, and cultivated her authority through the disorder of travel. The same Elizabeth so famously thrifty in other areas of her government—rewards, military support, and fiscal reform—nonetheless paid for the benefits that came to her from the problematic and expensive progresses. As William Harrison aptly observed of the travelling Queen, 'every nobleman's house is her palace, where she continueth during pleasure and till she return again to some of her own'.[74] Through four decades of arrivals, visits, and departures, Elizabeth in her progresses embraced a style of personal, mobile monarchy that has echoed through the centuries as an intrinsic part of her legacy.

[73] *HMC . . . Salisbury*, x (1904), 180.   [74] Harrison, *Description of England*, 227.

3

Giving and Receiving on Royal Progress

Felicity Heal

COSTS AND BENEFITS

The subject of the Elizabethan progresses has provoked some historians to express profound disapproval of the Virgin Queen. In Lawrence Stone's memorable language: 'erratic and destructive as a hurricane, summer after summer Elizabeth wandered about the English countryside bringing ruin in her train, while apprehensive noblemen abandoned their homes and fled at the mere rumour of her approach'.[1] Stone's is merely the most trenchant version of a more general view that any benefits derived from these summer eruptions tended to be outweighed by the problems. E. K. Chambers, who devoted such careful attention to the pattern and pageantry of royal progresses, reflected that in the end they were of little advantage to those who received the Queen. Elizabeth's unpredictability made the planning of her entertainment a logistic nightmare; the host often had to vacate his own dwelling to make space; the court, when it came, destroyed lawns and gardens and pilfered furnishings.[2] As for the supposed benefit: 'you probably got knighted, if you were not a knight already, which cost you some fees, and you received some sugared royal compliments on the excellence of your entertainment and the appropriateness of your "devices" '.[3]

Chambers and Stone could point to plenty of evidence to reinforce these negative views of progresses. There were anxious letters from potential hosts to Burghley, or the Lord Chamberlain, seeking advice on how to manage a visit, or politely suggesting that the Queen might be happier going elsewhere, coming

---

[1] Lawrence Stone, *The Crisis of the Aristocracy, 1558–1641* (Oxford: Clarendon Press, 1965), 453–4.

[2] In 1526, one of Henry VIII's household ordinances acknowledged this last problem, threatening dire royal displeasure against those who wasted the commodities of a host's estate or stole doors, locks, tables, etc. (*Letters and Papers, Foreign and Domestic, of the Reign of Henry VIII, 1509–1547*, ed. J. S. Brewer et al., 21 vols. (London: Longman, 1862–1932), IV.i. 862).

[3] E. K. Chambers, *The Elizabethan Stage*, 4 vols. (Oxford: Clarendon Press, 1923), i. 113.

another year when building was finished, and so forth. Then there were the groans of the government officials and courtiers who did not see the merits of constant movement. Thomas Smith, Elizabeth's Secretary of State, writing to Burghley while on the 1575 progress, moaned that the Queen was thinking of moving on from Worcester to Shrewsbury although 'men are weary, the way and the wether fowle, the countrey sore vexed with cariage'.[4] The same summer, Sir Francis Walsingham took a sour view of the time wasted in entertainment, complaining from Lichfield that 'we are altogether given to banquettinge and pastime'.[5] Moreover, there were complaints aplenty from petitioners who found themselves unable to press their suits, or at least were unanswered: 'her Matie [is] in progresse, a tyme very unfitt for negotiation', William Tresham told John Loke in 1601.[6] And finally there was the costliness of the whole exercise: such great expense to hosts, especially if they had to build for the Queen, and such relatively high charge to the impecunious Exchequer.[7] It may be that Elizabeth herself acknowledged the issue of cost: it was partly the need to save money that limited the ambition and geographical range of progresses in the 1580s.[8]

However, there have always been those who have argued that the political benefits of Elizabeth's contact with her realm far outweighed any inconvenience associated with her restless journeying. John Nichols's fascination with progresses and gifts marks the earliest stages of a historiographical perception that Elizabeth's behaviour provides an outstanding example of cultural politics.[9] Town entries, the constant acceptance of hospitality from subjects, and calculated accessibility were activities elevated to art forms by the Queen. In recent studies, Elizabeth's journeys have been read as social drama, enacting the monarch's symbolic and physical possession of her realm, and as exchanges of power and influence with her elites.[10] It is the purpose of this essay to isolate one aspect of this social

---

[4] British Library, London [BL], Harleian MS 6992, fo. 10.

[5] The National Archives, London [NA], SP 12/45/30.   [6] NA, SP 12/282/94.

[7] In 1573, for example, Burghley, who was trying to persuade the Queen to economize, calculated that at least £1,000 per season could be saved if the court did not migrate; by 1576, an 'overlong' progress had cost an extra £2,000 (BL, Lansdowne MS 21, fos. 130, 139ᵛ; Chambers, *Elizabethan Stage*, i. 118).

[8] Simon Adams, *Leicester and the Court: Essays on Elizabethan Politics* (Manchester: Manchester University Press, 2002), 27.

[9] The most balanced view, which affirms the political value of the progresses, is Mary Hill Cole, *The Portable Queen: Elizabeth I and the Politics of Ceremony* (Amherst: University of Massachusetts Press, 1999). Among the general biographies of the Queen, Alison Weir's *Elizabeth the Queen* (London: Jonathan Cape, 1998) provides the best attempt to integrate the progresses into the political narrative of the reign.

[10] See particularly Louis A. Montrose, 'Gifts and Reasons: The Contexts of Peele's *Araygnement of Paris*', *English Literary History*, 47 (1980), 433–61; Louis A. Montrose, ' "Eliza, Queene of shepheardes", and the Pastoral of Power', *English Literary Renaissance*, 10 (1980), 153–82; David Bergeron, *English Civic Pageantry 1558–1642* (London: Edward Arnold, 1971; repr. Tempe: Arizona State Medieval and Renaissance Studies, 2003); Jean Wilson, *Entertainments for Elizabeth I* (Woodbridge: Boydell, 1980); and Patricia Fumerton, *Cultural Aesthetics: Renaissance Literature and the Practice of Social Ornamentation* (Chicago: University of Chicago Press, 1991), 31–43.

drama, the giving and receiving of hospitality and the gifts that accompanied it. Patterns of giving and receiving had long been at the heart of monarchical progresses.[11] Elizabeth and her leading subjects took these traditional forms of behaviour, and moulded them to new political and cultural purposes. Hospitality acquired an intensified theatricality; gift-giving increasingly combined public gestures of loyalty with claims of personal intimacy associated with the offering of jewels, clothing, and the like.

A broad political ideal of the circulation of benefits between monarch and subjects was reified in the welcome provided by the Queen's hosts and in the thanks that she offered in return. The method by which this was expressed was that of total prestation, the surrender of all the resources of an individual or community to the visiting sovereign. William Harrison in his *Description of England* observed that 'every nobleman's house is her palace, where she continueth during pleasure and till return again to some of her own'.[12] The Earl of Leicester's pageant-makers used the same idea with romantic double entendre in the Kenilworth entertainment of 1575: the Earl 'gave him selfe and all. | A worthy gift to be received, | and so I trust it shall'.[13] The Queen was invited to consume that which was her subjects' but also her own. This could be no arbitrary imposition, since it was part of a dialectic of giving freely and receiving with gratitude that which was offered. And, as this was an open exchange, it affirmed the loyalty of subject to monarch, and the assurance of good lordship from monarch to subject. One of the features of Elizabeth's use of language on progress was that it was designed to acknowledge the contract implied in giving and receiving, to accept offerings as the proper manifestation of obedience and to return appropriate thanks as the prerogative of kingship.

When subjects considered benefits they thought not only of giving and receiving graciously, but also of reciprocation. The metaphor used was that of the Three Graces, whose joined hands represented the proper form of exchange.[14] Seneca taught the Elizabethans that the Graces expressed the essence of beneficence.[15] The three, said Spenser, show 'that men first ought to be gracious and bountiful to other freely, then to receive benefits at other mens hands curteously, and thirdly to requite them thankfully'.[16] At Elvetham in 1591,

---

[11] Since this essay considers all hospitality and gift-giving that the Queen experienced, it does not differentiate between long summer visits and trips of a day or two, or even for one meal, which she took away from court. On the problems of defining a progress, see Cole, *Portable Queen*, 22–4.

[12] William Harrison, *Description of England*, ed. G. Edelen (Ithaca, NY: Cornell University Press, 1968), 227.

[13] *The Progresses and Public Processions of Queen Elizabeth*, ed. John Nichols, 2nd edn., 3 vols. (London: John Nichols, 1823), i. 496.

[14] The key study for the iconography and importance of the Graces in Renaissance culture is Edgar Wind, *Pagan Mysteries of the Renaissance* (London: Faber and Faber, 1958), 26–52.

[15] Seneca, *De Beneficiis*, trans. J. W. Basore (London: William Heinemann, 1935), 13–15.

[16] The 'Aprill' eclogue of Edmund Spenser, *Shepheardes Calender*, in *The Yale Edition of the Shorter Poems of Edmund Spenser*, ed. William A. Oram et al. (New Haven: Yale University Press, 1989), 82.

the Graces danced before the Queen, removing blocks to her entrance to the Earl of Hertford's house and no doubt reminding her of the circulation of benefits embedded in the occasion.[17] The cycle of giving had to be sustained by the passing on of the benefit received, and the gift had to circulate to achieve its full efficacy.

In Marcel Mauss's classic account of the gift, its importance lies in the circulation of social energy. It not only articulates a bond between giver and recipient: it should ensure that there is a return to its sender, a return that is not immediate but one that fructifies the relationship between them.[18] This provided what Pierre Bourdieu has memorably called a 'gentle, invisible form of violence' in which honour is bound up in the giving and receiving of benefits, binding the parties more closely together than any direct commercial exchange.[19] The giving, receiving, and rewarding that are integral to Elizabeth's progresses had to appear to model themselves on the free-flowing generosity of the Graces' gestures. However, they also had to point constantly to the asymmetry of exchange. While beneficence, in its Senecan sense, could not normally be demanded by the recipient, the Queen's status legitimized a form of asking that could not be refused. In return, the hierarchical principle was upheld, and the essentially conservative nature of the transactions was directed at the stabilization and enhancement of the existing communities of honour that the Queen encountered. Anthropologists talk of the paradox of 'giving-while-keeping', displaying generosity in order to have one's essential social claims upheld, and this, we shall see, was a key feature of the exchanges that marked the monarch's progress through her realm.[20]

PATTERNS OF GIVING AND RECEIVING

The Queen's entertainment on progresses and visits conformed to a general model. There were ceremonies of greeting: first the hosts would meet the royal party at the boundary of a jurisdiction or estate, then the symbols of urban power or household authority would be surrendered, the Queen would graciously return them, and a speech or drama of welcome would be made.[21] The giving of gifts

---

[17] *Progresses*, ed. Nichols, 2nd edn., iii. 108–9.

[18] Marcel Mauss, *The Gift: Forms and Functions of Exchange in Archaic Societies*, trans. Ian Cunnison (New York: W. W. Norton, 1967).

[19] Pierre Bourdieu, *The Outline of a Theory of Practice*, trans. Richard Nice (Cambridge: Cambridge University Press, 1977), 192. See also L. M. Klein, ' "Your humble handmaid": Elizabethan Gifts of Needlework', *Renaissance Quarterly*, 50 (1997), 463–71.

[20] On giving-while-keeping see, in particular, A. B. Weiner, *Inalienable Possessions: The Paradox of Keeping-While-Giving* (Berkeley, and Los Angeles: University of California Press, 1992).

[21] The surrender of authority by private hosts is not always easy to trace, but is expressed particularly dramatically at Kenilworth in 1575 and at Cowdray in 1591, when Hercules appears in the initial pageants and offers keys to the Queen. (*Progresses*, ed. John Nichols, 2nd edn., i. 430; iii. 90.) The significance of greeting ceremonies is illuminated by Esther Goody, ' "Greeting",

was associated above all with the process of greeting, though not exclusively
confined to that moment. What followed was the provision of feasts—both in
the usual sense of food offered and also that of entertainment given—hunting,
masques, and music for the individual host—pageants and shows for the
town—disputations and sermons when the universities were visited. Then there
were the reverse ceremonies of withdrawal, often accompanied by speeches of grief
and loss. Inevitably, it is the grand entries and the most pompous celebrations
that made their mark on the records: hosts who had invested lavishly in display,
and authors who had cudgelled their wits to write masques, often celebrated in
print. The simpler exchanges were rarely noted for posterity, but in essence the
pattern of greeting, entertainment, and farewell probably held true.

Cities and towns had long experience of the duty to greet and entertain
monarchs. Richard III, Henry VII, and Henry VIII had all expected their citizens
to display loyalty by the formality and warmth of their welcomes.[22] Monasteries,
bishops, and courtiers were natural targets for monarchs who travelled the country
to assess the dutifulness of subjects, or who simply sought the pleasures of hunting
and an escape from the environment of London. Henry VIII, especially during
the first half of his reign, continued an earlier pattern of peripatetic monarchy:
travelling from manor to manor in the London area in winter and spring, and
somewhat further afield in summer. Henry's passion for hunting determined
many of his routes, and in summer he often travelled with a relatively small riding
household for the chase.[23] When Elizabeth began her travels, she therefore had
existing models of behaviour that she adopted, and adapted, to meet her own
political needs. On the whole it was the formal and public qualities of earlier
entertainments that she chose. While the holiday aspect of progress was not
forgotten, the Queen chose to emphasize the public and performative aspects of
her visits. This meant that, though the court was reduced in scale for its summer
travels, it remained larger than a riding household, and accumulated a train of
courtiers and great men as it lumbered from one location to another.[24]

"Begging" and the Presentation of Respect', in J. S. La Fontaine (ed.), *The Interpretation of Ritual:
Essays in Honour of A. I. Richards* (London: Tavistock Publications, 1972), 39–71.

[22] On the history of royal welcomes, see Lorraine Attreed, 'The Politics of Welcome: Ceremonies
and Constitutional Development in Late Medieval English Towns', in B. Hanawalt and K. L.
Reyerson (eds.), *City and Spectacle in Medieval Europe* (Minneapolis: University of Minnesota Press,
1994), 208–31. Sydney Anglo, *Spectacle, Pageantry and Early Tudor Policy* (Oxford: Clarendon
Press, 1969).

[23] Neil Samman, 'The Progresses of Henry VIII, 1509–1529', in Diarmaid MacCulloch (ed.),
The Reign of Henry VIII: Politics, Policy and Piety (Basingstoke: Macmillan, 1995), 59–73. On
Henry's use of the riding household in summer progresses, see Fiona Kisby, 'Kingship and the Royal
Itinerary: A Study of the Peripatetic Household of the Early Tudor Kings, 1485–1547', *Court
Historian*, 4.1 (1999), 29–39.

[24] Though the royal household was reduced in scale on progress—for example, by halving the
size of the Chapel Royal establishment—the scale of what was still required is indicated by the 1575
visit to Worcester, when fourteen noblemen, ten ladies of honour, and six bishops were present
(*Progresses*, ed. Nichols, 2nd edn., ii. 544–5).

Towns and cities swiftly responded to this royal concern for formality and display. In 1575, for example, Worcester planned for the Queen's August visit with a city ordinance of 16 July. Its fifteen clauses ordered the cleaning of streets, decorating of houses, gilding of the city regalia, organizing a speech of welcome by Mr Bell, deputy to the Recorder, preparation of two pageants, proper dress for the aldermen and others, and funding of an appropriate gift. But more telling than the practical costs and details of such visits, noted in many a set of town records, is the development of the process of describing the rituals and the royal response. Though royal entries to London and York already had a history of textual dissemination, such descriptions now became a feature of the self-imaging of a number of provincial centres. It was both the form of giving and the form of receiving that were felt worthy of note. At Worcester, Norwich, Coventry, and in the two universities of Oxford and Cambridge, Elizabeth's every gesture was recorded for a wider audience. The Queen herself was acutely aware of the significance of the word of a prince and of the fact that the language of gratitude had the power to intensify loyal identity. This is particularly clear in the rhetoric and gesture she used in response to urban greetings and farewells. At her departure from Worcester, for example, she told the accompanying train of townsmen that 'you all pray so hartily for me, as I fear you will by your prayers make me lyve too long', and rode away 'with teres in her eyes'.[25]

The scripts to be used for visits to private hosts were less well rehearsed. The variable interests of individual monarchs meant that their courtiers needed flexibility to judge the royal will correctly, and Elizabeth's preferences remained for some time an uncertain novelty. Nicholas Bacon, writing to Burghley in 1572, reflected a general anxiety when he asked for advice on how to behave when the Queen visited, since 'no man is more rawe in suche a matter then myselfe'.[26] There were, however, plenty of courtly brokers who claimed understanding of the Queen's will and made it their business to ensure it was achieved. The basic structure was a formal reception by the host, the surrender of the house, and a display of hospitality with the organizational and financial assistance of the Lord Chamberlain's office. When Thomas Churchyard described the reception by individual hosts on the 1578 progress to East Anglia, he used phrases such as: the Queen was 'nobly entertained' or 'worthily feasted', or they offered 'a franke house'. Not everyone managed even this display of generosity: Churchyard also noted that at Hide Hall in Essex, home of Sir Thomas Jocelyn, 'I heard of no greate cheere nor bankketing'.[27]

Increasingly, hosts felt that they had to do more than merely make available their houses and provide a portion of the feasting. They sought at least to

[25] Ibid. 543.

[26] *Original Letters Illustrative of English History*, ed. Henry Ellis, 3 vols. (London: Harding, Triphook, and Lepard, 1824), ii. 264.

[27] *Progresses*, ed. Nichols, 2nd edn., ii. 214–16, 219–20. On managing the costs of such a visit, see Cole, *Portable Queen*, 40–6.

appropriate some of the ideas used by the towns and cities in welcoming pageants, or, more ambitiously, to provide a courtly mode of masque entertainment. The Earl of Leicester provided the model and his great Kenilworth entertainment of the Queen in 1575 set the standard to emulate.[28] By the second great progress period in the last fifteen years of the reign, such pageants were commonplace. Their specific messages were various, but all worked within the ideal paradigm of the greatness of the honour accorded the host by the Queen's presence. Elizabeth revived the 'enchanted' knight at the gates of Sir Henry Lee's Ditchley estate, and he in turn claimed that he 'lyved' by her presence. The welcomers at the Harefield entertainment of 1602 referred to Elizabeth as 'the mistress of this faire company, though she know the way to all men's hearts, yet she knows the way to few men's houses, except she love them very well' (one of the least accurate statements ever made about the entertainment of the Queen!).[29]

No allusions to any direct material advantages that might derive from hosting the court were permitted to disturb the courtly rhetoric of these receptions. Self-interest had to be cloaked in the language of deference, and specific suits uncoupled from the royal visit. Sir William Cornwallis, an assiduous entertainer of the Queen, remarked to Sir Robert Cecil in 1601 that he could not 'move recompense' in his suit so soon after a progress 'like [a] waterman that calls presently for . . . hire after labour'.[30] There was, though, a morally coercive edge to the gestures: the consumption of hospitality created what Blau calls a 'diffuse future obligation' to reciprocate.[31] Welcoming and entertaining gave hosts an opportunity to sketch the form that that reciprocation might take. In 1591 and again in 1594, Burghley used Theobalds welcomes to make a case for his own retirement and the elevation of his son Robert to the secretaryship of state. The Earl of Hertford's Elvetham entertainment pointed the Queen towards support of his cautious naval policy as Lord Admiral. And, most famously, Leicester probably hoped to use his last Kenilworth pageant to persuade the Queen to marry him, or release him to marry elsewhere.[32] The benefit of progress was that it offered different opportunities for visibility and accessibility from normal courtly life, and these could occasionally be parlayed into material reward. Sir Edward Dyer, out of favour for several years in the early 1570s, seems to have effected this trick

[28] Robert Langham, *A Letter: Whearin, part of the Entertainment unto the Queenz Maiesty, at Killingworth Castl . . . is signified*, ed. R. J. P. Kuin (Leiden: Brill, 1983).

[29] E. K. Chambers, *Sir Henry Lee* (Oxford: Clarendon Press, 1936), 276. Jean Wilson, 'The Harefield Entertainment and the Cult of Elizabeth I', *Antiquaries Journal*, 66 (1986), 315–29 (p. 319).

[30] *HMC Calendar of the Manuscripts of the Most Hon. the Marquis of Salisbury*, 25 vols. (London: HMSO, 1888–1976), xi (1906), 397.

[31] Peter Blau, *Exchange and Power in Social Life* (New York: Wiley, 1964), 93.

[32] James M. Sutton, 'The Retiring Patron: William Cecil and the Cultivation of Retirement, 1590–98', in Pauline Croft (ed.), *Patronage, Culture and Power: The Early Cecils* (New Haven: Yale University Press/The Paul Mellon Centre for Studies in British Art, 2002), 159–80; H. H. Boyle, 'Elizabeth's Entertainment at Elvetham: War Policy in Pageantry', *Studies in Philology*, 68 (1971), 146–66; and Simon Adams, 'Robert Dudley', *New Oxford DNB*.

with his performance in the mournful 'Song of the Oke' at Woodstock in 1575. He was able to return to court, and then next year received more than gracious words: the monopolistic right to regulate tanners.[33] Towns might take advantage of the established convention that subjects could petition to draw attention to the decay of their industries or the problems of their schools. But even towns rarely presented direct requests: instead, they approached the councillors travelling with the Queen, or persuaded the local bishop to speak on their behalf.[34]

Elizabeth was, of course, alert both to the reasonably direct requests of the towns and to the more general desire to manipulate her through compliment. On the rare occasions when her words to individual hosts were recorded, she seems to have sought to manage the circulatory pressure of the Graces' dance with warm thanks and praise. One reading of Senecan ethics legitimized the idea that 'he who receives a benefit gladly has already returned it'.[35] Elizabeth's pleasure at her reception is repeatedly reported by the narrators of visits. Sometimes a step further was needed, as when she told the Earl of Hertford in 1591 that his entertainment had been 'so honorable, she would not forget the same', yet her remembrance held out no explicit promise of reward.[36] As a material, but costless, gesture she knighted hosts or members of their family. At Basing in 1601, for example, eleven men were knighted and Richard White, with whom she dined next day, had the same honour 'overlaid . . . his weak shoulders' 'to make up a full dozen'.[37] None of this was conceived as binding the royal will, nor did it do much to change the image of a royal progress as an occasion on which hosts gave and the Queen graciously received.

THE MATERIAL GIFT

Both urban and individual hosts who engaged in elaborate ceremonies of welcome and entertainment presumably viewed the performance as holistic, as an integrated series of actions adding up to the full prestation of loyal subjects. We can, however, isolate individual elements within the performance, and these provide a means of understanding the nature of giving and the ways in which

[33] Ralph M. Sargent, *At the Court of Elizabeth: The Life and Lyrics of Sir Edward Dyer* (Oxford: Oxford University Press, 1935), 28–35.

[34] *Progresses*, ed. Nichols, 2nd edn., i. 339; ii. 275, 543–4, 195–6. Coventry did succeed in gaining support in its suit against John Hales by such a direct approach: Benjamin Poole, *Coventry: Its History and Antiquities* (London: J. R. Smith, 1870), 246–8. Stafford, petitioning for the return of the assizes and for cap making, succeeded in at least the first part of its request: *Acts of the Privy Council of England: New Series . . . 1575–7*, ed. J. R. Dasent (London: HMSO, 1890), 36; *Acts of the Privy Council of England: New Series . . . 1577–8*, ed. J. R. Dasent (London: HMSO, 1890), 341. *HMC . . . Salisbury*, iii (1889), 116.

[35] Seneca, *De Beneficiis*, 113.   [36] *Progresses*, ed. Nichols, 2nd edn., iii. 121

[37] Thomas Tooke relates this to Mr John Hubberd, 19 Sept. 1601 (*The Court of James I*, ed. J. S. Brewer, 2 vols. (London: R. Bentley, 1839), ii. 22).

it transmuted over time. The most obvious item that always had to be offered was the material gift. Monarchs expected more than fair words from their subjects, and hospitality therefore merged into presentation. Cities and towns gave foodstuffs to visiting kings and nobles: York was still doing this in 1541 when Henry VIII's grand visit was received with the municipal gift of twenty fat oxen and one hundred sheep.[38] Money or plate might also be offered, though the very detailed Canterbury records suggest that this was not automatically the case.[39] As for the private giving to monarchs on progress, the surviving Privy Purse accounts for 1529–32 show that summer gifts were often hawks and hounds, as well as food suitable for making merry in Henry's travels. When the King was at the Vyne, Hampshire, in August 1531, he received hounds from the Marquess of Exeter. A month earlier, Thomas Heneage had given him a greyhound.[40] Henry in his turn could be beneficent and sometimes reciprocated his welcome by offering venison to those who demonstrated loyalty by appearing on the progress. William Fitzwilliam, treasurer of the household, reported to Wolsey in 1521 that all those who had 'repaired unto his grace's presence' had been given gracious words and venison 'to their singular comfort'.[41] While the Henrician court was the site of elaborate and costly gift exchange and of displays of magnificence, the King's progresses do not seem to have assumed great importance as moments of grand giving.

From the beginning of Elizabeth's reign, the records indicate intensified emphasis on the material gift. Urban and academic gift gestures might still include texts, notably the Bible, or clothing such as gloves. But they were unlikely any longer to consist of foodstuffs; these were now reserved for the accompanying courtiers.[42] Elizabeth was almost invariably offered money and plate by her loyal townsmen. From the very beginning of the reign, when London gave a gift of 1,000 gold marks during the 1559 entry, the Queen anticipated and received cups of gold or silver gilt or purses containing sovereigns. When the city of Oxford gave a cup and £30 (or £40) in gold in 1566, it was noted that this was a change from earlier custom and was instituted by the steward

[38] *York Civic Records*, ed. Angelo Raine, 8 vols. (Wakefield: The Yorkshire Archaeological Society, 1939–53), i (1939), 150–9.

[39] *9ᵗʰ Report of the Royal Commission on Historical Manuscripts. Part I. Appendix* (London: HMSO, 1883), 145–9. Richard III refused money gifts, but cups with money in them were given to Henry VII in 1504 and Katherine of Aragon in 1513.

[40] *The Privy Purse Expences of King Henry VIII: November MDXXIX to December MDXXXII*, ed. H. Nicolas (London: W. Pickering, 1827), 152, 154.

[41] *Letters and Papers, Foreign and Domestic, of the Reign of Henry VIII, 1509–47*, ed. J. S. Brewer et al. (London: Longman, 1862–1932), iv. ii. 2368.

[42] On at least two occasions, the giving of Scripture was important—when the Queen made her first entry into London and in 1575 when Laurence Humphrey presented her with an Irish text on her visit to Woodstock (*Progresses*, ed. Nichols, 2nd edn., i. 60, 597–8; Sir William Croft, *Croftus sive Hibernia Liber*, ed. A. Keaveney and J. A. Madden (Dublin: Irish Manuscripts Commission, 1992), 99). For examples of gifts to courtiers at Worcester in 1575, see *Progresses*, ed. Nichols, 2nd edn., i. 531–41.

and courtier Sir Francis Knollys.[43] While Elizabeth might occasionally disclaim any interest in the financial gift, she clearly encouraged a pattern of behaviour in which such giving became essential to the honour of the town.

Honour also demanded proper rhetorical strategies in presenting and accepting the gift. In Norwich in 1578, the Mayor in his oration surrendered the sword of the city and offered 'this treasure [as] a pledge of our good wills and habilitie: which all how great or little soever they be, we poure down at your pleasure'. In response, Elizabeth, thanking the corporation for their tokens of goodwill, asserted that 'Princes have no neede of money', but that she took the loyalty of her subjects as the greatest riches of the kingdom.[44] In 1572, she assured the Warwick bailiff that 'it is not the maner to be always presented with gifts [but] . . . a myte of their haunds is as much as a thowsand pounds of some others'.[45] Of course, the gift itself mattered, but when at Coventry the Queen temporarily became too interested in the money—'I have but few such', she said, referring to the gold sovereigns—the Mayor felt moved to prompt her scripted response saying that what she was being offered was 'the faithfull harts of all your true loveing subjects'. The tone of Elizabeth's return—'Wee thanke you Mr Maior . . . it is indeed a greate deale more'—was unlikely to have been warm.[46]

Private hosts also recognized that the Queen expected gifts that were more durable than consumables to make merry or even offerings to assist the hunt. At the very beginning of the reign, the Earl of Arundel, hoping for the Queen's hand in marriage, gave her a 'cupboard of plate' when she first visited Nonsuch.[47] By 1573, when the Queen visited Kent, hosts were regularly imitating towns in giving plate: a standing cup of crystal and silver-gilt from Sir Richard Baker at Sissinghurst, and three bowls of silver and gilt embossed with the Queen's arms from Mr Tufton who was her host for two days in August.[48] Thereafter hosts were gradually emboldened to offer more intimate presents in the form of jewels and elaborate clothing. In 1574 Mary Ratcliffe, the keeper of the Queen's jewels, recorded a series of gifts on the progress to Bristol: a salamander and phoenix jewel from Sir John Young at Bristol, and a dolphin in mother-of-pearl garnished with gold from Sir John Sherington.[49] This coincided with a better-documented change in the New Year gifts given to Elizabeth.[50] Leicester, who certainly gave

[43] *Progresses*, ed. Nichols, 2nd edn., i. 141, 208. For other examples, see Cole, *Portable Queen*, 101.

[44] *Progresses*, ed. Nichols, 2nd edn., ii. 140–1.   [45] Ibid. i. 315.

[46] William Dugdale, *Antiquities of Warwickshire*, 2nd edn., 2 vols. (London: John Osborn and Thomas Longman, 1730), i. 149.

[47] On Arundel, see Andrew Boyle, 'Henry Fitzalan, 12th Earl of Arundel, Politics and Culture in the Tudor Nobility' (unpublished doctoral dissertation, University of Oxford, 2002), 205–6.

[48] BL, Stowe MS 555, fo. 138ʳ, printed in A. J. Collins, *Jewels and Plate of Queen Elizabeth I* (London: British Museum, 1955), 544–5.

[49] BL, Harleian MS 4698, fos. 22–4.

[50] On New Year gifts, see Collins, *Jewels and Plate of Queen Elizabeth*, 109–10; Diana Scarisbrick, *Jewellery in Britain 1066–1837* (Wilby: Michael Russell, 1994); Janet Arnold, *Queen Elizabeth's Wardrobe Unlock'd* (Leeds: Maney, 1988), 93–8.

Elizabeth gifts of jewels from an early date, is credited with initiating the change, but the development of such intimacy must essentially be explained by the Queen's own preferences.[51] So commonplace did this eventually seem that, looking back, Burghley's biographer John Clapham described how 'in times of Progress there was no person who entertained her but . . . he bestowed a jewel on her; a custom in former times begun by her special favourites that (having in great measure tasted of her bounty) did give her only of her own'.[52]

The growing value and permanence of the gifts offered to the Queen were matched by the elaboration of their forms of presentation. When Lord Keeper Puckering was to receive the Queen in 1594, it appeared he was more concerned about this aspect of the visit than any other. His second note in a list of plans read, 'What present shalbe given by my Lord, when and by whome it shalbe presented, and whether more then one.' This note was followed by three further items addressing the question of what gifts to give.[53] Giving was more tightly incorporated into drama, either that of welcome, or in the later shows prepared for the royal party. Jewels were presented by sea Titans at Elvetham in 1591, by Ceres in a crown of wheat at Bisham in 1592, and by a dairymaid who gave a jewelled fork and rake at Sir Thomas Egerton's at Harefield in 1602.[54] These receptions followed patterns already established at court, especially the Accession Day tilts developed by Sir Henry Lee, and Lee was also one of those who invested heavily in ceremony when the Queen was on progress.[55] Giving was often both concealed and revealed by artfulness. The occasion of the offering was partially public, in an entertainment that was played out before court and bystanders, with the actors making specific allusions to what was offered. Courtiers and others in their turn conveyed excited and sometimes exaggerated descriptions of the great gifts to their correspondents.[56] Offerings played to the relationship between the Queen and her host, and could be expected to redound to the honour of both. Some presentations, notably those of clothing, were made in the even more private environment of the Queen's lodgings. Puckering's main gift at her 1595 visit to Kew was a fine gown given to Elizabeth in her private apartment.

The rhetorical strategy used in the presentation of these gifts was to stress their inadequacy in the face of majesty. The 'old man' who spoke for Lord North at the Queen's Rycote reception in 1592 offered a gown—'this trifle; and with this

[51] Scarisbrick, *Jewellery in Britain 1066–1837*, p. 133.

[52] *Elizabeth's England: Certain Observations Concerning the Life and Reign of Queen Elizabeth by John Clapham*, ed. E. P. Read and C. Read (Philadelphia: University of Pennsylvania Press, 1951), 87–8.

[53] BL, Harleian MS 6850, fo. 91.   [54] *Progresses*, ed. Nichols, 2nd edn., iii. 111, 135–6, 588.

[55] Chambers, *Sir Henry Lee*, 276; Roy Strong, *The Cult of Elizabeth: Elizabethan Portraiture and Pageantry* (London: Thames and Hudson, 1977), 129–63. Accession Day tilts also involved gift-giving.

[56] Gabriel Heaton, 'Performing Gifts: The Manuscript Circulation of Elizabethan and Early Stuart Courtly Entertainments' (unpublished doctoral dissertation, University of Cambridge, 2003), 62–93.

my heart, the greatest gift I can offer, and the chiefest that I ought'.[57] The gift, in this hierarchical world, could never be adequate, and hosts had reason to point to the disequilibrium involved.[58] Despite this formal disparity, jewels and clothes had great value as mnemonic devices keeping the giver in the consciousness of the royal recipient.[59] This was sometimes immediately visible, as in the case of the gold bowl embossed with the Queen's arms and the Gresham grasshoppers, almost certainly given to her by Sir Thomas Gresham.[60] Such directness was not, on the whole, the courtly way. Instead there were jewelled hearts from Sir Henry Lee and Sir Thomas Egerton, and mermaids and eagles from the Earl and Countess of Pembroke.[61] Elizabeth, always aware of the importance of the public manipulation of symbols, sometimes responded by drawing attention to her use of these personal gifts. She wore gowns and jewels, pointing out, as she did to the Countess of Rutland in 1583, that she held a present 'in great good favour'.[62] Elizabeth commonly played this ritual game at court, sometimes adding a counter-gift. Sir Thomas Heneage presented the Queen with a bodkin and pendant: she responded that she would wear it 'on that eare that shoulde heare nothing that sholde hurte him', but in practice she closed the giving circle by returning a butterfly of mother of pearl 'that he might allowayes remember her that sent ytt'.[63] But nothing in the structure of progress entertainment obliged the Queen to make an immediate counter-gift. The host who chose to do more than simply make his home available to the court had to do so within the conventions of hospitality in which any return, except rewards to servants, would have been dishonourable.[64]

A CRISIS OF GENEROSITY?

In a Christmas masque of 1604, the Three Graces again danced, this time before King James I, celebrating a new regime and singing:

> Desert, Reward and Gratitude,
> The Graces of Society,
> Do here with hand in hand conclude

[57] *Progresses*, ed. Nichols, iii. 168.   [58] Heaton, 'Performing Gifts', 44–6.

[59] On the use of needlework as such a mnemonic device, see Klein, ' "Your humble handmaid" ', 472–6.

[60] Collins, *Jewels and Plate of Queen Elizabeth*, 286.

[61] *Progresses*, ed. Nichols, 2nd edn., iii. 590; BL, Stowe MS 555, fo. 137.

[62] Examples come from general court exchanges, rather than progresses. *The Manuscripts of His Grace the Duke of Rutland, G.C.B., preserved at Belvoir Castle*, ed. Maxwell Lyte et al., 4 vols. (London: HMSO, 1888–1905), i (1888), 94, 153.

[63] Quoted in Klein, ' "Your humble handmaid" ', 474.

[64] Felicity Heal, *Hospitality in Early Modern England* (Oxford: Clarendon Press, 1990), 12–15. Rewards to servants and to performers were common. In 1575, the Queen went beyond the usual payments and gave Sir John Hubard, constable of Kenilworth, a jewel shaped like a greyhound (BL, Harleian MS 4698, fo. 9).

> The blessed chaine of amity.
> 1. For I deserve. 2. I give. 3. I thank:[65]

James, on his progress south to assume the throne, had shown that this was precisely how he understood the cycle of beneficence. Hosts entertained him with great lavishness, and the reciprocation was now often immediate, since it behoved the prince to be generous to his deserving subjects. In *Basilikon Doron*, the King had already counselled his son to 'use true liberality in rewarding the good and bestowing frankly for your honour and weal'.[66] And so the movement of the Graces was reversed—good hospitality might still be a trigger, but the substantive initiation of reward for the worthy was now the most visible part of the gift cycle.[67] The Venetian Ambassador, commenting on James's progress south to take the throne, noted his magnanimity and judgement, displayed in his refusal to take costly gifts from the hosts who entertained him.[68] This does not seem to have been true, but at least the perception of royal behaviour had changed.

This shower of largesse served to cast the 1590s in a peculiarly gloomy light as a period when the Queen had allowed the fountains of patronage to run dry. The decade was marked by strains in government, the withering of patronage under the financial pressure of the Armada wars, and the growth of factional divisions between Essex and the Cecilians. Since these were also the years when elaborate progresses began again after a prolonged pause, it is important to consider whether such political difficulties are actually reflected in changes in the cycle of benefits and giving. Change there certainly appears to have been, though on close inspection it does not all indicate political or social strain. Men of power were still eager to gratify the Queen, and indeed most of the truly grand progress visits, apart from Kenilworth in 1575, took place during these late years.

The giving of presents and the performance of ceremonial welcomes culminated in that fully documented entertainment at Harefield in 1602, given by Lord Keeper Egerton and his wife Alice, Countess of Derby.[69] One of the numerous accounts of this event is preserved in Archbishop Matthew Hutton's papers and is of particular interest since it records the cost that the writer thought had been bestowed on gifts to the Queen. The first offering, of a jewelled rake and fork, was followed by a diamond heart worth £300; a rainbow gown and sleeves valued

[65] *The Progresses and Public Processions of King James I*, ed. John Nichols, 3 vols. (London: John Nichols, 1828), i. 309.

[66] James I, *Basilikon Doron*, in *The Political Works of James I*, ed. C. H. McIlwain (Cambridge, Mass.: Harvard University Press, 1918, repr. 1952), 52.

[67] Linda Levy Peck, ' "For a King not to be bountiful were a fault": Perspectives on Court Patronage in Early Stuart England', *Journal of British Studies*, 25 (1986), 31–61.

[68] Giovanni Carlo Scaramelli, Venetian Secretary in England, letter dated 15 May 1603, in *Manuscripts, Existing in the Archives and Collections of Venice, and in Other Libraries of Northern Italy. 1603–1607*, ed. Horatio F. Brown et al., 37 vols. (London: HMSO, 1864–1947), x (1900), 25.

[69] This is one of the examples of hosts or their circle disseminating narratives of a successful entertainment as a means of enhancing reputation (Heaton, 'Performing Gifts', 62–92).

at £340; the jewels designed for Elizabeth from the lottery box that occupied the evening of the visit, another £600; and a final anchor jewel at her departure, worth 100 marks.[70] A different account, sent from Sir Henry Savile to the Earl of Shrewsbury, reinforced the view that this complex entertainment was primarily about gifts: 'your lordship may see the manner of presentinge the giftes which wear many and great'.[71] This was the last of a series of prestations by lawyers that impressed the court gossips. Lord Keeper Puckering, Sir Edward Coke, and Sir Julius Caesar had all competed to show the Queen extravagant generosity. This imposed a strain on others who sought to maintain their visibility through entertainment. Sir William Cornwallis, 'to whom the entertainment of a prince hath been but a pastime', pursued his campaign for favour with hospitality at Highgate, spending, according to his father, £200 on gifts in 1594. The last example is most indicative of the pressures of giving: Sir Thomas caustically remarked that 'hys vanitye and pryde wyll cause wyse men to laugh at hym and all other men to dysdane his presumptuous prodigalitye'.[72] Sir Francis Carew, whose Beddington home was a favourite target for the Queen, told Robert Cecil in 1596 that he was reluctant to seek the Queen's help in a suit, because she would expect 'greater entertainment and gifts at my hands'.[73]

These examples suggest that prodigality was now the expected norm for the Queen's hosts, and that courtiers had to engage in increasingly ferocious competition to impress. But the evidence should be treated with caution. In practice Sir Francis Carew managed to delight his monarch without great gifts by charming with his garden, his orangery, and his ability to delay the ripening of cherries for her benefit.[74] Michael Hickes, Burghley's secretary, was advised in 1597 that he could cope with a royal visit by simply providing some personal gift: 'sum fine wastcoate, or fine ruffe, or like thinge which . . . would be acceptablies taken as if it weare of great price'.[75] Moreover we may be misled by the volume of courtly correspondence in these years: writers of news not only gave a much more personal view of progresses than was possible during the earlier decades, they also instinctively sought out the sensational and atypical to report. They were certainly at times prone to excited exaggeration of the lavishness of visits. Rowland Whyte, for example, reported that Lord Keeper Puckering gave the Queen a jewel valued at £400, whereas the accounts give a value of only £90.[76]

---

[70] *The Correspondence of Dr Matthew Hutton*, ed. J. Raine (Durham: Surtees Society, 1843), 278. The edited narrative does not include the first figures, which are taken from Heaton's reading of the original MS (Heaton, 'Performing Gifts', 66–7).

[71] Lambeth Palace Library, London, MS 3201, fo. 43.

[72] *Court of James I*, ed. Brewer, ii. 21. Cambridge University Library, Hengrave MS 88/2, no. 82.

[73] *HMC . . . Salisbury*, vi (1895), 139.

[74] *Diary of Baron Waldstein: An Elizabethan Traveller in England*, ed. G. W. Groos (London: Thames and Hudson, 1981), 164–5.

[75] Ellis, *Original Letters*, ii. 275–6.

[76] *Letters and Memorials of State . . . by Sir Henry Sydney*, ed. Arthur Collins, 2 vols. (London: T. Osborne, 1746), ii. 376; BL, Harleian MS 6850, fo. 89. For some discussion of this issue see

Savile was even more astray in describing Harefield, where he valued one jewel at £1,000.[77] Both the hosts and the Queen had motives to heighten the drama of these entertainments, and the costliness was in some measure in the eye of the bedazzled spectators.

Yet we cannot quite infer that all was well in the relationship between the Queen and the subjects who entertained her. The last decade of the reign was a time of intense political and economic competition, with spectacular winners and losers. One obvious means of seeking to manipulate the Queen was to act with great generosity in the hope of favour, either favour newly given, or favour restored after disgrace. The Earl of Hertford's spectacle at Elvetham was aimed partly at his full restoration to the Queen's love, and Egerton's Harefield extravaganza in 1602 had as an objective his final return to grace after the Essex affair. Such gestures were not guaranteed success: Whyte reported of Egerton that 'all here are not confident that the same will procure an abolition of former unkindness'.[78]

The Essex crisis, in particular, was marked by attempts to persuade Elizabeth to accept presents and return favour, though not necessarily in the context of progresses. In November 1599, Lady Essex sent a jewel 'but it would not be accepted'; a very rich jewel was presented on the Earl's behalf in January 1600, and 'it was neither received nor rejected', and in February Lady Leicester, Essex's mother, produced a spectacular gown costing '£100 at least', which again the Queen neither accepted nor rejected but remarked 'that it was not fit for her to desire what she did'.[79] In November 1599, Elizabeth had explicitly refused a pearl from Egerton at a time when he was still in some measure identified with Essex, saying that she returned thanks, 'butt that her mynde was as greate to refuse as hys was to gyve'.[80] Sir Robert Cecil sought both to capitalize on the crisis and to distract the Queen with generous New Year gifts in 1600 and with good entertainment at Theobalds.[81]

There is also ample evidence of resentment at the lack of material reward deriving from loyal entertainment. The best-known case is that of Sir Henry Lee, who had led the courtly dance around Elizabeth and whose disillusion towards the end of the reign is palpable. In 1596, Rowland Whyte drew a picture of Lee and Lord North playing at cards with the Queen: 'that is like to be all the Honor that will fall unto them this year'.[82] Lee's complaints about benefits gone wrong focus partly on the progresses. Writing to Cecil in 1600, he hoped to stave off

Queen Elizabeth's Entertainment at Mitcham, ed. Leslie Hotson (New Haven: Yale University Press, 1953), 9–10.

[77] Lambeth Palace Library, MS 3201, fo. 43.

[78] Edmund Lodge, *Illustrations of British History*, 3 vols. (London: G. Nicol, 1791), iii. 135. If this was an important aspect of the Harefield visit, then the anchor given to the Queen at departure would have symbolized hope for Egerton.

[79] *Report on the Manuscripts of Lord De L'Isle & Dudley Preserved in Penshurst Place*, ed. C. L. Kingsford et al., 6 vols. (London: HMSO, 1925–66), ii (1934), 418, 427–8, 436.

[80] Lodge, *Illustrations*, iii. 105.   [81] *HMC . . . Salisbury*, xii (1910), 560.

[82] *Letters and Memorials of State*, ed. Collins, ii. 382.

another royal visit to Ditchley: his estate was impoverished, he claimed, and he had entertained the Queen many times before but no 'part of her Highness's many promises performed'.[83] Though Elizabeth had tried to console Lee with the gift of membership of the Order of the Garter, for a time this seems merely to have reminded him of the lack of tangible profit from his years of service.[84] In another incident in these last years, the entertainment offered by the Lord Admiral at Christmas 1602 seems to show resentment at the Queen's rapacity. According to John Chamberlain, the hospitality was not extraordinary, 'neither were his presents so precious as was expected, being only a whole suit of apparell; whereas it was thought he wold have bestowed his rich hangings of all the fights with the Spanish Armada in eightie-eight'.[85] At Basing in 1601, there was much complaint that Elizabeth had offloaded the cost of entertaining the French embassy onto her hostess.[86] All of this was set in a context of growing arbitrariness of behaviour on the Queen's part. Chamberlain complained in 1599 that the 'court . . . commonly knows not overnight what shalbe don in the morning': in an extreme case Sir Julius Caesar's opportunity to act as a lavish host in 1598 came after he had prepared fruitlessly for the Queen on at least five previous occasions.[87]

Elizabeth's method of managing progresses always had this potential to create the resentments associated with 'gifts gone wrong'. In her dealings with individual hosts, she relied upon an exchange offering honour in return for mandatory hospitality. Her great courtiers then encouraged her in the belief that lavish and enduring gifts, as well as consumables, were a natural part of the honourable exchange of 'keeping-while-giving'. Progresses were episodic and unpredictable: in this sense, Stone's hurricane image is apt. Most of this held true throughout the reign. The Queen, as John Clapham observed, 'loved to be sued unto and to be gratified with rewards', or, in the case of progresses, lavishly received and then gratified.[88] There is some evidence that the preoccupation with extravagance in both entertainment and gifts was a greater feature of the last years than of the 1560s and 1570s, and that these changes were played out against a growing background of resentment about failure in the allocation of rewards. Access to the Queen was a diminishing asset, and Clapham may well be correct in arguing that lesser men came to resent the burdens of largesse. Yet, even in these last years, Queen and hosts conspired to conceal the strains in the dance of the Graces: the pattern by which political and social authority had been confirmed to both parties in the exchange of honour survived as the legacy of Elizabeth's form of royal progress.

---

[83] *HMC . . . Salisbury*, x (1904), 180.   [84] Chambers, *Sir Henry Lee*, 177.

[85] *The Letters of John Chamberlain during the Reign of Queen Elizabeth*, ed. Sarah Williams (London: Camden Society, 1861), 169–70. It is worth noting that the coming of James loosened some of these purse strings again. Lee, for example, returned to acting with some enthusiasm as a host.

[86] Brewer, *Court of James I*, ii. 21–2.   [87] Chamberlain, *Letters*, ed. Williams, 37, 19.

[88] *Elizabeth's England*, ed. Read and Read, 86.

PART II

CIVIC AND ACADEMIC RECEPTIONS FOR QUEEN ELIZABETH I

4

Location as Metaphor in Queen Elizabeth's Coronation Entry (1559): *Veritas Temporis Filia*

Hester Lees-Jeffries

When Elizabeth Tudor made her ceremonial entry into the city of London on 14 January 1559, the day before her coronation, her procession followed a route from the Tower of London to Westminster that had become standard on such occasions, stopping at particular points to admire tableaux, watch brief pageants, and have their symbolism explained in speeches in English and Latin. The climax of the procession, in formal terms if not in spectacle, was the speech of welcome by the Recorder of London and the presentation of a gift from city to prince. The ceremonial purpose of the procession was a formal welcome and declaration of fealty by citizens to monarch, but it was also a process whereby, beneath the ritualized, conventionally adulatory surface, the complex relationship between crown and city was enacted and worked out. Through specially erected stages, triumphal arches, and tableaux, Elizabeth's presence was absorbed, albeit temporarily, into the very fabric of the city. More permanently, if less tangibly, she became part of London's history and mythology, in the commemorative account of the entry that was quickly published by Richard Mulcaster[1] and, later, in histories and 'surveys' such as John Stow's. While every word and gesture made by Elizabeth was carefully recorded, and while she was on occasion accorded transformative powers over the various symbolic landscapes presented in the tableaux that greeted her, she remained a spectator rather than a participant. Although she was in some respects an actor in the pageants that she witnessed, she was an actor largely without agency, subject above all to the 'direction' of the topography and physicality of London itself.

---

[1] A critical edition of Mulcaster's pamphlet, together with other documents related to the entry and a lengthy introduction, has recently been published: *The Queen's Majesty's Passage and Related Documents*, ed. Germaine Warkentin (Toronto: Centre for Reformation and Renaissance Studies, 2004). All references are taken from this edition.

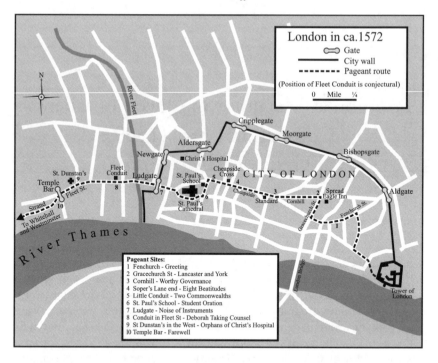

Map 4.1. A map of London, showing the route of Elizabeth I's coronation procession of 1559. Drawn by Nigel James.

Many of the pageant stages were set up at the conduits, London's public water cisterns. Implicitly in Elizabeth's entry, as explicitly in the coronation entries of some of her predecessors, the pageant devisers employed the imagery and symbolism of fountains. London, as it was 'entered' by its prince throughout the medieval and early modern period, was not an empty stage or a blank page, but a palimpsestic conglomeration of landscape and monuments inscribed and re-inscribed with the 'texts' of historical association, communal memory, and accumulated civic pride and idealism. As William Hardin argues, '[d]uring London's development as the major trading and industrial center of England, its conduits, springs, and market crosses acquired special significance as sites at which the city government staged emblematic displays of how it wished London to be perceived, using motifs of the city's history and traditions to mark these locations with the stamp of civic authority'.[2] In its own way, the cityscape through which Elizabeth processed was as densely immanent as the more conventionally numinous landscape of the pastoral or the romance or, indeed, the 'landscape

[2] William Hardin, ' "Pipe-Pilgrimages" and "Fruitfull Rivers": Thomas Middleton's Civic Entertainments and the Water Supply of Early Stuart London', *Renaissance Papers* (1993), 63–73 (p. 63).

entertainment'. Because the conduits were such a focus of civic identity and values at the same time as the fountain was a vital image of both monarchical power and the new English translations of the Scriptures,[3] the conjunction of these two symbolic economies at the conduits during Elizabeth's coronation entry made them points and moments where the nature of the relationship between crown and city was scrutinized, and revealed to be one of interdependence and reciprocity, multivalence and ambivalence.

The focus of this discussion is just one pageant in Elizabeth's coronation entry, *Veritas Temporis Filia*, 'Truth the Daughter of Time'. In this pageant, the penultimate in the sequence that greeted the Queen, a figure representing Time led his daughter Truth out of a cave, to present the Queen with an English Bible and draw her attention to the principles of good government which would ensure the well-being and prosperity of the city and the nation. This essay suggests that the fountain metaphor that underpinned the pageant was implicitly expressed through its location at the Little Conduit in Cheapside, at the end of St Paul's Churchyard. The first part of this essay contextualizes London's conduits and the part they played in royal pageantry; this draws on previous work by Sydney Anglo, Gordon Kipling, Lawrence Manley, and others, bringing together knowledge of the specifics of early modern pageantry and the evolving understanding of the early modern cultural geography of London. The second part discusses Anne Boleyn's coronation entry in 1533 and its possible influence on that of Elizabeth. In the third part, the relationship between conduits running with wine and ritual gift-giving is considered. The fourth and longest section addresses *Veritas Temporis Filia* itself, while the final section briefly considers some late Elizabethan and early Jacobean recurrences of its imagery and ideological agenda.

LONDON'S CONDUITS AND ROYAL PAGEANTRY

There were a number of practical reasons why the conduits had long been focal points in royal entries. Probably the most important was their location: in a city of narrow, crowded streets, the conduits stood in relatively open spaces. This was particularly the case in Cheapside, where three—the Great Conduit, the Little Conduit, and the Standard—were located. Cheapside was a natural choice as a processional route: it was long, relatively straight, and (by London standards) especially wide; Michael Berlin has described Cheapside as London's closest equivalent to a 'public ritual space' such as Venice's St Mark's Square.[4] It also

[3] See chapters 2 and 3 of my 'Fountains in Renaissance Literature' (unpublished doctoral thesis, University of Cambridge, 2002), 68–112, 122–69.
[4] Michael Berlin, 'Civic Ceremony in Early Modern London', *Urban History Yearbook*, 13 (1986), 15–27 (p. 21).

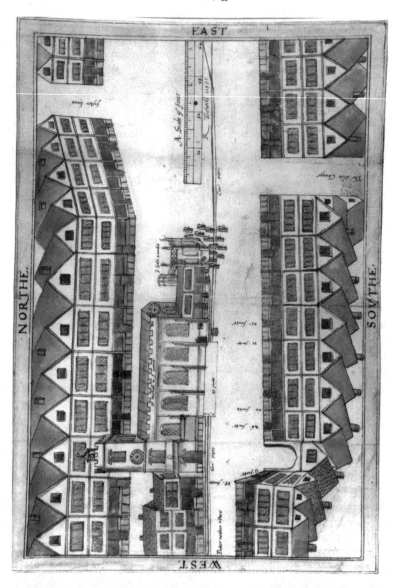

Figure 4.1. *Bird's eye view of the church of St Michael le Querne and the Little Conduit,* by Ralph Treswell. 1585. Pen and ink, and watercolour, on paper; signed, dated, and inscribed in black ink with place names, measurements, scale, and compass bearings. 39.3 × 27.1 cm. (© The Trustees of the British Museum, London)

took in some of London's most expensive shops, notably goldsmiths, and so could be relied upon to make a fine display along its street frontage. Lawrence Manley describes the stretch of Cheapside between Cornhill and the Little Conduit as 'a cultural *limen*, a site of political negotiation';[5] he also comments succinctly on the place of the conduits in pageantry:

A basic syntax of pageant stations was clearly laid out around the same invariant landmarks, the cisterns—the Conduit in Cornhill, the Great Conduit at the head of Cheapside, the Little Conduit at Paul's Gate—and the standards—the Standard and the Cross in Cheapside—that punctuated the route. At these stations, and chiefly at the cisterns—where normally the city's life welled up to be gathered by apprentices of a morning, and where water turned to wine during entries—nature, culture, and grace converged in pageant form.[6]

Most practically, the conduits also provided a solid foundation against, around, or on top of which a scaffold stage, triumphal arch, or other monumental scenic device could easily be constructed. As is apparent from descriptions and the rare surviving illustrations of the conduits, they were essentially little towers containing cisterns, frequently castellated and with tiled roofs. They would therefore have provided an ideal base upon which to construct the elaborate stages which the pageants required. On some occasions, even when a separate platform stage was constructed beside the conduit, the conduit itself functioned as a musicians' gallery. In addition, the conduits were a long-established focal point in the city, where proclamations were issued and punishments were carried out: for example, following the suppression of Wyatt's rebellion in 1554, the bodies of the executed rebels had been set up at various of the conduits, as at other public places in the city.[7] They were an accustomed meeting place, a familiar site for all kinds of dramas.

ANNE BOLEYN'S CORONATION ENTRY (1533) AS A SOURCE FOR ELIZABETH'S

Elizabeth's entry into London was of course not the first of its kind, and it had features common to most royal entries. It is particularly interesting, however, to speculate as to what influence Anne Boleyn's coronation entry in 1533 might have had on that of her daughter twenty-six years later. Anne's coronation entry had been organized, on the specific orders of Henry VIII, in a very short space of time. A printed account of the event survives (and is reproduced in other sources), but the pamphlet itself is extremely rare. The most

---

[5] Lawrence Manley, *Literature and Culture in Early Modern London* (Cambridge: Cambridge University Press, 1995), 241.
[6] Ibid. 225. [7] John Stow, *Annales* (London: R. Newbery, 1592), sig. Yyy7ᵛ.

recent, and probably the fullest, account of the entry is by Gordon Kipling, and the entry is also extensively discussed by Sydney Anglo and others.[8] While Anglo is ultimately dismissive of what he describes as its 'superficial' humanism, 'a self-conscious Latinity and a thin veneer of commonplace literary allusions covering what is, for the most part, a dull, trite and lamentably repetitious pageant series', he still admits that in 1533 'for the first time England witnessed a pageant series which seemed truly classical'.[9] For this reason, and for the fact that it was put together by the city authorities (probably with considerable assistance from various officers of the court) in just over two weeks, it is quite remarkable. A sketch by Holbein, which features Apollo and the Muses seated on Parnassus with a fountain at their feet, is almost certainly connected to the second pageant in the series; indeed, it may have taken the form of a triumphal arch.[10] In Kipling's reading, this device acts as a frame for the entire sequence:

this pageant rightly stands at the head of the series as a statement of the show's theme: Anne's entry into London inspires a new outpouring of the Muses; a new Golden Age of the arts springs forth as she marches to her coronation. A series of emblematic wellsprings further carries this theme throughout the pageant series. The literary wellspring at the fountain of Helicon, which figures so centrally in Holbein's design, is succeeded at the next pageant by a genealogical 'spring' as St. Anne and her progeny prophesy the coming of a Protestant king. The Three Graces sit behind another 'spring of Grace' at the conduit in Cornhill, which runs continuously with wine. Anne's reign, the Graces tell her, is to be the source of gladness, honour, and success, just as the conduit is the source of the continuous stream of wine. Finally, at the Conduit in Cornhill, another fountain accompanies an outpouring of melody and verse, thus recalling once again the literary fountain of Helicon at the first pageant station. Again and again, the pageants seek to dramatize the springing forth of the new Golden Age occasioned by the queen's coronation.[11]

As would be the case in the pageant of *Veritas Temporis Filia* that greeted her daughter, the message at Anne Boleyn's coronation entry was one of transformation and renewal, conventional but still highly complimentary and effective, especially in the way in which it was expressed through the physical transformation of the city's landscape and monuments. As well as marking the introduction

---

[8] Gordon Kipling, ' "He That Saw It Would Not Believe It": Anne Boleyn's Royal Entry into London', in Alexandra F. Johnston and Wim Hüsken (eds.), *Civic Ritual and Drama* (Amsterdam: Rodopi, 1997), 39–76. The best single-volume source for descriptions and interpretation of these earlier pageants remains Sydney Anglo, *Spectacle, Pageantry, and Early Tudor Policy* (Oxford: Clarendon Press, 1969; repr. 1997).

[9] Anglo, *Spectacle*, 248.

[10] Anglo notes that this is the only surviving illustration of a Tudor civic pageant (p. 5). However, it is unclear 'whether it was made merely as a record of the proceedings, or whether it should be interpreted as evidence that Holbein himself designed the pageant of Parnassus' (Susan Foister, *Holbein and England* (New Haven: Yale University Press/The Paul Mellon Centre for Studies in British Art, 2004), 129).

[11] Kipling, 'Anne Boleyn', 64–5.

Figure 4.2. *Apollo and the Muses on Parnassus*, by Hans Holbein the Younger. *c*.1533. Ink and wash on paper. 42.3 × 38.4 cm. (© Kupferstichkabinett, Staatliche Museen, Berlin)

of classicism into English civic pageantry—however superficially—Anne's entry also drew on familiar medieval religious motifs, some only very slightly Protestantized. Most drew attention to her status as the mother of the hoped-for and expected future king (she was pregnant with Elizabeth at the time). As Kipling points out, this pageant was the last in a long series which welcomed queens to their coronations as types of the Virgin Mary, in particular at her Assumption and Coronation:

As the queen progresses through the streets of the city, she thus imaginatively ascends to the New Jerusalem, where the holy Sponsa awaits to crown her Queen of Heaven. By virtue of such pageants, the queen enters the Celestial City as a bearer of Grace, chaste virgin, holy childbearer, Celestial Mediatrix, Mother and Spouse of the royal saviour.[12]

Certainly by the late sixteenth century, the conduits and its generally well-irrigated situation (at least in accounts such as Stow's) were important to London's self-appointed identity as a New Jerusalem, and Kipling notes that 'from the first appearance of a single pageant in 1377 during Richard II's coronation entry to Edward VI's coronation triumph of 1547, each London royal entry included at least one pageant representation of the New Jerusalem'.[13] These usually took the form of 'celestial castles' from which angels descended and heavenly music was heard, which were frequently erected on the conduits. Indeed, the conduits appear to have been the starting point and perhaps even the conceptual centre of the pageantry for Anne's coronation entry in general. Kipling records:

when the Court of Aldermen met on Wednesday, 14 May, it agreed to provide a water show for the 29th and royal entry pageants for the 31st . . . only these pageants were agreed for the new Queen's civic triumph, and the city seems to have envisioned these as little more than decorated civic conduits[14] running with wine rather than water: 'one at the ledenhill the second at the standerd yn chepe to be goodly hangyd & garnysshed w*ith* mynstralsy & chyldern syngyng at eu*er*y of the sayd conduytes And also at the standerd aforesayd wyne rennyng'.[15]

It is surely not overdetermined, therefore, to interpret these three conduits, on this evidence, as the symbolic heart of the city to which the new queen consort was to be welcomed, and it is not surprising that they were also the pageants' thematic centre.

Anne Boleyn did in fact 'appear' in her daughter's coronation entry in 1559. In the tableau of the Tudor succession in Gracechurch Street, she was seated beside Henry VIII, who himself sat in the rose growing out of the united stock of Lancaster and York: 'by him sat one representing the right worthy Lady Queen Anne, wife to the said King Henry the eighth and mother to our most sovereign Lady Queen Elizabeth that now is' (p. 78). Tactfully, the main point of this tableau was the connection between Elizabeth of York and her granddaughter Elizabeth Tudor as bringers of peace and unity, thus drawing attention away from the somewhat problematic nature (and outcome) of the relationship between Henry VIII and the latter's mother. In Anne Boleyn's coronation entry, the classical ideal of the return of the Golden Age had been elided with the traditional Christian goal of the Celestial City. This had been expressed in the palimpsestic layering and juxtaposition of the physical features of an idealized and totemic classical site (the fountain of Helicon) with traditional aspects of the New Jerusalem. The two were connected not only through the figure of the

---

[12] Kipling, 'Anne Boleyn', 52.   [13] Ibid.
[14] Kipling's specific designation of the conduits here as 'civic' is interesting.
[15] Kipling, 'Anne Boleyn', 45–6.

Queen, as she made her linear progression from one to the next, but through their shared occasion and location in the London streets. As will be seen, this emphasis on the symbolic and associative valency of location was a vital feature of Elizabeth's entry and, although the wine-fountain's conventional nature makes it difficult to argue that there was a deeper underlying connection between the apparently shared thematic significance of fountains in the coronation entries of Elizabeth and her mother, it is certainly not impossible that the more explicitly Protestant content of Elizabeth's entry, especially in *Veritas Temporis Filia*, had been grounded on the humanist themes and underlying metaphors of Anne Boleyn's.[16]

FOUNTAINS OF WINE AND GIFTS TO THE PRINCE

Making some or all of the conduits to run with wine was a traditional aspect of royal entries, and, it appears, of some mayoral pageants too. By way of a brief excursus here, I want to consider the custom as part of the wider context of gift-giving in coronation entries. Stow's *Survay* (1598) notes that in Westminster, outside the Palace of Westminster, 'standeth a Fountaine, which at the Coronations, and other great triumphes, is made to run with wine out of diuers spouts' (Cc4ᵛ). The records of the Office of the King's Works include among the preparations for Anne Boleyn's coronation the repainting of the fountains at Westminster Palace, and give some idea of the mechanics of the wine-fountain process:

Outside in New Palace Yard the conduit was similarly embellished, and connected by a pipe to a cistern in the Clock Tower which was filled with wine. Five more pipes syphoned the wine from the conduit into five 'sestrons new made to receyve the said wynne standing without the pales of the said conduit for people to resort unto'.[17]

In Shakespeare's *2 Henry VI*, the rebel leader Jack Cade asserts his newly won authority thus: 'Now is Mortimer lord of this city. And, here sitting upon London Stone,[18] I charge and command that, of the city's cost, the Pissing

---

[16] Rather oddly, there is no mention of wine flowing from the conduits in any of the surviving accounts of Elizabeth's coronation entry or the related documents (see *The Queen's Majesty's Passage*, ed. Warkentin, 75–125). My assumption, however, is that it did, but from the London (and Westminster) conduits not directly involved in the pageants' action, such as the one described below.

[17] H. M. Colvin et al., *The History of the King's Works*, 6 vols. (London: HMSO, 1963-82), iv.2 (1982), 291.

[18] This was possibly the original Roman milestone, from which distances were measured, and hence the symbolic centre of the city. It stood in the middle of what is now Cannon Street, near London Bridge, until 1742, when it was moved and built into the wall of St Swithin's church. It survived the church's destruction in the Blitz, and is now visible in a niche in the wall of the Bank of China, in Cannon Street, as noted by Peter Ackroyd in *London: The Biography* (London: Vintage, 2001), 18–19.

Conduit run nothing but claret wine this first year of our reign. And now henceforward it shall be treason for any that calls me otherwise than Lord Mortimer' (iv. vi. 1–6).[19] In this particular context, this is clearly a populist gesture, and one which foreshadows Cade's increasingly violent megalomaniac excesses. As Stow's note shows, on many other royal and civic occasions it appears simply to have been a standard and unelaborated—and crowd-pleasing—feature of the celebrations: the continuation of Stow's *Annales* (1605) records that when James was making his progress from Scotland in 1603 the celebrations organized in York on 16 April included 'a Conduict that all the day ranne White wine, and Claret, euery man to drinke as much as he listed' (Ssss7ᵛ). Stephen Harrison, the designer of the arches that formed the pageant stages for James's coronation entry in 1604, records in his 'Lectori Candido' at the end of *The Arches of Triumph* (1604) that '[t]he Conduits of *Cornehill*, of *Cheape*, and of *Fleetestreete*, that day ran Claret wine very plenteously', and adds (in an observation that could no doubt have been applied to all such occasions) that the wine '(by reason of so much excellent Musicke, that sounded foorth not onely from each seuerall *Pegme*, but also from diuerse other places) ran the faster and more merrily downe into some bodies bellies' (K1). An excellent pictorial record or reconstruction of fountains running wine—and their potential ill effects—can be seen in the well-known painting of the Field of the Cloth of Gold, in 1520.[20] But Cade's gesture in *Henry VI* is also an obvious and powerful appropriation of civic—and royal—authority and its symbolic prerogatives.

Some of the more elaborate instances of the wine-fountain device that had appeared in the coronation entries of a number of Elizabeth's predecessors had even used the turning of ordinary conduit water into wine as a sign of the quasi-miraculous, transformative power of the prince's presence, a version of Christ's miracle at Cana; indeed, the same symbolism was also perhaps behind its simpler manifestations, however remotely. Discussing Henry VI's entry in 1432, Gordon Kipling notes the imagery of Epiphany drawn on in many of the medieval pageants, and locates the transformation of water into wine specifically within this tradition:

Since the liturgy of Epiphany celebrates three of Christ's Epiphanies—the Magi, the baptism, and the wedding at Cana—and suggests many other prefigurations and types, pageant devisers found in it great scope for their ingenuity . . . The staged offering of a gift, like the gift of the Magi, symbolized the citizens' acclamation of the king and their faithful submission to him . . . Water turned to wine at the royal

---

[19] See *The Arden Shakespeare: Complete Works*, ed. Richard Proudfoot, Ann Thompson, and David Scott Kastan (London: Thomson Learning, 1998; rev. edn. 2001), 522–3.

[20] This is discussed by Anglo, *Spectacle*, 142. A detail of this painting, executed *c*.1545 and now in the Royal Collection, is reproduced in colour in Paula Henderson, *The Tudor House and Garden: Architecture and Landscape in the Sixteenth and Seventeenth Centuries* (New Haven: Yale University Press/The Paul Mellon Centre for Studies in British Art, 2005), 185 (fig. 211).

advent in almost every civic triumph, sometimes specifically alluding to the wedding at Cana.[21]

It seems unlikely either that this symbolism was ever appreciated by more than a select few, or, indeed, that it endured undimmed in the pageantry of increasingly Protestant London as the sixteenth century progressed. But the association that Kipling makes, through Epiphany, between ritual gift-giving and the conduits running with wine in the royal presence is a suggestive one. The prince him- or herself did not usually partake of the wine that flowed from the conduits, or at least not in any of the accounts of sixteenth-century royal entries; indeed, given the presumed quality of any wine made so freely available and on such a scale, this was probably wise. Yet it was still occasioned by their presence and, as such, on one level appeared as a royal gift to the city and citizens, a sign and promise of royal favour in the future.

Balancing this foretaste of plenty was the gift from city to prince which was usually staged between the conduits in Cheapside, probably primarily for reasons of space. When she had passed the Cross in Cheapside, Elizabeth was formally welcomed by the aldermen and 'the right worshipful master Ranulph Cholmley, Recorder of the City', who made a speech professing the city's loyalty and presented her with 'a purse of crimson satin richly wrought with gold, wherein the City gave unto the Queen's Majesty a thousand marks in gold' (p. 86). The Queen accepted the gift graciously and answered the Recorder in terms which made clear the reciprocal nature of her relationship with the city:

I thank my lord mayor, his brethren, and you all. And whereas your request is that I should continue your good lady and Queen, be ye ensured, that I will be as good unto you, as ever Queen was to her people. No will in me can lack, neither do I trust shall there lack any power. And persuade your selves that for the safety and quietness of you all, I will not spare, if need be, to spend my blood. God thank you all. (pp. 86–7)

The gift-giving that took place during Elizabeth's coronation entry exemplified the contractual, bond-building nature of gift exchange outlined by anthropologists such as Marcel Mauss, and explored, in the context of the Elizabethan progresses, elsewhere in this volume by Felicity Heal.[22] It would be interesting to know whether the wine that flowed from the conduits on occasions such as this was perceived as a gift from monarch to people, or from the city itself to its citizens in the prince's honour. If it were the former, a sign of royal beneficence and generosity, then it was of a different symbolic order to the gifts given by the city to the prince; it could in fact be seen as an anticipatory response to those gifts. The monarch would continue to bestow her favour and bounty upon her

[21] Gordon Kipling, 'Wonderfull Spectacles: Theater and Civic Culture', in John D. Cox and David Scott Kastan (eds.), *A New History of Early English Drama* (New York: Columbia University Press, 1997), 153–71 (pp. 159, 161).

[22] See pp. 46–61, above.

subjects, the loyal citizens of London, because she had already been seen to do so, and had been praised for it.

Even in the most conventional and formal presentation of gifts to the monarch in the context of his or her coronation entry or other civic welcome, the relationship between royal bounty and favour and civic loyalty and adulation was thus a closely intertwined one. As Evelyn B. Tribble puts it, 'the "entertainment" or pageant presented to the visiting monarch could work both to honor the passing monarch and to display precisely the source of that honor: the good will of her subjects . . . ceremony and civic pageantry, far from being monolithic or merely adulatory, could provide a subtle and flexible forum for negotiation between subject and monarch'.[23] A relationship was therefore enacted between crown and city which was reciprocal, but also in some respects conditional. This was a particularly obvious principle (and tension) in the didacticism of Elizabeth's 1559 entry, where Elizabeth's power—although a power able to transform the very city streets, and to restore and nourish an ailing realm—was predicated upon that of the city, because it was represented as ultimately being drawn from something that the city specifically appropriated into its gift.

ELIZABETH'S CORONATION ENTRY AND THE LITTLE CONDUIT

There were seven tableaux in Elizabeth's coronation entry. Although Mulcaster records that the conduits not directly involved in the pageant 'action' were decorated, that in Cornhill being 'curiously trimmed against that time with rich banners adorned, and a noise of loud instruments upon the top thereof' (p. 81) and the Great Conduit in Cheap 'beautified with pictures and sentences accordingly against her Grace's coming thither' (p. 83), the final two pageants in the series both took place at conduits. Mulcaster himself makes clear that the two were closely related, but he gives more prominence to the first of the two, at the Little Conduit. This is not least because it was the one in which the Queen took the most active part; it was the most overtly political. It represented the thematic climax of the coronation entry and its constituent pageants' dramatization of London's spaces and monuments, as the presentation of the purse had been its symbolic climax, and this thematic climax itself reached its height with a second gift from the city to the Queen, presented as part of the pageant's action. In Mulcaster's text, the pageant at the Little Conduit in Cheap is given a considerable build-up, because '[s]oon after that her Grace passed the cross [in

[23] Evelyn B. Tribble, ' "We Will Do No Harm With Our Swords": Royal Representation, Civic Pageantry, and the Displacement of Popular Protest in Thomas Deloney's *Jacke of Newberie*', in Alvin Vos (ed.), *Place and Displacement in the Renaissance* (Binghamton: State University of New York, 1995), 147–57 (p. 148).

Cheap], she had espied the pageant erected at the Little Conduit in Cheap, and incontinent required to know what it might signify' (p. 85). Although she was given an explanation, she had first to be formally welcomed, and given the city's gift. But after this, the Queen was allowed, finally, to approach the pageant at the Little Conduit.

It seems from Mulcaster's description that the pageant stage or scenery may in fact have integrated the conduit itself into its structure: he states that it was 'a pageant with square proportion, *standing directly before the same conduit, with battlements accordingly*' (p. 87; my emphasis). The staging consisted of two hills:

The one of them being on the north side of the same pageant was made cragged, barren and stony, in the which was erected one tree artificially made, all withered and dead, with branches accordingly . . . The other hill on the south side was made fair, fresh, green and beautiful, the ground thereof full of flowers and beauty, and on the same was erected also one tree very fresh and fair. (p. 87)

Beside each tree was an appropriately dressed 'personage', and the first hill was labelled (in English and Latin) '*Ruinosa Respublica*' and the second '*Respublica bene instituta*'. Each tree displayed further 'tables', which gave the various reasons for their respective states: 'Causes of a ruinous commonweal are these: *Want of the fear of God. Disobedience to rulers. Blindness of guides. Bribery in magistrates. Rebellion in subjects. Civil disagreement. Flattering of princes. Unmercifulness in rulers. Unthankfulness in subjects.* Causes of a flourishing commonweal. *Fear of God. A wise prince. Learned rulers. Obedience to officers. Obedient subjects. Lovers of the common weal. Virtue rewarded. Vice chastened*' (p. 89). Between these two hills (and, therefore, presumably directly in front of the conduit itself):

was made artificially one hollow place or cave, with [a] door and lock enclosed, out of the which, a little before the Queen's highness's coming thither, issued one personage whose name was *Time*, apparelled as an old man with a scythe in his hand, having wings artificially made, leading a personage of lesser stature than himself, which was finely and well apparelled, all clad in white silk, and directly over her head was set her name and title in Latin and English, *Temporis filia*, the Daughter of Time. Which two so appointed, went forward toward the south side of the pageant. And on her breast was written her proper name, which was *Veritas*, Truth who held a book in her hand upon the which was written *Verbum veritatis*, the Word of Truth. (pp. 87–8)

The book held by Truth was an English Bible. It was let down 'by a silken lace' (p. 86) and passed by Sir John Perrot, one of the attendant gentlemen, to the Queen.[24] This action, more than any other, was the most densely symbolic moment of the entire entry.

Discussing the importance of the Bible in English Renaissance civic pageants, David Bergeron argues that 'biblical references in the pageants serve political

---

[24] *The Queen's Majesty's Passage*, ed. Warkentin (59–61) suggests that Perrot was an illegitimate son of Henry VIII and therefore Elizabeth's half-brother; this legend is denied by his most recent biographer in the *Oxford DNB*.

purposes, offering in various ways support for the state . . . [and] making the sacred reinforce the secular'.[25] This is obvious from pageants such as the pageant of the Beatitudes (at the end of Soper Lane) and the tableau of Deborah (at the conduit in Fleet Street) in Elizabeth's entry, and numerous others of this more traditional medieval type: all took a biblical text as a theme for illustration and explication. They therefore treated the Bible as a collection of *sententiae* to be mined. But the pageant of *Veritas Temporis Filia* and the appearance of the English Bible within it can also be read and interpreted in terms of what Mark Breitenberg discusses (with particular reference to *Gorboduc*) as 'cultural fashioning . . . depend[ing] on a complex intermingling of iconic and verbal representation, what one might call the iconicity of texts and the textuality of icons'.[26] In the pageant the Bible was not simply an iconic text, but a material and functional object. Because it had all these qualities, it was able to be the focus of both an ideological statement and a transaction. Its materiality and its status as a gift perhaps made its didacticism more obliquely acceptable, less likely to offend or anger the Queen. The symbolic centre of this pageant was not the device of the two hills, not yet even the revelation of Time and his daughter Truth. Rather it was the gift of the book, a gift which breached the notional fourth wall of the pageant's symbolic staging and drew the Queen into its action. The Queen played her part perfectly, and it would not be surprising if she had been instructed in what she should do beforehand, in addition to her questions about the nature of the pageant when she first saw it in the distance (p. 85): 'she as soon as she had received the book, kissed it, and with both her hands held up the same, and so laid it upon her breast, with great thanks to the city therefor' (p. 88). In Gordon Kipling's interpretation of this action,

the queen necessarily performed a crucial emblematic action that revealed her nature as a Protestant ruler: she received the Word on behalf of her Reformed people . . . The magically altered garden manifested the power of the Word, for only the Word offered in the English Bible had the power to reform the landscape.[27]

This pageant was thus at the ideological and programmatic heart of the Queen's civic welcome and, in itself and in combination with the other tableaux, it expressed particular hopes for Elizabeth's reign.

The complex symbolism of the pageant and Elizabeth's response to it was intimately related to its setting at the Little Conduit, which functioned as a material metaphor for its action. As I have discussed elsewhere, in relation to Spenser's *Faerie Queene*,[28] a very common image applied to the English Bible

---

[25] David M. Bergeron, 'The Bible in English Renaissance Civic Pageantry', *Comparative Drama*, 20 (1986), 160–70 (p. 161).

[26] Mark Breitenberg, 'Reading Elizabethan Iconicity: *Gorboduc* and the Semiotics of Reform', *English Literary Renaissance*, 18 (1988), 194–217 (p. 195).

[27] Kipling, 'Wonderfull Spectacles', 169.

[28] See my discussions in 'Fountains in Renaissance Literature', 68–112 and in 'From the Fountain to the Well: Redcrosse Learns to Read', *Studies in Philology*, 100 (2003), 135–76.

in this period was the fountain, which denoted the new translation from the original sources without the corrupt mediation of the Vulgate (the humanist principle of the return *ad fontes*), as well as its function as an agent of spiritual refreshment and renewal akin to baptism. In the pageant of *Veritas Temporis Filia*, the English Bible was thus the metaphorical fountain that would restore the barren commonwealth and sustain the fertile, through the agency of the rightful and godly prince. Furthermore, the fountain was also a commonplace humanist image for the operation of monarchical government, and the device of the two hills was clearly concerned with the nature of good government. Thus, Elizabeth's mediation and fulfilment of the English Bible to her people was to ensure the well-being of her realm. She herself was to be a fountain.

Perhaps explicitly bringing together these two symbolic economies in an analogous way to the coronation entry, a Flemish medal produced in 1565 in fact depicted Elizabeth as 'Divine fountain of the realm' (ZAΘEH.BA[Σ]IΛIHΣ.Λ IBAΣ),[29] an anagram in Greek of 'Elizabeth the Queen' devised by Charles Utenhove, a Flemish humanist connected with the French embassy in London. Since it was first discussed by Jan Van Dorsten in the 1960s,[30] little scholarly attention has been paid to this medal, and to my knowledge no one has sought to connect it with the coronation pageant at the Little Conduit. The medal (the unique example of which, found in a ploughed field in Norfolk in 1962, is now in the National Portrait Gallery) has a portrait head of Elizabeth on one side; the reverse portrays Faith as a woman seated beside a fountain. Roy Strong describes it as 'the best medallic portrait of [Elizabeth] prior to the advent of Hilliard'.[31] As John King notes, '[t]he medal compliments the queen, who incorporated Protestant theology into her settlement in religion, by identifying Faith as one who drinks pure waters that find their source in Elizabeth herself'.[32] Although there is no scenic fountain mentioned in Mulcaster's detailed account of the pageant's staging, there was undeniably one present, in the pageant's location at the Little Conduit. The physical presence of the conduit thus materialized and unified the metaphor that underpinned both strands of the pageant, its concern with right (Protestant) religion and good government.

Veritas Temporis Filia also made pointed reference to the reign of Elizabeth's immediate predecessor, her half-sister Mary, who had herself used 'Veritas

---

[29] There are letters missing from the inscription on the reverse, and also that on the obverse, ELIZABETH.D.G.AN[GLI]Æ.ET HIBE[RNIÆ.R]EGINA, because the medal has been damaged and also because it has a hole bored in it to allow for suspension.

[30] See Jan Van Dorsten, 'Steven Van Herwyck's Elizabeth (1565): A Franco-Flemish Political Medal', *Burlington Magazine*, 111 (1969), 143–7; and Jan Van Dorsten, *The Radical Arts: First Decade of an Elizabethan Renaissance* (Leiden: Leiden University Press/Oxford University Press, 1970), 42–5. Drawing on Van Dorsten, the medal is noted by Roy Strong in *Gloriana: The Portraits of Queen Elizabeth I* (London: Thames and Hudson, 1987; repr. London: Pimlico, 2003), 62–3.

[31] Roy Strong, *Tudor and Jacobean Portraits*, 2 vols. (London: HMSO, 1969), i. 101.

[32] John N. King, *Tudor Royal Iconography: Literature and Art in an Age of Religious Crisis* (Princeton: Princeton University Press, 1989), 107.

Figure 4.3. *Queen Elizabeth I,* by Steven van Herwyck (after a programme by Charles Utenhove). 1565. Lead medal (Obverse: Elizabeth I). Diameter 4.8 cm. (The National Portrait Gallery, London)

Figure 4.4. *Queen Elizabeth I,* by Steven van Herwyck (after a programme by Charles Utenhove). 1565. Lead medal (Reverse: Faith seated by a Fountain). Diameter 4.8 cm. (The National Portrait Gallery, London)

Temporis Filia' as a motto. 'Veritas' had appeared as a character in *Respublica*, the interlude performed before Mary at Christmas 1553; it may originally have been written as part of her coronation festivities the previous October.[33] Furthermore, chronicles record a notorious incident in the entry of Mary and Philip into London after their marriage in August 1554: Stephen Gardiner, Bishop of

[33] Dawn Massey, '*Veritas Filia Temporis*: Apocalyptic Polemics in the Drama of the English Reformation', *Comparative Drama*, 32 (1998–9), 146–75 (p. 151).

Winchester and Lord Chancellor, ordered the hasty alteration of a painted representation of Henry VIII, which had depicted him holding a book similarly labelled '*Verbum Dei*', lest the Catholic monarchs be offended by the sight of a Bible (albeit possibly a Latin one) in the hands of a heretic and schismatic.[34]

Drawing on all these particular aspects of its symbolism and associations, the pageant of *Veritas Temporis Filia* at the Little Conduit made fundamental points about the nature of good government and the proper ordering of relationships in a flourishing commonwealth. After explaining the characters of the tableau, the child orator pointed out its moral, and applied it directly to the Queen:

> . . . Now since that Time again his daughter Truth hath brought
> We trust O worthy Queen, thou wilt this truth embrace.
> And since thou understandst the good estate and nought
> We trust wealth thou wilt plant, and barrenness displace.
>
> But for to heal the sore, and cure that is not seen,
> Which thing the book of truth doth teach in writing plain:
> She doth present to thee the same, O worthy Queen,
> For that, that words do fly, but writing doth remain. (p. 88)[35]

The written word of the English Bible was thus accorded a permanence because it was material. In addition, in this particular tableau it was strongly associated with physical landscape, a landscape which was itself written on and inscribed. In Stow's *Survay*, in a way perhaps analogous to their appearances in coronation entries such as Anne Boleyn's as well as that of her daughter, the conduits are points where London is at its most richly palimpsestic, not only physically, but temporally. One of the aspects of the conduits to which Stow pays most attention is their prominence in the records of public charity, and it is in that record (as well as, on occasion, in inscriptions placed upon the conduits themselves) that the names and eulogies of community benefactors endure, forming an idealized

---

[34] The incident is recorded by John Foxe, *Actes and Monuments* (London, 1583): 'From London Bridge they passed to the Conduit in Gracious streete whiche was finely painted, and among other thinges, the ix worthies, whereof king Henry the 8. was one. He was paynted in harnesse hauing in one hand a sworde, and in the other hand a booke, wherupon was written *Verbum Dei*, deliuering the same booke (as it were) to his sonne king Edward, who was paynted in a corner by him. But hereupon was no small matter made, for the Bishop of Winchester Lord Chauncellour, sent for the painter and not onely called him knaue for paynting a booke in K. Henries hand, and specially for writing therupon *Verbum Dei*, but also rancke Traytour and Villaine, saying to hym that he should rather haue put the booke into the Queenes hand (who was also paynted there) for that she had reformed the church and religion, with other things according to the pure and sincere word of God in deede. The Paynter answered and sayd, that if he had knowen that that had bene the matter wherfore his Lordship sent for him, he coulde haue remedied it, and not haue troubled his Lordship. The bishop answered & said, that it was the Queenes maiesties will and commaundement that he shoulde send for him: and so commaunding him to wype out the booke and *Verbum Dei* too: he sent him home. So the Paynter departed, but fearing least he should leaue some part eyther of the booke, or of *Verbum Dei*, in king Henries hand: hee wiped away a piece of his fingers withal', p. 1472 [Pppp6]. The incident's reworking in 1559 is noted by Manley, *Literature and Culture*, 249.

[35] These are the last two stanzas of four.

and transhistorical community of benevolence that, in turn, becomes 'attached' to the physical conduit. Forty years before Stow, in Elizabeth's coronation entry, both book and setting existed in terms that were at once textual and material, at the same time as they suggested the possibility of an ideology of unity and community that could transcend the limitations of time and place.

Using terminology that would soon become familiar through the Elizabethan homilies on obedience, the descriptions of the ruined and the flourishing commonwealths affixed to the two trees made clear the absolute interdependence of spiritual and temporal order, and the mutual obligations of ruler and subjects in pursuing them. Elizabeth was presented with a didactic and even-handed prescription for government, warning her that the commonweal could be destroyed by '*Blindness of guides*' and '*Unmercifulness in rulers*' as much as by '*Rebellion in subjects*' and '*Unthankfulness in subjects*' (p. 89). Like the relationship between city and prince, enacted in both the gift of the Bible and the gift of the gold-filled purse which immediately preceded this particular pageant, the ideal relationship between monarch and subjects is a reciprocal one of mutual obligation, grounded in truth, the Word, and the fear of God. According to Mulcaster, '[t]he matter of this pageant dependeth of them that went before' (p. 89). It looked back to the third pageant, in Cornhill, which had represented the Queen herself, sitting on '*The seat of worthy governance*':

stayed by lively personages, which personages were in number four . . . whereof every one had a table to express their effects which are virtues, namely *Pure religion, Love of subjects, Wisdom,* and *Justice,* which did tread their contrary vices under their feet. That is to wit, *Pure religion,* did tread upon *Rebellion* and *Insolence, Wisdom* did tread upon *Folly* and *Vainglory, Justice* did tread upon *Adulation* and *Bribery.* (p. 82)

And it also looked back to the fourth pageant, at the end of Soper Lane, in which eight child actors portrayed the Beatitudes (Matthew 5: 3–11). The pageant of *Veritas Temporis Filia* was therefore the most prescriptive of the series in political and religious terms, the culmination of a series of didactic tableaux. Unlike the tableaux that had preceded it, however, it made particular and pointed use of its location at the conduit as a metaphor, in a way that could be seen as a refinement of the 'London as New Jerusalem' imagery of Anne Boleyn's entry a quarter of a century before.

Yet the Little Conduit also provided another gloss upon the pageant and its action. This particular pageant was prefaced by the formal welcoming of Elizabeth by the city officials, and by the presentation of their gift to her. The Bible, too, was specifically the gift of the city. As Stow made clear in the record of benefactions that accompanied his descriptions of conduits, they were civic and popular sites, set up, maintained, repaired, and utilized by ordinary people in the most mundane way possible and located in the ordinary city streets, freely available to all. They were not the signs of royal munificence, but of civic and community pride and benevolence. They were a focal point of community identity for Londoners both as they lived and as they liked to see themselves. The Little Conduit as it appeared in the pageant of *Veritas Temporis Filia* might well have been doing service as a religious and monarchical symbol, but it also remained a public, civic, and communal one. Even in its expressions of adulation and loyalty to the new Queen, the city was expressing something of its autonomous identity and its power.

The final tableau was similarly didactic in intention to its precursor at the Little Conduit, and was closely related to it. It was staged at the Conduit in Fleet Street, and depicted Deborah, seated on a throne and 'richly apparelled in parliament robes' (p. 91), surrounded by representatives of the nobility, the Church, and the commons. The whole was labelled: '*Deborah with her estates, consulting for the good government of Israel*' (p. 91). Mulcaster noted that:

The ground of this last pageant was, that forasmuch as the next pageant before had set before her Grace's eyes the flourishing and desolate states of a commonweal, she might by this be put in remembrance to consult for the worthy government of her people. (p. 92)

Both culminating pageants, therefore, were concerned with the communal and reciprocal nature of good government, the first demonstrating the need for the successful ruler to look to the Scriptures for guidance, and the second her obligation to seek and heed advice from those around her. As Sydney Anglo has observed, 'there is one feature of the pageants for Elizabeth which marks them off from their predecessors. This is the degree to which they not merely praise the monarch, or exhort her to behave well, but also give her advice on a right course of action. To a certain extent most civic pageantry includes this element, *laudando praecipere*—but rarely in so emphatic a fashion.'[36]t could also be observed that it is particularly striking in the number of levels upon which this didactic principle operates: speeches, texts, visual symbols, and (in the case of the gift of the English Bible) physical transactions, all enacted in civic locations with their own associative density.

The Queen's formal entry into London, therefore, was a process whereby she was welcomed into a particular relationship with the city through her negotiation of the city's symbolically enhanced landscape. It was a journey designed, in its didactic intent, to transform as well as to flatter her: above all, it attested to the contingent nature of her relationship with the city. Writing specifically about the entertainments presented to Elizabeth in provincial towns, Mary Hill Cole has observed, 'Although the towns owed allegiance to Elizabeth for their civic rights, she did not have official status within the corporation . . . Even though she ruled the country, as an outsider to the town, the queen needed to undergo

---

[36] Anglo, *Spectacle*, 357.

a process of inclusion.'[37] Even in her coronation entry, the Queen remained the city's (honoured) guest, as she was a guest actor, in the performance of an action the outcome of which was undeniably beneficial to all concerned, but which nonetheless consisted of responsibilities as well as rights and obligations that were mutual; power relationships that were reciprocal but not necessarily always constructed in the monarch's favour. After all, the support of the city for Mary only five years before had been crucial. In the pageant at the Little Conduit, Elizabeth might well have been figured as Truth, the daughter of Time who was to bring peace and prosperity to the realm, but the Book from which she was to draw her strength and right was the city's gift, and the place where it was presented to her was a location loaded with civic and community significance.

CONCLUSION: THE 'AFTERLIFE' OF VERITAS TEMPORIS FILIA

Elizabeth's entry into London in January 1559 had a considerable 'afterlife', and the pageant which appears to have had the most impact was *Veritas Temporis Filia*. A number of late Elizabethan and early Jacobean pageants and plays, for example, reworked it: these included George Peele's Spenserian mayoral pageant *Descensus Astraeae* (1591), in which the nymph Astraea defended the fountain of Protestantism;[38] the dumb-show of Time and Truth which begins Dekker's *The Whore of Babylon* (1607); and the presentation of the Bible to Elizabeth by the Mayor, in the highly condensed version of her coronation entry that concludes the first part of Thomas Heywood's *If you know not me, you know no bodie* (1606).[39] In the speech given by Heywood to the Queen in response to the city's gifts, there is a reflection of both the fountain imagery and the theme of communality that are implicit in *Veritas Temporis Filia*. Heywood's Elizabeth says of the Bible:

> This is true foode for rich men and for poore,
> Who drinkes of this is certaine ne're to perish
> This will the soule with heauenly vertue cherish,
> Lay hand vppon this Anchor euery soule,

[37] Mary Hill Cole, 'Ceremonial Dialogue between Elizabeth I and her Civic Hosts', in Douglas F. Rutledge (ed.), *Ceremony and Text in the Renaissance* (Newark: University of Delaware Press, 1996), 84–100 (pp. 86–7).

[38] I have discussed these at more length, together with the coronation entry of James VI and I in 1604, in 'Fountains in Renaissance Literature', 208–19.

[39] See the discussion of this scene by Jonathan Gil Harris, 'This Is Not a Pipe: Water Supply, Incontinent Sources, and the Leaky Body Politic', in Richard Burt and John Michael Archer (eds.), *Enclosure Acts: Sexuality, Property and Culture in Early Modern England* (Ithaca, NY: Cornell University Press, 1994), 203–28.

Your names shalbe in an eternall scrowle;
Who builds on this dwel's in a happy state,
This is the fountaine cleere imaculate,
That happy yssue that shall vs succeed,
And in our populous Kingdome this booke read. (F3ᵛ – F4ʳ)

Here, the image of the fountain implicit in the conduit location and the gift of the Bible in 1559 is made explicit: Heywood has Elizabeth use the image of the fountain to endorse the English Bible as a source of both spiritual sustenance and, perhaps even more importantly, community cohesion; she implicitly identifies herself with the fountain also. The image so central to the negotiation, in 1559, of the relationship between Elizabeth and the city of London, and enacted at that time in material terms, remained a potent and enduring one in her cultural memory.

5

Spectator and Spectacle: Royal Entertainments at the Universities in the 1560s

Siobhan Keenan

Few of Elizabeth I's early progress visits are well documented. Her visits to the universities of Cambridge (1564) and Oxford (1566) are, however, notable exceptions. Thanks to the survival of several contemporary accounts, we know a great deal about the lavish welcomes she received and the programme of recreations with which she was entertained, the highlight of which was a series of play performances. For Elizabeth, her Oxford and Cambridge visits were a way of inspecting the universities and complimenting the noblemen who oversaw them. For her hosts, they provided a chance to win the Queen's favour. It was not an opportunity either university took lightly. But a royal visit also provided a chance to counsel the Queen. Would the scholars take advantage of this fact, too?

In the 1560s, it seems that they did. Between them, the universities implicitly offered the Queen advice on the three issues that dominated early Elizabethan politics and the parliaments of 1563 and 1566: religious conformity, the royal succession, and the Queen's marriage.[1] In choosing to offer Elizabeth counsel on such issues, especially through theatre, the scholars followed the example of her courtiers and lawyers. In 1562, Lord Robert Dudley had used the court masque of *Desire and Lady Beauty* to encourage the Queen to marry and choose him as her consort.[2] He appears to have sponsored the Inner Temple and court performances of Thomas Norton's and Thomas Sackville's *The Tragedie of Gorboduc* (1561–2) for similar reasons. Although superficially a neoclassical tragedy about the downfall of an ancient British king, Gorboduc's story was used by Norton and Sackville to emphasize the importance of establishing the royal succession with the agreement of parliament, and, it seems, to offer

---

[1] See, for example, T. E. Hartley, *Proceedings in the Parliaments of Elizabeth I* (Leicester: Leicester University Press, 1981), i: *1558–1581*, 58–62; 90–3.

[2] See Marie Axton, *The Queen's Two Bodies: Drama and the Elizabethan Succession* (London: Royal Historical Society, 1977), 40.

covert support to Dudley's marriage suit.[3] In 1565, the members of Gray's Inn would broach the issue of the Queen's marriage again in a play of Juno and Diana. The drama debated 'the pros and cons of marriage' and 'ended with Jupiter's ruling in favour of matrimony'. On this occasion Elizabeth was only too well aware that the lawyers were seeking to influence her, reportedly observing that 'This is all against me'.[4] Building on the work of earlier scholars such as Frederick S. Boas, Alan H. Nelson, and John R. Elliott Jr., this essay re-examines Elizabeth's early visits to Cambridge and Oxford and the plays performed before her, considering how the programme of entertainments was arranged, and what these royal visits and performances have to reveal about the relationship between the universities and the monarch, and the functions of her progress visits.

CAMBRIDGE, 1564: LEARNING AND ORDER

Elizabeth's decision to visit Cambridge was momentous, for 'not since 1522 had a monarch paid a formal visit to the University and the town'.[5] One testimony to the interest the visit produced is the series of contemporary accounts it prompted. The three main descriptions are by Cambridge graduates: Matthew Stokys (King's College), Nicholas Robinson (Queens' College), and Abraham Hartwell (King's College).[6] Stokys's manuscript account is written in English;[7] while Robinson's *Commentarii Hexameri Rerum Cantabrigiae Actarum* and Hartwell's *Regina Literata* are both Latin texts.[8]

Stokys appears to have compiled his account in his joint capacity as University Registrary and esquire bedell. The latter were officials who 'supervised university ceremonies' and therefore sometimes kept books 'which recorded details of such events as . . . royal visits'.[9] These books were mainly intended to provide guidance for the organization of similar events in the future and were not usually publicly circulated. Robinson's description is, likewise, unpublished, forming part of a manuscript miscellany he wrote to commemorate the royal

[3] Norman Jones and Paul Whitfield White, '*Gorboduc* and Royal Marriage Politics: An Elizabethan Playgoer's Report of the Premiere Performance', *English Literary Renaissance*, 26.1 (1996), 3–16 (pp. 3–4).

[4] Ros King (ed.), *The Works of Richard Edwards: Politics, Poetry and Performance in Sixteenth Century England* (Manchester: Manchester University Press, 2001), 85.

[5] Alan H. Nelson, *Early Cambridge Theatres: College, University and Town Stages, 1464–1720* (Cambridge: Cambridge University Press, 1994), 10.

[6] Frederick S. Boas, *University Drama in the Tudor Age* (Oxford: Clarendon Press, 1914), 90.

[7] Stokys's Book, Cambridge University Archives, Misc. Collection, fo. 4. Quotations from this manuscript appear by permission of the Syndics of Cambridge University Library.

[8] Boas, *University Drama*, 90.

[9] *Records of Early English Drama: Cambridge*, ed. Alan H. Nelson, 2 vols. (Toronto, London: University of Toronto Press, 1989), ii. 794.

visit.[10] Robinson was a graduate of Queens' College, where he had been involved in several plays in the 1550s—a fact that may have contributed to his special interest in the University's entertainment of the Queen and his wish to memorialize the visit.[11] Hartwell's poetic description of the visit was the only one to be published (1565), implicitly with the support of the University and its noble patrons, as is reflected in its full title and preface. In the latter, Hartwell is careful to praise both the University's powerful Chancellor (Sir William Cecil) and its High Steward (Lord Robert Dudley); while the title dedicates the description to Walter Haddon, the well-respected courtier and scholar who had been closely involved in the preparations for the Queen, and alludes to it having been specifically prepared for handing 'down to posterity'.[12] Publishing such an account in Latin verse was a way of both commemorating the Queen's visit and displaying the learning of Cambridge's scholars.

Elizabeth was to arrive in Cambridge after a brief progress through Hertfordshire and Middlesex; and continued from the city into other parts of Cambridgeshire, Huntingdonshire, Leicestershire, Northamptonshire, Buckinghamshire, Bedfordshire, and Middlesex.[13] John Nichols assumed that the visit was a compliment to the University's Chancellor and leading statesman, Sir William Cecil; but contextual evidence suggests that it was also a political and religious inspection.[14] 'As the potential breeding places of enlightened rulers and of scholars who would become the religious leaders, teachers, poets, and propagandists of England', the universities were 'a highly important adjunct to the state', and Elizabeth needed to know she could count on their members' loyalty and obedience.[15] Such an agenda is implied by Cecil's anxious first letter to the Vice-Chancellor in which he articulated his wish that 'two things maye speciallye appeare in that Universitye: order and lerninge. And for order I meane bothe for Religion and civill behaviour.'[16] Given Elizabeth's implied ulterior motive for visiting Cambridge, Cecil's concern is not surprising. Whereas Oxford's Chancellor would have to

[10] Robinson's Book is held in the Folger Shakespeare Library, as MS V.a.176; see also *REED: Cambridge*, ii. 796.

[11] *REED: Cambridge*, i. 168, 182, 186.

[12] Abraham Hartwell, *Regina Literata siue De serenissimæ Dominæ Elizabethæ Angliæ, Franciæ & Hiberniæ, fidei defensione illustriss. in Academiam Cantabrigiensem aduentu. &c. anno. 1564. Aug. 5. narratio Abraham Hartuelli Cantabrigiensis Ad clariss. virum D. Gualterum Haddonum Regiæ Maiestati a supplicum libellis tunc temporis conscripta, nunc demum posteris tradita* (London, 1565), sig. Bi. The author would like to thank Frank Beetham for his translation.

[13] Mary Hill Cole, *The Portable Queen: Elizabeth I and the Politics of Ceremony* (Amherst: University of Massachusetts Press, 1999), 181.

[14] *The Progresses and Public Processions of Queen Elizabeth*, ed. John Nichols, 3 vols. (London: John Nichols & Son, 1823), i, p. xxviii.

[15] Eleanor Rosenberg, *Leicester: Patron of Letters* (New York: Columbia University Press, 1958), 121; Claire Cross, 'Oxford and the Tudor State from the Accession of Henry VIII to the Death of Mary I', in James McConica (ed.), *The History of the University of Oxford*, iii: *The Collegiate University* (Oxford: Clarendon Press, 1986), 117–49 (p. 149).

[16] *Progresses*, ed. Nichols, i. 151–2.

wrestle initially with lingering Catholicism, in Cambridge Cecil faced difficulties with radical Protestantism.[17] Ensuring religious 'order' might not be easy.

The first news of Elizabeth's visit came in July 1564 when the Vice-Chancellor received a letter from Cecil notifying him of the Queen's intended trip.[18] Such a letter was to become the customary means by which notice of a royal visit was given. At Cecil's suggestion, the University sent three men to London to consult with him and a group of senior clerics and courtiers (including Walter Haddon) about the preparations to be made.[19] The group discussed how members of the University should dress and behave; the programme of entertainments for the Queen, including 'thorder of co*m*modies and tragedies'; and the compilation of a book describing 'ye founders and benefactors of every colledge & what gret lerned men and servaunt*es* to ye prynce or co*m*mon wheale had been brought vp in ye same'; the latter a gesture clearly intended to emphasize the University's importance as a nursery for future scholars and statesmen.[20]

It was agreed that the Queen and the plays would be hosted by King's College. Initially, it was intended that the latter take place in the college hall and a great stage was built therein, but 'by cause it was iudged by divers to be to Lytle and to cloose for her highnes and her co*m*panye & also to farre from her Lodgynge it was taken downe'.[21] A new stage was constructed by the Queen's Surveyor in the college chapel. This afforded a much larger performance space, measuring 40 by 120 feet 'in the antechapel alone'.[22] Such a space was more capacious than many of the royal halls used for plays, including that at Whitehall Palace (measuring 90 feet by 40 feet), which was the venue for the 1562 productions of *Gorboduc* and *Desire and Beauty*.[23] Such court intervention in the preparations for a progress entertainment was unusual and probably orchestrated by Cecil. It suggests not only his determination that the Queen be well entertained, but also that the University performances were perceived to be an extension of court theatre, in which the appropriate display of the Queen's power was as significant as the quality of the entertainment offered her.

The stage constructed was impressive in scale, 'co*n*teyning ye breadth of ye churche from thone syde vnto thother' and running the length of 'twoe of the Loer chapels'. According to Alan Nelson, this would have produced a 'playing platform 40′ wide by nearly 50′ deep'.[24] Special seating was also constructed. This included a raised chair on the south wall for the Queen, seats on the rood loft for the court ladies, and two tables below the loft for the 'choise officers

---

[17] See C. M. Dent, *Protestant Reformers in Elizabethan Oxford* (Oxford: Oxford University Press, 1983), 18; H. C. Porter, *Reformation and Reaction in Tudor Cambridge* (Hamden, Conn.: Archon Books, 1972), 112.

[18] *REED: Cambridge*, i. 227.   [19] *Progresses*, ed. Nichols, i. 153.

[20] Stokys's Book, fo. 63ᵛ.   [21] Ibid. 70ᵛ.

[22] Nelson, *Early Cambridge Theatres*, 10, 13.

[23] John Astington, *English Court Theatre, 1558–1642* (Cambridge: Cambridge University Press, 1999), 44.

[24] Stokys's Book, fo. 70ᵛ; Nelson, *Early Cambridge Theatres*, 13.

of ye courte'. As this reveals, the seating was hierarchical, with the highest, most visually prominent seat reserved for the Queen, as was customary at court performances. There was no place for students. After welcoming Elizabeth they were ordered to 'quietly & orderlye . . . departe home to their colledg*es*'.[25] This was presumably one of the ways in which the University intended to preserve, as well as to display, order.

THE VISIT

The Queen arrived on Saturday, 5 August and departed on Thursday, 10 August. Having been greeted on the outskirts of the city by the Mayor, she was led to King's College where her welcome involved a carefully choreographed display of order. At two o'clock the University assembled in full academic dress to line the road from Queens' College to King's College Chapel: the Scholars and Bachelors stood furthest from the church, and the Doctors and Vice-Chancellor closest. At the door of the Chapel the Queen was greeted with an oration. The speaker, William Master, began by commending Elizabeth's virtues and virginity, and declaring the University's joy at her visit. This was followed by a brief account of Cambridge's antiquity, and praise for Elizabeth's two leading courtiers, Cecil and Dudley. Master chose his matter well. It was intended to flatter and impress the Queen. Contemporary report suggests that he was successful. His praise of virginity proved especially welcome, reportedly prompting the Queen to interject, 'god*es* blessing of thyne harte: there co*n*tynue'.[26] Elizabeth had declared her preference for a virgin life as early as 1559; her warm response to Master's oration confirmed this preference to the scholars and did not bode well for those who were advocating that she marry soon.[27]

Each day of Elizabeth's visit was to be marked in similar fashion, with lectures and disputations planned for the daytime, and a play for the evening. Each event was designed to display the scholars' learning and to entertain the Queen; but topical issues were to be broached, too, as the scholars sought to counsel as well as to impress the monarch.

THE ENTERTAINMENT

Most of the plays performed at the Elizabethan universities were classical and didactic, as the main motive for encouraging academic drama was pedagogical. Classical learning was at the heart of the Renaissance curriculum. Studying

---

[25] Stokys's Book, fos. 70ᵛ, 66.   [26] Ibid. 68.

[27] See Raphael Holinshed, *Chronicles of England, Scotland and Ireland*, 6 vols. (1st edn. 1577) (New York: AMS Press, 1965), iv. 178.

classical plays was perceived as a way of enhancing students' knowledge of the literature of antiquity, while performing them provided training in oratory and rhetoric and improved their fluency in Latin. Students performed a variety of plays, but tragedy was the most prestigious dramatic genre. When Cecil and his associates first began planning the Queen's visit, it is therefore unsurprising that they proposed the provision of 'some Princely Tragedye' for her entertainment, and suggested two classical plays, 'Hercules furens' and 'Troas' (probably Seneca's *Troades*).[28] Performing such works was a way of displaying the scholars' learning and flattering that of the Queen. Although neither play was chosen, the four dramas planned for the Queen's visit did include two tragedies, presumably for this reason.[29] But Elizabeth was to be offered a taste of the diversity of academic drama, too: she would sample each of the three major dramatic genres (tragedy, comedy, history), and would be entertained with old and new, classical and non-classical, Latin and English drama. Each would have a lesson to teach.

The dramatic programme began with an evening performance of Plautus' Latin comedy *Aulularia* (6 August). The play tells the story of Euclio, a miser who is robbed of his riches, only to have them restored by a young man to whom he gives his wealth and his daughter in marriage as a reward.[30] It thus teaches a playful lesson about the dangers of miserliness and ends with the restoration of social 'order'. Performing such a comedy was a way of starting the festivities on a light-hearted rather than an obviously topical note, and played to the scholars' strengths: Plautus was popular with student performers, his plays being performed more often than any other playwright's at Elizabethan Cambridge.[31] The eyewitnesses do not describe the performance in detail, but we know that it was staged in costume and with props and that the side chapels probably served as stage 'houses'. The students would have been accustomed to acting against such a backdrop, most classical comedies featuring a similar street scene. But the performance was not necessarily wholly classical. Several payments relating to morris bells suggest that the wedding was celebrated with morris dancing.[32] This would represent a fascinating fusion between classical and native traditions. An Anglicized bridal party may also have been a tactful way of alluding to the prospect of another hoped-for English wedding: Elizabeth's. Whether or not there was an intentional allusion to this desired event, Elizabeth appears to have enjoyed the comedy, unlike some of her courtiers, who 'whether accustomed to sleep (at that hour) or by lack of skill in Latin dialogue, took the squandering of so many hours amiss'.[33]

---

[28] See *REED: Cambridge*, i. 229.

[29] Who finally chose the plays is undocumented, although Cecil is likely to have been involved.

[30] The play does not survive complete. See Plautus, *The Pot of Gold and Other Plays*, ed. E. F. Watling (London: Penguin, 1965), 9.

[31] *REED: Cambridge*, ii. 968–74. [32] Ibid. ii. 1215.

[33] Robinson, trans. ibid. 1136–7.

The themes for the next day's recreations (Monday, 7 August) were to be more conspicuously relevant to the Queen. The first questions to be debated during the afternoon disputations dealt with issues of rule: 'Monarchy is the best condition of the body politic' and 'Frequent change of the laws is dangerous'.[34] Disputing these points provided an opportunity to show support for the monarchy and to offer Elizabeth political counsel; counsel which she appears to have welcomed. Indeed, the Queen was reportedly so pleased by some of the scholars' replies that 'she by divers gestures declared ye same and sondere tymes stayed ye proctors' from interrupting them.[35]

That evening's play was to address an even more topical issue: royal marriage. The play chosen was a Latin adaptation of Virgil's tragic tale of Dido and Aeneas by former King's College Fellow Edward Halliwell. His *Dido* is no longer extant but was reportedly 'made up in large part of verses from Virgil' and thus a work that embodied the classical learning which Cambridge scholars prided themselves on possessing.[36] In choosing to perform a tragedy, the actors opted for the most 'princely' genre, while their choice of story may have had a didactic function, like the afternoon debates about governance. Dido's tragic love affair with Aeneas offered a potential warning to the Queen about the dangers of choosing a foreign prince as consort; a warning earlier offered by *Gorboduc*, and to the tastes of Dudley, Elizabeth's chief English suitor, if not the Chancellor. (Cecil was currently engaged in marriage negotiations with Charles, Archduke of Austria.[37]) That the King's scholars may have favoured the suit of their High Steward despite Cecil's preferences is potential testimony to the royal favourite's growing power and could explain why Cecil joined Dudley in standing on stage during the performance: it allowed Cecil to keep a close eye on his courtly rival and the audience. Yet, if there was an element of contemporary political allegory in the performance, none of the eyewitnesses mentioned it, nor does it appear to have spoilt Elizabeth's enjoyment of the production. Indeed, she was so impressed with the performance of Thomas Preston that she reportedly awarded him an annual pension.[38] It is tempting to speculate that he played Dido, and that part of his reward was for playing a woman of political power akin to Elizabeth's own. If Elizabeth did draw parallels between herself and Dido, rewarding her actor may also have been a way of symbolically rejecting the performance's 'lesson' and asserting her right to choose a partner independently.

On Tuesday, 8 August, the Queen was only to watch *Ezechias*, a biblical history play by Nicholas Udall, one-time headmaster of Eton and author of *Ralph Roister Doister* (first performed *c.*1552); the afternoon disputations were deferred until Wednesday. Given that Udall died in 1556 and was an Oxford, rather than a

[34] Stokys's Book, fo. 73, trans. Frank Beetham.   [35] Ibid.

[36] Robinson, trans. in *REED: Cambridge*, ii. 1137.

[37] Susan Doran, 'Juno versus Diana: The Treatment of Elizabeth's Marriage in Plays and Entertainments, 1561–1581', *Historical Journal*, 38.2 (1995), 257–74 (p. 263).

[38] *REED: Cambridge*, i. 243.

Cambridge, graduate, the choice of his play for such a prestigious occasion might seem surprising. Boas speculates that it was familiar to some of the scholars from their Eton days.[39] The subject of the now-lost English drama provides another explanation. It told the story of its eponymous biblical king, Hezekiah, famous for his quest to purify religion of idolatry, and included well-known episodes from this quest, such as Hezekiah's iconoclastic shattering of the serpent in the temple.[40] The King's College actors were implicitly paying a compliment to their Protestant monarch, inviting the audience and the Queen to recognize Elizabeth as a modern-day Hezekiah, as Udall invited his contemporaries to see Henry VIII as 'oure Ezechias' sent 'to roote vp all Idolatry'.[41] The play was probably also intended to demonstrate the University's Protestantism, although the reform-minded may have hoped that it would have a more radical function, encouraging Elizabeth to extend her own attack on idolatrous, 'popish' practices. That contemporary analogies did suggest themselves is hinted at in Hartwell's account: he writes of Hezekiah restoring 'the way of true religion', the latter a phrase regularly used by Protestants to distinguish themselves from the Catholic Church.[42]

Religion was, again, the scholars' theme when Elizabeth attended the deferred disputations in divinity on Wednesday afternoon (9 August). Like Udall's play, the questions chosen were topical: 'the authority of scripture is greater than that of the church', and 'a civil magistrate has authority in ecclesiastical matters'.[43] Debating the first question, in particular, afforded a chance to display the University's Protestant credentials, a belief in the virtue of scriptural study underpinning Protestantism. But a contemporary allusion suggests that all did not go smoothly. According to the Spanish Ambassador, one of the scholars spoke so well on behalf of Catholicism that he was 'attacked by those who presided, in order to avoid having to give him the prize'.[44] The controversial nature of the disputations may help to explain why Elizabeth chose not to attend the play scheduled for that evening, for she was not a monarch who welcomed arguments about religion. But there was no note of reproof in the oration she delivered at the end of the disputations. After modestly protesting her reluctance to address the scholars, Elizabeth used her carefully crafted Latin speech to declare her support for learning and her wish to 'leave some famous monument behind' at the University in the manner of her royal forebears.[45]

The scholars had planned to close their dramatic programme with Sophocles' *Ajax Flagellifer*, the play that tells the story of Ajax's madness and suicide; but the

[39] Boas, *University Drama*, 94–5.

[40] The biblical reference is to 2 Kings 18: 4: see *The Bible* (*Authorized King James Version*), ed. Robert Carroll and Stephen Prickett (Oxford: Oxford University Press, 1997), 470.

[41] Preface to Erasmus' paraphrase of the Gospel of St Luke, *The first tome or volume of the Paraphrases of Erasmus vpon the newe testament*, trans. Nicholas Udall (London: Edward Whitchurch, 1552), fo. Aiii[v].

[42] Trans. in *REED: Cambridge*, ii. 1140.

[43] Stokys's Book, fo. 75, trans. Frank Beetham.

[44] Trans. in *REED: Cambridge*, ii. 1143.

[45] Trans. in *Progresses*, ed. Nichols, i. 178.

performance was cancelled when Elizabeth declined to attend.[46] In this instance, *Ajax* appears to have been selected for its cultural prestige. As a well-regarded classical tragedy, it was the kind of 'princely' play Cecil and his associates deemed especially appropriate for a royal performance, while the story of Ajax's madness following his failed attempt to win the arms of Achilles from the learned and eloquent Ulysses demonstrated the dangers of pride and wrath, and the value of wisdom. Such a lesson was calculated to appeal to 'courtly and academic ears and minds', as was recognized when the same play was performed before King James VI and I at Oxford (1605).[47]

On the final morning of the Queen's visit (10 August), the University granted MAs to many of the noblemen in Elizabeth's train, while the Queen departed early for the Bishop of Ely's house at Stanton, and then Hinchinbrook.[48] If the Spanish Ambassador is to be believed, a group of Cambridge scholars followed her to Hinchinbrook with a further unscripted show attacking transubstantiation. His description reveals how ill calculated it was to please a monarch with a distaste for religious irreverence: 'First came the Bishop of London carrying a lamb in his hands as if he were eating it as he walked along, and then others with different devices, one being in the figure of a dog with the Host in his mouth.' The Queen reportedly stormed from the room in anger.[49] If true, the incident suggests that Cecil's carefully maintained religious 'order' faltered at the last.

Despite this allegedly controversial epilogue, Elizabeth's visit was generally deemed a success. Yet the Queen would not return to Cambridge; and there is little evidence that she was influenced by the advice she was offered on issues such as religion or marriage. She would not fulfil her promised investment in the University either. But there were rewards for some of the individuals involved in the royal welcome. Shortly afterwards, Elizabeth finally elevated her royal favourite to the peerage, creating Dudley Earl of Leicester (September 1564). By the end of the year, he had been appointed Chancellor of the University of Oxford, too.[50] The University's hospitable entertainment of the royal entourage earned Cambridge friends amongst Elizabeth's nobles, as well. Thomas Howard, Duke of Norfolk, subsequently agreed to give Magdalene forty pounds a year 'till they had builded the quadrant of their College' and promised that 'he would endow them with land for the encrease of their number and studys'.[51] More generally, the Queen's symbolic support for learning at the University appears to have contributed to a subsequent rise in student numbers.

---

[46] *REED: Cambridge*, i. 235.

[47] Trans. in *Records of Early English Drama: Oxford*, ed. John R. Elliott Jr. and Alan H. Nelson (University); Alexandra F. Johnston and Diana Wyatt (City), 2 vols. (Toronto: University of Toronto Press, 2004), ii. 1023.

[48] *Progresses*, ed. Nichols, i. 180, 179.   [49] Trans. in *REED: Cambridge*, ii. 1143.

[50] Rosenberg, *Leicester*, 22.   [51] *Progresses*, ed. Nichols, i. 182.

OXFORD, 1566: COURTSHIP AND COUNSEL

The royal visit to Cambridge was followed by a longer trip to Oxford in 1566: the Queen arrived on Saturday, 31 August and departed on Friday, 6 September. The visit marked the culmination of a two-month progress through Middlesex, Northamptonshire, and Warwickshire. Afterwards, Elizabeth would travel briefly into Oxfordshire, Buckinghamshire, and Surrey before returning to London for the 1566 parliament.[52] During this controversial session, Elizabeth was to be petitioned even more outspokenly than in 1563 about the importance of settling the royal succession, reportedly with the support of the University's Chancellor, Dudley.[53]

Again, we have several contemporary accounts of the visit. The most detailed are those written by John Bereblock (Exeter College), Nicholas Robinson (Bishop of Bangor and Cambridge graduate), and Miles Windsor (Corpus Christi).[54] Bereblock's Latin account appears to have been written shortly after the visit and circulated in manuscript, with several copies being produced of a now-lost original.[55] Like Nicholas Robinson (1564), Bereblock appears to have been keen to memorialize his University's display of learning and hospitality. The fact that he had participated in the royal welcome perhaps contributed to this desire. He delivered one of the welcoming orations at Christ Church and was 'responsible for . . . drawings of the colleges' included in 'a book of Latin verses praising' Oxford 'by Thomas Neale and presented' to Elizabeth during the visit.[56] Robinson's description of the Oxford visit is less detailed and less flattering, mainly serving as a foil to his unpublished manuscript account of the royal progress to Cambridge.[57] Windsor's version, too, is unpublished, surviving in two versions, one a draft, and the other a fair copy: both are preserved in an antiquarian manuscript miscellany about the history of the University of Oxford prepared by Brian Twyne.[58] Windsor appears to have left his papers to Twyne before his death. Like Bereblock, Windsor appears to have been prompted to memorialize the visit by the fact that he and his family were involved in it: he

[52] Cole, *Portable Queen*, 182.

[53] See *Calendar of Letters and State Papers Relating to English Affairs: Spanish Papers*, ed. Martin A. S. Hume (London: HMSO, 1892), 577.

[54] See Boas, *University Drama*, 98–9.

[55] Bereblock's account is found in Bodleian MS Additional a. 63; Bodleian MS Rawlinson d. 1071; Folger Shakespeare Library MS V.a.109. See John R. Elliott Jr., 'Drama', in Nicholas Tyacke (ed.), *The History of the University of Oxford*, iv: *Seventeenth-Century Oxford* (Oxford: Clarendon Press, 1997), 641–58 (p. 645).

[56] King (ed.), *Richard Edwards*, 67.   [57] *REED: Oxford*, ii. 697.

[58] Miles Windsor, 'Gestes of ye Quenes Maiesties receavinge in oxfourde', held in the archives of Corpus Christi College, Oxford, as CCC MS 257, fos. 104–14 (fair copy); fos. 115–23 (draft). Quotations from this manuscript appear with the permission of the President and Fellows of Corpus Christi College, Oxford.

was one of the actors, and his great-uncle, the third Lord Windsor, accompanied Elizabeth to the city and was to entertain her 'at his country estate the following week'.[59]

As in 1564, preparations for Elizabeth's arrival commenced with the Vice-Chancellor's receipt of a letter from the Chancellor announcing the visit. A programme of entertainments was then devised that included orations, sermons, disputations, and plays, with the University assuming corporate responsibility for the theatrical entertainments, and elected individuals taking charge of the practical arrangements.[60]   One of those commissioned to assist with these preparations was the Oxford graduate and Master of the Chapel Royal Richard Edwards. He was invited to write a new play and to oversee the performances. Implicitly, the University was capitalizing on his experience of producing courtly plays with the Chapel Children; but it also set a precedent for commissioning professional and/or courtier writers to produce progress entertainments.[61] For Edwards, involvement in the royal entertainment provided a way of honouring his old college, and a valuable opportunity to win the favour of Elizabeth and her courtiers.

****Christ Church was to host the Queen and the University plays, as was to become customary, 'both because Christ Church as a royal foundation traditionally acted as host to the sovereign, and because its hall was the largest in either Oxford or . . . Cambridge', measuring approximately 115 feet by 40 feet.[62] No effort was spared when it came to ensuring the Queen's comfort. This included engaging in extensive building and cleaning work, and ensuring that Christ Church visually acknowledged its royal associations. Thus, Michael Herne was paid for 'makinge the Quenes armes to sett on the porche'.[63]

The University was keen to surpass Cambridge's efforts in its entertainments, too, creating an impressive temporary theatre in the college hall. A wooden stage was built at the upper end, as was common for court performances, 'with a throne at the centre for Elizabeth, who sat facing the audience'.[64] Bereblock describes how this magnificent chair of state was 'provided with pillows and tapestries and covered with a golden canopy'.[65] This prominent position ensured that the Queen could see, and be seen. As at Cambridge, the latter was as significant as the former. Other spectators were accommodated on scaffolds 'placed at one end of the hall and along each of the side walls', with special boxes at the top of them for 'the more important spectators'. Others were able to stand around the platform.[66] Such hierarchical seating arrangements resembled those common for court entertainments, and provided a visual display of social order, as in 1564.

[59] King (ed.), *Richard Edwards*, 67, 66.   [60] Elliott, 'Drama', 645.
[61] King (ed.), *Richard Edwards*, 3, 6–7.   [62] Elliott, 'Drama', 644.
[63] *REED: Oxford*, i. 113–23, 122.   [64] Elliott, 'Drama', 645–6.
[65] Trans. in *REED: Oxford*, ii. 979.   [66] Elliott, 'Drama', 645.

On stage were several stage houses. As well as providing a scenic backdrop these served as the actors' temporary tiring houses. They were decorated to resemble 'magnificent palaces', while the ceiling of the hall was 'gilded' and 'panelled' so that the chamber resembled an 'ancient Roman palace'.[67] The overall effect was spectacular. Its magnificence was heightened by the 'princelie' lighting provided by numerous candles and lights hung from the walls and ceiling. These were kept burning continuously during the plays so that lights 'provyded for v night*es* woulde serve but one nighte'.[68] Such dazzling illumination was customary for royal festive occasions.[69] Fortunately for Christ Church, the court appears to have borne the costs of this display of conspicuous consumption.[70] Still, such entertainment did not come cheaply: Christ Church spent nearly £150, a figure less than the cost of Elizabeth's visits to several private hosts in the 1560s, but higher than most civic hosts spent on royal entertainments in the same period.[71] Despite being the richest of the colleges, Christ Church complained that this was more than it could afford, and was later partially reimbursed. From this time, it became customary for the University to fund royal entertainments collectively, as did many of the corporations who hosted Elizabeth on progress.[72]

THE VISIT

Arriving on Oxford's outskirts with her retinue (31 August), the Queen was met with orations by civic and University representatives.[73] As she proceeded into the city, past the assembled scholars, Elizabeth was welcomed with a series of further speeches, the final of which was spoken by Thomas Kingsmill at Christ Church. As in 1564, this formalized welcome was intended to impress the monarch with the University's order and scholarship. In practice, there were some tense moments, as when Elizabeth was introduced to Laurence Humphrey, one of the Oxford dons who had gone into continental exile during the Marian era. On Elizabeth's accession Humphrey was invited to return to Oxford as Regius Professor of Divinity, but by 1566 Elizabeth was known to be displeased with him. He had become well known for his 'sympathies with . . . radical' Protestants and their calls for further church reform, including their wish to abandon traditional clerical dress.[74] Elizabeth's own position was firm: she had no plans for further reform, and was not ready to compromise on the question of clerical attire. Meeting Humphrey provided an opportunity to make this clear to the next generation of university-trained clerics. Noticing that he wore his

---

[67] Bereblock, trans. in *REED: Oxford*, ii. 979.   [68] Windsor, 'Gestes', fos. 118ᵛ, 107ᵛ.
[69] See Astington, *English Court Theatre*, 96.   [70] *REED: Oxford*, i. 121.
[71] See Cole, *Portable Queen*, 75, 103–4.
[72] See Elliott, 'Drama', 645; Cole, *Portable Queen*, 104–6.
[73] *Progresses*, ed. Nichols, i. 208.   [74] See Dent, *Protestant Reformers*, 35–8.

regulation gown, she reportedly remarked to him: 'me thinckethe yis gowne becu*m*meth you verye well & I m*a*ruell y*a*t you ar so straighte laced in these poynt*es*'.[75] Elizabeth was similarly acerbic in her response to Kingsmill's oration, in which he tactlessly praised the Queen for appointing Humphrey, reportedly remarking that: 'You would have done well, had you had good matter.' This discordant beginning perhaps contributed to the Queen's decision to keep to her rooms the following day, missing the morning and afternoon sermons in Christ Church, and the first play.[76]

The programme of recreations for the Queen's visit was much like that at Cambridge. Most days there were lectures and disputations and a play in the evening; some were topical in theme. But whereas religion had been a recurring theme at Cambridge, the Oxford scholars largely avoided theology. Instead, they addressed the issues of marriage and the royal succession. This was in keeping with their Chancellor's political agenda. Indeed, as on previous occasions at court, Dudley was arguably using the Oxford entertainments to present himself as would-be royal consort and solution to the succession issue.

THE ENTERTAINMENT

The choice of plays was probably made by the University delegation which oversaw the preparations for the royal visit, but no evidence survives of 'what options they were given', 'how they made their decisions', or whether Dudley was involved in the process.[77] As in 1564, the planned theatrical programme was didactic but diverse, including history, tragedy, and comedy; and Latin and English, neoclassical and non-classical drama. However, whereas the Cambridge plays included works by ancient authors, the Oxford dramas were all by contemporary graduates. This may have been a way of distinguishing the 1566 entertainments from those of 1564 and of suggesting that Oxford was home to native talent comparable with that of the ancients.

The first play (which the Queen did not attend) was *Marcus Geminus* (1 September), a Roman history play by Tobie Matthew (Christ Church). It is Matthew's only known drama and now lost, but the Latin play told the story of the false accusation of Geminus Campanus 'because of envy and emulation'. Bereblock describes how Campanus was eventually exonerated thanks to the intervention of some 'honourable freedmen . . . whom neither penalty nor bribery could bring to an unjust accusation'.[78] Although comic in places, the play had a serious lesson to teach about the dangers of flattery and corruption amongst politicians. Implicitly, its choice for performance before Elizabeth was didactic. Matthew was clearly attuned to the possibility of using the royal

[75] *REED: Oxford*, i. 127.   [76] *Progresses*, ed. Nichols, i. 209.
[77] Elliott, 'Drama', 645.   [78] Trans. in *REED: Oxford*, ii. 979.

entertainments to offer counsel as he was also one of the participants in the Tuesday afternoon disputations in moral philosophy where the first question was of immediate political relevance: 'A prince must be proclaimed by succession, not by election.'[79] The debate raised the issue of parliament's possible role in choosing the monarch at a time when politicians were, again, preparing to petition the Queen to settle the succession through parliament.[80] Matthew was one of those who argued on the more controversial side of the question against succession, apparently with great success. As Ros King notes, 'this might initially seem to be quite a feat, appearing as he was before a monarch who claimed the right of succession from her father'; but 'if Elizabeth were not to marry and produce an heir . . . as she had already indicated that she might not' it was possible that her successor would need to be elected. It was thus a debate worth her hearing.[81]

The following evening (2 September) saw the performance of part I of Richard Edwards's *Palamon and Arcite*; part II was performed on Wednesday (4 September). Edwards's English play does not survive but appears to have been based on Chaucer's Knight's Tale. This tells the story of Palamon and Arcite, two kinsmen, who become mortal enemies after they fall in love with the same woman (Emily, or Emilia in Edwards's version) while prisoners of Duke Theseus of Athens.[82] In choosing to dramatize a medieval tale about a virgin princess wooed by two knightly suitors, Edwards offered the Queen a mirror for her own situation, a fact which would have been emphasized visually by her sharing of the actors' stage. He also anticipated the common use of stories and tropes from medieval romance to flatter and allude to Elizabeth in later court and progress entertainments.[83] Like Emilia, Elizabeth found herself the object of competing lovers' suits (those of Dudley and Charles, Archduke of Austria) and under pressure to marry, despite a preference for a virgin life.[84] Emilia's association with Diana, goddess of chastity, reinforced the parallel: Elizabeth had also been identified with the goddess, as in the Gray's Inn play of *Juno and Diana* (1565).[85] Emilia prays to Diana 'for a solitary life and perpetual chastity', but learns that the goddess is unable to help and that she is destined for marriage.[86] Edwards's romance implicitly counselled the Queen to accept the same destiny.

Bereblock's description suggests that the play followed the structure of Chaucer's tale, and dramatized at least some of its major scenes. In part I, this included the woodland dispute of Palamon and Arcite, which is interrupted

[79] Windsor, 'Gestes', fo. 109ᵛ, trans. Frank Beetham.
[80] See Hartley, *Proceedings*, 129–39.   [81] King (ed.), *Richard Edwards*, 77–8.
[82] Geoffrey Chaucer, *The Canterbury Tales*, ed. F. N. Robinson, 3rd edn. (Oxford: Oxford University Press, 1998), 37–68.
[83] See Malcolm Smuts, 'Progresses and Court Entertainments', in Arthur F. Kinney (ed.), *A Companion to Renaissance Drama* (Oxford: Blackwell, 2004), 281–93 (pp. 288–9).
[84] King (ed.), *Richard Edwards*, 64.   [85] Axton, *Queen's Two Bodies*, 49.
[86] Bereblock, trans. in *REED: Oxford*, ii. 981.

by Theseus while out hunting.[87] Special efforts were made to mimic the sound of
the latter's off-stage pursuit, the performers sounding hunting horns and bringing
live dogs into the quad outside the hall. This prompted much excitement: audience members 'hallowed' and cried out 'nowe nowe' at the window, prompting
the Queen to exclaim, 'O excellent . . . those boys are readye to leape owte at [the]
wyndowe to the howndes.'[88] The second half of the play appears to have been
similarly ambitious in its staging, opening with the return of the two knights
ready for battle. The knights' ensuing duel was performed in visually thrilling
fashion, as was Arcite's subsequent destruction by fire and his cremation.[89]
Indeed, his on-stage pyre was allegedly so realistic that a spectator tried to prevent
one of the players from throwing a borrowed cloak onto it, remarking: 'God*es*
woundes . . . what mean ye? will ye burn ye K*ing* E*dward* cloake in ye fyer?'
Edwards was quick to berate the intrusive 'stander by', but it was not the only
'hitch' in the performance. John Dalaper, who played Lord Trevatio (a character
not found in Chaucer), apparently forgot his lines with similarly embarrassing
consequences: 'beinge owte of his p*ar*te & missinge his kewe' he offered 'his
servise to ye ladyes swearinge by ye masse or Got*es* blutt I am owte', prompting
the Queen to reprove him: 'Goo thy waye; God*es* pitty . . . what a knave it tis.'[90]

Interruptions aside, the performance was successful. Its conclusion with the
betrothal of Emilia and Palamon proved especially popular, being greeted 'with
incredible shouting and applause'; a rapturous reception that perhaps signalled
the scholars' desire to see their Queen similarly happily married, as much as their
enjoyment of the performance.[91] But Edwards's play earned him royal approval,
too. The Queen reportedly 'laughed . . . hartelie', gave him 'great thanck*es*', and
bantered with him about his male leads, describing Arcite as 'a righte marciall
knighte, whoe had in deede a swarse & manly cowtenance', and observing of
Palamon, 'I warrant hym hee dalyethe not in love when hee was in love in
deede'.[92] Elizabeth was impressed with the men who played Edwards's leading
women, too, rewarding John Rainolds (Hippolita) and Emilia's performer with
eight angels each; a display of generosity which perhaps had as much to do with
their performance of female roles with which the Queen felt some sympathy as
with their 'relative acting skills'.[93]

On Thursday (5 September) Elizabeth spent the afternoon listening to
disputations, including the debate about succession. The topicality of the
disputations does not appear to have troubled her; and, at the conclusion of the
session, she delivered a short Latin oration in which she praised, and expressed
her support for, the University, as in 1564.[94] A performance that evening of
James Calfhill's Latin tragedy *Progne* was to provide the finale of the week's

---

[87] *REED: Oxford*, i. 138–9.   [88] Windsor, 'Gestes', fo. 110[v].
[89] See Bereblock in *REED: Oxford*, i. 140.   [90] Windsor, 'Gestes', fo. 118.
[91] Bereblock, trans. in *REED: Oxford*, ii. 982.   [92] Windsor, 'Gestes', fos. 108[v], 110[v], 121.
[93] King (ed.), *Richard Edwards*, 85.   [94] See *Progresses*, ed. Nichols, i. 214–15.

entertainments. Calfhill's lost play is thought to have been an adaptation of Gregorio Coraro's 1558 dramatization of Ovid's tale of Procne's revenge for her sister's rape.[95] In closing their dramatic programme with a classically derived tragedy, the Oxford scholars followed Cambridge's example, ending with a culturally prestigious, rather than a topical, work. It was a tragedy implicitly intended to display the learning of Oxford's scholars and to flatter that of the Queen, while also offering a poignant lesson about the tragic consequences of moral transgression. The performance itself is not described in detail, but Robinson emphasizes its 'princely' quality, reporting that 'all (was put on) with the finest preparation and in truly royal style'.[96]

The final morning of the Queen's visit (6 September) was dedicated to hospitable gift-giving and leave-taking. Following Cambridge's example, the University created a number of the Queen's nobles MAs, and gave them and Elizabeth presents: she reportedly left well satisfied.[97] Indeed, after a shaky start the Queen's Oxford visit arguably proved more successful than that to Cambridge. It is perhaps no coincidence that the scholars generally avoided the issue of religion, focusing instead on secular topics such as the royal succession and marriage. These were issues on which Elizabeth was accustomed to receiving advice in courtly entertainments. As such, the counsel the University tactfully offered about marrying and settling the succession does not appear to have offended her in the way that the direct petitions of her 1566 parliamentarians would.

As well as rewarding several individuals, Elizabeth later confirmed the 'power and privileges of the University' and lent her name to the founding of a new college in 1571 (Jesus). This was a mark of favour she did not show any similar Cambridge institution.[98] Elizabeth's Oxford visit may have had indirect benefits for the University, too, apparently contributing to a rise in student numbers, as at Cambridge.[99] The visit was not without its rewards for the Oxford Puritans, either. She may have shown them short shrift during her stay, but soon after the Royal Commissioners clamped down on colleges that continued to retain superstitious monuments.[100] Elizabeth may not have wished to engage in a dialogue about religion with the Oxford scholars, but she would act to ensure religious order there, as well as at Cambridge.

CONCLUSIONS

Elizabeth later described monarchs as princes 'set on stages' (1586).[101] During her visits to the universities, this theatrical metaphor was vividly realized, as the

[95] Boas, *University Drama*, 104. [96] Trans. in *REED: Oxford*, ii. 978.
[97] *Progresses*, ed. Nichols, i. 217.
[98] King (ed.), *Richard Edwards*, 64; Rosenberg, *Leicester*, 129–30.
[99] Rosenberg, *Leicester*, 132. [100] See *Progresses*, ed. Nichols, i. 327.
[101] Holinshed, *Chronicles*, iv. 934.

Queen 'took her place on a variety of' platforms.[102] At each event, Elizabeth was the chief spectator and spectacle. This was usual in progress entertainments. The court's extended involvement in the Cambridge and Oxford visits was less so. Although it was common for the Queen to contribute to the costs of accommodating and feeding herself and her retinue on progress, there is less evidence of royal contributions to her entertainment. This was more usually organized and funded by the host.[103] While this difference could be attributed to the influence of the universities' powerful chancellors and their wish to impress their mistress, it suggests Elizabeth's early visits to Cambridge and Oxford were seen as uniquely important occasions for the monarch, too, providing an opportunity for the Queen not only to display her power, but to scrutinize and instruct the next generation of politicians and clerics in her views on subjects ranging from chastity to religious conformity. Like so many of Elizabeth's progress visits, those to Cambridge and Oxford were occasions for the dissemination of royal propaganda. That Elizabeth felt both institutions merited such politic visits early in her reign is a testimony to their special importance as adjuncts of the state.

The universities made great efforts to please and impress the Queen, as they courted her support for their institutions. Using the cultural smokescreens of disputations and plays, they sought to counsel her, too. Thus, at Cambridge, the scholars used their entertainments to encourage the Queen in her reform of the Church; while at Oxford, the scholars used their 'princely' shows to advocate Elizabeth's marriage and the settling of the royal succession. In both cases, scholarship was deployed to lend weight to the counsel offered. Elizabeth was not to heed the scholars' advice: she never chose to engage in wide-ranging religious reform, nor would she marry or nominate a successor, until her death. The universities' entertainments were not, therefore, wholly effective as didactic shows; but they did have political and practical rewards, securing Elizabeth's symbolic support for scholarship and the traditional privileges of the universities: this strengthened both institutions and appears to have contributed to an increase in their populations.

Given Elizabeth's superficial satisfaction with her 1560s visits, it might seem surprising that she did not visit the universities more often: she did not return to Cambridge and paid only one later visit to Oxford (1592). This could be a sign that she was happy with her early inspections and trusted the two chancellors to supervise them thereafter; or perhaps that she resented the scholars' counsel more than she had appeared to do. There may even have been a pragmatic reason for staying away: she may not have wished to be reminded of her promised investment in the universities. But Elizabeth's visits, though rare, revived the tradition of royal progresses to Oxford and Cambridge and showed them to be potentially powerful theatres in which the monarch could

---

[102] King (ed.), *Richard Edwards*, 66.   [103] See Cole, *Portable Queen*, 72–3.

stage his/her power and views, *and* engage in a mutually instructive dialogue with the country's next generation of thinkers and doers. James I and Charles I would both exploit this fact as they made royal visits to Cambridge and Oxford a regular event and forged even closer links between the universities and the state.

6

Mysteries, Musters, and Masque: The Import(s) of Elizabethan Civic Entertainments

C. E. McGee

'I have much marvelled at these strange Pageantries,' wrote Sir John Harington of the shows at Theobalds in 1607, 'and they do bring to my remembrance what passed of this sort in our Queen's days . . . but I never did see such lack of good order, discretion, and sobriety as I have now done.'[1] Had Harington been in London on 14 January 1604, he might also have noted not a collapse of decorum such as he witnessed at Theobalds, but a new style in English civic pageantry as King James VI and I processed through a series of classical arches modelled on European triumphal entries.[2] This essay takes yet another step back, to the 1570s, where we can see civic theatre in the provinces transformed for, and by, Elizabethan progresses. The shows that provincial towns and cities produced for Elizabeth I in those years differed in crucial ways from those that they presented to her forebears. Norwich and Bristol, not trusting to their own playwrights or to local theatrical resources (especially the mystery plays that smacked of Catholicism), imported outsiders to write their shows, imported courtly forms of entertainment to replace civic drama, and privileged the monarch's agenda as if it were more important than their own. The result was a militarization of provincial civic pageantry and theatre in accordance with the Elizabethan project of building, and defending, a strong Protestant nation. In the 1570s, civic pageantry for royal entries, like the procession, ceremonies, feasting, and drama of Corpus Christi, was caught up in an important shift unfolding over the course of the sixteenth century, a shift, in the words of Louis A. Montrose, 'from a culture focused upon social dynamics within the local

---

[1] *The Progresses, Processions, and Magnificent Festivities, of King James the First*, ed. John Nichols, 4 vols. (London: J. B. Nichols, 1828), ii. 73.

[2] See especially Stephen Harrison, *Arches of Triumph* (London: J. Windet, 1604), which, in publishing engravings of the arches, emulates European books documenting royal entries just as London's triumphal arches imitated European ones.

community to one that incorporates the local within and subordinates it to the centre'.³

The shows presented by Sandwich, Norwich, and Bristol in the 1570s confirm this general claim, but the forces that gave each community its distinctive character also complicated the change in civic pageantry. Two caveats are in order as a result. First, the 'local' and the 'centre' were not simply and necessarily at odds. The needs and desires of the two might overlap, as they did, for example, in cities like Bristol that depended on foreign trade for their prosperity. These cities desired the peace for which Queen Elizabeth prayed, even as she ordered the citizenry to arm and train.⁴ Secondly, the subordination of the local was never total: civic receptions, civic pageants in particular, remained a discursive space in which towns and cities could publicly fashion their relationship with the crown in ways consistent with local aspirations and civic pride of place. The port of Sandwich, which Elizabeth visited in 1573, is a case in point.

The entertainment of Elizabeth there, for which we have a description but no script of pageant speeches, presented a collage highlighting key features of the town's complex ceremonial, military, social, and economic life. The opening ceremonies on 31 August and the next day's entertainment responded to the anxieties of the central government by displaying the town's loyalty and military resources. The town donned the Queen's colours: in accordance with orders of the town council, the people painted their houses black and white, adorned routes with black and white bays, and marshalled an armed guard, 300-strong, in black stockings with white garters and white doublets with black and white ribbons. Part of the official welcoming party, the armed guards were led by three captains with drum and ensign and all the men carried firearms, which they discharged at Sandowne Gate. When the town mace was delivered to the Queen, the great ordnance was fired too, and so impressively that the Queen and some of her noblemen commended the civic officials for having their guns

---

³ 'A Kingdom of Shadows', in *The Theatrical City: Culture, Theatre and Politics in London, 1576–1649* (Cambridge: Cambridge University Press, 1995), 72. On the interaction between the central government and provincial towns and on the impact of that interaction on local culture, see also Mervyn James, *Society, Politics and Culture: Studies in Early Modern England* (Cambridge: Cambridge University Press, 1986), 26–47; Philip Corrigan and Derek Sayer, *The Great Arch: English State Formation as Cultural Revolution* (Oxford: Basil Blackwell, 1985), 55–72; Robert Tittler, *The Reformation and the Towns of England: Politics and Political Culture, c.1540–1640* (Oxford: Clarendon Press, 1998), 305–34; Vanessa Harding, 'Reformation and Culture 1540–1700', in Peter Clark (ed.), *The Cambridge Urban History of Britain*, ii (Cambridge: Cambridge University Press, 2000), 263–88; Penry Williams, *The Tudor Regime* (Oxford: Clarendon Press, 1979), 305–10; David Harris Sacks, *The Widening Gate: Bristol and the Atlantic Economy 1450–1700* (Berkeley and Los Angeles: University of California Press, 1991); Muriel C. McClendon, *The Quiet Reformation: Magistrates and the Emergence of Protestantism in Tudor Norwich* (Stanford, Calif: Stanford University Press, 1999).

⁴ Elizabeth's prayer thanking God for her safe journey to Bristol in 1574 ends with her petition that she preserve 'a peacable, quiett, & well ordered state & Kingdome, as also a perfect reformed church to ye furtherance of thy Glory', in the State Papers, Domestic Series 12/98/13 (15 Aug. 1574).

in such good order.[5] Besides this welcome, the town devoted the full first day
of its entertainment to military exercises. These began with a comic tourney in
which two Walloons, perched on platforms at the stern of two boats, fought with
wooden staffs and shields until 'one of them did over throwe an other At which
the Quene had good sport' (p. 858). Then followed the assault on a fort, built for
the occasion across the harbour at Stonor. In contrast to the Walloons' parodic
tiff, this siege displayed tactics and weaponry closer to those of real combat,
so that the entertainment that occupied most of the day clearly displayed the
military skill, preparedness, and loyalty of the citizenry.

Balancing the military exercises and games, Sandwich presented two shows
that spotlighted aspects of its distinctive local scene. On 2 September, the Queen
attended a banquet and made merry with the wives of the civic leaders, and the
next day she saw a pageant with 'dyvers Children Englishe and dutche to the
nomber of Cth or vj score all spynning of fyne baye yarne a thing well Lyked both
of her Maiestie and of the nobilletie and Ladies' (p. 859). While the town's public
expressions of strength, loyalty, hospitality, and industry were being presented
in its shows, the city fathers worked the political backrooms to secure financial
assistance for dredging the harbour. 'My Lord Threasorer my Lord Admyrall my
Lord chamberleyn and my Lord of Leycester' had been 'made pryvie to the suyt'
during the course of the royal visit, and the Mayor made public the town's cause
by exhibiting 'vnto her highnes a supplicacion for the Havon' (p. 859) as she
departed. With this petition added to the town's various other kinds of shows,
Sandwich's entertainment of Elizabeth I seems to be a complex balancing act on
the part of a town proud of its local heritage and alert to the anxieties and the
aims of the Queen.

But in most Elizabethan civic pageants the balance between local concerns and
causes and those of the centre tipped in favour of the latter. To understand this
change in civic theatre, we must of necessity focus on the work of soldier-poet
Thomas Churchyard, the cities of Bristol and Norwich, and the 1570s. By Mary
Hill Cole's count, Elizabeth made eighty-three visits to fifty-one towns and cities
(London excluded) over the course of her reign, but scripts of the dramatic
devices prepared to receive and entertain her survive for only two, Bristol in 1574
and Norwich in 1578.[6] Thomas Churchyard played a leading role in writing,
directing, and publishing accounts of both entertainments.[7] After 1578, pageants

[5] *Records of Early English Drama: Kent: Diocese of Canterbury*, ed. James M. Gibson (Toronto:
University of Toronto Press, 2002), 857; parenthetical references in this section are to this edition.

[6] The list of town and city visits is part of appendix 2 of *The Portable Queen: Elizabeth I and the
Politics of Ceremony* (Amherst: University of Massachusetts Press, 1999), 204–5 (table 4). The city
of Worcester also produced pageants for Queen Elizabeth's visit in 1575, but the boys' speeches,
once to be found on the first leaves of the *Chamber Order Book 1*, are now missing (*Records of Early
English Drama: Herefordshire and Worcestershire*, ed. David N. Klausner (Toronto: University of
Toronto Press, 1990), 310).

[7] For Churchyard and the 1578 Norwich pageant, see David M. Bergeron's essay in this volume,
pp. 142–59.

and other theatrical forms enlivened, ennobled, and articulated the meanings of Accession Day tilts, manor house shows, aristocratic weddings, and mayoral inaugurations, but no provincial town or city produced a dramatic device to welcome the Queen or entertain her during the course of her stay.

Norwich and Bristol, the provincial capitals of the eastern and western regions of the realm, were obvious destinations for a monarch intent on using progresses to consolidate her power. Both cities, the second and third largest in England, were centres of commercial, judicial, ecclesiastical, and military business. They had the buildings needed to accommodate the Queen and her highest-ranking courtiers, as well as sufficient open lands within their precincts for the encampment of the rest of her retinue. Located 'at nodal points of transport networks, especially those formed by navigable rivers',[8] both cities were well situated to supply the extraordinary provisions required by a progress and to facilitate the court's effort to conduct its ongoing business. Located on rivers giving access to the sea, Norwich and Bristol also had strategic importance, so that Bristol Castle and the Castle of Blanche Floure stood as symbols of England's defence against invasions from abroad, potent symbols in the early 1570s when Protestant England felt threatened by Catholic forces on the Continent. Bernard Garter underscored this aspect of Norwich in 1578 by stationing the first pageantic character, the legendary founder of the city, King Gurgunt—mounted, in armour, and wearing both the family colours of the Tudors and the personal colours of the Queen—'within a flight shot or two of the city, where the Castle of Blaunche Flowre was in moste beautifull prospect'.[9] Even if Elizabeth I had had no specific political concerns about Norwich or Bristol,[10] the status each city enjoyed within its region invited a royal visit so that the Queen might confirm by her presence the citizens' due love and dread of the monarch.

Norwich and Bristol could also be counted on to provide a properly grand reception and entertainment because both cities had strong local traditions of music and drama. Mystery plays, the guild-sponsored dramatizations of biblical stories and saints' lives, had been one part of both their traditions. School drama was another part: local schoolmasters wrote plays and pageants, which their pupils performed not only in school as part of their training, but also in public to enhance the celebration of political events. On such an occasion, civic pageants could give the city the ear of a mayor celebrating his election or that of a monarch on a provincial progress. On such an occasion, civic pageants and other

---

[8] Peter Clark and Paul Slack, *English Towns in Transition 1500–1700* (Oxford: Oxford University Press, 1976), 47.

[9] *Records of Early English Drama: Norwich 1540–1642*, ed. David Galloway (Toronto: University of Toronto Press, 1984), 249.

[10] Elizabeth's progresses were motivated in part by just such concerns, political and religious, as other papers presented at the Elizabethan Progresses Conference (Stratford-upon-Avon, 16–17 April 2004), such as Professor Patrick Collinson's 'Pulling the Strings: Religion and Politics in the Progress of 1578', showed: see also Professor Collinson's essay in this volume, pp. 122–41.

theatrical devices could gather together royal visitors, courtiers, local dignitaries, and citizenry into the real, and symbolically useful, unity of an audience. In Bristol and in Norwich in the 1570s, civic pageants could have produced some of the same effects as they had in the past, but in authorship, form, and content the shows they produced for Elizabeth I were remarkably different from their precedents.

PRECEDENTS: EARLY TUDOR CIVIC PAGEANTS

Of the earliest Tudor civic pageantry, John Meagher argues that the 'language of pageantic display was a remarkably versatile instrument in the service of royal propaganda and of civic diplomacy', because 'in a pageantic show, a city could create a privileged meeting place between itself and its king and define the real relationship between them in ways that transcended both the neutrality of convention and the tact of silence'.[11] Sensitive to the insecurity of Henry VII's situation in the year following his victory at Bosworth Field, the towns and cities he visited on his first progress affirmed what the new monarch hoped to hear: his regime was legitimate, his accession a joyous occasion, and their loyalty assured. Even if towns and cities had prospered under Edward IV or Richard III, Henry VII was now king *de facto* and *his* rule was publicly to be confirmed with customary festivity. At the same time however, York, Worcester, and Bristol seized the opportunity provided by his royal entry to pursue their own goals, appealing respectively for a reduction in the fee-farm rent, a pardon for alleged treason, and a subsidy for local industries damaged by economic setbacks and natural disasters. Portraying Henry VII as the gracious ruler they hoped he would prove to be, the cities admitted their needs and petitioned for relief, and they did so with a strong sense of local pride and autonomy.[12]

York was most emphatic about its independence in its dealings with the new King. When Lord Clifford offered to advise the city on how best to receive Henry in 1486, the city council rejected the offer and informed him that they would comport themselves in accordance with their 'knawledge by presidences remanyng of record in the Register of the said Citie'.[13] What was true of the planning of the reception was true of the performance as well.[14] In York, local clerics wrote, directed, and acted in the shows, employing local minstrels to

---

[11] John C. Meagher, to whose memory this work is dedicated, 'The First Progress of Henry VII', *Renaissance Drama*, ns 1 (1968), 48.

[12] Sacks, *The Widening Gate*, 177–80, emphasizes this aspect of Bristol's entertainment of Henry VII in 1486.

[13] *York Civic Records*, ed. Angelo Raine, The Yorkshire Archaeological Society, Record Series (Wakefield: West Yorkshire Printing Company, 1939–45), i. 154.

[14] For the details of the royal entry into York that follow, see *Records of Early English Drama: York*, ed. Alexandra F. Johnston and Margaret Rogerson, 2 vols. (Toronto: University of Toronto Press, 1979), i. 137–52.

provide music and local children to sing and deliver pageant speeches. These speeches celebrated the city's distinctive history, and the procession through the town to York Minster drew attention to impressive features of the cityscape. In the first show, King Ebraucus, York's legendary founder, embodied the ancient dignity of the place as he told the story of its recent past, stressing York's loyalty to the forebears of Henry VII while hushing up the regret the city council recorded in its minutes when it received the news of the death of Richard III.[15] The city also relied on its own theatrical resources for the reception of the King by adapting for this occasion some of the pageants normally seen in its cycle of Corpus Christi plays. To the Plasterers' pageant of the Creation, they added a red rose tree and a white rose tree, to which 'all other floures' on the pageant stage were to 'lowte and evidently yeue sufffrantie'.[16] And from the heavens of the Weavers' pageant of the Assumption, Our Lady descended to welcome the King and to assure him that the citizens of York were devoted to her, to Christ, and to 'his knyght',[17] that is, to Henry VII himself.

Bristol and Coventry, like York, enhanced their receptions of royal visitors by drawing on their own traditions of religious drama. For Henry VII's entry in 1486, Bristol displayed the Shipwrights' pageant and another pageant (presumably that of a guild) of an elephant and castle, with a picture of Christ's resurrection, and in the highest tower 'certeyne Imagerye smyting bellis'.[18] When Prince Arthur visited Coventry in 1498, the city erected stages for shows at the Spoon Street Gate, the conduit, and the high cross, but they also set forth the Barkers' pageant with a speech by 'the Quene of fortune' written for the occasion.[19] Similarly, in 1526 Coventry used the Mercers' pageant for the welcome of Princess Mary, and, forty years later, the city set forth the pageants of the Drapers, Smiths, and Tanners when Elizabeth arrived. During this royal entry, Coventry's Recorder, John Throgmorton, brought to the Queen's attention another important part of Coventry's history and theatrical heritage. He included among his list of the town's worthy achievements its defeat of the Danes and reminded the Queen that 'a memoriall' of this event 'is kept vnto this day by certaine open shewes in this Citty yearely'.[20] Local theatrical resources served these cities well not only when first receiving royal visitors, but also when the monarchs extended their stay and

---

[15] See *York Civic Records*, i. 119–53; the 'spin' that York's pageants put on its recent history was consistent with its negotiations with Henry VII throughout the first year of his reign; see C. E. McGee, 'Politics and Platitudes: Sources of Civic Pageantry, 1486', *Renaissance Studies*, 3.1 (1989), 29–34.

[16] *REED: York*, 139.   [17] Ibid. 143.

[18] *Records of Early English Drama: Bristol*, ed. Mark C. Pilkinton (Toronto: University of Toronto Press, 1997), 13. Indeed, Bristol's guilds regularly paraded their pageants to celebrate good news at court, such as the marriage of a princess in 1508–9 (p. 21) or the birth of a prince in 1510–11 (p. 22).

[19] *Records of Early English Drama: Coventry*, ed. R. W. Ingram (Toronto: University of Toronto Press, 1981), 89.

[20] Ibid. 125, 234, and 233; Coventry also set forth three pageants for the visit of Henry VIII and Katherine of Aragon in 1511; none is identified by reference to the guild that sponsored it, but

desired, or required, or commanded, further entertainment; so the city fathers
of York presented Richard III with a performance of their Creed Play in 1483
and in 1487 mounted 'by the kinges Commaundement' a production of their
Corpus Christi plays for Henry VII's second visit there.[21] All these provincial
towns and cities acknowledged the political needs and aims of the monarch,
but local culture—its writers, actors, singers, musicians, theatrical resources,
traditions of religious drama, even features of the cityscape—predominated, as
did the advancement of the political and economic goals of the boroughs.

MYSTERIES' END

Noting that the pageants of Coventry's Drapers, Smiths, and Tanners were
presented as part of the reception of Elizabeth I in 1566, Montrose argues
that civic religious drama was 'not wholly suppressed by the royal government
but . . . selectively appropriated'.[22] Like some civic rituals, which were reinvented
or adapted for different occasions, the mystery plays were revised in ways
appropriate to a Protestant regime. As such they survived, but only temporarily.[23]
After 1566, no English city would roll out a Corpus Christi pageant or stage a
Creed, Pater Noster, or Hocktide play for a *civic* reception or entertainment of
the monarch. Coventry did produce its Hocktide play once more for Elizabeth,
but at Kenilworth, not Coventry, and as part of their (temporarily successful)
lobbying 'that they might haue theyr playz vp agayn'.[24] Cities which struggled to
maintain their local theatrical activity through the 1570s, as York and Coventry
did, never again had the opportunity to entertain the monarch in this way:
Elizabeth made no more visits to Coventry and progressed no further north than
Stafford.[25] The city of Bristol, which did have the chance to use its pageants again
when Elizabeth visited in 1574, carefully kept them in storage since such devices
were seen as relics of Catholicism, and Bristol's entertainment explicitly rejected
'roemish dregs' that might cause dissension.[26] When the last cycle of mystery
plays was 'laid down' in 1579,[27] provincial towns and cities lost a theatrical
resource by which to make a special occasion like a royal entry even more special,
as well as more explicitly, precisely meaningful.

The end of the mystery plays was one factor that helped to change the
character of civic shows for Elizabeth I and facilitated the subordination of local

---

that which included 'the 9 orders of Angells' (p. 107) was probably one of the city's Corpus Christi
pageants of the Creation.

[21] *REED: York*, 130–1; 155.   [22] 'A Kingdom of Shadows', 72.

[23] See Paul Whitfield White, 'Reforming Mysteries' End: A New Look at Protestant Intervention
in English Provincial Drama', *Journal of Medieval and Early Modern Studies*, 29.1 (1999), 121–47.

[24] *REED: Coventry*, 273, which excerpts *Robert Laneham's Letter* (London, [1575]), 32–8.

[25] See Cole, *Portable Queen*, appendix 2.

[26] *REED: Bristol*, 96.   [27] *REED: Coventry*, 294.

culture to that of the centre. So too did the surprising unwillingness of the city governors to rely on local writers when planning for a royal visit. In Coventry, Shrewsbury, Bristol, Norwich, and other towns and cities, local schoolmasters regularly received rewards for writing and directing plays at Christmas and for special events on the civic calendar,[28] but they were not entrusted with devising the receptions for the Queen. Instead, the city fathers, as modern bureaucrats might say, 'outsourced' the writing and direction of their shows. Although Norwich licensed its company of waits to perform comedies, tragedies, and interludes in 1576,[29] two years later the city hired poets with connections at court—Bernard Garter, Henry Goldingham, and Thomas Churchyard—to create the shows for Elizabeth I's reception and entertainment. Presumably, had the Queen's projected visit come to pass in 1575, Shrewsbury would have performed the devices proposed by Churchyard, for which he received five marks from the borough.[30] In Bristol in 1574, Mr Thomas Dunne, master of the free school of St Bartholomew, contributed some form of entertainment or at least a performance space, for he was paid £1 7*s*. 6*d*. for charges related to 'his stage at the schole dore'.[31] Evidently that was not enough for Mr Dunne, who sabotaged other shows because, not entrusted to oversee the entire event, he 'enuied that any stranger should set forth these shoes'.[32] So, at least, claimed Thomas Churchyard, the poet whom the council brought in, and paid, 'for his travayle bothe in the ffortes and concernyng oracions', five times what Dunne received.[33]

Besides Churchyard, Bristol hired Captain John Shute, 'a gunner of the Tower of London and yeoman of the ordnance for life',[34] to serve as 'generall of all the armye'[35] that conducted the mock siege with which they entertained the Queen. Perhaps he, or Churchyard, or both of them, arranged for courtiers not only to watch the military exercises, but also to participate in them. Negotiations with the court must have occurred, for on the second day of the mock siege 'cam diuers gentilmen of good callynge from the Court, which maed the shoe very gallant'.[36] On the next day too, the plot took a decisive turn when, just before the final assault, 'nue suckors commyng from the Courte to the Forts great comfort, the enemye agred on a parley'.[37] Shute, Churchyard, Goldingham, and Garter, all purveyors of court culture to the provinces, were also the instruments

---

[28] *REED: Bristol*, 78, 85, 113, 117, 145, 147; *REED: Norwich*, 21, 38–43, 52, 53–4; *REED: Coventry*, xx and xxii; and *Records of Early English Drama: Shropshire*, ed. J. Alan B. Somerset (Toronto: University of Toronto Press, 1994), 228–31.

[29] *REED: Norwich*, 57. [30] *REED: Shropshire*, 220.

[31] *REED: Bristol*, 88. [32] Ibid. 109. [33] Ibid. 88.

[34] E. Lord, 'Shute, John (*fl.* 1557–1598)', *Oxford Dictionary of National Biography* (Oxford: Oxford University Press, 2004); 20 Dec. 2004, www.oxforddnb.com/view/article/25484. With Shute, artillery from the court might also have been provided, as the Tower provided mortars and battering rams for the mock siege at Warwick Castle in 1572; see *The Progresses and Public Processions of Queen Elizabeth*, ed. John Nichols, 2nd edn., 3 vols. (London: J. Nichols, 1823), i. 319.

[35] *REED: Bristol*, 88. [36] Ibid. 102. [37] Ibid. 107.

by which powerful courtiers shaped provincial civic pageantry. The records of Shrewsbury make this explicit: twice in 1575 the town rewarded Thomas Churchyard, both times noting that he was 'sent hether by my Lord president'.[38] Unlike York, which in 1486 rejected Clifford's offer of advice about how best to welcome the King, in the 1570s Bristol, Shrewsbury, and Norwich accepted the influence of non-local poets and their patrons as they prepared to entertain the Queen.

MILITARIZING CIVIC SHOWS

If provincial towns and cities would not entrust to local playwrights the theatrical devices for a royal entry and could not draw on the resources of their traditional religious drama, how would the towns receive and entertain a visiting monarch? William Pelham, lieutenant-general of the Ordnance Office, had an idea of how provincial civic entertainments *should* be transformed. In 1567, he recommended the establishment of a Society of Harquebusiers, with units throughout the realm, whose military exercises would supplant traditional local festivities. He proposed specifically that 'At the tymes hertofore vsed for the sportes of Robyn Hood midsomer Lordes and Ladyes, so nowe that fellowshipe only to be permitted, in thosse accustemed seasons on the festevall dayes within the presynke of their Libertyes to shewe them selves with drome & fyfe and other Musyke, and non other.'[39] Though the Council never implemented this scheme, Pelham's thinking exemplifies the operations of 'a culture... that incorporates the local within and subordinates it to the centre'. The history of York's drama epitomizes the change Pelham envisioned: its Corpus Christi plays died, its Corpus Christi ridings lived on, and thrived as part of the musters of local militia. A similar pattern may be seen in Coventry drama. After the suppression of its religious plays, the city produced, or offered to produce, plays that included mock battles: *The Conquest of the Danes*, *The Destruction of Jerusalem*, and a history of Edward IV. The last example of civic drama there was the most obviously militaristic: in 1614 'a Squadron in warlike manner', with English, Irish, Scottish, and Spanish soldiers, mustered at the high cross

---

[38] *REED: Shropshire*, 220. The court (particularly Sir Christopher Hatton, Vice-Chamberlain from 1577 until his death in 1591, and, in this role, one of the courtiers responsible for organizing progresses) may have influenced the design of the entertainment at Bristol if Churchyard got the commission for the show in Bristol as he would in Shrewsbury, that is, through the direct recommendation of a nobleman at court. For an analogous case, Sir Henry Killigrew's recommendation, probably for an entertainment at Kenilworth in the 1560s, of an Italian master of fireworks to the Earl of Leicester, see C. E. McGee, 'Fireworks for Elizabeth', *Malone Society Collections XV* (1993), 85–8.

[39] State Papers, Domestic Series 12/44/60 (3 Nov. 1567); abbreviations in the manuscript have been silently expanded. This and related schemes are discussed in Lindsay Boynton, *The Elizabethan Militia* (Newton Abbot: David & Charles, 1971), 59–76.

for 'a very tough Skermidg . . . in which Battell death leech was fained to be slayne'.[40]

Elizabeth herself encouraged the militarization of civic pageantry. On 3 July 1559, the city of London brought a muster of 1,400 armed men to Greenwich where, in the presence of the new Queen, noble attendants, and foreign ambassadors, the men skirmished 'in imitation of close fight'.[41] A week later, she proceeded with lords, ladies, and foreign ambassadors to the Park Gate at Greenwich to watch the military exercises of the Earl of Ormond, Sir John Perrot, Mr North, and her pensioners. In the encouragement that Elizabeth gave to these martial sports, in her willingness to see the displays and to be seen at them, John Strype saw evidence of what was 'undoubtedly the Queen's policy, to accustom her Nobles and subjects to arms, and to give all countenance to the exercise of warfare, having such a prospect of enemies round about her'.[42]

In the late 1560s and early 1570s especially, such a policy seemed prudent, for Elizabeth was no less at risk from foreign foes or fraudulent 'friends' then than she felt she had been in 1559. She had survived the Northern Rebellion and the Ridolfi plot, but Mary Queen of Scots remained alive, with a claim to the throne of England that made her a magnet for those who would unseat Elizabeth. Across the English Channel, Elizabeth faced two staunch Catholic powers, France and Spain, which had recently deployed in the Netherlands a force of over 10,000 soldiers under the Duke of Alva. Pope Pius V urged both of these countries to depose Elizabeth when he promulgated a bull in 1570 that excommunicated her, declared her illegitimate, and absolved her subjects from allegiance to her.[43] Given these threats, military preparedness was a matter of urgency. In 1569, the Queen ordered certain gentlemen in every county and the sheriffs there to take musters of the men, horses, ships, armour, weapons, and munitions in their jurisdictions.[44] Whereas anxiety about danger in or from the north prompted this effort, concern about an invasion from Europe motivated the general musters of 1572, 1573, and 1574.[45]

This context made martial sports and exercises more significant. Musters, marches in the town harness, shooting practice and competitions, and the *jeux des armes* of the tournaments had been promoted as forms of training for real combat. In 1507, a challenge affirmed that the projected tournament aimed 'to

[40] *REED: Coventry*, 332, 390; see also pp. xxiii–xiv of that volume and R. W. Ingram, '1579 and the Decline of Civic Religious Drama in Coventry', *Elizabethan Theatre*, 8 (1979), 114–28.

[41] *Progresses*, ed. Nichols, i. 72 (n. 33); the account of the show occupies pp. 69–72.

[42] Ibid. 73.

[43] I am indebted here to Susan Doran, *England and Europe in the Sixteenth Century* (New York: St Martin's, 1999); Carole Levin, *The Reign of Elizabeth I* (Basingstoke: Palgrave, 2002); and Paul E. J. Hammer, *Elizabeth's Wars: War, Government and Society in Tudor England, 1544–1604* (Basingstoke: Palgrave, 2003), esp. pp. 78–115.

[44] *Calendar of State Papers, Domestic Series, 1547–80*, ed. R. Lemon (London: HMSO, 1856), 331 (item 49).

[45] Ibid. 450–94 *passim*.

make folkes more apte to serue ther prince when cawses shall require'.[46] In 1540, a challenge claimed that such feats of arms had 'raised men to honour, both in God's service against his infidel enemies and in serving their princes'.[47] And in Bristol at the time of Elizabeth's visit in 1574, Protestant preachers such as John Northbrooke, who would have castigated the city fathers for presenting 'vain plays' that took citizens away from work, recommended military games as a way of ' "trayning vp men in the knowledge of martiall and warrelike affaires and exercising" and imparting "knowledge to handle weapons" ' .[48]

As a training ground, the mock siege was particularly useful because the combatants had to display a wide range of military skills and coordinate their efforts in action. At the Tudor court, examples of the device—in great hall, park, tiltyard, and on the Thames—can be found from 1501, when the Knights of the Mount of Love assaulted a castle as part of the celebration of the marriage of Prince Arthur and Katherine of Aragon, until at least 1581, when the Four Foster Children of Desire besieged the Fortress of Perfect Beauty. During the reign of Henry VIII, similarly romantic castle sieges occurred at court in 1512, 1515, 1516, 1520, 1522, and 1524. Edward VI witnessed a fort holding on land in 1548 and on the Thames in 1550. During the latter, the combatants in four pinnaces, having first forced the one ship defending the fort to flee, attacked the fort 'with cloddes, scuibes, canes of fire, cartes made for the nonce, and bombardes' and levelled it.[49] In 1572, Ambrose Dudley, Earl of Warwick (and, appropriately for such a show, Master of the Ordnance), entertained Elizabeth at Warwick Castle with a mock siege that came to a climax when a fireworks dragon flew into the castle and set it ablaze. Clearly courtly forms of entertainment, the mock siege and other martial sports, would become the stuff of civic shows in the 1570s. Besides helping to develop the local militia, such displays of military force affirmed for the benefit of foreign ambassadors in the audience that Elizabeth I had the power to resist a foreign enemy or back an ally.

Given these various conditions—the perceived threats at home and abroad to the Queen and the realm, the commitment to improve military preparedness, the belief that military games developed military skills, the tradition of such games at court and of musters in the provinces, and the availability of a soldier-poet such as Thomas Churchyard—it is not surprising that provincial towns and

[46] Alan Young, *Tudor and Jacobean Tournaments* (London: George Philip, 1987), 23, quoting College of Arms MS R36, fo. 124ᵛ; see also *Here begynneth the iustes of maye* (*STC* 3543), ll. 152–72, in *Remains of the Early Popular Poetry of England*, ed. W. Hazlitt, 4 vols. (London, J. R. Smith, 1866), ii. 119.

[47] *Letters and Papers, Foreign and Domestic, of the Reign of Henry VIII, 1509–47*, ed. J. S. Brewer, J. Gairdner, and R. H. Brodie, 21 vols. (London, 1862–1910), xv. 300 (item 616).

[48] Quoted by Sacks, *The Widening Gate*, 192.

[49] *Literary Remains of King Edward the Sixth*, ed. John Gough Nichols, 2 vols. (London: Roxburghe Club, 1857), ii. 279. On this form of entertainment, see Philip Butterworth, 'Royal Firework Theater: The Fort Holding, Part I', *Research Opportunities in Renaissance Drama*, 34 (1995), 145–66; 'Part II', *RORD*, 35 (1996), 17–31; 'Part III', *RORD*, 37 (1998), 99–110.

cities also militarized their shows for Elizabeth. Like Sandwich, Bristol and Norwich certainly did, though in combination with other speeches, ceremonies, and theatrical devices so that the balance between the agenda of the central government and the importance of local interests varied in each case.

BRISTOL, 1574

In Bristol's shows for the Queen's visit in 1574, there is nothing like Sandwich's formal appeal for help with its harbour, nothing like Bristol's own use of a pageant in 1486 to appeal for financial aid.[50] Instead, the efforts of the Queen and her Council to provide for the defence of the realm seem to overwhelm the city's concerns, hopes, and sources of pride. Bristol's reception and entertainment included the traditional bell-ringing, gift-giving, ceremonies of obeisance, official speeches, pageants of welcome, and a mock siege or fort holding. But the last of these—that most closely associated with aristocratic devices of the tiltyard and with the Queen's agenda—dominated the event. The mock siege lasted three days of the Queen's four-day stay, employed over 400 armed men fighting on land and sea, and featured the razing of one fort, the defence of another. Probably because the soldier-poet Churchyard had responsibility for the entertainment as a whole, the siege invaded even the speeches of the civic pageants of welcome. In the first, at the high cross, Fame spent three-quarters of his speech on the customary business of welcoming the Queen to the town, extolling her virtues, and expressing the joy of the inhabitants, but, in closing, Fame announced that there would be 'warlike pastimes playn. | As shalbe seen to morn in feeld, | if that your highnes pleas'.[51] On the next pageant, Salutation, having explained that the bells ringing throughout Bristol symbolized the popular joy prompted by the Queen's arrival, devoted the entire second half to the projected military exercises, supplying some of the allegory of the 'matter moud tween Peace and warre' (p. 95). Finally, Gratulation, after only four lines of a forty-line speech, provided a detailed interpretation of the future siege and completed the process of constructing Elizabeth's roles implied by the fiction of that show: first as a spectator, then as the arbiter of the dispute, finally as the city's 'suer . . . staye: | That shall surseace Bellonas brags, | and end our fearfull fray' (p. 96). While performing some of the traditional duties of civic pageants, the *series* of pageant speeches reveals

---

[50] *REED: Bristol*, 11–12; parenthetical references in this section are to this edition.

[51] Ibid. 94. The change for which I am arguing is well illustrated by the contrast between this pageant at the high cross and that held there in 1486. Unlike the 1574 pageant, which directed attention to the future war games, the 1486 pageant ended with a prayer to 'Crist therfor that on crosse diede' and to the 'holy seintes all' (Ibid. 12). These words, perhaps underscored by a simple gesture, focused attention on impressive architectural features of Bristol—on the cross, on the images of saints that adorned it, and on the adjacent church of All Saints.

Churchyard's increasing appropriation of these civic shows for the purposes of his grand courtly device.

But Bristol's entertainment of the Queen was more complex than a binary opposition between civic shows and courtly devices (and, implicit in it, the opposition between local aims and the royal agenda) suggests. The city probably took pride in its ability to stage the massive military and naval exercises that Churchyard designed. Unlike many cities, Bristol had responded quickly and effectively to the 1569 order for musters. In 1570, it had successfully petitioned the Council for permission to marshal its bands separately from the county of Gloucestershire, and that year 'the city was spending £65 on equipping 160 soldiers'.[52] The Council repaired the city armour, purchased drums, and made an ensign in fine silk of the city's colours. In August 1573, the Mayor and his brethren reported that they had executed the commission for musters as required, and attached a certificate of the musters of able men from the ages of 16 to 60.[53] Whereas civic religious drama had provided the theatrical raw material for royal entries in the past, the customary local practice of marching in the city harness and mustering trained bands, a custom recharged and galvanized by royal command, gave Bristol the resources it needed to receive Elizabeth I with an unparalleled display of armed force and skill. In 1574, she was conducted through Bristol to her lodging by a guard of 300 soldiers, whose discharge of 300 small shot was answered by the firing of over 100 pieces of ordnance. Then came the three-day fort holding or siege, exhibiting the soldiers, sailors, ships, armour, weaponry, munitions, firepower, and battlefield expertise that Bristol could place at the Queen's disposal. This western port, like Dover and Sandwich on the east coast, had done what the Queen had required of it and readied itself for the defence of the realm.[54] The city's ceremonies and shows were the proof.

Churchyard, though an outsider and a poet of soldiery, ultimately served the city well by establishing quite clearly in the resolution of the action what Bristol—or at least its political and financial elite—valued.[55] Bristol's fort holding ended by means of a treaty, with neither real harmony nor military victory achieved.[56] Neither side won the day, not the soldiers who took the Queen's part and defended the castle of Peace, nor the armies of War and the 'wicked world' (p. 96). Harmony was not really achieved either, since War,

[52] Boynton, *Elizabethan Militia*, 59; and for an account of the difficult effort to develop armed forces and the qualified success, see pp. 53–125.

[53] *CSP, Domestic, 1547–80*, 467 (item 22).

[54] Although no Dover records document the Queen's visit there in 1572, Sandwich provided that town with a hundred armed men for four or five days, as requested by the Lord Warden of Dover Castle; see *REED: Kent*, 856; Dover too, it seems, militarized its entertainment then.

[55] As the speech of The City proceeds, this allegorical character identifies the entire city of Bristol with its political and financial elite. The 'we' of its speech refers not to the citizenry at large, but to the lawgivers, law enforcers, and merchant adventurers. For evidence that men in Bristol's leading families played a large role in financing and producing the entertainment, see *REED: Bristol*, 282–4.

[56] Cf. Cole, *Portable Queen*, 157.

by definition unharmonious, remained one of the parties to the treaty, which it celebrated with a triumphant blast of its artillery. Instead, both sides in the combat happily accepted a diplomatic deal based on another political fiction, the invincibility of the alliance of 'the corrage of good people, & the force of a mighty prince' (p. 108). Conflict within the show giving way to compliment of the most important person in its audience, the plot culminated in the achievement of peace and equilibrium.

Equilibrium is typical of the ways the City represents itself in the final speech of the show, the speech of 'The City'. This character, the ultimate spokesperson for the besieged fortress of Peace/the Queen/the City, prizes soldiers whose noble acts spring from noble minds, but not extremists who 'glory all in warres, and peace disdayns in deed' (p. 107). Similarly admirable are well-balanced merchants who keep their shops and maintain their households, while remaining ready and willing to 'blaed hit with the best, when cawse of contrey coms' (p. 106). The City draws attention to the massive gathering of troops in the show, the 'soldyars as you see' (p. 106), as a sign of its commitment to military vigilance and might. And while the citizens of Bristol value those qualities, they prefer, The City affirms, peace, because of the 'welth and gain' (p. 106) it brings. For Bristol, a hub for its hinterland and a busy port for overseas trade, peace was invaluable. War cost the Merchant Adventurers and other wealthy retailers engaged in foreign trade money, manpower, and ships, the means by which they plied their trade. They lost these in times of war because ships were attacked by enemies or conscripted for use by the English navy.[57] After three days of 'warlike pastimes' (p. 94) that should have reassured Elizabeth that Bristol was responsive to the current anxieties of the central government, Churchyard gave the last word to The City. The City emphatically repeated in the last speech what Bristol most desired—that is, peace—by praising Elizabeth as 'a Prince, by whom our peace is kept', urging all England to celebrate her for keeping 'her country thus. In peace and rest', and concluding with a prayer to 'the god of peace', that 'In peace by peace our peace presarue' (p. 107).

In Bristol's entertainment of Elizabeth I in 1574, the local culture seems overwhelmed by that of the centre. The city hired Thomas Churchyard, staged a grand courtly device, and embraced in it the Queen's and Privy Council's policy objectives. Nor did the city use its shows to lobby for specific local projects, celebrate local history, or point out beauties and amenities of the place. A strong sense of the city ultimately emerges from Churchyard's dramatic efforts neverthe-less. Given Bristol's investment in the development of its local militia, the mock siege enacted before the Queen might be seen not only as an endorsement of her agenda, but also as a celebration of what had become a proud part of the city's

---

[57] On Bristol's Merchant Venturers and their conflict, especially intense between 1566 and 1571, with wealthy retailers who also wanted the right to trade abroad, see Patrick McGrath, *The Merchant Venturers of Bristol* (Bristol: The Society of Merchant Venturers of the City of Bristol, 1975), 13–17.

culture. This show also went beyond a simple endorsement of militarization: in the end, peace is prized above all. War games are entertaining, not wars. In Bristol's entertainment, the concerns of the centre and those of this provincial city are intertwined in complex ways. We have neither a clear case of the centre subordinating the local, nor one of a city appropriating national policy initiatives for its own ends, but rather a careful alignment of common interests and aspirations.

NORWICH, 1578

The local concerns of Norwich fade out most fully from the civic shows this city produced for the entertainment of Elizabeth in 1578. Like Sandwich, Norwich presented various kinds of drama—traditional street pageants, military games, and a masque—and commissioned three different poets, none home-based there, to compose and direct the shows. In the pageants written by Bernard Garter, 'Citizen of London',[58] the city pursued no particular local causes, but these shows did acknowledge in passing Norwich's history, geography, industry, ideals of government, and, most importantly, its strong commitment to the Protestantism that the city shared with the Queen. In the last respect, the pageants announced the dominant theme of the orations of the Mayor, the minister of the Dutch church, and the schoolmaster, that while careful of her 'Maiesties health, honour, and pleasure', they cherished as an even higher priority 'Gods glory and true religion' (p. 251). Norwich, like Bristol, aligned its local self-understanding with a crucial aspect of the religious aims of the monarch, aims that she was pursuing on her progress into East Anglia in 1578.

After the royal entry proper, however, court culture took over Norwich's entertainment of the Queen. Thomas Churchyard served up yet another tournament device in his 'Shew of Manhode and Dezartes'. This device, written to be performed outdoors by four men and a boy, presented an allegorical 'controuersie' (p. 318) among Manhood, Desert, and Good Favour, all rivals for the love of Lady Beauty. Beauty had secured the Queen as audience and defined Elizabeth's roles by appealing to her to protect Beauty/beauty, save lives, and administer justice in this case. Before this judgement could occur however, Good Fortune, or Destiny, entered, refuted the claims of the others, seized Lady Beauty, and proposed to defend his right by force of arms. When Manhood, Desert, and Good Favour affirmed their readiness to take up Good Fortune's challenge, it becomes clear that the purpose of this fictive conflict was to set up a display of martial arts:

And yet to shew that Destenie, (and who best can conquer) shal gouerne all, . . . sexe Gentlamen on either side with rebated swords and targets (only in dublet and hose, and

---

[58] Garter identifies himself in this way on the title page of his account of the entertainment; see *REED: Norwich*, 247. Parenthetical references in this section are to this edition.

Morion on head) approached, and woulde clayme the combat, and deale togither twelue blowes a peece, and in the ende Fortune should be victor . . . (p. 317)

Like traditional challenges for such devices at court, this one prescribed the number of combatants, the weapons to be used, the armour to be worn, and the number of blows to be exchanged. If Lady Beauty were construed to be a representation of Elizabeth, as she was in the romantic allegories of the Accession Day tilts, the victory of Good Fortune effected by this formalized combat might be taken as proof that no nobleman of the English court and no foreign prince, no matter how courageous, handsome, or deserving he might be, could win her. The show implies that in matters of love and marriage in Elizabeth's life, man doth purpose (to vary Churchyard's phrasing), but Destiny doth dispose.

Churchyard, however, extended the action of this show in a way that complicated the import of the device. After the firing of a shot, the significance of which was deliberately mistaken, a mêlée, another tournament event, occurred. All the armed men were to 'fall at variaunce so sharpely . . . that Fortunes side should triumph and march ouer the bellies of their enimies: in which time was legges and armes of men (well and liuely wrought) to be let fall in numbers on the grounde, as bloudy as mighte be' (p. 317). Was this spectacle of violence a *reductio ad absurdum*, a scene so exaggerated that it was fit only to stir up laughter? Or was it a warning that to trust to Destiny was to risk losing the service of men who are manly, well favoured, and truly deserving? The show ends, after all, not with the triumphal exit of Good Fortune but with 'a dolefull song for the death of Manhood, Fauour, and Dezartes' (p. 317). Whatever the meaning of this device, for which we have only Churchyard's scenario rather than the speeches that might have made explicit the significance, the show illustrates clearly Churchyard's importation of tournament devices for an urban entertainment in the provinces.

Norwich also brought in for Queen Elizabeth's entertainment the most courtly of all theatrical forms: the masque. Henry Goldingham devised this show, which, with its consort of musicians, procession of torchbearers, and presentations of speeches and gifts by classical deities, was a masque in its simplest form.[59] This courtly device, created by a poet with connections at court, also engaged not the local political concerns of Norwich, but those of the Queen and the Privy Council. Speeches by Mercury and Cupid, which frame the main action of the masque, advert to a crucial topic at court during the 1578 progress, Elizabeth's marriage negotiations. Mercury begins by apologizing for the absence of certain deities: Ceres, Bacchus, Pomona (all of whom are said to be busy

---

[59] This masque, like other Elizabethan ones, is simpler when compared to the Jonsonian form, its derivatives, and the great state occasions on which Jacobean and Caroline masques were performed. In its simpler form, the performance of a masque was often a gift in itself and a means of presenting gifts, as at Norwich in 1578. With this form and function, it persists at least until the 1620s; see, for instance, C. E. McGee, ' "The Visit of the Nine Goddesses": A Masque at Sir John Crofts' House', *English Literary Renaissance*, 21 (1991), 371–84.

with the year's harvest), and Hymen, who 'denyeth his good wil, eyther in presence, or in person' (p. 272). Because of this recalcitrance on the part of the god of marriage, Diana has, Mercury says, 'countrechecked him' so that 'he shall euer hereafter be at your [Elizabeth's] commaundement' (p. 272). When it comes to marriage, the speeches imply, Elizabeth herself is in charge. Cupid confirms the Queen's power and independence in matrimonial matters, by giving her a golden arrow and counselling her to 'Shoote but this shafte at King or Caesar: . . . | And he is thine, and if yout wilte allowe' (p. 276). With its array of classical deities, Goldingham's masque seems out of place in the context of Norwich, a sturdily Protestant city where one would expect biblical, legendary, and allegorical characters representing the city, as they did on the pageants Bernard Garter prepared for the Queen's reception. Goldingham's subtle, topical device was, in Garter's words, 'an excellent Princely Maske' (p. 271), but it was not a piece of court culture brought to Norwich *by* the court *for* the court, as the court brought its business along and, if necessary, its beer. The masque, despite its exotic character, was sponsored by the city and clearly received as a *civic* production, for after the deities departed from the Queen's presence, she 'called to hir Maister Robert Wood, the Mayor of Norwich, whome first she hartily thanked: and toke by the hande, and vsed secret conference, but what, I know not. And thus this delightfull night passed, to the ioy of all whiche sawe hir Grace in so pleasant plight' (p. 276).

CONCLUSION

When Elizabeth went on progress in the 1570s, so too did court forms of drama, with Thomas Churchyard as their chief purveyor. Perhaps the resilient Churchyard himself epitomizes best the character of civic receptions of the Queen at this time. Chaplinesque in making the best of bad situations, Churchyard could transform a show of water nymphs, drenched by a thunderstorm one day, into a show of the Queen of Fairies and her train the next,[60] or turn a rudimentary dramaturgical *faux pas* into a unforgettable feat.[61] Provincial towns and cities faced with a royal visit in the 1570s had to be similarly resourceful in producing theatrical devices to welcome and entertain the Queen. For their shows, they relied in part, and increasingly, on imports, which in turn determined the import of their reception and entertainment of the monarch. The city fathers, perhaps unwittingly, furthered the professionalization of the theatre by hiring

---

[60] *REED: Norwich*, 328.
[61] *REED: Bristol*, 102–3: those directing the mock siege at Bristol made the basic mistake of staging the show too far from the Queen; because the speeches could not be heard, Mr John Roberts, barrister and later Mayor of Bristol, swam fully clothed across the Avon River to present the Queen with a book of all the speeches, petitioned for her aid in their military effort, and plunged back in to return to the siege.

poets without local connections to write and direct the shows. Civic leaders might have followed their own precedents and trusted to local amateurs, such as the schoolmasters who served as playwrights for big events on the civic calendar, but they did not. Provincial cities such as Bristol and Norwich also facilitated the subordination of local culture to that of the centre, the Queen and her Council, which, in general, preferred to control drama rather than to ban it.[62] Unable or unwilling to use the civic religious drama that had served them well in the past, the towns and cities brought in theatrical devices native to the court or the tiltyard and they developed, especially if the central government impelled them to do so, customary forms of local pageantry to deploy on the occasion of a royal visit. In so doing, provincial towns and cities demonstrated that Tudor civic drama, pageantry, and ceremony remained a versatile instrument by which the provinces could define their relationships with the monarch in terms beneficial to both. The civic drama of Sandwich, Bristol, and Norwich in the 1570s advanced the policy objectives of those building and defending a Protestant nation while providing those towns and cities with the opportunity to affirm their sturdy, loyal, and productive place within it.

[62] Alexandra F. Johnston, 'Tudor Drama, Theatre and Society', in Robert Tittler and Norman Jones (eds.), *A Companion to Tudor Britain* (Malden: Blackwell, 2004), 441.

7

Pulling the Strings:
Religion and Politics in the Progress of 1578

Patrick Collinson

I

In July and August 1578, Elizabeth I and her court went on progress deep into East Anglia, the only extensive royal tour of that region. From 16 to 22 August the great travelling show reached the second city of the kingdom, Norwich, referred to by the Spanish Ambassador as 'the North'.[1] There are a number of episodes in the course of the 1578 progress which have made it into many accounts of Elizabethan history and culture, some of them literary. There was the encounter at Audley End with the University of Cambridge, when Gabriel Harvey, in Thomas Nashe's hostile account 'ruffling it out huffty tuffty in his suit of velvet', made a favourable impression on the Queen, who said that he looked 'something like an Italian', which Harvey was not sure was entirely a compliment, but to which he responded with a published volume of verses, *Gratulationum Valdinensium libri quatuor* (1578).[2] Then came a strange little iconoclastic drama played out at Euston, near Newmarket, which seems to have signalled a sea change in the politics of East Anglia. The climax was reached in elaborate celebrations at Norwich, stage-managed and choreographed by Thomas Churchyard, a native of the

I am grateful to Dr Simon Adams for his comments and suggestions on this essay.

[1] *Calendar of Letters and State Papers . . . in the Archives of Simanacs, 1568–79*, ed. Martin A. S. Hume, 4 vols. (London: HMSO, 1892–9), ii (1894), 606–7, 613. Dr Adams has suggested to me that one reason why Elizabeth never penetrated into the true 'North' was that for many years that would have entailed a meeting with Mary Queen of Scots, something which, for contrary diplomatic reasons, she could neither undertake nor be seen, if in the vicinity, not to undertake.

[2] Cambridge University Library, University Archives, Letters B9, B13 a–c; *The Progresses and Public Processions of Queen Elizabeth*, ed. John Nichols, 2nd edn., 3 vols. (London: John Nichols, 1823), iii. 109–15; Virginia F. Stern, *Gabriel Harvey: His Life, Marginalia and Library* (Oxford: Clarendon Press, 1980), 39–46.

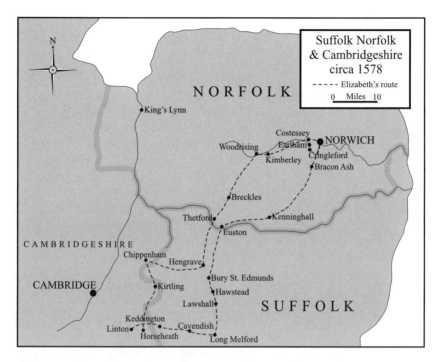

Map 7.1. A map of Suffolk, Norfolk, and Cambridgeshire, showing sites visited by Elizabeth I on her 1578 progress through East Anglia. Drawn by Nigel James.

city, which may have had a serious and substantial political purpose. The twin panegyric accounts of the Queen in Norwich composed by Churchyard and Bernard Garter,[3] rushed to the press immediately after the events they celebrated, make this one of the best recorded of all Elizabethan progresses. It is the only one to have been the subject of a monograph: *An Elizabethan Progress*, in which Zillah Dovey provides an account of the people and places visited in this progress.[4] In this essay, I will address the politics—and, in particular, the religious factor in the politics—of the 1578 progress.

---

[3] Bernard Garter, *The ioyfvll receyuing of the queenes most excellent maiestie into hir highnesse citie of Norwich* (London: Henrie Bynneman, 30 Aug. 1578); Thomas Churchyard, *A discovrse of the queenes maiesties entertainment in Suffolk and Norffolk* (London: Henrie Bynneman, 20 Sept. 1578). Both texts are available in *Records of Early English Drama: Norwich 1540–1642*, ed. David Galloway (Toronto: University of Toronto Press, 1984), 243–330.

[4] Zillah Dovey, *An Elizabethan Progress: The Queen's Journey into East Anglia, 1578* (Stroud: Alan Sutton, 1996). But see, more generally, Mary Hill Cole, *The Portable Queen: Elizabeth I and the Politics of Ceremony* (Amherst: University of Massachusetts Press, 1999), 141–4.

Elizabethan history is in the course of being rewritten—not, of course, for the first time.[5] The essence of this new approach, reflected, very variously, in the work of Simon Adams, Stephen Alford, Susan Doran, John Guy, Anne MacLaren, and to a modest extent in some of my own writings, is to be less Queen-fixated.[6] Much of this new Elizabethan history explores the major fault-line in the polity, a line often dividing the Queen from her councillors and other policy-makers. It was out of the East Anglian progress of 1578, from Bury St Edmunds, that the Earl of Leicester wrote: 'Our conference with Her Majesty about affairs is both seldom and slender.'[7] But that must mean, because a great deal was going on, internationally, in the summer of 1578, that the conference of Privy Counsellors like Leicester, without the benefit of the Queen's presence and participation, must have been far from seldom and slender. Never before or after, in their correspondence among themselves, did the governors of Elizabethan England do less to disguise the fact that they had the greatest difficulty in inclining the Queen to their way of thinking. The conundrum of counsel, which was the greatest political problem of an age which brought into uncomfortable partnership nearly absolute monarchy and a civic-minded humanism, was never more nakedly exposed. East Anglia in 1578 is where historical geology is best able to uncover the fundamental fault-line in Elizabethan politics.

Given the marked policy differences between the Queen and many of her councillors and courtiers, it sometimes looks as if there were two governments, not one, in mid-Elizabethan England. The issues included policy towards the Netherlands (where it could be said that events were coming to a moment of crisis in the months of the 1578 progress, if that were not the normal state of Dutch affairs), and also towards Scotland; the problem of both recusant and non-recusant Catholicism; religious affairs more generally (overshadowed in 1578 by the continued suspension and disgrace of Archbishop Edmund Grindal); what to do with and about Mary Queen of Scots; and the perennial operatic question

---

[5] Patrick Collinson, 'Elizabeth I and the Verdicts of History', *Historical Research*, 76 (2003), 469–91.

[6] Simon Adams, *Leicester and the Court: Essays on Elizabethan Politics* (Manchester: Manchester University Press, 2002); Stephen Alford, *The Early Elizabethan Polity: William Cecil and the British Succession Crisis, 1558–1569* (Cambridge: Cambridge University Press, 1998); Susan Doran, *Monarchy and Matrimony: The Courtships of Elizabeth I* (London: Routledge, 1996); Susan Doran and Thomas S. Freeman (eds.), *The Myth of Elizabeth I* (Basingstoke: Palgrave Macmillan, 2003); John Guy (ed.), *The Tudor Monarchy* (London: Arnold, 1997); John Guy (ed.), *The Reign of Elizabeth I: Court and Culture in the Last Decade* (Cambridge: Cambridge University Press, 1995); A. N. McLaren, *Political Culture in the Reign of Elizabeth I: Queen and Commonwealth 1558–1585* (Cambridge: Cambridge University Press, 1999); Patrick Collinson, 'The Monarchical Republic of Queen Elizabeth I', in Guy (ed.), *The Tudor Monarchy*, 110–34; Patrick Collinson, 'The Elizabethan Exclusion Crisis and the Elizabethan Polity: The Raleigh Lecture 1993', *Proceedings of the British Academy*, 84 (1994); Julia Walker (ed.), *Dissing Elizabeth: Negative Representations of Gloriana* (Durham, NC: Duke University Press, 1998).

[7] Leicester to Sir Francis Walsingham, 1 Aug. 1578, 'in much haste, her Majesty ready to horseback, at Bury': *Relations politiques des Pays-Bas at de l'Angleterre sous le règne de Philippe II*, ed. Kervyn de Lettenhove, 11 vols. (Brussels: n.p., 1882–1900), x. 678–80.

of a royal marriage, now building up to the last act, the affair of 'Monsieur', as the duc d'Alençon and Anjou was known. On all these momentous matters it was a question of proposing and disposing; often the Council proposing and the Queen disposing—although in the case of the Anjou match the reverse would be true. The overture to that last act was performed at Norwich.

II

The route and destination of the 1578 progress, as of all the summer progresses undertaken by Elizabeth, was in itself a matter which was not merely personal to the Queen, nor solely the concern of the Lord Chamberlain, who was formally responsible for what were called the Queen's 'gests'. There were negotiations and decisions within the courtly as well as conciliar machinery of government which are mostly concealed from us. For 1578, the question is: did the Queen take her court and Council to East Anglia or did they take her? If the latter scenario is the more likely, why? Who decided on the exact itinerary, and again, why?

To know when, and by whom, the final decisions about a summer progress were taken, we should need to be privy to the processes of decision-making. In July 1576, Gilbert Talbot told his father, the Earl of Shrewsbury, that there was 'no certainty' about the itinerary for that summer: 'For these two or three days it hath changed every five hours.'[8] On how far the East Anglian tour of July to September 1578 was known, how early, and to whom of the interested parties (thinking especially of the involuntary hosts in the country), the evidence is not consistent. Already in May of that year Talbot reported to his father: 'It is thought her Majesty will go in progress to Norfolk this year, but there is no certain determination thereof as yet.'[9] On 18 June, the Earl of Leicester was concerned that his friend Lord North had no time 'to furnish his house according to his duty and honourable good will'.[10] In the event, North came over from his house to pay his respects at Audley End, and it was only on the return leg of the progress, five weeks later, that he played host at Kirtling, having in the meantime built new kitchens and refurbished other rooms.[11] Thomas Churchyard, who arrived in Norwich on 25 July to oversee the pageants which would greet the Queen, thought that Norfolk and Suffolk had 'but small warning' of the event.[12] In fact, Norwich had received due warning in mid-June.[13] But in mid-July Sir Nicholas Bacon, the Lord Keeper, was uncertain whether the Queen would progress as far as Suffolk, while as late

---

[8] Edmund Lodge, *Illustrations of British History*, 3 vols. (London: G. Nicol, 1791), ii. 150.
[9] Ibid. 171.
[10] Sir Christopher Hatton to Leicester, 18 June 1578; Longleat House, MS Dudley II, fo. 178. I owe this reference to Simon Adams.
[11] Dovey, *An Elizabethan Progress*, 114–18; *Progresses*, ed. Nichols, 2nd edn. ii. 236–46.
[12] *REED: Norwich*, 295.   [13] Dovey, *An Elizabethan Progress*, 17–18.

as 20 July the Norfolk gentleman Sir Christopher Heydon hinted in a letter to Bacon's son Nathaniel of Stiffkey that the Queen might not be coming as far as Norwich after all, 'if the bird sing truly that I heard this day'.[14] The next day, the Earl of Northumberland was asking Burghley for news of 'the certainty of Her Majesty's progress'.[15] Whether these conflicting reports reflect a simple muddle or something more significant and political, we cannot say. But given almost everything that happened in the course of the progress, we are entitled to suspect that the decision to head for Norwich, through Suffolk, was taken by the dominant group in the Privy Council, and perhaps more personally by Robert Dudley, Earl of Leicester, whose interests, in several dimensions, were most affected; although we cannot discount disagreements within the Council itself over the route to be followed.[16]

III

In taking the heart of government, court and Council, into East Anglia, those whose business was government must have known that they were entering a region of delicate instability, still trying to adjust to the spectacular fall of its greatest magnate, Thomas Howard, Duke of Norfolk, executed only six years earlier. Behind the Howards remained what was left of the affinity of Mary Tudor, whose 1553 *coup d'état* had been mounted from Suffolk. Howard had left behind a political detritus in patterns and networks of office-holding, patronage, and social prestige. This was a region whose very soul was at stake, as progressive, Protestantizing, elements competed for the upper hand with conservative, Catholic, or crypto-Catholic forces.[17] The Queen was lodged, it might have seemed indiscriminately, in the houses of Protestants, Catholics, and crypto-Catholics. But that did not mean that her government intended to be religiously neutral: quite the opposite.

[14] *The Papers of Nathaniel Bacon of Stiffkey*, ed. A. Hassell Smith and Gillian M. Baker, 4 vols. (Norwich: Centre of East Anglian Studies, University of Norwich, 1983), ii. 19.
[15] *Calendar of the Manuscripts of the Most Hon. the Marquis of Salisbury . . . Preserved at Hatfield House, Hertfordshire*, 14 vols. (London: HMSO, 1883–1923), ii (1888), 189–90.
[16] A footnote on p. 196 of Diarmaid MacCulloch, *Suffolk and the Tudors: Politics and Religion in an English County, 1500–1600* (Oxford: Clarendon Press, 1986), reporting a communication from Simon Adams, has been hardened up into an over-confident assertion that Leicester was 'involved in the planning of the progress' (Susan Doran, 'Juno vs Diana: The Treatment of Elizabeth's Marriage Plans in Plays and Entertainments, 1561–1581', *Historical Journal*, 36 (1995), 257–74 (p. 271); Doran, *Monarchy and Matrimony*, p. 150). He may well have been. But Dr Adams knows of no surviving evidence that Leicester's role was central or decisive.
[17] For the background, and much of the content, of what follows, see Diarmaid MacCulloch, 'Catholic and Puritan in Elizabethan Suffolk: A County Community Polarises', *Archiv für Reformationsgeschichte*, 72 (1981), 232–89; MacCulloch, *Suffolk and the Tudors*; A. Hassell Smith, *County and Court: Government and Politics in Norfolk 1558–1603* (Oxford: Clarendon Press, 1974).

The diocese of Norwich, consisting of Norfolk and Suffolk, was described by Gabriel Harvey's enemy Andrew Perne, Master of Peterhouse, one of the heads of Cambridge houses who would have kissed the Queen's hand at Audley End on 27 July 1578 and himself a Norfolk man, as 'that great disordered diocess'.[18] One of the issues defining the fault-line between Queen and Council was how to address that disorder. The instinct of the Privy Council, or at least of the Leicesterians within it, which was also the agenda for the 1578 progress, and there is no reason to suppose that Lord Burghley had a different agenda, was to complete the local revolution which Norfolk's downfall entailed by placing the government of the region in reliable Protestant hands. The Queen, on the other hand, like her late Archbishop of Canterbury, Matthew Parker (another Norfolk man), will have laid the blame for the disordered state of the diocese upon her first Bishop of Norwich, John Parkhurst. Parkhurst was a learned and dedicated Protestant evangelist, but he was a naive and incompetent administrator, too indulgent to radical Puritan tendencies but also weak in his dealings with Catholic elements which were more strongly entrenched in Norfolk than anywhere else in southern England, with the possible exception of Sussex.[19] With neither faction effectively disciplined, the result was polarization. Someone in Norfolk said that 'the state could not long stand thus, it would either to papistry or puritanism'.[20]

The Queen, determined that no such thing should happen, favoured the third way, which we may call, at the risk of perpetrating an anachronism, Anglicanism: strict conformity to the terms of the ecclesiastical settlement, Catholic and Puritan dissidence to be handled with equal severity. The improbable instrument she chose (or had chosen for her) was Edmund Freke, who was appointed Bishop of Norwich in 1575. Why improbable? Freke had a history of fellow travelling with Puritans. He was known to have opposed the imposition of vestments, and he had favoured the preaching conferences known as prophesyings, the defence of which had spelt nemesis for Archbishop Grindal. He seems to have owed his advancement from the bishopric of Rochester to Norwich in part to Leicester, and both Leicester and Burghley probably congratulated themselves on having avoided the appointment of one or other of the stern advocates of conformity (including John Whitgift) whom the late Archbishop Parker had put on his own

[18] Quoted (from Inner Temple Library, MS Petyt 538/47, fo. 494) in Patrick Collinson, 'Perne the Turncoat: An Elizabethan Reputation', in Collinson, *Elizabethan Essays* (London: Hambledon, 1994), 179–218 (p. 181 n. 6).

[19] Smith, *County and Court*, 201–2. For the case of Sussex, which the Privy Council treated very differently, in effect deposing the Bishop of Chichester (Richard Curteys) for being too high-handed in his handling of the Catholic gentry, see Roger B. Manning, *Religion and Society in Elizabethan Sussex: A Study of the Enforcement of the Religious Settlement, 1558–1603* (Leicester: Leicester University Press, 1969).

[20] The National Archives, London [NA], SP 15/25/119, fo. 280ᵛ. SP 15/25/119 contains a fat little dossier (fos. 268–86) headed: 'The principal solicitors and instruments of the bishop of Norwich his unadvised dealings, detected by oath of discreet and faithful deponents, and by other apparent likelihoods plainly discovered.' This rather suspect dossier is the source for some of the circumstantial detail that follows.

short-list.²¹ But once at Norwich he changed his mind. This was perhaps thanks to the pressure placed upon him by two women: the Queen, whose almoner he was, which meant that he was regularly attendant upon her at court; and his wife, who had the Bishop firmly in her control. The result has been called by the latest historian of the Elizabethan episcopate 'the most calculated volte-face in the history of the Elizabethan church, a ruthless career-move'.²²

It didn't do Freke much good. In his first year, he suspended most of the leading nonconformist preachers in his diocese, reportedly 'putting down' as many as twenty exercises of preaching in Norwich alone. The most famous preacher of all, John More, the legendary 'apostle of Norwich', was among those silenced.²³ The leading Protestant gentry of the county were naturally alienated, and compromised by what was said about them at court. Reports reached the Queen that 'divers gentlemen' of Norfolk were 'anabaptists'; Nathaniel Bacon and his friend William Heydon were incensed and told Leicester so.²⁴ Bishop Freke, who could not survive without political allies and friends, was obliged to look for support on the other side of the fence. Norfolk was soon buzzing with rumours. Known Catholics were infiltrating the Bishop's household. Freke was careful when he dealt with recusancy, on one occasion calling a notorious recusant back into custody only because he had been put under pressure to do so, 'very sharp reprehension from my lords of the council for my lenity extended towards you and the rest in question for religion in these parts'.²⁵ A dinner party at the Bishop's country house was attended by known recusants and church papists, among them Sir Thomas Cornwallis, sometime comptroller of Mary Tudor's household and the principal agent to the Duke of Norfolk, now living quietly in political retirement, a moderate and reasonable recusant, popular with the Queen, and with friends across the politico-religious spectrum.²⁶ When Freke, who was short of money, confessed that he sought translation to a quieter diocese, Cornwallis was reported to have said: 'Nay that shall you not my lord', offering to subscribe to a fund to keep him at Norwich. Thus encouraged, the Bishop was said to have uttered 'in some rage': 'Nay, they say the puritans have removed me hence, but before God I will tarry here in despite of them all,

---

²¹ *Conferences and Combination Lectures in the Elizabethan Church: Dedham and Bury St Edmund's, 1582–1590*, ed. Patrick Collinson, John Craig, and Brett Usher (Woodbridge: Boydell [and] Church of England Record Society, 2003), pp. xlii–l.

²² Brett Usher, *William Cecil and Episcopacy, 1559–1577* (Aldershot: Ashgate, 2003), 118–19, 120–2.

²³ Patrick Collinson, *The Elizabethan Puritan Movement* (Oxford: Clarendon Press, 1990), 202–4; Smith, *County and Court*, 208–25; *Conferences and Combination Lectures*, ed. Collinson, Craig, and Usher, pp. xlvii–xlviii.

²⁴ Draft letter from Bacon to 'a noble lord', almost certainly Leicester, 24 Jan. [1578?]; Folger Shakespeare Library, Washington, DC, Case 1472, Bacon Folder 11. I owe this reference to Hassell Smith.

²⁵ Bishop Freke to Ferdinando Paris of Pudding Norton, 13 Mar. 1582; Pembroke College, Cambridge, MS Letter Book relating to the Paris family, fo. 46.

²⁶ MacCulloch, 'Catholic and Puritan', 235.

to plague the whole generation of them, striking the board with his fist very angrily.'

Meanwhile, Freke had fallen out with his diocesan chancellor, John Becon, a protégé of Bishop Parkhurst and a client of Leicester. This was far from a sideshow. As Freke struggled to get rid of Becon and as Becon, fiercely litigious, entrenched, it became a cause célèbre.[27] Becon was a near-presbyterian, well known as a leader of the Puritans in Cambridge in the early 1570s.[28] Cornwallis, who was accused of constant interference in the conduct of ecclesiastical justice, broadly in the Catholic interest, was working closely with Freke to replace Becon with William Masters, another suspected papist, whom Freke's predecessor, Bishop Parkhurst, had unwisely appointed to the office under pressure from Cornwallis.[29]

Both the cause of the Norwich preachers and the Becon affair had been brought to the attention of Leicester, Burghley, and other councillors before the royal progress reached Norwich in August 1578. In May, Dr Becon had discussed More's case with Leicester. He told Nathaniel Bacon that he would have to be content to be called a favourer of Puritans 'when generally all the good men in the country are calumniated that way'. But who was it, he asked, who for the last eighteen months had been spreading slanderous rumours about Puritanism as far as the court itself?[30] Radical Puritanism was not a paper tiger. In 1583, fewer than 175 citizens, 'with infinite more in this shire of Norfolk', were to petition the Queen in favour of a non-episcopal, presbyterian church settlement.[31] But the preferred policy of the Privy Council was to favour the middle ground, defusing a potentially dangerous situation with moderation, persuading the preachers to be somewhat conformable. This was where Leicester stood, and it was what the whole Council, Burghley in the forefront, tried to achieve when they reached Norwich in August 1578; whereas the Queen favoured a hard line, with a series of interventions in religious matters which the latest historian of the Elizabethan Church, Brett Usher, has censured: 'Her actions were more likely than not to exacerbate the tensions between her unnecessarily narrow conception of "Ecclesia Anglicana" and the moderate, evangelical tradition of Protestant churchmanship upon which her settlement principally relied for its survival and advancement.' Her interventions, Usher concludes, were 'invariably disastrous'.[32]

We need to join the progress at an earlier staging post along the road to Norwich: Euston Hall near Newmarket, the home of a wealthy young Catholic,

[27] Smith, *County and Court*, 210–23.
[28] Victor Morgan, *A History of the University of Cambridge*, 4 vols. (Cambridge: Cambridge University Press, 2004), ii. 71, 73.
[29] Smith, *County and Court*, 210, 216.
[30] John Becon to Nathaniel Bacon, 23 May 1578, *The Papers of Nathaniel Bacon*, ii. 8–9; Patrick Collinson, 'The Puritan Classical Movement in the Reign of Elizabeth I' (unpublished doctoral thesis, University of London, 1957), 312–19, 882–5; Smith, *County and Court*, 210–11.
[31] *The Seconde Parte of a Register*, ed. Albert Peel, 2 vols. (Cambridge: n.p., 1915), i. 157–60.
[32] Usher, *William Cecil and Episcopacy*, 182–3.

Edward Rokewood, whose family was closely allied to the Cornwallises.[33] And then we should backtrack to Bury St Edmunds, which the progress had left for Euston on 9 August. At Euston there was a sample of what was now to happen throughout East Anglia, a curious piece of carnivalesque theatre. For what took place as the Queen was saying her goodbyes and thankyous and preparing to leave Rokewood's house we are dependent, for better or worse, on a far from dispassionate account supplied to the Earl of Shrewsbury by Richard Topcliffe, the notorious papist-finder-general of Elizabethan England, whose evidence has to be evaluated with scepticism.[34] According to Topcliffe, a search for a piece of missing plate led to the discovery, in a hay-house, of an image of the Virgin Mary. Then, 'after a sort of country dances ended, in Her Majesty's sight the idol was set behind the people, who avoided'. The Queen commanded that the image be burned, 'which in her sight by the country folks was quickly done, to her content, and unspeakable joy of every one but some one or two who had sucked of the idol's poisoned milk'.

This curious piece of near-fiction raises more questions than we can hope to answer. How fortuitous was the discovery of the image? Had it perhaps been planted? What was the role of the country people? Would their dancing have happened, image or no image? What does 'who avoided' mean? Above all, what role was the Queen playing? Was it as active and as approving as Topcliffe suggests? Or was this not rather something arranged for her benefit? Is this evidence of conciliar manipulation, even of a plot hatched before the progress ever left Greenwich? Why had Euston been chosen as a staging post? The house was small and there were many more convenient places to stay in the vicinity. We can confirm what Topcliffe otherwise reports: Rokewood was later summoned to appear before the Privy Council at Norwich and committed to prison, the beginning of a long ordeal for the Rokewoods which would culminate in the involvement of another member of the family in the Gunpowder Plot of 1605. But whether at Euston there was a face-to-face encounter between Rokewood and Lord Chamberlain Sussex, who asked him how, as someone excommunicated for papistry, 'he durst presume to attempt' the Queen's royal presence, we cannot say. However, that something out of the ordinary happened at Euston may be confirmed by an even more garbled account from the Spanish Ambassador, who reported that at one of the houses which had received the Queen 'her people found an altar with all the ornaments thereupon ready for the celebration of Mass', and that the family had received the Queen 'with crucifixes round their necks'.[35]

The progress had come to Euston from Bury St Edmunds. This was another religious problem area, and was to become more so in the years immediately

---

[33] MacCulloch, *Suffolk and the Tudors*, 85, 187–8.
[34] Richard Topcliffe to Shrewsbury, 30 Aug 1578: Lodge, *Illustrations*, ii. 187–8.
[35] *CSP . . . Simanacs, 1568–79*, ed. Hume, ii (1894), 613.

following the progress of 1578.[36] In that summer, the events known to history as 'the Bury stirs' were only just beginning. Jurisdictionally, the stirs were problematic. Bishop Freke was trying to impose his ecclesiastical authority over the town through his commissary, which was opposed by the local archdeacon, the future Bishop John Still, a fellow traveller with the Suffolk Puritans, and by some of the local Protestant/Puritan gentry. At a later stage, the Bishop would be supported by the assize judges, his opponents by the Privy Council. At issue in 1578 was the religious ascendancy of two preachers, who were both nonconformists and associated with the exercise of prophesying which Bishop Parkhurst had authorized. Bury was beginning to polarize between two leading townsmen, Thomas Badby, a Puritan, who had turned the ruins of the abbey into a stately home, and the religiously conservative Thomas Andrews. In the years to come, the Privy Council would normally support the Puritan faction in its feud with Bishop Freke and his supporters. But in August 1578 there was perhaps an attempt at even-handedness. While the Queen was lodged with Badby in the abbey, Burghley and Leicester stayed with Andrews.[37] From a petition sent to Burghley a few days after the royal party had left Bury, it appears that one of the preachers, John Handson, had been examined by Burghley and others upon complaints of his nonconformity. But it also appears that the result was that for the time being Handson was left undisturbed.[38] And Robert Jermyn of Rushbrooke, Badby's nephew, the leader of the up-and-coming Puritan gentry of West Suffolk, was among the Suffolk gentry now knighted.[39]

And so to Norwich. Much more happened in Norwich in August 1578 than what a Victorian author unkindly called 'absurd speeches' and 'grotesque pageants'.[40] The Privy Council addressed the struggle between Bishop Freke and the Norwich preachers, imposing a settlement which was better news for the preachers than for Freke. Freke was forced to accept a promise of limited conformity from the nonconformists, led by the 'apostle' John More; although others more radical and unreconciled soon headed out of Norwich in a southerly direction, to establish on the borders of Suffolk and Essex what history knows as the Dedham classis.[41] Two years later, when Freke tried to extricate himself, he was given a sharp reminder from the Privy Council that he ought to handle the preachers 'as charitably as becometh a man of his profession'.[42] The

[36] The latest and best account of the 'Bury stirs' is in John Craig, *Reformation, Politics and Polemics: The Growth of Protestantism in East Anglian Market Towns, 1500–1610* (Aldershot: Ashgate, 2001).
[37] Dovey, *An Elizabethan Progress*, 47–8.
[38] Craig, *Reformation, Politics and Polemics*, 90–1.
[39] MacCulloch, *Suffolk and the Tudors*, 196; Collinson, 'The Puritan Classical Movement', 866–930.
[40] Augustus Jessopp, *One Generation of a Norfolk House: A Contribution to Elizabethan History*, 3rd edn. (London: Fisher Unwin, 1913), 95.
[41] *Conferences and Combination Lectures*, ed. Collinson, Craig, and Usher, pp. xlvii–xlviii.
[42] Collinson, *The Elizabethan Puritan Movement*, p. 203.

Council also threw its weight behind Dr Becon in his struggle with Freke. Burghley filed away Becon's plan for a church constitution (supplied to him by Freke's enemies), which would combine the best elements of episcopacy and presbyterianism, 'a form of government' which, the Lord Treasurer was led to believe, was evidence of 'his desire of good proceedings'.[43] Thanks to the patronage of Leicester and Walsingham, Becon was rapidly advanced to the chancellorships of, in succession, Chichester and Coventry and Lichfield, where further trouble ensued.[44] A commission composed of Protestant/Puritan loyalists appointed to look into the affair after the court had left Norwich produced a copious if suspect dossier on Freke's dealings with a number of papists and crypto-papists, headed by Cornwallis. It was said in Norfolk that Becon owed his position to the Council, Masters, his rival for the post, to the Queen.[45] This was just one of the many little cracks that ran out from the fault-line in the Elizabethan polity.

Meanwhile, it was a time of judgement for the religious conservatives among the governors of Elizabethan Norfolk and Suffolk. Edward Rokewood was only one of twenty-three recusants and suspected recusants, all ranking gentlemen, who were summoned to appear before the Privy Council in Norwich. One list of culprits, and what was done with them, is in Burghley's own hand.[46] Rokewood and Robert Downes, the man who had boasted that he had the Bishop on his side, faced a lifetime of intermittent imprisonment. Others were bailed and put under house arrest. The elderly and immensely wealthy Sir Henry Bedingfield, once a Privy Counsellor to Queen Mary, failed to appear, but was seen two days later at the next stopover on the progress, and bound over.[47] From Hengrave, at the end of the month, the Council wrote to the Bishop 'touching such order as is to be taken by him with the papists in Suffolk'.[48] Although the Privy Council knew better than to lay hands on the Queen's friend Sir Thomas Cornwallis, it was a clear victory for the evangelical cause. While the papists were discountenanced, several gentlemen of proven Protestant credentials had been countenanced, indeed knighted.[49] By early September, Leicester was able to tell Sir Nicholas Bacon that his sons Nicholas and Nathaniel were back in good favour with the Queen. Sir Thomas Heneage, not known as a Puritan, wrote to Walsingham: 'My lords, with the rest of the council, have most considerately straightened divers obstinate and arch Papists, that would not come to church; and by some good means Her Majesty has been brought to believe well of

---

[43] *HMC . . . Salisbury*, ii (1888), 195–8; Collinson, 'The Puritan Classical Movement', 236–9, 883–5.

[44] Manning, *Religion and Society in Elizabethan Sussex*, 118–19; Collinson, *The Elizabethan Puritan Movement*, 183–7.

[45] NA, SP 12/126/3, 6, 19, 23, 41, 41I; SP 15/25/119, 120.

[46] Reproduced from a Hatfield House MS as a facsimile in Dovey, *An Elizabethan Progress*, 90.

[47] *Acts of the Privy Council of England*, ed. John R. Dasent, 25 vols. (London: HMSO, 1890–1964), x (1895), 310–16.

[48] Ibid. 317.   [49] MacCulloch, *Suffolk and the Tudors*, 196–7.

divers loyal and zealous gentlemen of Suffolk and Norfolk, whom the foolish Bishop had maliciously complained of to her as hinderers of her proceedings, and favourers of Presbyterians and Puritans.'[50] We can guess what those 'good means' were. Nathaniel Bacon now wrote to Leicester: 'The especial prayer of us all is that God will with his spirit guide your lordship both in this and all other your actions.'[51] Here were the origins of a potent legend: that when Elizabeth had crossed into Suffolk, to be met by the gentlemen of the county, all accompanied by their preachers, she had declared: 'Now I have learned why my County of Suffolk is so well governed, it is because the Magistrates and Ministers go together.'[52] I am sure that she said no such thing, but East Anglia now looked forward to a century of government by those heavenly twins, godly magistracy and ministry.[53] To coin a phrase, the purpose of the 1578 progress appears to have been regime change.

IV

Thus far, I have discussed what went on in Suffolk and Norfolk in the course of the 1578 progress, publicly and politically, as if it had to do only with religion. But 'only with religion' is, for the sixteenth century, an oxymoron. The religious issues were the political issues, and vice versa. I have explored, on an earlier occasion, the considerable political implications of the sequestration and threatened deprivation of the Archbishop of Canterbury, Edmund Grindal, which was interpreted at the time as symbolic of a general reaction in policy.[54] In January 1578, Sir Francis Knollys, a councillor privileged by his blood relationship to the Queen, had written a letter in which religious and political motives were inextricably linked: 'The avoiding of her Majesty's danger doth consist in the preventing of the conquest of the Low Countries betimes; secondly, in preventing of the revolt of Scotland from her Majesty's devotion unto the French and the Queen of Scots; and thirdly, in the timely preventing of the contemptuous growing of the disobedient papists here in England.' He added: 'But if the bishop of Canterbury shall be deprived, then up starts the pride and the practice of the papists. And then King Richard the Second's men [i.e. flatterers

---

[50] *The Papers of Nathaniel Bacon*, ii. 20; *Calendar of State Papers, Domestic Series, Addenda, 1566–1579*, ed. Mary Anne Everett Green (London: HMSO, 1871), 548.

[51] A draft letter from Bacon to Leicester (Folger Shakespeare Library, Bacon Papers). I owe this reference to Hassell Smith.

[52] William Gurnall, *The Magistrates Pourtraiture* (London: printed for Ralph Smith, 1656), 38.

[53] Patrick Collinson, *The Religion of Protestants: The Church in English Society, 1559–1625* (Oxford: Clarendon Press, 1982); Patrick Collinson, 'Magistracy and Ministry: A Suffolk Miniature', in Collinson, *Godly People: Essays on English Protestantism and Puritanism* (London: Hambledon Press, 1983), 445–66.

[54] Patrick Collinson, 'The Downfall of Archbishop Grindal and its Place in Elizabethan Political and Ecclesiastical History', in Collinson, *Godly People*, 371–97.

and false counsellors] will flock into Court apace and will show themselves in their colours.'⁵⁵

The politics of the perilous situation in the Low Countries, a conflict suffused with religion, was what mainly preoccupied Elizabeth's ministers as they trailed around behind and before her. When Leicester complained, from Bury St Edmunds, that conference with the Queen was but seldom and slender, it was that politics to which he referred. If what happened in the summer of 1578 in East Anglia, the most prosperous of all English regions, would determine its politics for the next century, what was at stake in the Netherlands, the most advanced economy of the world of its time, was the future of Europe itself for the next three hundred years.⁵⁶ In the immediate aftermath of the disastrous defeat of Gembloux, before which a united and embryonic Netherlands state had seemed a realistic possibility, the Privy Council was as nearly united as it could ever be on the need to come to the aid of the Dutch, and to prop up the shaky fortunes of William of Orange. Even Sir Nicholas Bacon, hardly a Puritan hothead, wrote: 'I see no way so sure for your Majesty as to keep the Prince of Orange in heart and life.'⁵⁷ The immediate need was for money, and it was money, or the lack of it, which dominated the diplomatic correspondence of that summer. But the decision to intervene had already been taken, certainly by Leicester and his friends. The Queen was of another persuasion, and military intervention would be delayed for another seven years. As early as 1577, rumour had it that Leicester was about to cross the North Sea with an expeditionary force: 'This is his full determination, but yet unknown unto her Highness, neither shall she be acquainted with it until she be fully resolved to send.'⁵⁸ Elizabeth, of course, was not so resolved, and the result has been called a set of 'strange diplomatic quadrilles'.⁵⁹

The interventionist majority on the Privy Council stood between what might be called the militant tendency on the left and on the right the conservatism, religious and otherwise, of, amongst others, the Queen, just as it did in addressing the religious differences in Norfolk and Suffolk. William Davison was Ambassador in the Netherlands, and very much part of the militant tendency. In his dispatches to the Queen he allowed his own ideological commitment to colour his advice. When he cooperated with the Puritan divine Walter Travers in establishing a presbyterian form of worship in the church of the English merchants in Antwerp, Sir Francis Walsingham warned him: 'If you knew with what difficulty we retain what we have, and that the seeking of more might hazard

⁵⁵ Knollys to Secretary Wilson, 9 Jan. 1578; British Library, London [BL], Harleian MS 6992, no. 44, fo. 89.

⁵⁶ Charles Wilson, *Queen Elizabeth and the Revolt of the Netherlands* (London: Macmillan, 1970), 43.

⁵⁷ NA, SP 12/115/24. See Robert Tittler, *Nicholas Bacon: The Making of a Tudor Statesman* (London: Cape, 1976), 168–86.

⁵⁸ NA, SP 15/25/35.   ⁵⁹ Wilson, *Queen Elizabeth and the Revolt of the Netherlands*, 59.

(according to man's understanding) that, you would then, Mr Davison, deal warily in this time, when policy carries more sway than zeal.'[60] A few days earlier, Walsingham had had occasion to write to Davison: 'You shall do well hereafter to forbear to set down your private opinion in the public letters you send us the Secretaries, for that some give out that you are more curious in setting down your own discourses (a matter not incident to your charge) than in searching out the bottom of the proceedings there and advertising such particularities as were fit for Her Majesty's knowledge.'[61] Secretary Wilson wrote: 'You are to be commanded, and bound to follow the bounds of your charge by just limitation. And, although things be sometimes ordered much against your mind, yet you must submit yourself to the same.'[62] Davison, 'I living here where I see and observe how things pass',[63] thought that he knew what had to be done: keep out the French, drive out the Spaniards, and secure the cause of religion and liberty. But, he added, 'I do live here utterly ignorant of the success of things in our Court.'[64]

Throughout the months of the progress, Walsingham, with Lord Cobham, a finely balanced duo of Protestant and near-Catholic, was himself in the Nether-lands, engaged in a critical diplomatic mission ostensibly aimed at pacifying and neutralizing this region, but with more than one agenda, a mission which was so frustrating, as the Queen continually and repeatedly reneged on what many on that side of the North Sea were expecting of her, that by September he was on the verge of resignation, resolved to give up diplomacy as a bad job: 'God send me well to return and I will hereafter take my leave of foreign service.'[65] He whimsically suggested that he and Cobham would be hanged on their return, he hoped after due trial, where the gravest charge would be that they had had more regard for the Queen's honour and safety than for her finances. 'There is a difference between serving with a cheerful and languishing mind.'[66] Those travelling with the Queen shared his deep frustration, so that the letters passing between Walsingham in Antwerp and the court in East Anglia are some of the best evidence we have of the deep division between the Queen and her Privy Council on the most salient issue in foreign policy. Never before or after were the inmost thoughts of Privy Counsellors committed to paper as they were in the summer of 1578, unless it was at the time of the trial of Mary Queen of Scots eight years later, when Walsingham was moved to write: 'I would to God

[60] Conyers Read, *Mr Secretary Walsingham and the Policy of Queen Elizabeth*, 3 vols. (Oxford, Clarendon Press, 1925), ii. 265.

[61] Walsingham to Davison, 2 May 1578 (*Relations politiques*, ed. de Lettenhove, x. 438–9).

[62] Wilson to Davison, 6 May 1578 (ibid. 449–50).

[63] Davison to Walsingham, 11 May 1578 (ibid. 461).

[64] Davison to Walsingham and Wilson, 8 May 1578 (ibid. 453–5).

[65] Ibid. 813–19. See Walsingham to Heneage, 2 Sept. 1578: 'God send me well to return, and I will henceforth take my leave of foreign service': Read, *Mr Secretary Walsingham*, i. 422.

[66] Walsingham to Hatton, Walsingham to Thomas Randolph, both 29 July 1578; *Relations politiques*, ed. de Lettenhove, x. 664–5; quoted in Read, *Mr Secretary Walsingham*, i. 393–4.

her Majesty would be content to refer these things to them that can best judge of them, as other princes do.'[67] Normally the Ambassador, Davison, would have been in regular communication with the Secretaries of State, Walsingham and Sir Thomas Wilson. But with the principal Secretary of State thrust into the unwelcome role of ambassador, it was Walsingham himself who was corresponding with Burghley, Leicester, Sussex, and the up-and-coming star, Christopher Hatton.

When Leicester came down from Buxton to join the progress in late July, he told Walsingham that the Queen's mind had recently changed, and that he had gone almost beyond the limits of the protocols of counsel in trying to persuade her where her best interests lay, Walsingham hoping that his 'wonted manner of plainness in causes that so deeply touch Her Majesty' would have the desired effect.[68] Burghley wrote in similar terms from Audley End on 29 July: 'All this and much more alleged with all manner of ernestness and importunity, to her displeasure . . . A strange thing it is to see God's goodness, so abundantly offered for Her Majesty's surety, to be so daintily hearkened unto.'[69] On 6 August, the Earl of Sussex wrote from Bury: 'It resteth in God to dispose her heart as shall please him.' Sussex thought that by trying to please the Queen there was a risk of dividing 'the good of her from the good of the realm, and so the ill of her from the ill of the realm', which in the end would deceive both her and the realm.[70] Plain speaking from someone on the far right of our politico-religious spectrum! The next day Leicester wrote to Walsingham of the Queen: 'It is no small alteration I find in Her Majesty's disposition . . . How loth she is to come to any manner of dealing that way, specially to be at any charges, it is very strange.'[71] On 9 August, Secretary Wilson wrote from Thetford: 'Temporising hath been thought heretofore good policy. There was never so dangerous a time as this is, and temporising will no longer serve.'[72]

On the same day, Burghley wrote to the ambassadors: 'It is at this present determined here that, if, upon your answer, necessity shall induce Her Majesty to send forces, my Lord of Lecester will come over without delay and the army shal follow. Nevertheless, though this be for the present ernestly meant, I can assure nothing, but this only that I am here uncertain of much.'[73] Leicester told Davison that at Norwich they were almost close enough to hear 'the voice of that people'. 'Well', he commented, 'God help them and us too, fearing our need will

---

[67] J. E. Neale, *Queen Elizabeth* (London: Jonathan Cape, 1934), 274.
[68] Leicester to Walsingham, 20 July 1578, Walsingham to Leicester, 23 July 1578 (*Relations politiques*, ed. de Lettenhove, x. 613–15, 630).
[69] Burghley to Cobham and Walsingham, 29 July 1578 (ibid. 659–61).
[70] Sussex to Walsingham, 6 Aug. 1578 (ibid. 696–7).
[71] Leicester to Walsingham (ibid. 678–80). This letter is dated 1 Aug. in de Lettenhove.
[72] Wilson to Walsingham, 9 Aug. 1578 (ibid. 710–11).
[73] Burghley to Cobham and Walsingham, 9 Aug. 1578 (ibid. 710).

be more than theirs.'[74] On 29 August, Leicester wrote to Walsingham: 'It were needless to discourse at large to you what dealings here hath been on all sides to further this good cause, because there followeth so small fruit thereof.'[75] Two days later, Burghley told Walsingham that 'we of her council are forced greatly to offend [the Queen] in these and Scotland matters'.[76] By early September, Walsingham was warning Burghley that by whatever advice the Queen had been directed to deal so hardly with the Dutch, 'depending as they do chiefly upon her favour in their necessity', the result would prove so perilous to herself and to the reputation of her realm 'that she will curse them that were authors of the advice when she perceives that they had more regard to some private profit... than to her safety'.[77] I think that this was aimed at Sussex, or at Hatton, who was finding that to be an echo to the Queen's thoughts and fears was a safe road to advancement.

V

Thus far I have not mentioned the role of François, duc d'Alençon and Anjou, 'Monsieur'. Yet Anjou, in his absence, was central to the politics of the progress, as he was to the diplomacy of the English ambassadors, which was aimed at preventing him from filling the dangerous vacuum in the Netherlands by coming to terms with the Estates.[78] His representatives were part of the progress, witnesses to all that went on. What did Anjou signify? Would he keep the French out of the Netherlands, or would he draw them in? Did policy demand that the Queen marry Anjou, or would his role in the Netherlands be an alternative to marriage? Was Anjou serious in his marriage overtures, or was he double-dealing? Was the Queen engaging in sincere courtship behind the backs of her ministers? The letters passing to and fro in July to September 1578 make it clear that no one at the heart of government had any idea how to answer those questions. Sometimes Anjou was seen as part of the problem, sometimes as the solution. When Walsingham wrote to Burghley on 28 August, it is clear that he was thoroughly confused: 'I find that Venus is presently ascendant in your climate. But when I consider the retrograde aspects that the present cause in hand is subject unto, I can hope after no great good. I pray God there ensue no harm thereof.'[79] William Davison made it clear, in all his dispatches, that he regarded Anjou as bad news. For the Dutch, Davison reported, it was 'a question in policy very hard to discuss whether were better to accept or reject him... The

---

[74] Leicester to Davison, 18 Aug. 1578 (ibid. 741).
[75] Leicester to Walsingham, 29 Aug. 1578 (ibid. 772–3).
[76] Burghley to Walsingham, 31 Aug. 1578 (ibid. 783).
[77] Walsingham to Burghley, 2 Sept. 1578, quoted in Read, *Mr Secretary Walsingham*, i. 416–18.
[78] Read, *Mr Secretary Walsingham*, i. 373–422.
[79] Walsingham to Burghley, 28 Aug. 1578 (*Relations politiques*, ed. de Lettenhove, x. 766–7).

question is then what shall be done with him.'[80] Walsingham believed that
Monsieur was deceiving the Queen.[81] Leicester's advice was that Walsingham
should neither seem to favour nor to oppose the marriage, since the Queen's own
intentions were obscure.[82] Sussex was no less sceptical.[83] But in mid-August,
Walsingham told Leicester that 'the match were not to be misliked, seeing the
necessity Her Majesty and the realm hath of the same'.[84] Yet he would be loath
'to lay any great wager on the matter'.[85] But in writing to Walsingham in late
August, Leicester expressed regret that the Queen had done nothing to satisfy
Monsieur's expectation 'in the matter of marriage', which might have given her
some security. Beyond that he had no advice to offer.[86] Just before she left
Norwich, Elizabeth received advice from Sussex about the benefits which might
grow 'by this marriage at this time', and about the perils which would follow 'if
she married not at all'.[87]

VI

To marry not at all? It was in the cultural context of the 1578 progress,
and in Thomas Churchyard's Norwich, that Elizabeth I was first publicly
celebrated as the Virgin Queen. The allegorical symbolism was transparent in the
entertainment staged by Churchyard on the fourth day of the visit, 'Tuesday's
Device'. Churchyard claimed that this playlet was almost improvised, taking
the opportunity of the Queen passing on a certain route to her dinner, and
perhaps seizing the advantage of one of the few fine days in a sodden week,
when most events were rained off. Churchyard, disregarding the 'many doubts'
expressed, 'many men persuaded to tarry a better time', 'hastily prepared my
boys and men, with all their furnitures'. But there must have been more to it
than that. The plot concerned a series of encounters between Venus and her
son Cupid, both 'thrust out of Heaven', a grey-headed Philosopher, and Dame
Chastity, accompanied by her maids, Modesty, Temperance, Good Exercise,
and Shamefastness. Elizabeth was thoroughly involved in the action. Chastity,
claiming that the Queen had chosen the best life, that is, one of celibacy, handed
her Cupid's bow to shoot with as she pleased, since 'none could wound her
highness's heart'. 'Then sith (o Queen) chaste life is thus thy choice, | And that

[80] Davison to Leicester, 18 July 1578 (ibid. 606).
[81] Walsingham to Leicester, 29 July 1578 (ibid. 662–3).
[82] Leicester to Walsingham, 1 Aug. 1578 (ibid. 679–80); quoted in Read, *Mr Secretary Walsingham*, i. 402 n. 3.
[83] Sussex to Walsingham, 6 Aug. 1578 (*Relations politiques*, ed. de Lettenhove, x. 696–7).
[84] Walsingham to Leicester, 18 Aug. 1578 (ibid. 744); quoted in Read, *Mr Secretary Walsingham*, i. 402–3.
[85] Walsingham to Leicester, 28 Aug. 1578 (*Relations politiques*, ed. de Lettenhove, x. 765).
[86] Leicester to Walsingham, 29 Aug. 1578 (ibid. 772–3).
[87] Sussex to Walsingham, 29 Aug. 1578 (ibid. 774–5).

thy heart is free from bondage yoke, | Thou shalt (good Queen) by my consent and voice, | Have half the spoil, take either bow or cloak.' The song sung by Chastity's 'maids' reiterated in line after line 'chaste life', contrasted with 'lewd life'. 'Chaste life a precious pearl, | doth shin as bright as Sun.' In Bernard Garter's account of the Saturday pageant, in which Cupid's golden arrow was again handed to the Queen, Diana, presenting her with a bow and silver-tipped arrows, used the phrase 'Virgin Queen', which we do not find in Churchyard: 'Who ever found on Earth a constant friend, | That may compare with this my Virgin Queen?' 'The Virgin's state DIANA still did praise.' Garter's account of the Monday proceedings contains a further reference to the Queen as 'a Virgin pure, which is, and ever was'.[88]

Churchyard claimed that, following his Tuesday show, 'I had gracious words of the Queen openly and often pronounced by her Highness.' Before reading on, he wrote, 'you must thoroughly note what my discourse thereof hath been'.[89] Whose 'discourse' was it? Who had put Churchyard up to it? It is easy to conclude, as Susan Doran has done, that the Norwich shows were devised by opponents of the Anjou match, perhaps in particular by Leicester, whose opposition to the match would become rather more clear in 1579 and 1580; perhaps even that the whole libretto of the progress, Leicester's libretto, had this anti-Anjou purpose.[90] But as we have seen, in August 1578 everyone, including Leicester, was in at least two minds about Anjou. As was the Queen, which may explain why she congratulated Churchyard on his drama of Venus, Cupid, and Chastity. We can assume that a marriage between Elizabeth and Leicester was no longer likely, and had not been, at least since 1575 and Kenilworth. That was not the message of Philip Sidney's masque 'The Lady of May', performed in the Queen's presence at Wanstead earlier in the summer of 1578; although the contested politics of intervention in the Netherlands probably was.[91] That Leicester was about to marry the widowed Countess of Essex was a secret already leaking in several directions, although not apparently in the direction of Gabriel Harvey, for all that he was Leicester's man.[92] Book II of his *Gratulationum Valdinensium libri quatuor*, presented to the Queen in manuscript at Audley End and in print at Hadham on 15 September, was one of the last literary attempts to promote a marriage between Elizabeth and Leicester.[93] What was going on in Norwich during those rainy August days was an expression of widely shared doubts and fears about the Anjou match. Opinions ranged from an open-minded scepticism

[88] *REED: Norwich*, 304–14, 261, 275, 287.   [89] Ibid. 305–6.

[90] Doran, 'Juno vs Diana', 270–2; Doran, *Monarchy and Matrimony*, 150–2.

[91] Doran, 'Juno vs Diana', 269–70.

[92] On 22 Aug. 1578, William Fulke, master of Pembroke Hall, wrote to the Fellows from Norwich, instructing them to renew Harvey's fellowship for another year, at 'the ernest request' of Leicester. *Letter-Book of Gabriel Harvey, A.D. 1573–1580*, ed. E. J. L. Scott (London: Camden Society, 1884), 88.

[93] Stern, *Gabriel Harvey*, 40–6.

(which the Queen certainly shared) to the downright hostility of those who thought like Davison, and his close friend John Stubbs, whose *The discoverie of a gaping gulf wherinto England is like to be swallowed by an other French mariage* would be published exactly a year later.[94] Stubbs had written to Davison on 30 April 1578: 'The Lord knit us faster and faster in our faith and love and hope of our everlasting life', wishing him 'happy success' in his 'godly endeavors': the authentic voice of political Puritanism, which was one of the most insistent voices of that summer of 1578.[95]

VII

I end with a coda. Among his other qualities, the Earl of Leicester was given to writing revealing letters, self-promoting, self-protecting, self-righteous, full of injured pride. On 27 September 1578, Leicester wrote such a letter to his colleague and, I think we can say, friend, Lord Burghley. The letter had to do with matters concerning the Mint, on which Leicester had not been properly consulted, perhaps because in July he had been out of touch, at Buxton. Hatton wrote to Burghley on 28 September saying that he had heard that he was in trouble with Leicester, 'his taking offence towards you in that he was not made privy to this last warrant for the coining of money', and that in Hatton's opinion it was much ado about nothing, which does indeed seem to have been the case.[96] Nevertheless, Leicester believed that he had been shabbily treated, something he could neither understand nor accept. He and Burghley had been together for weeks, so why had nothing been said? 'For we began our service with our sovereign together, and have long continued hitherto together, and touching your fortune I am sure your self cannot have a thought that ever I was enemy to it.' 'Your lordship hath been acquainted with me now almost thirty years, and these twenty years in service together. What opinions you have in deed of me, I may for these considerations alleged somewhat doubt, though I promise you I know no cause in the world in my self that I have given you other than good.' No one had ever deserved so well at Burghley's hands as Leicester. So why this opposition? 'Well, my Lord, you may suppose this to be a strange humour in me to write thus and in this sort to you, having never done the like before.'[97] The notion of Conyers Read that Burghley and Leicester represented polar opposites in the Elizabethan polity, forever repelling each other, fails to convince. But this letter is evidence that it was always an uneasy relationship.

[94] *John Stubbs's 'Gaping Gulf' with Letters and Other Relevant Documents*, ed. Lloyd E. Berry (Charlottesville: University of Virginia Press, 1968).
  [95] Ibid. 106–7.
  [96] Hatton to Burghley, 28 Sept. 1578; *HMC . . . Salisbury*, ii (1888), 208.
  [97] Leicester to Burghley, 27 Sept. 1578 (NA, SP 12/125/73).

Yet it is altogether understandable that Leicester should have been agitated on 27 September. Four days earlier, he had entertained the Queen to lunch at his great house at Wanstead, the final event in that marathon of a progress, which had started out ten weeks earlier. Three days before that, he had been quietly married, in that same house, to Lettice, Countess of Essex. The Queen was not supposed to know and she may not have known. Everyone must have been feeling the strain of those long July, August, and September days: the strains of travelling and of hectic and mostly abortive diplomacy. As Gabriel Harvey's enemy Thomas Nashe might have put it, Leicester's odd letter was that summer's last will and testament. In that entertainment, Nashe's Summer declares that he would have already died, but that 'Eliza' had bidden him to 'live and linger' until 'her joyful progress was expired'.[98]

---

[98] Charles Nicholl, *A Cup of News: The Life of Thomas Nashe* (London: Routledge & Kegan Paul, 1984), 135–6.

8

The 'I' of the Beholder: Thomas Churchyard and the 1578 Norwich Pageant

David M. Bergeron

The Prologue speaker in Shakespeare's *Troilus and Cressida* says that he comes 'armed, but not in confidence | Of author's pen or actor's voice'.[1] Yet Thomas Churchyard, in his account of Queen Elizabeth I's progress through Norfolk and Suffolk and particularly the pageant presented to her at Norwich in August 1578, can claim that he comes confidently with author's pen, actor's voice, and beholder's perspective as he constructs the text. In fact, we see (hear) the author's voice immediately on the title page: 'Deuised by THOMAS CHVRCHYARDE, Gent. with diuers shewes of his own inuention sette out at Norwich'.[2] Churchyard invented several of the pageant devices in Norwich, he acted in them, he reports what he has seen and heard about them, and he puts together this elaborate text. He self-consciously constructs his persona, the 'I' of the beholder who fashions his discursive discourse about this pageant. This essay argues that Churchyard astutely, relentlessly, and purposely shapes the pageant text to put himself in the best possible light as reporter and author. Throughout the text, he creates a self-image that conveys his accomplishment and his moral concern for the commonwealth.

As Daryl Palmer reminds us, 'Unlike the playwright who produces a text for performance, the author of the progress narrative asserts that his text will do business in the culture, recording the culture's practices of hospitality and the rewards of royal power.'[3] Churchyard ratifies this observation through his

---

[1] See 'Prologue', ll. 23–4, in *The Arden Shakespeare: Complete Works*, ed. Richard Proudfoot, Ann Thompson, and David Scott Kastan (London: Thomson Learning, 1998; rev. edn. 2001), 1155.

[2] Thomas Churchyard, *A Discovrse of the Queenes Maiesties entertainment in Suffolk and Norffolk* (London: Henrie Bynneman, 1578), sig. A1ʳ. Most subsequent references to this work will be noted parenthetically in the main text above. For a discussion of this pageant and the others mentioned here, see my *English Civic Pageantry 1558–1642*, 2nd edn., rev. the author (Tempe: Arizona State Medieval and Renaissance Studies, 2003).

[3] Daryl W. Palmer, *Hospitable Performances: Dramatic Genre and Cultural Practices in Early Modern England* (West Lafayette, Ind.: Purdue University Press, 1992), 123, and, for his discussion

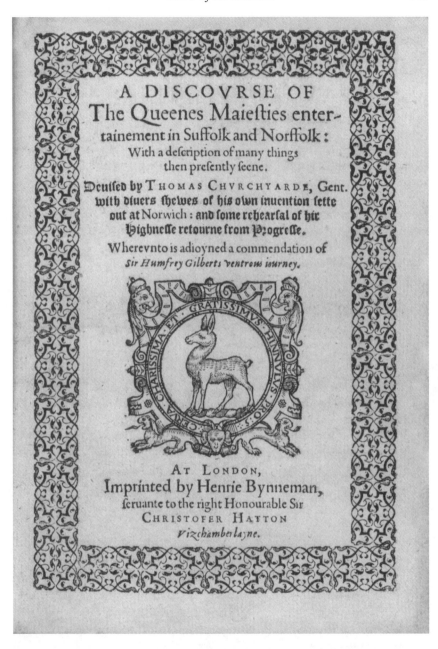

Figure 8.1. Title page of Thomas Churchyard's *Discovrse of the Queenes Maiesties entertainement in Suffolk and Norffolk* (London: Henrie Bynneman, 1578). (By permission of the British Library, London, shelfmark G.11238)

embracing a social purpose. He also senses the boundaries of the discourse appropriate to a pageant text. But for a writer 'well bounde to wryte', as he says near the end of the text, we can readily understand his desire to test the bounds of discourse (L4^r). Churchyard in many ways is shaping the nature of the Elizabethan pageant text, stretching its boundaries and enlarging its scope, offering a discourse of diverse parts and multiple purposes.

This pageant text, a multi-part discourse full of social and moral purpose, celebrates what Churchyard calls a 'commendation of courtesie' with its focus on the political and practical purposes of 'hospitalitie' (B2^r). In reading this text, we latter-day readers learn that we stand in the presence of the beholder's eye and benefit from this reliable 'I' who reports and constructs this text. With this 'I' we cross social boundaries (the author/actor conversing with no less than the Queen), and feel bound to the festive community that first engaged his artistic services. Through his carefully constructed persona, Churchyard guides and binds us to his writerly purpose in this discursive discourse. In what follows, I shall examine the cultural contexts, Churchyard's self-conscious prefatory material, and his construction of the text. Through his efforts, Churchyard fashions himself through the text, making Stephen Greenblatt's point that self-fashioning comes through language.[4]

I

Certainly the trip to Suffolk and Norfolk took Queen Elizabeth far beyond her usual geographical limits for a summer provincial tour (see Map 7.1). Mary Hill Cole and Patrick Collinson, in particular, have called attention to the complex religious reasons for Elizabeth's trip.[5] As always, such a progress also carried with it ongoing political issues—chiefly, in this case, the question of whether England ought to intervene in the United Provinces' revolt against Spain. Lurking in the background of the eastern 1578 progress, the marriage question also received attention, as C. E. McGee and Patrick Collinson point out elsewhere in this volume.[6]

---

of pageants, pp. 119–55. For another discussion of pageant texts, see Wendy Wall, *The Imprint of Gender: Authorship and Publication in the English Renaissance* (Ithaca, NY: Cornell University Press, 1993), 111–67. For a discussion of prefatory matter in dramatic texts, specifically epistles dedicatory and addresses to readers, see my *Textual Patronage in English Drama, 1570–1640* (Aldershot: Ashgate, 2006).

[4] Stephen Greenblatt, *Renaissance Self-Fashioning: From More to Shakespeare* (Chicago: University of Chicago Press, 1980), 9.

[5] Mary Hill Cole, *The Portable Queen: Elizabeth I and the Politics of Ceremony* (Amherst: University of Massachusetts Press, 1999), 141–4; and Patrick Collinson, pp. 122–41, above. A thorough description of the 1578 trip also can be found in Zillah Dovey, *An Elizabethan Progress: The Queen's Journey into East Anglia, 1578* (Madison, NJ: Farleigh Dickinson University Press, 1996).

[6] For McGee's essay, see pp. 104–21, above; for Collinson's essay, see pp. 122–41, above.

The cultural contexts for this progress obviously also include other pageant entertainments, and I start with Churchyard's earlier account of the entertainment for Elizabeth's reception into Bristol in 1574. The text for this entertainment comes as the last item in *The Firste Parte of Churchyardes Chippes, contayning twelve severall Labours* (London, 1575; 2nd edn., London, 1578, the year of the Norwich show). Churchyard dedicates the entire *Chippes* to Sir Christopher Hatton, but the pageant text itself does not carry its own dedication. In fact, this text, which Churchyard calls *The Whole Order howe oure Soveraigne Lady Queene Elizabeth, was received into the Cite of Bristow,* looks rather spare and straightforward. For example, Churchyard plunges right into the show: 'At the High Crosse, in a disguised manner, stood Faem, very orderly set forth, and spoke as followeth.'[7] He offers no elaborate description or commentary, mainly providing only the speeches and sufficient connectives—nothing in the way of rumination about the events and their social or political significance. This pageant text resembles many other Elizabethan ones in its simplicity and efficiency. By 1578, however, as we shall see, Churchyard has learned to create a text with multiple functions and one that revels in digressions, expositions, and moral conclusions. The 'I' has become a beholder with a purpose, a writer willing to put himself forward and one supremely aware that he is fashioning a literary text. This text will simultaneously report the event and transcend it, creating what I have elsewhere called 'textual performance'.[8]

The context for Churchyard's Norwich pageant includes another text, *The Ioyfvll Receyuing of the Queenes most excellent Maiestie into hir Highnesse Citie of NORWICH* (STC 11627), also printed by Bynneman in 1578. Bernard Garter, self-described 'Citizen of London', dedicates the text to Sir Owen Hopton, 'Lieutenante of hir highnes Tower of London', who, according to Garter, had requested such a report of the pageant.[9] Presumably, Garter did not initiate the project, but instead responded to Hopton's desire. Mainly on the strength of this dedication, the editors of the *Short Title Catalogue* grant Garter authorship of the text, though the title page indicates no author.[10] Thus, the complementary text for the Norwich pageant blurs the matter of authorship—unlike Churchyard's, the title page of which proudly announces him as author. Garter's text includes the designation 'FINIS B.G.' after each speech or section which he wrote, but curiously resorts to the passive construction to introduce the speech that he

[7] *The Progresses and Public Processions of Queen Elizabeth*, ed. John Nichols, 2nd edn., 3 vols. (London: John Nichols, 1823), i. 396.
[8] See my 'Stuart Civic Pageants and Textual Performance', *Renaissance Quarterly*, 51 (1998), 163–83.
[9] Bernard Garter, *The Ioyfvll Receyuing of the Queenes most excellent Maiestie into hir Highnesse Citie of NORWICH* (London: Henry Bynneman, 1578), sig. A2ʳ. Most subsequent references to this work will be noted parenthetically in the main text above.
[10] *A Short-Title Catalogue of Books Printed in England, Scotland and Ireland and of English Books Printed Abroad, 1475–1640*, ed. A. W. Pollard and G. R. Redgrave, 2nd edn., rev. W. A. Jackson, F. S. Ferguson, and Katherine Pantzer, 3 vols. (London: Bibliographical Society, 1986), i. 515.

actually gave to the Queen: 'the speache was thus vttered vnto hir' (E4ʳ).[11] The
text also includes designations for the sections prepared by Henry Goldingham.
Readers thus gain information, but the effect of this publication strategy lessens
the impact of authorship.

Garter does provide an absolutely crucial account of the dramatic festivities in
Norwich; indeed, his and Churchyard's texts must be placed together in order
to get a full picture of what took place.[12] For example, Garter offers an extensive
description of the royal entry that took place in Norwich on 16 August, when
Elizabeth arrived. Churchyard, by contrast, includes only a song and activity at
the end of that day. Likewise, Garter's text contains an elaborate description of
the masque presented on Thursday night, containing various mythological gods
and goddesses. Churchyard remains silent about this event. One also detects a
generous spirit in Garter's several references to Churchyard, as if alerting us to
the necessity and desirability of conferring with Churchyard's text. For example,
Garter writes, 'Upon the Monday following, M. Churchyard brought Mercurie
in a gallant coatch' (C3ᵛ), adding that on Tuesday Churchyard 'performed a very
prety pleasant shew before hir highnesse without S. Benets gates' (C3ᵛ–C4ʳ).
Garter notes how bad weather cancelled Churchyard's effort for one day. And
he observes about the Queen's departure from Norwich on Friday, 22 August:
'within a flight shot or little more whereof, Maister Churchyarde had another
shewe, whiche I leaue to himself to vtter: bycause my hope is, he will manifest that
among the rest shortly' (E4ᵛ). We can therefore infer that the Garter text, which
seems to anticipate Churchyard's, was written first. This is corroborated by the
Stationers' Register, which records an entry on 30 August 1578 for Garter's text;
nearly a month later, on 20 September, it shows an entry for Churchyard's text.[13]
The Ioyfvll Receyuing thus seems to pave the way for Churchyard's account, one
in which this author will repeatedly call attention to himself as he indulges in a
version of self-fashioning.

Clearly Churchyard has an authorial vision, starting with the title page, the first
pageant text that reveals the author's identity. He seems fascinated with the idea
of 'discourse', a word that he uses some ten times in the text,[14] a frequency that

[11] The text of Churchyard's speech to the Queen is framed by passive constructions, for the
usual 'ꜰɪɴɪꜱ B.G.' is, in this case, supplemented by the following: '*and spoken by himselfe, to whome
hir Maiestie saide: We thanke you hartely*' (E4ᵛ).

[12] The 1578 Norwich pageant is unique amongst Elizabethan civic entertainments in having
been commemorated by two printed accounts. In this respect, however, it echoes the Earl of
Leicester's Kenilworth festivities of 1575, which also had been the subject of two printed pamphlets
(and alluded to in a third, now lost). As with the Norwich pageant texts, the printed descriptions
of the Kenilworth entertainments provide a description of the festivities from the points of view
of both spectator and deviser and thus, when read together, provide a wealth of descriptive detail.
See Stephen Orgel, *The Jonsonian Masque* (Cambridge, Mass.: Harvard University Press, 1967;
repr. New York: Columbia University Press, 1981), 37.

[13] *A Transcript of the Registers of the Company of Stationers of London, 1554–1640 A.D.*, ed.
Edward Arber, 5 vols. (London: printed privately, 1875–94), ii. 336, 338.

[14] See, e.g., sigs. A1ʳ, A2ᵛ, A4ʳ, B1ʳ, B2ʳ, D1ʳ, D1ᵛ, E3ʳ, F4ᵛ (twice), G4ᵛ (twice), H1ʳ, and L4ᵛ.

I do not find matched by other Elizabethan pageant texts.[15] He seems to intend multiple meanings of 'discourse', as attested by other sixteenth-century usage: a narrative or account, serious written treatment of a subject, and a succession of time, events, and action.[16] Although this may be a pageant text, Churchyard envisions serious purposes for it. We can see his conscious division of the text, a measure of a structure befitting a worthy document and a specialized meaning of 'discourse' as Churchyard understands the term. Just as *Churchyardes Chippes* had its twelve parts, so here the writer divides prefatory material from text proper. Within the text itself, Churchyard, with the cooperation of the printer, imposes headings for each day's entertainment, as in 'Mondayes Device', 'Tuesdayes Device', and so forth, each beginning on a new page. Printer's ornaments help delineate these divisions further.[17] In short, Churchyard wants the text to appear in a certain way, creating an impression of a worthwhile text, subject to logical divisions—the sort of structure a 'discourse' would have. When we behold this text, we see a writer at work busily shaping the appearance of it. The 'I' wants us to appreciate and appropriate this discourse, sent, as the epistle dedicatory says, as a 'signe of good will' (A2^r).

II

Another sign of self-conscious authorship can be found in Churchyard's prefatory material—an epistle dedicatory and an address to the reader, forms that had become increasingly common in other kinds of books, as Wendy Wall has richly documented.[18] Indeed, Churchyard's Norwich text is not only the first civic pageant text to have the author's name on the title page, but also the first to include such extensive prefatory matter. These self-conscious moves anticipate what would become, in the Jacobean period, more commonplace, as for example in the printed texts of the Lord Mayors' Shows, starting in 1612 with Thomas Dekker's *Troi-Nova Triumphans*.[19] All such prefaces reflect a writer fully aware of constructing a book that puts him front and centre. These prefaces reflect

---

[15] The word does not appear at all in Churchyard's account of the Queen's 1574 visit to Bristol, while it is used only once in Garter's account of the 1578 Norwich entry (sig. C2^v).

[16] Significantly, Churchyard's use of 'discourse' in the sense of 'a dissertation, treatise, homily, sermon, or the like' pre-dates the earliest such usage (1581) recorded in the *Oxford English Dictionary*. Churchyard's understanding of 'discourse' as 'a narrative, tale, account' is also comparatively early, the first such usage recorded in the *OED* being Sir Thomas Smith's of 1572. See *OED*, 2nd edn., iv. 750–1.

[17] See, e.g., sigs. C3^v, E3^r, G3^r, and H1^v.   [18] Wall, *The Imprint of Gender*, 169–226.

[19] John Marston's *The Malcontent* (1604) is the first significant address to the reader found in a play intended for the public theatre. The 1630s has the largest number of epistles dedicatory in regular playtexts, seeking aristocratic support, despite well-established theatres, audiences, and acting companies. These matters I explore in depth in chapter 2 of my *Textual Patronage in English Drama*, which focuses on prefatory material in masque and pageant texts.

and create a social and literary energy, linked to patronage. They underscore, reinforce, and acknowledge various modes of patronage. Churchyard, helping pave the way for such epistles and addresses, embraces a social purpose in his dedication to Sir Gilbert Gerard, the Queen's Attorney General, and in the address to the reader. The author ponders what binds the community together and how certain moments (such as the pageant entertainment) cross several boundaries. The prefatory material itself helps the reader cross the boundary into the text proper; in it, we hear the author's unmediated voice.

In the epistle dedicatory, Churchyard suggests that this book of the pageants might provide some recreation for a busy man like Gerard. But it also strives to make a 'report' of the Queen's reception in Suffolk and Norfolk with the surrounding circumstances (A2ᵛ). Because, Churchyard writes, 'I sawe most of it, or heard it so credibly rehearsed, as I know it to be true, I meane to make it a mirror and shining glasse, that al the whole land may loke into, or vse it for an example' (A2ᵛ). As Churchyard establishes his *ethos*, he claims that if the pageant can be a 'mirror', then so must be the text itself. And he adds that all shires may see the entertainment here and 'striue to follow this lanterne when occasion is offered' (A3ʳ). Thus, we can see the pageant and the text as both mirror and lamp, reflecting and guiding. Having available a reliable text constitutes the only way to make this culturally and practically possible.

The playwright in the dedication nods in the direction of the text in terms of its faithfulness; he admits his own involvement in writing, several times consciously referring to the 'vse [of] my penne' and 'this exercise of pen' and 'I will boldly hold on my matter which I haue penned' (A3ʳ, A3ᵛ). 'I haue presumed', Churchyard writes, 'to sette out these things, . . . bycause at Norwich I was employed to sette forth some shewes, which heere I haue imprinted, as well those that hir Highnesse sawe not, by meanes of euill weather' (A3ᵛ). This text records what might have been as well as what actually took place; and Churchyard, not typically to be understood as a 'professional' dramatist, has no hesitancy about publishing: indeed, he sees this task as a responsibility, anticipating his final statement about writing: 'I am . . . well *bounde* to wryte' (L4ʳ; emphasis added). He confronts the possible charge that he does 'enterlard this discourse' with words and sentences that 'may seeme to degresse from my purposed cause'; but his judgement, he says, 'is carried by circumstances, to treate at large those things, that shortnesse of speeche will not suffer' (A3ʳ). The writer thus faces head-on a potential complaint by offering a rhetorical rationale for what he has done, allowing the discursive possibilities of discourse. In fact, preparing the pageant text seems to have liberated Churchyard, as it will many of his successors, to explore all kinds of topics through digression and dilation, offering social commentary and a model for behaviour.[20]

---

[20] An earlier example of a digressive pageant text is, of course, the Kenilworth *Letter*, though it—unlike Churchyard's *Discourse*— does not claim to offer a model for behaviour.

As outlined in the epistle dedicatory, the text becomes for Churchyard, then, not only a representation of the event but also a blueprint for other places to imitate when entertaining the Queen, reinforcing the text's social work beyond this pageant. He praises the 'hospitalitie' of the good people of this region (A2ᵛ), and the text becomes 'a guerdon due for their worthy & honest dezerts' (A3ʳ). Churchyard has penned this text 'for those people that dwell farre off the Court, that they may see with what maiestie a Prince raigneth, and with what obedience and loue good Subiectes do receiue hir' (A3ᵛ). In Churchyard's not completely unbiased view, no other entertainment has surpassed this one. His efforts proceed from his moral stance and the good will that he bears to all 'vertuous actions'; therefore, he commends this 'small Booke' to Gerard's good will, joining all those who 'speaketh well' of this courtier (A4ʳ). Churchyard adds, 'I shall find my selfe greatly bound vnto you therefore' (A4ʳ). Binding oneself to a worthy patron defines an ancient and still flourishing system of patronage, especially sought by writers wanting status and protection in this early era of publishing. This text also binds us, as readers, to the community and to the event which it sponsored, as we join the circulation of social energy that the pageant and text spark.

In 'To the Reader', Churchyard concentrates on the social circumstances of the entertainment, developing what he had hinted at in the dedication, suggesting that his effort to provide delight springs from the desire to 'shew thee the good disposition of some people' (B1ʳ). Only tangentially can one claim that he responds to the dramatic entertainment itself. Instead, Churchyard offers a somewhat romanticized and idealized account of social behaviour, of 'people nurtured farre from Courte' who yet 'vse muche courtesie' (B1ʳ). Churchyard will prove 'by the humblenesse of the common people, where lately the Prince hath passed, that if in a manner all ciuilitie were vtterly decayed, it might haue bin found freshly florishing in many of those parties and places specifyed before' (B1ʳ). As soon as the Queen entered 'their boundes', these common people responded with duty and obedience, 'not with feyned ceremonies, but with friendlye entertaynemente' (B1ʳ, B1ᵛ). The Queen crosses the boundaries of geographical location and enters into a bond with the community. The 'inwarde affections of the people', Churchyard insists, were 'playnely expressed by their outward apparance, and manifest curtesies' (B1ᵛ). In Churchyard's view, the Queen has not only been received within 'their boundes', but also within their hearts. In fact, some social boundaries have been blurred by the remarkable behaviour of the people: even in Norwich, 'where the entertainemente was so greate, that all degrees, from the highest to the lowest, were had in such admiration, that it seemed another worlde to beholde' (B1ᵛ). Churchyard has been the 'beholder': his eyes have beheld the event, and his 'I' constructs an account.

The admirable behaviour of these people far from the court serves as a rebuke to the 'stiffe-necked behauiour of some places', Churchyard observes (B1ᵛ). If they but looked on the shires far from court, 'they might soone bee learned to

clappe on more comelynesse, and vse lesse obstinacie' (B2ʳ). Thus Churchyard
continues in this vein in what he calls his 'commendation of courtesie' (B2ʳ).
Only at the end does the playwright turn his attention to the condition of the
text, as Churchyard claims to 'haue rehearsed a peece of those thinges I sawe in
Suffolke and Norffolke, to further thy delight towards the reading of my simple
Booke' (B2ʳ–B2ᵛ). He even promises another book that will presumably provide
'the rest of that Progresse' (B2ᵛ). Churchyard has produced a text in his address
to the reader that has much to do with courtesy, behaviour, and duty but little to
do with the pageant. This becomes a kind of free-standing text that commends
courtesy and provides social discourse that just happens to batten itself onto the
pageant event.

These prefatory documents, unique in civic pageant texts up to this time,
underscore the multi-faceted purposes that dramatists and other writers chose
in writing dedicatory epistles and addresses to readers. In Churchyard's hands,
his 'discourses' display the writer as one who assumes a platform of moral
understanding and instruction. Not so much a rationale for the pageant drama
as a forum for judgement, these prefatory items offer guidance and a transition
into the text proper, preparing us to understand the mirror and lamp functions
of the entertainment itself.

Churchyard, the playwright and social observer, takes the reader into his
confidence in order to comment on behaviour and to exalt the pattern found
among the common folk in distant shires. Clearly, Churchyard fulfils the text's
purpose by 'recording the culture's practices of hospitality and the rewards of
royal power', in Daryl Palmer's words.[21] Commending courtesy and seeing it
embodied first in Sir Gilbert Gerard, the dedicatee of the text, and then in
the citizens of Norfolk and Suffolk, Churchyard constructs a text that surely
complements the state while complimenting social behaviour. All these elements
bind the community of spectators and readers, now prepared to cross the
boundary into the text. Such defines Churchyard's circulation of authority and
energy. His textual economy has everything to do with social purpose and moral
judgement, reinforcing the *ethos* and persona that Churchyard has created, the
'I' of the beholder.

III

From the beginning of the text proper, we find Churchyard conveying several of
the qualities already seen in the prefatory material. The opening three pages, with
their copious details, contrast with the immediate plunging into the speeches of
the Bristol pageant in 1574. In the opening of the Norwich text, Churchyard

---

[21] Palmer, *Hospitable Performances*, 123.

presents himself as a reporter of events, one who engages in a conversation with readers, a moral commentator on the purpose and effect of the entertainments, and an artist whose services the city sought. He also provides the text of the song and speech given at the end of the long first day's entertainment, the fuller account to be found in the Garter text.

The writer takes us into his confidence from the beginning, when he confronts the limits of what he can do: 'To wright of the receiuing of hir highnesse into Suffolke and Norffolke in euery poynte, as matter may moue me, woulde conteyne a great time, in making a iust rehearsall thereof' (B3ʳ). Earlier, in the Dedicatory Epistle, he says, 'I mind to wrighte what truely happeneth' (A3ᵛ). This blurring between 'write' and 'wright' may imply an awareness of the craft involved in shaping this discourse. Churchyard 'will but briefely recite' the events, committing the 'circumstance and manner of the same, to your discretion and iudgement' (B3ʳ). Indeed, as he closes this long introduction, he refers to his intention 'to set forth other workes as tyme will permitte'; such proposed writing 'shall hold you longer tacke, and better please you' (B4ᵛ). Meanwhile, 'I pray you take in worth and good part my little paynes and greate good will, and reade (as your fansie fauoures) the Verses and Deuises that followe' (B4ᵛ). The writer self-consciously recognizes the imagined presence of readers (those referred to as 'you'), contemplates additional writing, and engages in this conversation with the readers. The first-person voice continues from the dedication and address.

'As I hearde': Churchyard several times uses this rhetorical formula,[22] indicating his role as reporter, even of events that he has not personally witnessed. Such happens in the rendition of the preparations and entertainments that occurred in Suffolk. Churchyard has heard of the 200 young gentlemen clad in white velvet and 300 in black velvet coats, along with 1,500 'seruing men' on horseback, all ready for Elizabeth's arrival into Suffolk (B3ʳ). Churchyard has learned of and therefore reports the sumptuous feasting that took place first in Suffolk and then in Norfolk, long before the Queen's arrival in Norwich. These people 'kept great houses', and offered bountiful hospitality to the Queen and others (B3ᵛ). Indeed, it seems that the noblemen of Norfolk sought to outdo their neighbours. Churchyard writes: 'in good sooth (as I haue heard credibly spoken) the bankets and feastes began heere afresh, and all kind of triumphes that might be deuised, were put in practise and proofe' (B3ᵛ). For example, the Earl of Surrey 'did shewe most sumptuous cheere, in whose Parke were speeches well sette out, & a speciall Deuice much commended' (B3ᵛ). Many others, 'whose names I haue not', responded similarly (B3ᵛ).

The Mayor and aldermen of Norwich, meanwhile, had determined that the Queen should be the recipient of shows and devices 'for six dayes togither' and made plans accordingly (B4ʳ). Such preparations and expenditures on the part of Norwich create good will, and their 'courtesie . . . shall remayne in perpetuall

---

22 See, e.g., sigs. B3ʳ, B3ᵛ, D4ᵛ, and G2ᵛ.

memorie, whiles the walles of their Citie standeth' (B4^r). Churchyard writes that he cannot 'but gyue them due laude and reputation, as farre as my penne or reporte may doe them goode, and stretche out theyr credite'—hence, this text (B4^r). Further, this manifestation of hospitality and civic pride has 'taughte and learned all the Townes and Cities in Englande a lesson, howe to behaue themselues in such like seruices and actions' (B4^r). Just as Churchyard had in the prefatory matter found the shining examples of courtesy and hospitality admirable and commendable, so here. The pageant text helps perpetuate memory and underscores the social and moral example that the nobles and citizens have offered, even as it mirrors the prefaces.

In the final section of this 'introduction', Churchyard talks about himself and his involvement with the Norwich planners. But first he explains the text: 'Nowe to returne to the Shewes and purposed matter penned out by me . . . I thoughte it conueniente to printe them in order, as they were inuented' (B4^r). Clearly Churchyard has made an authorial and editorial choice about how the text will be constructed and presented. He also observes that he 'was the fyrste that was called, and came to Norwiche aboute that businesse, and remayned there three long weekes before the Courte came thyther, deuising and studying the best I coulde for the Citie' (B4^r). Churchyard acknowledges the work of others, such as 'Maister Goldingham, Maister Garter, and others, [who] dyd steppe in after, and broughte to passe that alreadye is sette in Print in a Booke' (B4^r). He modestly refers to his own accomplishment, having published this text 'onely that myne honest intente may bee thereby expressed' (B4^r). The writer not only reports on events and draws conclusions about them, but he also celebrates his own artistic 'invention', even as he recognizes the work and text of others. This section of the text thus underscores the multiple tasks that a pageant dramatist might expect to fulfil, including but not limited to preparing dramatic devices and publishing a text.

Churchyard includes a song sung by the 'Waytes and best voyces in the Citie' in the late evening of that first Saturday of Elizabeth's arrival (B4^v). He characterizes the performance as 'maruellous sweete and good', but notes that the 'rudenesse of some ringer of belles did somewhat hinder the noyse and harmonie'—a detail that seems to be an attempt at accuracy and completeness (C1^r). He also tells us of a boy, 'wel and gallantly decked, in a long white roabe of Taffata, a Crimson Skarfe wrought with gold, folded on the Turkishe fashion aboute his browes', who stood at the door of Master Peck's (the Mayor's) house on a scaffold, itself beautifully decorated, Churchyard's eye beholding and recording (C1^r). When the music ended, the boy stepped forward and addressed the Queen in words of generous welcome, asserting that the city belongs to the Queen 'in heart, in word, and deede' (C1^v). Churchyard adds: '*The Boy therevpon flang vp his Garlande, and the Queenes Highnesse sayd*, This Deuice is fine' (C1^v). The writer has captured a rare moment of presumably direct quotation from the Queen, thereby enhancing his account, making it rich with concrete detail. The

Queen tarried a bit and then moved on to the cathedral. Sunday she spent with 'Sermons, and laudable exercises', Churchyard reports (C1ᵛ).

But the dramatist spent the day watching for a 'conuenient season, where and how might be vttered the things that were prepared for pastime' (C1ᵛ). Monday, 18 August, provided Churchyard the opportunity: 'And so vpon Monday before supper, I made a Deuice, as though MERCVRIE had bin sente from the Gods, to request the Queene to come abroade, and behold what was deuised for hir welcome' (C1ᵛ). The text then typographically sets off this device of Mercury, as Churchyard somewhat consistently distinguishes his commentary from the actual dramatic scene. One thing becomes clear early on in his text: the dramatist must be ready at any given moment to provide entertainment; he must therefore be innovative and somewhat spontaneous, no matter how much preparation may have gone on beforehand.

In an exceptionally elaborate coach, Mercury, following the sounding of trumpets, drew near the place where the Queen stood at a window. In a charming fusion of actor with fictional character, Churchyard writes: 'When MERCVRIE hadde espyed hir highnesse, he skipped out of the Coatche, and being on the grounde, gaue a iump or two, and aduanced himselfe in suche a sorte, that the Queene smiled at the boldnesse of the Boy' (C2ʳ). This boy/Mercury then spoke nearly 100 lines, offering expected praise of Elizabeth and the good wishes of the gods, who promise assistance to 'Vphold hir raigne, maynteyne hir regall state, | Find out false harts, and make of subiectes true, | Plant perfite peace, and roote vp all debate' (C3ᵛ). The speech, Churchyard writes, 'as I knowe' was 'very well taken and vnderstoode' by the Queen (C4ʳ). From his eyewitness vantage point and from having devised the event, Churchyard offers an extended description of the coach, 'made and framed on such a fashion, as few men haue seene', being covered with birds and naked sprites hanging by the heels in the air and clouds (C4ʳ). In the middle of the coach stood a tower, decked with golden jewels, 'in the top whereof was placed a faire plume of whyte feathers' (C4ʳ). Mercury himself (the actor playing Mercury) wore a blue satin outfit, lined with cloth of gold, with wings on his heels and carrying a golden rod. Clearly, the beholder's eye marvels at the spectacle. Churchyard closes the account by suggesting that not everyone expected entertainment at this moment ('a great number looked not for any shew'); indeed, things were not ready 'as some thoughte' (C4ʳ). Nevertheless, he presented the dramatic scene to the Queen's delight: 'all was well taken, and construed to the best meaning of the Deuisor' (C4ʳ).

Such good will must have spurred Churchyard on for Tuesday's device, a veritable morality play representing the conflict between Cupid, Wantonness, and Riot and the forces of Chastity, including Modesty, Temperance, Good Exercise, and Shamefastness. No one can doubt the outcome and its appeal to Elizabeth as the embodiment of Chastity and its several virtues. But Churchyard first focuses on the logistical and practical problems of mounting this show:

'although I was not well prouided of thinges necessarye for a Shewe (by meane of some crossing causes in the Citie)' (C4^v). The artist confronts political and social realities. Yet Churchyard, with the help of friends, remained determined to 'venter the hazzard of a Shewe' (C4^v). Thus he ascertains the path that Elizabeth will take on her way to dinner: 'I hastily prepared my Boyes and Men, with al their furnitures, and so sette forward with two Coatches' (C4^v). He settled for an open field where a crowd was already gathering in anticipation of a show: 'The common people beholding the manner thereof, and greedie to gaze on' (C4^v). As seen earlier, no matter how much planning has taken place, the playwright must be prepared to adjust quickly and find the appropriate venue for drama, a place compatible with the Queen's presence.

Churchyard's interest does not stop with mounting the show; he exhibits equal concern for the reader of his text. He writes: 'that you shall (and please you) imagine you see the thing, I haue heere set downe the whole manner of the Shew, and after that euery part as they were played, shall be heere expressed' (C4^v). He begins: 'First, there is a fayned deuice, that VENVS and CVPID were thrust out of Heauen, and walking on the earth, mette a Philosopher, who demaunded from whence they came' (C4^v). Churchyard follows with an extensive, two-page summary of the drama—in a word, a plot outline—which has no particular theatrical value; instead, it focuses on the reader in this self-conscious move to construct a 'literary' text (the sort of thing that Churchyard had not done in the text of the Bristol pageant).

He notes that, having driven away Cupid, Chastity and her maids arrive in a coach to Elizabeth 'and rehearsed what had happened' (D1^r). Churchyard adds the subordinate, parenthetical clause: 'although this was done in hir view' (D1^r). Despite the Queen's having already witnessed the action, these virtues thought it necessary to tell her what had happened. This seeming duplication (presentation and recounting) one often encounters in drama, of course; but Churchyard is being particularly self-aware about his craft, occupying the position of spectator, presumably reporting what actually happened.

After a song that contrasts the chaste life with the lewd life, Modesty serves as the final speaker: she 'spake to the Queene a good season' (D1^v). Thus the pageant scene ends; and Churchyard comments: 'for the whiche Shew, I had gracious words of the Queene openly and often pronounced by hir Highnesse' (D1^v). The writer has received his reward, and this expression of gratitude he wants his readers to know about. Before releasing readers to peruse the actual speeches, songs, and stage directions, Churchyard has a final admonition: 'Nowe before you reade the partes, you must throughly note what my discourse thereof hathe bin'—reinforcing Churchyard's sense that a discourse has parts, punning on divisions and on actors' roles (D1^v). We must presumably carefully read the author's summary before plunging into the text of the dramatic scene—a most unusual request and command. Churchyard adds: 'and carrying that care and good will with you, the matter shall seeme to haue the better life, and I shall thinke my labour & studie well bestowed' (D1ᵛ). The writer blatantly wants to guide the reader in the confrontation and experience with the text as we hear his insistent first-person voice, asserting a prerogative to intersect and shape the reader's experience and acknowledging his shaping a literary text open to interpretation.

Great frustration and disappointment followed on Wednesday, 20 August. The Queen dined at the Earl of Surrey's, and Churchyard readied a show about Manhood and Desert to present for her. He waited anxiously 'at my Lorde of Surreys backe dore, going to the Queenes Barge' (E3ʳ). But insufficient room made it impossible for all the participants to see and actors to perform; and therefore, 'we toke Boats, and conueyed our people downe the water, towards a landing place that we hoped the Queene would come vnto' (E3ʳ). But, having 'hoouered on the water three long houres', Churchyard and his players finally gave up as night fell (E3ʳ). No matter the plans, if the Queen does not appear, entertainment becomes impossible and pointless. The author can only wait for another time, which would come the next day 'by the Queenes Maiesties owne good motion, who tolde me she woulde see what pastimes were prepared' (E3ʳ). This prospect offers solace to a playwright and producer who has anxiously waited at a back door and then down the river for some three hours, and it places the 'I' in a favourable light. We readers 'shall perceyue by the discourse of these matters that I meane to make, and by this Shewe of MANHODE, and the Shewe of the NYMPHES, which I minde fully and truely to treate of' (E3ʳ). Such will follow in the text. But the writer has offered what surely seems to be a truthful account of his plight, inviting understanding and sympathy by our sharing in his disappointment as we join in his discourse.

On Thursday, 21 August, Churchyard became a very busy man, having received warning from the Lord Chamberlain that the Queen would ride abroad in the afternoon: 'he commaunded me to be ready, dutifully to presente hir with some Shewe' (E3ᵛ). Thus begins some intense construction: 'I caused a place to be made and digged for the Nymphes of the water' (E3ᵛ). Churchyard gives precise measurements of how this hole was to be done, including covering it with a canvas 'paynted greene like the grasse, and at euery side on the Canuas, ranne a string through Curtayne rings, whiche string might easily be drawen any kinde of way', making possible the illusion that the earth did seem to open (E3ᵛ). Inside this cave Churchyard would place 'a noble noyse of Musicke of al kind of instruments' (E3ᵛ). This cave would also be the residence of the water nymphs, 'desguised or dressed most strangely', wearing white silk, carrying a bundle of bulrushes, and wearing a garland of ivy on the head (E3ᵛ). Churchyard claims: 'touching the beautie of the Nimphes, they seemed to be the chosen children of a world' (E3ᵛ). He anticipates that at the Queen's arrival 'one Nimph shoulde poppe vp out of the caue first, and salute the Queene with a speech, and then another, and so till four of them had finished their speeches' (E4ʳ). Music and dancing with timbrels would follow. 'So in order and readinesse stoode that Shew for the time'—a seeming stasis that will plunge into life (E4ʳ).

But Churchyard has not forgotten his plan for a show about Manhood and Desert; so he has that one ready also, to be presented before the water nymphs. This show is 'as well furnished as the other' (E4^r). He imagines another kind of morality drama, recalling Tuesday's entertainment: Manhood, Favour, and Desert did strive for Beauty, 'but good Fortune (as victor of all conquestes) was to come in, and ouerthrowe' them and all their powers (E4^r). Churchyard intends a battle among the forces, complete with swords, targets, and shot. Fortune's side 'should triumph and march ouer the bellies of their enimies: in which time was legges and armes of men (well and liuely wrought) to be let fall in numbers on the grounde, as bloudy as mighte be' (E4^v). The fired imagination of the beholder's eye creates an 'I' who captures the moment. Exactly how this vivid and vicious scene relates to the water nymphs Churchyard chooses not to say. Obviously his dramatic creativity has been working feverishly, and he has crafted technically difficult presentations.

There is only one problem: 'as the Queenes highnesse was appoynted to come to hir Coatch . . . there fell suche a shoure of rayne . . . that euery one of vs were driuen to seeke for couerte and most comfort' (E4^v). Churchyard tried to take refuge under a bridge, but 'we were all so dashed and washed, that it was a greater pastime to see vs looke like drowned Rattes' (E4^v). This experience leads Churchyard to articulate a general principle: 'a Shew in the open fielde is always subiect to the suddayne change of weather, and a number of more inconueniences than I expresse' (E4^v). The life of a playwright in Norwich has become difficult indeed. Churchyard also laments the loss to the city of 'Veluets, Silkes, Tinsels, and some cloth of golde, being cutte out for these purposes'—a reminder of the expense of costumes, the greatest investment for any acting company (E4^v). Bleakness settles on the occasion, as Churchyard captures the scene of disappointment: people feeling their sense of injury and misfortunes, silence gripping everyone, and finally 'euery person quietly passed to his lodging' (F1^r). All that preparation and construction has come to naught; Churchyard remains to document the loss, which he does in a poignant discourse. Perhaps such disappointment prevented Churchyard from recording Goldingham's masque of that evening.

But ever resourceful, as he must be, Churchyard contemplates a way of salvaging some of this effort for Friday's entertainment, the day scheduled for the Queen's departure. He writes: 'fearing that all my labour shoulde be loste, [I] deuised to conuert the Nimphes of the water, to the Fairies on the land' (F1^r). And why not? In the meantime, Churchyard's text becomes the vehicle for recording the speeches and events that *should* have taken place on Thursday.[23]

---

[23] In this, Churchyard may have been influenced by the example of *The Princelye pleasures, at the Courte at Kenelwoorth* (London: Richard Jones, 1576), which printed the texts of two masques devised for the 1575 Kenilworth festivities, but not, in the end, performed. For a discussion of the ways in which both the written and visual artefacts of the 1575 Kenilworth festivities may be seen to have functioned as records of the performances that should have taken place at the festivities themselves, see Elizabeth Goldring's essay in this volume, pp. 163–88, below.

In fact, this day's entertainment, not performed, occupies the largest portion of Churchyard's text. He writes: 'I haue sette downe the foure speeches that foure Nimphes shoulde haue spoken . . . . I haue written the order and parts of the Shew of MANHODE and DEZARTES, that no one thing that was well meante, should sleep in silence' (F1ʳ). Thus the parts 'are heere for you to reade at your leysure', following in considerable detail (F1ʳ). Dramatic parts parallel the parts of discourse. Having written, this writer does not intend to discard; after all, he is preparing a text for readers, one of the multiple tasks assumed by this author, whose voice we hear clearly. Performance disappointment can be trumped by textual preservation, a self-conscious awareness of authorship. We can scarcely keep track of the lessons that Thomas Churchyard, Gent. is learning.

Friday's 'device' might well be entitled 'The Transformation of Nymphs and Author'. Left to his 'owne inuentions' and bereft of his aides, Churchyard 'drewe my Boyes vnto me, that were the Nymphes on the water, and so departed the Citie' (G2ᵛ). He took with him such garments and other 'stuffe' as necessary and chose a ground 'by the which the Queene must passe' and gathered his actors in a corner of a field (G2ᵛ). And 'there some parts I made, whych the Boyes mighte misse, bycause the time was short for the learning of those parts' (G2ᵛ). Improvise, in other words. Churchyard writes that he was determined to make the Queen laugh and decided that seven of the boys 'should passe through a hedge from the place of oure abode . . . and deliuer seauen speeches' (G2ᵛ). These boys, dressed like nymphs, 'were to play by a deuice and degrees the Phayries, and to daunce . . . like the Phayries' (G2ᵛ). One day nymphs, the next fairies: the virtue of innovation and imagination. Their appearance indeed made the Queen laugh, Churchyard insists. And then he gets into the action: 'And I hearing this good hope, being apparelled like a water Sprite, beganne to sounde a Timbrell', with others joining in; the playwright then led them all into a dance, which found favour (G2ᵛ). The Queen experienced the event and then headed to her lodging. Churchyard says succinctly and pointedly: 'it was past fiue of the clocke'—what a telling, concrete detail that leaves open-ended the possible response to this day's entertainment as night falls (G3ʳ). In this, we hear the voice of the author-actor who shapes his discourse.

IV

Before presenting the speeches of the seven fairies, Churchyard pauses in the text to sum up what he has done: 'Thus haue you truly hearde the reporte of mine owne workes and inuentions, with the which did no any one deale but my selfe' (G3ʳ). Proprietary and solitary authorship Churchyard claims. After all, he has shaped the text and our response. He uses this section to anticipate the final report of the Queen's return from Norwich, passing along towards Cambridgeshire. He sketches the limits of what he can report: 'but those, in whose houses I was (and where I saw or heard any thing worthy memorie) I mind to speake of, and touch, praying you that shall reade the same' (G3ʳ). Only the 'wante of knowledge' prevents a thorough and complete report (G3ʳ). In order to maintain his pose as a faithful reporter of events, Churchyard must acknowledge his inability to know everything that transpired. This stance adds to his credibility. He closes with a hopeful wish for the Queen: 'sende oure Queene often to suche pleasant Progresses, and increase good people and louing subiects to shew the like dutie and order, as hathe bene orderly seene in thys season, and tyme of triumph' (G3ʳ). Such a resounding conclusion underscores the social purpose that Churchyard has envisioned from the prefatory material through the text, as this beholder documents a commendation of courtesy, a time of triumph indeed.

This attitude governs his report of the Queen's journey from Norwich, an account Churchyard finds 'as necessarie to be tolde, as the rest of matter penned before, not chiefely for the cheere and entertaynemente founde returning, but for other causes meete to be rehearsed' (G4ᵛ). He will therefore 'playnely fall to the troth of thinges that I meane to haue vnderstood' (G4ᵛ). So, he notes the Queen's entertainment along the route, commenting when he has actual knowledge or observing that others have told him about the feast ('The trayne haue tolde me') as he creates a catalogue of her progress (G4ᵛ). In the middle of this report, however, Churchyard pauses to transact other rhetorical business: 'But nowe to speake a little by the way of Gods mightie hande and power' that governed the Queen's reception (G4ᵛ). God's operation, Churchyard says, has enabled people to respond so positively to the sovereign and demonstrate their duty. Such a 'Soueraigne Ladye we haue, that can make the crooked pathes streighte where she commeth, and drawe the hearts of the people after hyr' (H1ʳ). Suddenly Churchyard catches himself in this moral digression: 'I had almost passed the boundes of my discourse' (H1ʳ). Such boundaries exist in the eye/I of the beholder, and they can be readily crossed if so desired.

At the end of the account of Elizabeth's journey from Norwich, we find this typographical feature at the bottom of the page: 'ꜰɪɴɪs *Tho. Churchyard*' (H1ʳ). Not only does this presumably announce the end of text, but also it reinforces the identity of the author. We may therefore be surprised to discover on the next page a brief note to the reader in which Churchyard produces a list of the gentlemen that the Queen made knights in Suffolk and Norfolk. Had he not remembered, Churchyard asserts, this oversight would have been a 'blotte and blemishe to my Booke, bycause hir Highnesse aduanced them to the more Worship, for that they should al their life time after, haue the greater regarde to God, and to their Prince' (H1ᵛ). Beyond what seems to be the end of his text Churchyard pushes the boundaries of his discourse yet again.

But in fact the *Discourse* does not end here either, for in signatures H2ʳ to L4ᵛ Churchyard includes two poems, the first touching the voyage of discovery of Sir Humphrey Gilbert and the second, the return of Master Frobisher from his journey. The first ends with the word 'FINIS' quite prominent on K3ᵛ, and the second ends with 'Thomas Churchyarde' (L4ᵛ). Possibly the printer had a surplus of paper available; possibly the author insisted on adding these poems which he just happened to have ready. For whatever reason, Churchyard's pageant text creates hospitable space for other discourses, a point that he acknowledges near the end of the epistle dedicatory where he states what he has done, suggesting: 'These paynes and purposes of myne, proceede onely on the good will I beare to al vertuous actions' (A4ʳ).

Against sometimes difficult odds, the playwright has prevailed through determination and innovation. His imagination makes possible, for example, the transformation of water nymphs into fairies. For good measure, Churchyard himself takes on the role of actor as a water sprite, prompting laughter from the Queen. He has faithfully reported the events in Norwich, acknowledging when he lacks sufficient information, as when the Queen returns from Norwich and visits many different noblemen. He emphasizes himself as solitary author, one sometimes abandoned by others and thus left to his own inventions. Surely this self-proclaimed authorship from title page throughout the text suggests an emerging sense in the late 1570s that one can and possibly should assert such authorship. Because he is a writer intimately involved in the publication of his text, he takes great pains and care to construct the text as he desires, full of rich details, descriptions of dramatic action, and speeches. Churchyard's *Discourse*/discourse tells a narrative, provides a sequence of events, and offers serious treatment of a worthy subject. Along the way, the writer indulges in self-fashioning and textual performance, enabling us to understand the 'I' of this particular beholder, Thomas Churchyard, Gent.

PART III

PRIVATE RECEPTIONS FOR QUEEN ELIZABETH I

9

Portraiture, Patronage, and the Progresses
Robert Dudley, Earl of Leicester, and the
Kenilworth Festivities of 1575

Elizabeth Goldring

It is well known that portraiture played a prominent part in the civic pageants staged for Elizabeth I. When, for example, the new Queen processed through the streets of London at her coronation entry of January 1559, she passed painted images of her predecessors.[1] For this type of display—designed to emphasize dynastic continuity and legitimacy—there were numerous precedents, both in England and on the Continent.[2] Relatively little scholarly attention has been paid, however, to the use of portraiture in the pageants and entertainments staged for Elizabeth by private, as opposed to civic, hosts. Yet new findings suggest that painted portraits played a much larger role in the Elizabethan progresses than previously has been believed. Surviving inventories reveal that the Queen's favourite, Robert Dudley, Earl of Leicester, displayed more than fifty pictures at Kenilworth Castle, Warwickshire, as early as *circa* 1578, while other sources suggest that the bulk of this substantial collection was in place for the famous festivities of July 1575.[3] Moreover, all the evidence indicates that Leicester's picture collection at the castle was dominated by four, life-sized

I am indebted to Ellen Chirelstein and Lucy Gent, each of whom commented on an early draft of this essay. Quotations from the De L'Isle Papers at the Centre for Kentish Studies, Maidstone, are provided by kind permission of the Viscount De L'Isle, while quotations from the Dudley Papers at Longleat are provided by kind permission of the Marquess of Bath. I would like to thank Kate Harris for her assistance in the archives at Longleat.

[1] *The Queen's Majesty's Passage and Related Documents*, ed. Germaine Warkentin (Toronto: Centre for Reformation and Renaissance Studies, 2004), 108. For Elizabeth's coronation entry, see Hester Lees-Jeffries's essay in this volume, pp. 65–85, above.

[2] See, e.g., Lorne Campbell, *Renaissance Portraits: European Portrait-Painting in the 14th, 15th and 16th Centuries* (New Haven: Yale University Press, 1990), 198–201; and Robert Tittler, *Civic Portraiture and Local Identity in Early Modern England* (Manchester: Manchester University Press, forthcoming), especially chapter 5.

[3] For the archival findings summarized in this paragraph and the next, see Elizabeth Goldring, 'Portraits of Queen Elizabeth I and the Earl of Leicester for Kenilworth Castle', *Burlington Magazine*, 147 (2005), 654–60.

portraits of himself and the Queen that had been specially commissioned for the 1575 revels.

Two of these—described in contemporary documents as a portrait of Leicester 'whole proporcion, . . . in armor' and its accompanying 'greate table' of the Queen[4] —are now known to correspond to images executed in the spring of 1575 by Federico Zuccaro, the Italian mannerist who, as has recently been established, travelled to England for the express purpose of executing portraits of Leicester and Elizabeth for the Kenilworth festivities. Although Zuccaro's paintings are not extant, his preliminary drawings are now in the British Museum. A second set of portraits commissioned for the festivities—one of Leicester 'whole proporcion, . . . in a sute of russet satten and velvet welted' together with an accompanying 'greate table' of the Queen[5] —are now known to correspond to paintings in the National Portrait Gallery (NPG) and the Reading Museum, executed *circa* 1575 by an unknown artist or artists. The NPG's painting of Leicester, though currently three-quarter length, has been cut down from full-length. Quite probably the portrait of Elizabeth in Reading also has been truncated, or is a copy of a now-lost original in full length.

So far as is known, Leicester is unique among Elizabethan courtiers in having commissioned and publicly displayed large-scale paintings of himself with complementary ones of the Queen.[6] He also seems to have been the first—though not, as we shall see, the last—Elizabethan progress host to have made portraiture central to the festivities provided for Elizabeth and her court. That the 1575 Kenilworth festivities should have acted as the catalyst for the production of such unprecedented images is not, perhaps, surprising, for these revels were innovative in several respects.[7] Moreover, as Susan Frye has rightly noted, these festivities functioned as 'the earl's staging of his importance as the man closest to the queen'.[8] It is the contention of this essay that the performance of this special relationship may be found not only in the festivities' courtly entertainments—as described in *The Princely Pleasures*, first printed in 1576—but also in the display of Leicester's picture collection at the castle. Or, to put it another way, the dramatic revels staged at Kenilworth provide a

---

⁴ BL, Add. MS 78176, fo. 41ᵛ.   ⁵ Ibid.

⁶ The only comparable example is the set of sculpture busts depicting Leicester and the Queen recorded in the Earl's possession in London *c*.1578 and again in 1580 (BL, Add. MS 78176, fo. 23ʳ; DP V, fo. 11ᵛ).

⁷ The 1575 Kenilworth festivities were both longer and more lavish than anything that had been attempted previously in the course of the Elizabethan progresses. They are also noteworthy for having constituted the first occasion on which the French and Italian tradition of the water fête was deployed in England, and for having been the first Elizabethan court festival to have been commemorated by multiple printed pamphlets.

⁸ Susan Frye, 'Entertainments at Court', in Susan Doran (ed.), *Elizabeth: The Exhibition at the National Maritime Museum* (London: Chatto & Windus, 2003), 73–80 (p. 79).

Figure 9.1. *Robert Dudley, Earl of Leicester,* by Federico Zuccaro. 1575. Black and red chalk on paper. 37.8 × 27.5 cm. (© The Trustees of the British Museum, London)

Figure 9.2. *Queen Elizabeth I*, by Federico Zuccaro. 1575. Black and red chalk on paper. 36.5 × 27.5 cm. (© The Trustees of the British Museum, London)

Figure 9.3. *Robert Dudley, Earl of Leicester*, anonymous. *c.*1575. Oil on panel. 108 × 82.5 cm. (The National Portrait Gallery, London)

Figure 9.4. *Queen Elizabeth I*, anonymous. *c.*1575. Oil on panel. 114.3 × 79.7 cm. (© Reading Museum Service, Reading Borough Council. All rights reserved)

Figure 9.5. Detail of Fig. 9.3, showing where the panel has been cut down at the bottom edge.

context for reading these portraits, and the portraits a context for rereading the revels.[9]

This interpretation is foregrounded in Susan Frye's characterization of the 1575 festivities as a 'competition for representation', in which the dramatic performances 'fell into two groups: those displaying Dudley's interests and those showing Elizabeth's'.[10] As Frye has forcefully demonstrated, the entertainments in the former category articulated Leicester's desire for equal status with the Queen through marriage, as well as for a militant Protestant foreign policy, while those in the latter asserted Elizabeth's autonomy by emphasizing Leicester's place beneath her in the hierarchy at court. Like the festivities' dramatic performances—some of which did not go entirely according to plan—the portraits of Leicester and Elizabeth commissioned for the 1575 revels may be seen as the site of a struggle between Leicester's personal and political agenda and that of the Queen.

---

[9] For another example of the ways in which Elizabethan literature can provide a context for reading Elizabethan portraiture, see Elizabeth Goldring, ' "So lively a portraiture of his miseries": Melancholy, Mourning and the Elizabethan Malady', *British Art Journal*, 6.2 (2005), 12–22.

[10] Susan Frye, *Elizabeth I: The Competition for Representation* (New York: Oxford University Press, 1993; repr. 1996), 56–96 (p. 62).

Building upon Peter Burke's analysis of early modern portraiture as a prop for 'the presentation of self' in which the relationship between sitter and portrait is akin to that between actor and role,[11] I would suggest that the castle and its picture gallery may be viewed as a stage on which Leicester sought—with varying degrees of success—to perform an agenda of personal and political self-fashioning before an audience consisting of the Queen and her court. To that end, this essay begins with an overview of the Earl's collection of paintings at Kenilworth, before offering a reading of its central quartet of portraits in the context of the entertainments occasioned by Elizabeth's 1575 visit. Finally, this essay considers the fate of Leicester's picture collection at Kenilworth after 1575, as well as its influence on subsequent Elizabethan progress entertainments, including those staged at Woodstock and Ditchley by Sir Henry Lee.

LEICESTER'S PICTURE COLLECTION AT KENILWORTH: AN OVERVIEW

As might be expected, the vast majority of Leicester's paintings at Kenilworth were portraits. The subjects depicted included members of the Earl's political and familial circle in England, contemporary continental figures of note, and heroes from antiquity. Unfortunately, extant sources do not reveal exactly where or how this picture collection was displayed, though the surviving evidence for Leicester's other primary residences is suggestive. At Leicester House, London, the bulk of the Earl's more than one hundred paintings and other works of art were concentrated in the 'High galerye', while at Wanstead Manor, Essex, virtually all of Leicester's nearly sixty paintings seem to have hung in the 'greate Gallerie'.[12] Thus, it seems likely that the Earl's pictures at Kenilworth would have been clustered together in an equivalent space. Although the castle does not appear to have had a long gallery in the sixteenth century,[13] the upper floor of the keep, known as 'Caesar's Tower', might have housed a number of Leicester's paintings, thereby functioning as a large room, if not a long one.[14]

The question of who had access to this picture collection over the course of the 1575 revels is an intriguing one. The mercer and minor court official Robert Langham (or Laneham), whose famous *Letter* provides a wealth of information

[11] Peter Burke, *The Historical Anthropology of Early Modern Italy: Essays on Perception and Communication* (Cambridge: Cambridge University Press, 1987), 150–67.

[12] DP IV, fo. 60ᵛ; NA, E/178/1446, no. 44; DP Xb, fo. 17ᵛ; BL, Harleian Roll D.35, fo. 26ʳ. These figures reflect the size and disposition of the Leicester House and Wanstead collections shortly after Leicester's death.

[13] Leicester's will of 1587 makes reference to 'the Gallery which [he] once intended' at Kenilworth, but never built. See *Letters and Memorials of State,* ed. Arthur Collins, 2 vols. (London: T. Osborne, 1746), i. 72.

[14] I am grateful to Richard Morris for this information.

regarding the appearance of the castle's exterior as well as its garden, nonetheless is disappointingly silent on the subject of Leicester's picture collection. Indeed, Langham makes relatively few comments about the interior of the castle, and what he does say lacks the detail found in his lengthy descriptions of the building's façade and grounds[15]—all of which might suggest that someone of Langham's modest status was not granted access to the castle's more important rooms.[16] It is almost certain, however, that the higher-ranking members of the court would have seen Leicester's picture collection and that they, together with the Queen, constituted the Earl's intended audience. Although the composition of the guest list at Kenilworth varied from day to day, leading courtiers known to have been present for all or part of the July 1575 festivities include the earls of Warwick, Sussex, Northumberland, Derby, Rutland, and Hertford; the Barons Burghley, North, Buckhurst, Hunsdon, and Lumley; as well as Sir Francis Knollys, Sir James Croft, Sir Henry Lee, Francis (later Sir Francis) Walsingham, and Philip (later Sir Philip) Sidney.[17]

As is clear from surviving inventories, virtually all of Leicester's paintings at Kenilworth—including the four with which this essay is primarily concerned—were displayed with curtains affixed to their frames, a not uncommon practice in Elizabethan England. Often made of silk, curtains served a practical, protective function, shielding pictures from dust, soot, and light.[18] In addition, curtains could be used to control access to a collection as a whole or to individual items within it. Curtains also lent a staged, theatrical quality to a picture gallery, for their colourful fabrics—set off against dark frames and dark panelling—could be drawn aside with a flourish to reveal previously hidden images.[19] Whether this was the case at Kenilworth in July 1575 is not recorded; but a dramatic unveiling of the portraits newly executed for these revels would

[15] I would like to thank Sir Roy Strong for discussing this issue with me.

[16] Even if, like Brian O'Kill and David Scott, one believes Langham's *Letter* to have been written by William Patten, the point made here concerning the relationship between status and access still stands. For debates concerning the authorship of the *Letter*, see the following: R. J. P. Kuin, 'Robert Langham and his "Letter" ', *Notes and Queries*, NS. 25 (1978), 426–7; id., 'Introduction', to Robert Langham, *A Letter*, ed. R. J. P. Kuin (Leiden: E. J. Brill, 1983), 1–32; id., 'The Purloined *Letter*: Evidence and Probability Regarding Robert Langham's Authorship', *The Library*, 6th ser. 7 (1985), 115–25; Brian O'Kill, 'The Printed Works of William Patten (c.1510–c.1600)', *Transactions of the Cambridge Bibliographical Society*, 7 (1977), 28–45; and David Scott, 'William Patten and the Authorship of "Robert Laneham's *Letter*" (1575)', *English Literary Renaissance*, 7 (1977), 297–306.

[17] A fuller list of those known to have attended the festivities will accompany my new editions of *The Princely Pleasures* and Langham's *Letter* in Jayne Archer et al. (eds.), *Court and Culture in the Reign of Queen Elizabeth I: A New Edition of John Nichols's 'Progresses of Queen Elizabeth'*, (Oxford: Oxford University Press, forthcoming).

[18] For the use of curtains in this period, see Jacob Simon, *The Art of the Picture Frame: Artists, Patrons and the Framing of Portraits in Britain* (London: National Portrait Gallery, 1996), 13–14.

[19] Compare *Twelfth Night*, I. v. 227, in which Olivia's face is likened to a painting, her veil to a curtain: 'we will draw the curtain, and show you the picture' (see *The Arden Shakespeare: Complete Works*, ed. Richard Proudfoot, Ann Thompson, and David Scott Kastan (London: Thomson Learning, 1998; rev. edn. 2001), 1197).

have been in keeping both with Leicester's flamboyant personality and with the displays of princely magnificence that characterized the proceedings as a whole.

PAGEANTRY, PORTRAITURE, AND PROPOSALS OF MARRIAGE

The Kenilworth festivities long have been interpreted as an extended proposal of marriage on the part of the Queen's ambitious favourite, whose use of court festivals to forward his marital suit may be traced to the Inner Temple Revels of 1561–2.[20] Although there is some debate as to how seriously Leicester intended the proposals proffered in July 1575 to be taken,[21] what cannot be denied is that several of the dramatic interludes performed at Kenilworth thematized the Earl's special relationship with the Queen or the subject of marriage itself. The elaborate welcome staged on the evening of 9 July included, for example, the assertion that 'The Lake, the Lodge, the Lord' were Elizabeth's 'for to command'.[22] This idea was reiterated in Eccho's exchange with the Savage Man, with its proclamation that the gifts given to the Queen on her arrival had been 'tokens of true love' from 'Dudley . . . [who] . . . gave himselfe and all' (p. 496). Other of the festivities not only championed marriage over chastity, but overtly urged aged maidens to wed. On 17 July, a mock folk wedding featuring a 35-year-old bride was enacted in the tiltyard. This brideale was to have been followed a few days later by a performance of George Gascoigne's masque of Zabeta, the tale of one of Diana's 'best-beloved Nimphes' who had resisted marriage for 'neere seventeen yeares past' (p. 502). Gascoigne's commentary on the Queen herself—'Zabeta' being a variation of 'Elizabeth', and seventeen the number of years she had then been on the throne—was to have included the following injunction, voiced by Juno's messenger, Iris: 'How necesserie were for worthy Queenes to wed, | That know you wel, whose life alwaies in learning hath beene led' (p. 514). Although this masque was not performed, almost certainly because it had been censored by the Queen,[23] its erotic imperative was articulated in

---

[20] See Marie Axton, 'Robert Dudley and the Inner Temple Revels', *Historical Journal*, 13.3 (1970), 365–78.

[21] For a range of views on this matter, see the following: Marie Axton, *The Queen's Two Bodies: Drama and the Elizabethan Succession* (London: Royal Historical Society, 1977), 63–6; Philippa Berry, *Of Chastity and Power: Elizabethan Literature and the Unmarried Queen* (London: Routledge, 1989), 99; Helen Cooper, 'Location and Meaning in Masque, Morality and Royal Entertainment', in David Lindley (ed.), *The Court Masque* (Manchester: Manchester University Press, 1984), 135–48 (pp. 141–3); Susan Doran, *Monarchy and Matrimony: The Courtships of Elizabeth I* (London: Routledge, 1996), 67–72; and John N. King, 'Queen Elizabeth I: Representations of the Virgin Queen', *Renaissance Quarterly*, 43 (1990), 30–74 (p. 45).

[22] *The Princely Pleasures*, in *The Progresses and Public Processions of Queen Elizabeth*, ed. John Nichols, 2nd edn., 3 vols. (London: Nichols, 1823), i. 492. All subsequent page references to *The Princely Pleasures* within the main text are to Nichols's edition.

[23] Although *The Princely Pleasures* attributes the masque's cancellation to 'lack of opportunity and seasonable weather' (*Progresses*, ed. Nichols, i. 515), it is generally agreed that the real reason

other ways. In a speech delivered at Elizabeth's departure, Gascoigne related how Zabeta had 'so obstinately and cruelly rejected' her 'noble and worthy' suitors that there were 'sundry famous and worthy persons, whome shee hath turned and converted into most monstrous shapes and proportions' (pp. 518, 519). The subsequent appearance of *Deepedesire*, a 'Hollybush; . . . furnished on every side with sharpe pricking leaves, to prove the restlesse prickes of his privie thoughts' (p. 520), offered Leicester one final opportunity to voice his desires:

> Vouchsafe, O comely Queene, yet longer to remaine,
> Or still to dwell amongst us here! O Queene commaunde againe
> This Castle and the Knight, which keepes the same for you;
> . . . Live here, good Queene, live here; . . . (p. 522)

Although chivalric protestations of devotion to the Queen were in some ways the stock-in-trade of Elizabethan progress entertainments, the declarations of affection voiced on Leicester's behalf at Kenilworth stand out both for their extravagance and for the force with which they were reiterated over the course of Elizabeth's nineteen-day visit.

The festivities' literary entertainments were not, however, the only forum for the expression of Leicester's marital ambitions. As more than one scholar has argued, several of the spectacles mounted at Kenilworth seem to have been designed to reinforce the proposals of marriage that formed the heart of so many of the dramatic performances. John N. King, for example, has read the fireworks display over the lake—in which flames 'would rise and mount out of the water againe, and burn very furiously untill they were utterly consumed' (p. 494)—as having 'advertised Leicester's devotion to the queen'.[24] Similarly, Michael Leslie has interpreted the Earl's garden—dominated by a fountain which, with its depictions of erotic Ovidian scenes, could both inflame and extinguish desire—as a 'statement of the relationship between the aging, frustrating Queen and aging, frustrated courtier'.[25] To this list, I would suggest, may be added the portraits of Leicester and Elizabeth executed for the 1575 revels. By virtue of the fact that they were displayed as a quartet, these images would have been a vivid means of articulating Leicester's privileged status as favourite. Moreover, in the case of the paintings now in Reading and the NPG, several of the attributes with which Elizabeth and Leicester are depicted appear to have been designed to advertise their special relationship.

As Susan Doran has observed of Elizabethan portraiture, courtiers who commissioned paintings of the Queen often sought to incorporate into the works

---

was the sensitivity of its subject matter (see, e.g., Cooper, 'Location', 142–3; J. W. Cunliffe, 'The Queenes Majesties Entertainment at Woodstocke', *PMLA*, 26 (1911), 92–141 (p. 130); Frye, *Competition*, 70; and King, 'Queen Elizabeth I', 46).

[24] King, 'Queen Elizabeth I', 46.

[25] Michael Leslie, 'Spenser, Sidney, and the Renaissance Garden', *English Literary Renaissance*, 22 (1992), 3–36 (p. 10).

'signs or symbols to denote their own status'.²⁶ Implicitly, such images are as much depictions of the aspirations and agendas of the men who commissioned them as they are representations of the Queen. In the case of the Reading portrait, Leicester's intimacy with Elizabeth is vividly proclaimed by the fact that she is shown wearing a jewel-encrusted doublet that he himself had given her in January 1575, described in that year's gift list as 'a Doublett of white Satten garnisshedd with goldesmithes worke and sett with Eighteene very fayre payre of claspes of goldsmithes worke enamuledd, every payre sett with fyve Dyamondes and Eight Rubyes, one Dyamonde in euery paire biggar then the rest . . . with a fayre pasmayne lace of Damaske golde and Damaske silver'.²⁷ Appropriately, the complementary portrait of Leicester depicts him with several of the tangible trappings of his privileged status at court. The Lesser George suspended from the bejewelled chain around Leicester's neck, together with the coat of arms and the Earl's coronet emblazoned in the painting's upper left corner, may be read as emblems of the gifts Elizabeth had bestowed upon her favourite: his installation as a Knight of the Garter in 1559; his (and his family's) restoration in blood in 1561; and his elevation to the earldom of Leicester in 1564.

These paintings, however, do not simply depict their subjects as Queen and favourite. Like the proposals of marriage voiced by the festivities' literary entertainments, these images may be seen to gesture towards a future in which Leicester is no longer an earl, but a prince consort or a king. As is clear from recent re-examination of the NPG panel, the painting in its original full-length format depicted Leicester clad from head to toe in red, his doublet paired with matching stockings.²⁸ Given the contemporary associations of red with both love and royalty, this portrait might be interpreted not only as a visual analogue for the 'fierie flames' of 'desire' alluded to in several of the festivities' literary entertainments (p. 496), but also as a vivid expression of the ways in which Leicester's ardour for Elizabeth was intertwined with his political ambitions.

The notion that this portrait casts Leicester in the role of consort *manqué* is reinforced by an examination of the compositional affinities between this painting and its complement. Both depict their subjects against a dark background: in Leicester's case, a green velvet curtain; in the Queen's, what appears to be wooden panelling. In both paintings, the sitter is flanked by a chair and pivoted slightly to the viewer's left. In Elizabeth's portrait, the chair in question, though only partly visible, is clearly a throne: half of the royal coat of arms may be seen, as may the 'R' in 'E[lizabetha] R[egina]'. By implication, the viewer would seem to be invited to interpret the chair in Leicester's portrait as a throne, or at least a

---

²⁶ Susan Doran, 'Virginity, Divinity and Power: The Portraits of Elizabeth I', in Susan Doran and Thomas S. Freeman (eds.), *The Myth of Elizabeth* (Basingstoke: Palgrave Macmillan, 2003), 171–99 (p. 190).

²⁷ BL, Harleian MS 4698, fo. 9ʳ. The connection between this doublet and the Reading portrait was first established in Goldring, 'Portraits for Kenilworth Castle', 657–8.

²⁸ I am grateful to Tarnya Cooper for this information.

potential throne. Not only is it positioned directly below the Earl's coat of arms and coronet, but its knobs, tassels, and rivets are virtually identical to those seen in the complementary portrait of the Queen—a point which suggests that the chair next to which Leicester poses is something more than the generic prop so often seen in portraits of this period.

Such a reading probably would have been reinforced, if not actively encouraged, at Kenilworth by the marriage proposals repeatedly voiced in the festivities' dramatic performances. Moreover, the contents of the castle's picture collection as a whole would have been suggestive, for Leicester's images of himself and the Queen constituted the core of a collection that also contained portraits of continental rulers and consorts, including Philip II and William of Orange with their respective wives. The viewer's experience of these images would have been inflected by the castle's internal decorative scheme, the unifying motif of which appears to have been the communication of a quasi-princely magnificence. Inventories record an abundance of luxury goods, including Flemish tapestries and Turkish carpets; in addition, these documents reveal that Leicester's initials, coat of arms, and personal emblem were inscribed in gold and silver thread on objects ranging from chairs to table linen to bed linen.[29] If, as I have suggested, the castle and its picture gallery functioned as a stage for the performance of Leicester's personal and political agenda, then props such as these must be seen as part and parcel of that performance.

Thus far, this essay has considered the ways in which Leicester may have attempted to use portraiture to articulate his marital ambitions at Kenilworth in 1575. Yet it would be naive to assume that the paintings of Leicester and Elizabeth commissioned for these festivities reflected only the Earl's wishes. Portraits are the product of a complex three-way exchange between patron, painter, and sitter. Just as the Queen did not hesitate to make her views known at the Kenilworth festivities, censoring the performances that broached subjects she did not wish to have addressed, so we would expect her to have held her own when sitting for her portrait, regardless of what Leicester may have had in mind. The draft proclamation 'Prohibiting Portraits of the Queen' (1563):

commandeth all manner of persons . . . to forbear from painting, graving, printing, or making of any portrait of her majesty until some special person, that shall be by her allowed, shall have first finished a portraiture thereof; after which finished, her majesty will be content that all other painters or gravers . . . shall and may at their pleasures follow the said patron or first portrayer.[30]

In 1596, the Privy Council issued a warrant ordering the destruction of paintings, engravings, and woodcuts 'of her Majesty's person and vysage, to her Majesty's great offence and disgrace' (which is to say, portraits depicting the Queen as an

[29] BL, Add. MS 78176, fos. 28^r–48^v.
[30] *Tudor Royal Proclamations*, ed. Paul L. Hughes and James F. Larkin, 3 vols. (New Haven: Yale University Press, 1969), ii. 240–1 (p. 241).

old woman).[31] Clearly, from the beginning of her reign to its end, Elizabeth was extremely interested in and adept at controlling her own image. Although Zuccaro's painting of the Queen is not known to survive, the fact that Elizabeth would in later years praise Italian painters (and, by implication, Zuccaro) suggests that she was not dissatisfied with the finished product.[32] Presumably, the same may be said of the Reading portrait, which, whether by accident or design, depicts the Queen beside a throne considerably larger than the putative one glimpsed in Leicester's portrait, her arm projecting somewhat unnaturally from the panel, as if to emphasize that the throne is hers and hers alone.[33]

What is almost certainly not the product of chance is the fact that, in all four of these portraits, Leicester and the Queen are depicted facing the same direction rather than each other. This may seem a minor point, but it is a significant one. To have been painted facing one another would have been to adopt the conventions of Renaissance marriage portraiture,[34] something that Leicester may well have wanted, but which the Queen never would have sanctioned in the case of images intended for public consumption.[35] Moreover, as is clear from surviving inventories, Leicester's 'greate' pictures of himself at the castle were displayed with 'j curteine to them', while those depicting Elizabeth shared a separate 'curteine of chaungeable silke'[36]—an arrangement which suggests that even the notoriously audacious Leicester dared not display portraits of himself and the Queen as pairs *per se*. Thus, just as the printed accounts of the festivities speak to the tensions that erupted when Leicester's proposals of marriage became too overt for Elizabeth's liking, so the portraits commissioned for the Kenilworth festivities may be seen to hint at the conflicting agendas of the Queen and her favourite.

PAGEANTRY, PORTRAITURE, AND PROTESTANTISM

The 1575 Kenilworth festivities were not designed simply to articulate Leicester's desire for marriage to the Queen and equality of status with her. These revels

---

[31] *Acts of the Privy Council of England, A.D. 1596–7*, ed. John Roche Dasent (London: HMSO, 1902), 69.

[32] Nicholas Hilliard, *A Treatise Concerning the Arte of Limning*, ed. R. K. R. Thornton and T. G. S. Cain (Manchester: Carcanet, 1992), 65. Zuccaro is the only Italian painter the Queen is known to have met.

[33] I owe this observation to Elaine Blake.

[34] For marriage portraits in sixteenth-century England, see Elizabeth Honig, 'In Memory: Lady Dacre and Pairing by Hans Eworth', in Lucy Gent and Nigel Llewellyn (eds.), *Renaissance Bodies: The Human Figure in English Culture, c.1540–1660* (London: Reaktion, 1990; repr. 1995), 60–85 (pp. 63–8).

[35] Compare the miniatures of Leicester and Elizabeth executed by Nicholas Hilliard, *c*.1575, which, though designed as private, intimate images, nonetheless depict the pair facing the same direction rather than each other (Roy Strong with V. J. Murrell, *Artists of the Tudor Court: The Portrait Miniature Rediscovered, 1520–1620* (London: V&A, 1983), catalogue nos. 185 and 186).

[36] BL, Add. MS 78176, fo. 41ᵛ.

also were intended as a means of advancing Leicester's religio-political agenda—namely, his vigorous, almost obsessive, advocacy of English intervention in the revolt of the Netherlands against Spain.[37] From 1572, the year in which revolt broke out, until 1585, the year in which Leicester was finally appointed to lead an English military expedition to the Low Countries, the Earl was the most vocal proponent of the Orangist cause at the Elizabethan court. In July 1575, there was a palpable urgency to the question of whether Elizabeth would formally involve herself in the affairs of the Low Countries, for in the late spring or early summer of that year she had been offered sovereignty over Holland and Zeeland.[38] Although the Queen would eventually decline this offer,[39] the possibility that she might be persuaded to accept must have seemed a very real one at the time of the Kenilworth festivities.

Leicester's European ambitions—both for himself and for England—were most vividly dramatized at Kenilworth in William Hunnis's fictions depicting the knight 'Sir Bruse sauns pittie' and his attempted rape of the Lady of the Lake.[40] On the evening of 18 July, Elizabeth was approached, on her return from hunting, by Triton, floating on a mermaid. After greeting the Queen with a blast on his trumpet, Triton related the story of Sir Bruse, who had imprisoned the Lady of the Lake with waves, seeking 'by force her virgin's state | full fowlie to deface'.[41] This tale of woe completed, Triton asked the Queen to free the Lady: 'Your presence onely shall suffice, | her enemies to convince' (p. 499). Then, acting on behalf of Neptune, Triton commanded the winds, waters, and fishes to retreat, before proclaiming 'the maide released be, | by soveraigne maiden's might' (p. 500). As has been observed on more than one occasion, the would-be rapist Sir Bruse doubtless was intended to represent Spain, and the innocent Lady of the Lake the Netherlands.[42]

Thus, in liberating the Lady, Elizabeth assumed (within the confines of the festivities' fictions) the role that Leicester and the Orangists fervently desired her to adopt in the real world: that of saviour of the beleaguered Netherlands.

Significantly, this performance was an abbreviated version of a much more elaborate scheme. According to *The Princely Pleasures*:

---

[37] For another English court festival produced under Leicester's aegis that argued the case for military intervention in the Low Countries, see Elizabeth Goldring, 'The Funeral of Sir Philip Sidney and the Politics of Elizabethan Festival', in J. R. Mulryne and Elizabeth Goldring (eds.), *Court Festivals of the European Renaissance: Art, Politics and Performance* (Aldershot: Ashgate, 2002), 199–224; and Elizabeth Goldring, 'The Death (1586) and Funeral (1587) of Sir Philip Sidney', in Archer et al. (eds.), *Court and Culture*.

[38] *Calendar of State Papers, Foreign Series, of the Reign of Elizabeth, 1575–1577*, ed. Allan James Crosby (London: Longman, 1880), 76–7.

[39] A decade later, the Dutch again would offer sovereignty unsuccessfully to Elizabeth. In 1586, Leicester would incur the Queen's wrath for accepting the post of Absolute Governor-General of the United Provinces without her permission or knowledge.

[40] According to *The Princely Pleasures*, the 'devise of the Ladie of the Lake' was Hunnis's, though the verses themselves 'were penned, some by Master Hunnes, some by Master [George] Ferrers, and some by Master [Henry] Goldingham' (*Progresses*, ed. Nichols, i. 501, 502).

[41] Ibid. 499.   [42] Frye, *Competition*, 78–86; Berry, *Of Chastity*, 98.

it was first devised, that (two dayes before the Ladie of the Lake's deliverie) a Captaine with twentie or thyrtie shotte shoulde have bene sent from the Hearon House . . . : and that Syr Bruse, shewing a great power upon the land, should have sent out as many or moe shot to surprise the sayde Captayne; and so they should have skirmished . . . At last (Syr Bruse his men being put to flight) the Captaine should have come to her Majestie at the Castell window, and have declared more plainly the distresse of his Mistresse, . . . and that thereupon he should have besought hyr Majestie to succour his Mistresse . . . (pp. 501–2)

In the cancelled skirmish, Leicester was to have played the politically charged role of the Captain, who is not only the opponent of Sir Bruse and the defender of the Lady of the Lake, but also the Lady's advocate before the Queen. For this performance, which would have articulated Leicester's brand of militant Protestant intervention in the Netherlands, the Earl is believed to have had a new suit of tilting armour made by the Royal Workshops at Greenwich.[43] The suit in question, executed *circa* 1575 and now in the Royal Armouries, is inscribed with the initials 'RD', as well as the Dudley bear and ragged staff, the collar of the Order of St Michael, and the badge of the Lesser George. Today, only the shaffron (the piece that protects the horse's forehead, nose and cheeks) betrays any evidence of gilt, but originally the entire suit would have been embossed with gold.

Although the skirmish with Sir Bruse was aborted—again, almost certainly because the Queen had censored it—the castle's picture collection may have afforded Leicester another means of advertising his religio-political agenda. A striking number of the portraits depicted figures who had played, or continued to play, a central role in the ongoing struggle between the Netherlands and Spain. Surviving inventories juxtapose pictures of William of Orange and his allies (including the counts of Brederode, Egmont, and Hoorne) with pictures of Philip II and his deputies in the Netherlands (including Cardinal Granvelle, the Duchess of Parma, and the Duke of Alva). Although it has not (yet) been possible to link any of these inventory entries to extant portraits, the possibility that one or more of these paintings depicted their subjects in armour is, in light of the politically charged tenor of the wider Kenilworth festivities, a tantalizingly provocative one. While Leicester's display of such images was doubtless, in part, a reflection of his embrace of the Italianate cult of *uomini famosi*, it may also be the case that he sought, in the context of the 1575 festivities, to devise a hanging scheme that would both thematize the struggle in the Netherlands and transmit a call for English military intervention.

If so, such messages almost certainly would have been reinforced by the twenty-three 'cardes or mappes of cuntreys' apparently displayed alongside pictures at

---

[43] Erik Blakeley, 'Tournament Garniture of Robert Dudley, Earl of Leicester', *Royal Armouries Yearbook*, 2 (1997), 55–63.

Figure 9.6. Tilt armour of Robert Dudley, Earl of Leicester, by the Royal Workshops at Greenwich. *c.*1575. Steel, etched, gilt, and embossed (shaffron only), leather. (© The Board of Trustees of the Royal Armouries, Leeds)

the castle.[44] Although surviving inventories do not specify the geographic regions depicted, an examination of the documentary evidence for Wanstead and Leicester House is instructive. At the former, where the Earl displayed only two maps, one depicted 'all the Lowe Cuntries'.[45] At the latter, where Leicester kept a map collection similar in size to that at Kenilworth, there were four general maps of the Low Countries, as well as four of Holland, two of Friesland, and one of Zeeland.[46] If, as seems probable, the collection at Kenilworth contained similar images, their display at the 1575 festivities would have been a vivid reminder, for those interested in seeing it, of Leicester's religio-political ambitions.

Zuccaro's portrait of Leicester also may be read as having articulated the Earl's brand of militant Protestantism. Not only is Leicester depicted as a soldier, but his armour is itself charged with political significance. To understand this last point, it is necessary to distinguish between Zuccaro's preliminary drawing and the full-length painting on panel that resulted from it. Although the painting was destroyed when Christie's was bombed in 1940,[47] its appearance is known through a surviving photograph, which, like the preliminary drawing, depicts an armour-clad Leicester with his left hand on his hip and his right hand resting on a table.[48] However, the suit of armour worn by Leicester in the painting is not the one he is seen wearing in Zuccaro's sketch. In the latter, Leicester wears a suit of russet steel with gilt engraving designed for field, tilt, and tourney course and known to have been executed for him early in Elizabeth's reign.[49] Although this particular suit is not extant, it is illustrated in the *Almain Armourer's Album*, a collection of designs from the Greenwich armour workshops compiled by Jacob Halder from *circa* 1560 onwards. By contrast, the suit of armour worn by Leicester in the painting is that now in the Royal Armouries, which, as noted, is believed to have been commissioned for his skirmish with Sir Bruse.[50] In other words, this painting depicted Leicester in the role censored by the Queen at the 1575 festivities: that of the heroic Captain who vanquishes Spain and liberates the Protestant Netherlands.

[44] BL, Add. MS 78176, fo. 42^r; BL, Add. MS 78177, unfol.; CKS De L'Isle U1475 E92, fo. 28^v; DP XI, fo. 21^v.

[45] DP XI, fo. 126^r; DP IX, fo. 20^v; DP VIII, fo. 33^r.   [46] DP VII, fo. 48^v; DP VI, fo. 38^v.

[47] I am grateful to Claude Blair for this information.

[48] E. K. Waterhouse was the first to make this connection. See his 'The Palazzo Zuccari', *Burlington Magazine*, 69 (1936), 133–4 (p. 134).

[49] Karen Hearn (ed.), *Dynasties: Painting in Tudor and Jacobean England, 1530–1630* (London: Tate, 1995), 152. See also J. A. Gere and Philip Pouncey, with the assistance of Rosalind Wood, *Italian Drawings in the Department of Prints and Drawings in the British Museum: Artists Working in Rome, c.1550 to c.1640* (London: British Museum, 1983), 191–3.

[50] Blakeley, 'Tournament Garniture', 57; Waterhouse, 'The Palazzo Zuccari', 134; and Roy Strong, *Tudor and Jacobean Portraits*, 2 vols. (London: HMSO, 1969), i. 195.

Figure 9.7. *Robert Dudley, Earl of Leicester*, by or after Federico Zuccaro. *c.*1575. Oil on panel. Dimensions unknown. (Destroyed during a German air raid over London, 1940; photograph © The National Portrait Gallery, London)

Figures 9.8 and 9.9. Designs for a suit of tilt armour for Robert Dudley, Earl of Leicester, as illustrated by Jacob Halder in *The Almain Armourer's Album*. *c.* 1560. Watercolour on paper. Each sheet 42.9 × 29 cm. (V&A Images, The Victoria and Albert Museum, London)

THE AFTERLIFE OF THE KENILWORTH FESTIVITIES: LEICESTER'S PICTURE COLLECTION AT THE CASTLE, 1575–1588

This, however, is only half the story, for, as Claude Blair first noted, the armour seen in the painting has been painted over another suit, which does in fact correspond to that depicted in Zuccaro's drawing and in the *Almain Armourer's Album*.[51] Precisely when the repainting occurred is unknown, though it is almost certain to have been undertaken after the conclusion of the July 1575 revels (and therefore by someone other than Zuccaro, who left England in early August of that year). Given that Leicester is the only person likely to have gone to the trouble of substituting one suit of armour for the other,[52] the repainting must have taken place prior to his death. Surviving inventories, which reveal Leicester's picture collection at Kenilworth to have been virtually static from *circa* 1578

---

[51] Dr Blair's views are summarized in Gere et al., *Italian Drawings*, 192.
[52] See ibid. 191–3.

onwards, permit the window to be narrowed to the years immediately following 1575. Quite probably, the Zuccaro portrait was repainted prior to the summer of 1577—or, in other words, at a time when it seemed likely that the Queen might return to Kenilworth on progress.[53]

The alteration of this painting is curious, for, in the main, Leicester sought to preserve Kenilworth exactly as it had been in July 1575. Not only does he seem to have acquired no more than a handful of new pictures after that date, but he went so far as to specify in his will that Kenilworth's contents were 'all to remain to the said Castle and House, and not to be altered or removed'.[54] As I have recently argued elsewhere, the deliberate fossilization of the castle and its picture collection suggests a desire to create a lasting memorial to the revels of 1575, which, for all their mishaps, nonetheless constituted Kenilworth's (and, to a certain extent, Leicester's) apotheosis.[55] How, then, is the repainting of the Zuccaro portrait to be explained?

I noted at the beginning of this essay, and I have sought to demonstrate throughout, that the dramatic entertainments occasioned by the 1575 festivities provide a context for reading Leicester's picture collection at the castle, and the pictures a context for rereading the entertainments. As we have seen, Leicester's proposals of marriage and his calls for military intervention in the Netherlands found expression both in the dramatic revels and in the paintings commissioned for the festivities. Yet, for all the ways in which word and image may be seen to have been intertwined at Kenilworth, it is important to remember that they are fundamentally different media. As Joanna Woodall rightly has observed of English court portraits of this period, 'there is not an exact correspondence between verbal and visual representation: there are things which could not be said . . . which might be represented visually, and vice-versa'.[56]

With this precept in mind, let us return to the altered Zuccaro painting: might it not be the case that Leicester instigated the repainting in an attempt to record for posterity that which had proved too politically contentious for overt expression in the festivities' dramatic performances? Like the printing, in 1576, of the censored entertainments, the repainting of the Zuccaro portrait—and, indeed, the continued display of the Kenilworth picture collection as a whole—would have been a means of giving the 1575 revels an afterlife they otherwise would have been denied. Moreover, this was an afterlife in which the festivities were preserved as Leicester originally had envisioned them—literally so in the case of the altered Zuccaro painting. The marriage masque and the skirmish with Sir

---

[53] For the evidence that Leicester invited Elizabeth to return to Kenilworth in 1577, see Simon Adams, *Leicester and the Court: Essays on Elizabethan Politics* (Manchester: Manchester University Press, 2002), 327.

[54] *Letters and Memorials*, ed. Collins, i. 72.

[55] Goldring, 'Portraits for Kenilworth Castle', 659–60.

[56] Joanna Woodall, 'An Exemplary Consort: Antonis Mor's Portrait of Mary Tudor', *Art History*, 14.2 (1991), 192–224 (p. 218).

Bruse may have been aborted, and Elizabeth may have elected to leave Kenilworth early. But the continued display of a group of pictures assembled in anticipation of the 1575 festivities and intimately bound up with their religio-political themes enabled Leicester to re-write history, casting himself for posterity in the two roles denied him at the festivities and, indeed, in life: royal consort and liberator of Protestant Europe.[57]

CONCLUSIONS: PORTRAITURE AND THE PROGRESSES, 1575–1603

If the self-conscious fossilization of the castle and its picture collection constitutes one type of afterlife, the influence of the 1575 Kenilworth festivities on subsequent Elizabethan progresses constitutes another. Although Leicester was not to host the Queen again at Kenilworth, there is reason to believe that her visits to him at Wanstead acted as the catalyst for the acquisition of numerous paintings. *Circa* 1578, Leicester bought some thirty new pictures, most of them portraits destined for the newly acquired Wanstead,[58] to which he was keen to lure the Queen on progress.[59] In addition, Marcus Gheeraerts the Elder's portrait of Elizabeth, executed *circa* 1580 and reputed to depict Wanstead garden in the background,[60] might conceivably have been painted to commemorate one of the Queen's visits on progress.

Further evidence of the imprint of the Kenilworth festivities on both portraiture and the progresses may be found by re-examining the entertainments staged at Woodstock, in Oxfordshire, in September 1575. As is well known, the revels at Kenilworth and Woodstock were intertwined on numerous levels.[61] Not only did the Woodstock festivities follow closely on the heels of those at Kenilworth,

---

[57] The audience for this performance would have ranged from Leicester himself, who returned to Kenilworth nearly annually (Adams, *Leicester and the Court*, 324); to members of his inner circle at the English court (CKS De L'Isle U1475 E93); to the delegation of French ambassadors who visited the castle in 1581 (*The Book of John Fisher, Town Clerk and Deputy Recorder of Warwick (1580–1588)*, ed. Thomas Kemp (Warwick: Henry T. Cooke and Son, n.d.), 71). For another perspective on the afterlife of the Kenilworth festivities, see James Knowles's essay in this volume, pp. 247–67, below.

[58] BL, Add. MS 78176, fo. 24ʳ.

[59] For Leicester's anxiety about receiving the Queen at Wanstead in an 'empty and unadorned house', see Mary Hill Cole, *The Portable Queen: Elizabeth I and the Politics of Ceremony* (Amherst: University of Massachusetts Press, 1999), 70. For her famous visit of May 1578, see Elizabeth Goldring, 'The Queen's Entertainment at Wanstead, 1578', in Archer et al. (eds.), *Court and Culture*.

[60] Hearn (ed.), *Dynasties*, 86–7.

[61] See, e.g., the following: David M. Bergeron, *English Civic Pageantry 1558–1642* (London: Edward Arnold, 1971), 35; Berry, *Of Chastity*, 100–1; Doran, *Monarchy and Matrimony*, 69; Richard C. McCoy, *The Rites of Knighthood: The Literature and Politics of Elizabethan Chivalry* (Berkeley and Los Angeles: University of California Press, 1989), 44–5; and Frances A. Yates, *Astraea: The Imperial Theme in the Sixteenth Century* (London: Routledge & Kegan Paul, 1975), 95–8.

Figure 9.10. *Queen Elizabeth I* (the 'Wanstead' Portrait), by Marcus Gheeraerts the Elder. *c.*1580. Oil on panel. 45.7 × 38.1 cm. (Private collection)

but Sir Henry Lee, Elizabeth's host, was a client of Leicester's. Lee seems to have taken his lead from the Earl, and indeed Leicester personally oversaw the last-minute preparations for the Queen's visit.[62] Moreover, the revels staged at

[62] See Leicester's letters from Woodstock of 4 and 6 September (*Calendar of State Papers, Domestic Series, of the Reigns of Edward VI, Mary, Elizabeth, 1547–1580*, ed. Robert Lemon (London: Longman, 1856), 503).

Woodstock functioned as a coda to those performed (and scheduled to have been performed) at Kenilworth, for once again the twin themes of marriage and military engagement dominated the festivities. The knight Contarenus, who appears in accounts of the Woodstock entertainments as both a suitor and a soldier, seems to have been intended as a Leicester figure, while Princess Gaudina, who rejects her lover Contarenus for reasons of state, appears to have been a thinly veiled allusion to Elizabeth herself. Although surviving accounts of the Woodstock entertainment are fragmentary, nonetheless it is clear that painting—and, in particular, portraiture—played a pivotal role at Woodstock, just as it had done at Kenilworth. When Hemetes led the Queen to his hermitage, he showed her 'A number of fine Pictures with posies of the Noble or men of great credite . . . in like sort hanginge there.'[63] These images, which possessed 'Allegories . . . hard to be vnderstood', were greatly admired—in particular, by the French Ambassador, who 'made greate suite to haue some of them'.[64]

Seventeen years later, when the Queen visited Lee at Ditchley for a series of entertainments self-consciously designed to evoke memories of her 1575 visit to Woodstock, painting again took centre stage, both during the festivities and afterwards, in a commemorative capacity. As had been the case at Kenilworth and Woodstock, painting was intertwined with the fictions and dramatic interludes in which the Queen was asked to participate. Accounts of the Ditchley festivities record that Elizabeth was led to a pavilion hung with allegorical paintings, where an old knight, who had fallen under the spell of 'thos charmed pictures on the wall', lay sleeping.[65] His page then addressed the Queen, requesting that she 'Drawe nere & take a vew of everie table' (p. 129). Only after Elizabeth had examined the 'enchaunted pictures' and their inscriptions 'of highe intention' did the knight awaken from his slumber, the spell broken (p. 130).[66] In gratitude, he proclaimed that the paintings in question—some of which may have been on display in the banqueting house at Woodstock in 1575[67]—should 'ever . . . tarrie' at Ditchley, 'never to departe' (p. 130). The day's festivities then concluded with a song of praise for 'She, with more than wisdomes head, | [who] Hath enchaunted tables read, | She, with more than vertues mighte, | [who] Hath restorid us to right' (p. 136). Marcus Gheeraerts the Younger's celebrated

[63] *The Queenes Maiesties Entertainement at Woodstock* (London: Thomas Cadman, 1585), sig. B4ᵛ.

[64] Ibid.

[65] Jean Wilson, *Entertainments for Elizabeth I* (Woodbridge: Brewer, 1980), 129. Subsequent quotations from this edition are noted parenthetically in the main text above.

[66] It has been suggested that the images referred to here—and, indeed, those described in the banqueting house at Woodstock—were emblems rather than full-scale paintings (Yates, *Astraea*, 105). However, the 'Ditchley' portrait, with its inscribed sonnet, perfectly fits the description of a 'Picture with posies of the Noble'.

[67] The tale told by the knight when he awakes would seem to imply that at least some of the 'enchaunted tables' at Ditchley corresponded to the pictures that had been at Woodstock in 1575 (Wilson, *Entertainments*, 129–31 and n. 26).

Figure 9.11. *Queen Elizabeth I* (the 'Rainbow' Portrait), attributed to Marcus Gheeraerts the Younger. *c.*1602. Oil on canvas. 127 × 99.1 cm. (By courtesy of the Marquess of Salisbury, Hatfield House, Hertfordshire)

'Ditchley' portrait almost certainly was executed in connection with Elizabeth's 1592 progress visit (see Fig. 1.1).[68] Formerly at Ditchley and now in the NPG,

[68] Strong, *Tudor and Jacobean Portraits,* i. 104–7; and id. *Gloriana: The Portraits of Queen Elizabeth I* (London: Thames and Hudson, 1987; repr. Pimlico, 2003), pp. 135–41. See also Yates, *Astraea,* 106.

this painting shows the Queen standing on a map of England, her feet firmly planted on Lee's native Oxfordshire. Indeed, this image, which depicts its subject banishing black storm clouds and ushering in the sun, may well have been one of the 'enchaunted pictures' upon which Elizabeth was asked to pass judgement during the revels themselves.[69]

The extent to which portraiture may have played a similar part in other of the Elizabethan progresses is at present unknown, though it remains a tantalizing possibility that might well reward further investigation. There is, for example, almost certainly more to be said about the 'Rainbow' portrait of Elizabeth, which, like the 'Ditchley', depicts its subject as a source of sunshine after storms. Now at Hatfield House, this painting tentatively has been linked to Elizabeth's visit to Sir Thomas Egerton at Harefield, Middlesex, in the summer of 1602, as well as to her visit to Sir Robert Cecil at Cecil House, London, in December of that year,[70] though additional research is required if a firm connection is to be established to either of these.

What is clear is that the 1575 Kenilworth festivities seem to have been the first—but by no means the last—occasion on which an Elizabethan progress host made portraiture an integral part of the pageantry offered to the Queen and her court. Not only did Leicester commission new paintings of himself and Elizabeth specifically for her visit of July 1575, but, as we have seen, these images seem to have been designed to articulate and reinforce the content of the festivities' dramatic entertainments. In this respect, a line of descent may be traced from Kenilworth to Ditchley, via Woodstock—not only, as has been done so many times before, in terms of their respective iconographic and religio-political programmes—but also in terms of the role of painting. At all three progress locations, painting and portraiture were intertwined with the dramas enacted before the Queen. Moreover, in the case of the festivities staged at Kenilworth and Ditchley, portraits executed in connection with Elizabeth's visits on progress remained *in situ* afterwards as vivid, semi-permanent memorials to ephemeral events. Thus, to the long list of ways in which the 1575 Kenilworth festivities were both innovative and influential may now be added the deployment of portraiture as a tool of political self-fashioning and legacy-making.

[69] For portraiture and the 1592 Ditchley festivities, see also Lucy Gent, 'Marcus Gheeraerdts's *Captain Thomas Lee*', in Caroline van Eck and Edward Winters (eds.), *Dealing with the Visual: Art History, Aesthetics and Visual Culture* (Aldershot: Ashgate, 2005), 85–103 (p. 93); and Gabriel Heaton's forthcoming edition of the Ditchley entertainment in Archer et al. (eds.), *Court and Culture*.

[70] For the former view, see Janet Arnold, *Queen Elizabeth's Wardrobe Unlock'd* (London: Maney, 1988), 83–4; for the latter, see Strong, *Gloriana*, 157–61; and Mary C. Erler, 'Sir John Davies and the Rainbow Portrait of Queen Elizabeth', *Modern Philology*, 84 (1987), 359–71.

10

Contesting Terms:
Loyal Catholicism and Lord Montague's
Entertainment at Cowdray, 1591

Elizabeth Heale

The route of Elizabeth's progress in the summer of 1591, through Surrey to the maritime county of Sussex and on to Portsmouth, was carefully planned. Elizabeth and her Council were anxiously watching developments across the Channel in France and Spain. In France, Spanish forces were established in Brittany as part of their intervention in the civil wars being fought out between the Protestant King Henri IV and the pro-Spanish Catholic League determined to prevent Henri's effective accession to the throne, while from Spain, reports were arriving of the gradual build-up of a new armada. From Saturday, 14 to Friday, 21 August, Elizabeth stayed at Cowdray in Sussex, the seat of Anthony Browne, first Viscount Montague. R. B. Wernham suggests that, at Cowdray, Elizabeth hoped to 'be able to keep in closer touch with [the Earl of] Essex and his forces' in France and, perhaps, to draw the French King Henri IV over the Channel for a short visit.[1] Elizabeth and her Council, however, had additional reasons to visit Lord Montague, for the eyes of the Council were not only turned without, across the Channel, but also within, to the activities of missionary priests and their Catholic supporters in England.

While revising this essay I benefited by being able to consult Dr Gabriel Heaton's edition of *The Honorable Entertainment Giuen to the Queenes Maiestie in progresse, at Cowdray in Sussex, by the Right Honorable the Lord Montecute. 1591*, which has been prepared for *Court and Culture in the Reign of Queen Elizabeth I: A New Edition of John Nichols's 'Progresses of Queen Elizabeth*, ed. Jayne Archer, Elizabeth Clarke, and Elizabeth Goldring, (Oxford: Oxford University Press, forthcoming). I am also indebted to the kindness of the General Editors, who enabled me to consult Dr Heaton's text before publication. Gabriel Heaton's notes, his comments on a draft of this essay, and suggestions made by the editors of the present volume, have all contributed greatly to improve it from its earlier state. Unless otherwise stated, all quotations from the Cowdray entertainment are taken from *The Honorable Entertainment Giuen to the Queenes Maiestie in Progresse, at Cowdrey in Sussex* (London: Thomas Scarlet for William Wright, 1591), STC 3907.5.

[1] For events in France, see R. B. Wernham, *After the Armada: Elizabethan England and the Struggle for Western Europe 1588–1595* (Oxford: Clarendon Press, 1984), 262–356 (p. 324).

Montague's position as a leading Catholic nobleman has been recognized as crucial for the understanding of the lavish entertainments he offered the Queen during her stay at Cowdray, but previous discussions have tended to find in the shows traces of a covert antagonism and even threat towards Elizabeth.[2] Such readings, however, ignore the delicate dynamics of power and persuasion that characterize Elizabethan entertainments. My own study considers the ways in which Montague's entertainment adeptly observes and uses the decorum of a royal visit.[3] In this entertainment it is through the language of loyalty itself, central to entertainments, that Montague seeks to challenge government policy towards his co-religionists.

Welcoming the monarch to one's country estate could affirm, as Felicity Heal argues elsewhere in this volume, 'the circulation of benefits between monarch and subjects'.[4] Elizabeth's visit could bestow honour and status on her host, while the host, in handing over his or her house and estate—symbolized in the Cowdray entertainment by the gift of a golden key—acknowledged the Queen's ultimate lordship and his or her own dependency on royal favour. On a more practical level, as Mary Hill Cole suggests, royal visits enhanced Elizabeth's 'style of personal monarchy that depended on direct contact with people important in their locality'.[5] Conversely, a royal visit could offer to the host exceptional opportunities for access to the Queen and her influential courtiers, and for self-promotion through shows and lavish hospitality. There were, however, dangers. The power relation between guest and host was by no means equal and Elizabeth did not always feel obliged to be gracious or grateful. Montague in 1591 may well have nervously recalled a progress Elizabeth had made to Suffolk and Norfolk thirteen years earlier in 1578. On 10 August 1578 she had stopped at the home of a Catholic recusant, Edward Rokewood (or Rookwood) of Euston Hall in

---

[2] Curtis Charles Breight, 'Caressing the Great: Viscount Montague's Entertainment of Elizabeth at Cowdray, 1591', *Sussex Archaeological Collections*, 127 (1989), 147-66, describes the entertainment as 'hosted by a discontented Roman Catholic' and characterized by 'a high level of tension' (pp. 147, 149). In two discussions of the entertainment, Michael Leslie recognizes that the key themes are loyalty and deception, but suggests that the entertainment puts the Queen in an 'exposed and ambiguous position', subject to 'moments of exquisite embarrassment' ('The *Hypnerotomachia Poliphili* and the Elizabethan Landscape Entertainments', *Word and Image*, 14 (1998), 130–44 (p. 140), and ' "Something nasty in the wilderness": Entertaining Queen Elizabeth on her Progresses', *Medieval and Renaissance Drama in England*, 10 (1998), 47–72 (pp. 63–71)).

[3] Michael Questier, in an important study of Montague's loyal Catholicism, 'Loyal to a Fault: Viscount Montague Explains Himself', *Historical Research*, 77 (2004), 225–53, follows Breight's account of the entertainment although he notes that it pushes the case for Montague's disaffection 'as far as it will go' (p. 236). My own reading draws on Questier's account of Montague's career, but reads the entertainment not only in terms of the career, but also of the contest over representation fought out, with particular intensity in the late 1580s and early 1590s, between the Elizabethan government and its Catholic subjects.

[4] Felicity Heal, 'Giving and Receiving on Royal Progress', pp. 46–61.

[5] For this and the previous point, see Mary Hill Cole, *The Portable Queen: Elizabeth I and the Politics of Ceremony* (Amherst: University of Massachusetts Press, 1999), 63, 65.

Suffolk, then or later married to Montague's niece.[6] While searching for a missing piece of plate, 'someone on going into the hay-house, found an image of the Holy Virgin, which was brought into the hall, and in the Queen's presence treated with the greatest possible indignities. Rokewood was at once arrested and compelled to attend the court at Norwich where he was committed to prison.'[7] Patrick Collinson is inclined to agree with Helen Hackett's suggestion that Elizabeth herself may have been in collusion with her Council to trap Rokewood, a known recusant.[8]

While it may have suited the Council's purposes to make an example of the recusant Rokewood in 1578, Lord Montague's status and value to the government in 1591 required very different treatment. A public, and publicized, demonstration of loyalty by a leading Catholic nobleman, and of her favour towards him, suited the purposes of the Queen and Council as they combated accusations of the cruel persecution of Catholics at home, and looked fearfully at Spanish activity across the Channel.[9] No images were found, although Montague maintained chapels at Cowdray and at his other residence of Battle Abbey; no hidden priests were exposed, although there was at least one normally in residence; and no priest-holes discovered, although there was at least one on the estate.[10]

The Queen and her Council winked at Lord Montague's activities and took no offence at the considerable special pleading the entertainment contains because he served their purposes as a prominent example of English Catholic loyalty. This was not the first time that the government had sought to use Montague as a token Catholic, nor was it the first time Montague had attempted to persuade the government to take seriously the case for the toleration of loyal Catholic

---

[6] For the Rokewood genealogy, see *The Visitation of Norfolk in the Year 1563*, ed. Revd G. H. Dashwood, 2 vols. (Norwich: Miller and Leavins, 1878), i. 143, where one of Rokewood's wives is named as Elizabeth Browne, the daughter of William Browne of Elsing, Norfolk. William Browne was a brother of Lord Montague. See William Berry, *County Genealogies. Pedigrees of the Families in the County of Sussex* (London: Sherwood, Gilbert, and Piper, 1830), 354. In a footnote on p. 60 of *Publications of the Catholic Record Society*, 22 (London: Catholic Record Society, 1921), Rokewood's wife is misidentified as a daughter of Lord Montague.

[7] Quoted from the account in *Publications of the Catholic Record Society*, 22, Miscellanea XII, p. 60. Richard Topcliffe's letter on which this account is based is printed, with a full discussion of the incident, by Helen Hackett in *Virgin Mother, Maiden Queen: Elizabeth I and the Cult of the Virgin Mary* (London: Macmillan, 1995), 1–6.

[8] Collinson discusses the incident in the context of religion and politics in Norfolk and Suffolk: see 'Pulling the Strings: Religion and Politics in the Progress of 1578', pp. 122–41; Hackett, *Virgin Mother, Maiden Queen*, 2.

[9] Thomas Scarlet published two editions of the entertainment in 1591. The second edition included three songs missing from the first.

[10] For detailed accounts of Montague's life and Catholic affiliations, see Roger B. Manning, 'Anthony Browne, 1st Viscount Montague: The Influence in County Politics of an Elizabethan Catholic Nobleman', *Sussex Archaeological Collections*, 106 (1968), 101–12; Roger B. Manning, *Religion and Society in Elizabethan Sussex: A Study of the Enforcement of the Religious Settlement 1558–1603* (Leicester: Leicester University Press, 1969), *passim*; and Questier, 'Loyal to a Fault'. For the priest-hole, see H. Willaert, *History of an Old Mission: Cowdray—Easebourne—Midhurst* (London: Burnes, Oates, and Washbourne, 1928), 18.

subjects. This chapter will attempt to read the imaginative, yet surprisingly bold, strategies of the 1591 entertainment, in terms of a contest over representations of Catholicism and of loyalty that had characterized Montague's relationship with the Elizabethan government from the earliest years of the reign. It was a contest in which neither side had any interest in provoking the other too far. However, as the entertainment acknowledged, the final power of representation lay with the Queen. If the royal party left Cowdray satisfied with their welcome, Montague must have reflected ruefully on the ineffectiveness of his own persuasions. A new anti-Catholic proclamation, dated 18 October 1591, further criminalized those who harboured Catholic priests.[11] The Council may well have been working on the wording of this proclamation as they enjoyed Montague's hospitality and listened, perhaps not always attentively, to his complaints about the treatment of Catholics in his entertainments staged two months earlier, in August 1591.

LORD MONTAGUE AND THE CONTEST OVER REPRESENTATION

As a number of scholars have documented, Montague had, throughout Elizabeth's reign, established a reputation as a staunch Roman Catholic who nevertheless regarded himself as a loyal subject.[12] He had consistently opposed the legislation re-establishing Protestantism on Elizabeth's accession, and had been the sole temporal peer to speak out against the Act of Supremacy in 1559. In 1563, he again spoke eloquently against a bill to penalize the refusal to swear the Oath of Supremacy. In spite of such open opposition to the government's religious programme, he served the Queen as ambassador to Spain in the 1560s, as a joint lieutenant for Sussex at the time of the Northern Rebellion in 1569 and for many years after, and as a commissioner to try Mary Queen of Scots in 1587—all prominent positions in which a visibly loyal Catholic peer had particular propaganda value for the government. After 1585, as war approached, he was no longer appointed to the lieutenancy. The government's trust of Montague clearly had its limits. Curtis Charles Breight argues that Montague particularly resented his loss of the lieutenancy and suggests, convincingly, that the oak, planted in the soil of Cowdray and bearing the escutcheons of local Sussex gentry, which features prominently in the entertainment, asserts Montague's position as the natural focus for the loyal service of local gentlemen.[13]

---

[11] *A declaration of great troubles pretended against the Realme by a number of seminarie Priests and Iesuists, sent, and very secretly dispersed in the same, to worke great Treasons under a false pretence of Religion, with a prouision very necessary for remedy thereof,* 18 Oct. 1591.

[12] The following discussion is particularly indebted to the accounts of Montague's life by Manning, 'Anthony Browne', and Questier, 'Loyal to a Fault'.

[13] Breight, 'Caressing', 149–50. Manning, 'Anthony Browne' (p. 109), gives an instance where the government was forced to recognize the strength of Montague's local influence, even in 1588.

Some of the arguments that Montague used in 1563, when opposing the death penalty for refusal to swear the Oath of Supremacy, resonate again in the entertainment he staged for the Queen at Cowdray eighteen years later. He insisted, as later Catholic polemicists were to do, on Roman Catholicism as the traditional religion of England, underpinning an older, better order associated with the maintenance of ancient laws, traditions, and hierarchies in opposition to the new breakdown of social distinctions and loyalties introduced by Protestantism. Roman Catholics, he claimed, 'disturb not, nor hinder the public affairs of the realm . . . they dispute not, they preach not, they disobey not the queen'; they bring into the realm 'no novelties in doctrine and religion'.[14] On the contrary, it is religious innovation that threatens the commonwealth: 'let them therefore take good heed', he warned his fellow peers, 'and not suffer themselves to be led by such men that are full of affection and passions, and that look to wax mighty, and of power, by the confiscation, spoil, and ruin of the houses of noble and ancient men'. Prophetically, he warns that the new legislation will compel Catholics 'to lie and swear, or else to die therefore . . . And it is to be feared rather than to die, they will seek to defend themselves.' The peace for which 'every good prince and well-advised commonwealth ought to seek and pretend' will be destroyed, not through any inherent disorderliness in Catholics, but by their very integrity, criminalized by government action.[15]

For the government, of course, it was the activity of Catholics, and especially those 'vagrant and counterfeit persons', the missionary priests, who threatened the peace of the realm.[16] Burghley accused the priests of being 'fugitives . . . stolen into the realm and dispersed in disguising habits to sow sedition', whose very disguise and secrecy proved their guilty and disorderly natures: 'as some priests in their secret profession, but all in their apparel as roisters or ruffians, some scholars, like to the basest common people'. Such men are 'spial[s]' and 'explorer[s] for the rebel or enemy' who 'secretly search and sound out the havens and creeks for landing, or measure the depths of ditches or height of bulwarks or walls'.[17] In reply, Catholic writers up to the mid-1580s protest Catholic loyalty to the Queen and point out that disguise is forced upon them.[18] William Allen in *A True*,

[14] John Strype, *Annals of the Reformation*, 4 vols. (Oxford: Clarendon Press, 1824), i. 442.
[15] Ibid. i.i. 445, 446.
[16] I quote from a 1582 proclamation 'Declaring Jesuits and Non-Returning Seminaries Traitors', in *Tudor Royal Proclamations*, ed. Paul L. Hughes and James F. Larkin, 3 vols. (New Haven: Yale University Press, 1969), ii. 489.
[17] *The Execution of Justice by William Cecil and A True, Sincere, and Modest Defense of English Catholics by William Allen*, ed. Robert M. Kingdon (Ithaca, NY: Cornell University Press, 1965), 34, 36.
[18] See, for example, *An Epistle of the Persecution of Catholickes in Englande. Translated owt of frenche into Englishe . . . by G.T.* [Robert Persons] (Douai, 1582), 8, 44–5. See also Peter Holmes, 'The Background to Non-Resistance', in his *Resistance and Compromise: The Political Thought of the Elizabethan Catholics* (Cambridge: Cambridge University Press, 1982), 63–78, for a discussion of Catholic defences up to the mid-1580s when Catholic polemic began to advocate resistance to the Elizabethan regime.

Sincere, and Modest Defense (1584) asserts, like Montague, that it is Catholicism
that guarantees order and obedience: 'whatsoever is or hath been singular to our
country's honor . . . all came of the Catholic religion . . . As, on the contrary, the
waste of all goodness is now by many years' experience found to proceed of the
Protestants' not only fruitless but pernicious preachers and doctrine.'[19]

Allen's treatise reiterates Montague's defence of loyal Catholicism, but it also
begins what Holmes describes as 'the change from non-resistance to resistance'
in Catholic writings which increasingly openly justify rebellion and the legality
of papal intervention. Holmes suggests that many—perhaps most—members
of the Catholic laity shared these views, but there is little sign that this was the
case with Montague.[20] He was, for example, no recusant, apparently attending
Anglican services when necessary, including a service that must have been held
on Sunday, 15 August 1591, when Elizabeth and her Council were staying on
his estate. Montague's conformism would have been substantially confirmed by
Alban Langdale, his chaplain until 1588. Langdale, who had been Archdeacon
of Chichester during Mary Tudor's reign, had been removed from office for
refusing to take the Oath of Supremacy. He is also thought to have been the
author of a tract written in 1580 and circulated in manuscript, which defended
the practice of occasional attendance of Anglican services in the interests of
political and personal peace: 'folly yt were for a man to seeke to exulcerat that
which he cannot heale, and yt is not every manns lott to purge the Churche of
chaffe: And for a matter which might be made indifferent, to sterr troble is not
the best corse to quietnes.'[21]

Walsham suggests Langdale's views were widely shared by the surviving
Marian priests as well as by many of the laity.[22] They were, however, vehe-
mently rejected by the Jesuits, an associate of whom complained that Langdale's
treatise offered a 'cushion' that 'such as be frayle would be glad to . . . put
under their elbowes, to ease there pressures'.[23] Dr Richard Smith, Bishop
of Chalcedon, in his hagiographic biography of Montague's wife Lady Magdalen, first printed in 1609, blamed Montague's occasional conformity on
Langdale's influence:

If sometime afterward he went to heretical churches, it was not so much to be imputed
to him as to his priest, a learned and pious man indeed, but too fearful, who, supposing
it expedient something to give to the time, durst not determine such a fact to be sin. For

[19] Quoted in *Execution of Justice*, ed. Kingdon, 114, 220. Peter Milward, *Religious Controversies
of the Elizabethan Age. A Survey of Printed Sources* (London: Scolar Press, 1978), 69, calls Allen's
work 'the principal controversial work from the Catholic side during the whole period'.
[20] Holmes, *Resistance and Compromise*, 131, 176–85.
[21] Quoted by Alexandra Walsham, *Church Papists: Catholicism, Conformity and Confessional
Polemic in Early Modern England* (Woodbridge: The Boydell Press for The Royal Historical
Association, 1993), 53. See also Holmes, *Resistance and Compromise*, 90–4.
[22] Walsham, *Church Papists*, 51.
[23] Ibid. 54. Also Holmes, *Resistance and Compromise*, 93–4.

when that priest being dead he had entertained another, who with priestly courage told him it was a grievous offence and hateful to God and the Church and pernicious to his soul to be present at heretical service, he was so far from defending his fact that (as I received from the mouth of one that was present), instantly putting off his hat and falling on his knees, both with gesture of his whole body and with his tongue he most humbly submitted himself to the censure of the Catholic Church and piously promised never thenceforward to be present at heretical service, which all the rest of his life he exactly observed.[24]

This new chaplain, probably Father Robert Gray, whom Michael Questier identifies as himself a Marian priest, was found to possess a manuscript copy of Langdale's book in 1593 when he was arrested.[25] It is possible, therefore, that he was less uncompromising than Dr Smith suggested.

It may have been expedient for Montague to conform by occasional attendance at Anglican services, but it may also have been a loyal and grateful gesture of obedience to the Queen. In a speech, recently discovered and printed by Questier, and delivered to assembled family members and local gentlemen on 27 January 1592, five months after the 1591 entertainment, Montague acknowledged the 'extraordynarye favor, the freedom of my conscyence' that Elizabeth had shown him. He goes on: 'I further protest that yf the Pope or the Kinge of Spayne or anye other forreyne Potentate shuld offer to invade this realme, for any cawse whatsoever, I woulde be one of the fyrst that shoulde beare armes agenst him or them for my prynce & cowntrye, to the uttermost of my power.'[26] There is no reason to doubt Montague's sincerity, although his speech may, as Questier remarks, have also sought to exonerate his family and those around him as he anticipated the persecution that 'was likely to happen to his household once he was gone'.[27]

Montague may have had good reason to be grateful for Elizabeth's favour. In his 1592 speech, he acknowledged that 'yt hath been tolde her maiestie that yt was dawngerous commynge to my house, & she was advysed at her peryll to take heede howe she cam to me to Cowdrye this sommer past . . . & that I kept in my house syx score recusantes that never cam to churche, a wonderfull untruthe'.[28] Whatever Montague's protestations, there is substantial evidence that throughout the 1580s and early 1590s, Montague's estates at Cowdray and Battle, and his London residence at St Mary Overy, offered protection for

---

[24] *An Elizabethan Recusant House, comprising The Life of the Lady Magdalen Viscountess Montague (1538–1608). Translated into English from the Original Latin of Fr Richard Smith, Bishop of Chalcedon, by Cuthbert Fursdon. OSB, in the year 1627*, ed. A. C. Southern (London: Sands, 1954), 19–20.

[25] Questier, 'Loyal to a Fault', 240, 249. But see Questier, *Conversion, Politics and Religion in England 1580–1625* (Cambridge: Cambridge University Press, 1996), 120, where Robert Gray is described as a 'perpetually conforming seminarist'.

[26] Questier, 'Loyal to a Fault', 251, 252. I omit Questier's editorial marks when quoting from his text of Montague's speech.

[27] Ibid. 233.   [28] Ibid. 251.

Catholics and were almost certainly crucial to the secret enterprise of harbouring and protecting disguised missionary priests and Jesuits as they entered England to minister to English Catholics.[29] When Robert Gray, Montague's chaplain, was examined by Richard Topcliffe in 1593, after the old lord's death, he stated that 'his Lordship would not have any Jesuits or seminary priests brought into his house'.[30] If so, it may be evidence, analogous to his occasional attendance of Anglican services, of Montague's obedience to the letter of the law while encouraging, or at least allowing, the efforts of family and household servants to support and protect Catholic priests, including Jesuits. [31]

If Montague's policy of supporting his faith while remaining loyal and obedient to Elizabeth had its value for the Catholic cause in England, the converse was also true; Montague was a useful propaganda instrument for Elizabeth's government. The Council certainly knew some, and no doubt suspected more of the covert activities going on under Montague's protection in Sussex and London. Nevertheless, a manifestly loyal and unpersecuted Catholic peer could be usefully deployed against those who argued that Elizabeth's government persecuted Catholics for their religious beliefs alone, rather than for their treasonous—or potentially treasonous—activities. In *The Execution of Justice*, Burghley claimed that priests and their harbourers were prosecuted for their covert and treasonous activity not for their faith and pointed to a number of Marian clergy as well as 'a great number of others, being laymen of good possessions and lands, men of good credit in their countries' who had not been accused of treason:

yet none of them have been sought hitherto to be impeached in any point or quarrel of treason, or of loss of life, member or inheritance, so as it may plainly appear that it is not nor hath been for contrarious opinions in religion or for the Pope's authority [alone], as the adversaries do boldly and falsely publish, that any persons have suffered death since Her Majesty's reign.[32]

With the open threat of Spanish invasion in 1588, the potential propaganda value to the government of a loyal Catholic nobleman like Montague grew. The seminary priests and Jesuits were accused of possessing, in the words of the 1591 Proclamation, 'certaine skrolles or beadrolles of names, of men dwelling in sundry partes of our Countries . . . but specially in the maritimes' who would be willing, or might be persuaded, 'to serue their purpose both with their forces,

---

[29] Manning, *Religion and Society*, 43, 157, 162; *Calendar of State Papers, Domestic Series . . . 1547 –1580*, ed. Robert Lemon (London: HMSO, 1856), 376; Willaert, *History of an Old Catholic Mission*, 18. See Breight, 'Caressing', 29.

[30] *Calendar of State Papers, Domestic Series . . . 1591–1594*, ed. Mary Anne Everett Green (London: HMSO, 1867), 380–1; Questier, 'Loyal to a Fault', esp. p. 236.

[31] For Questier's careful analysis of Montague's position, and for evidence of the very active Catholicism of most of Montague's family, see 'Loyal to a Fault', 239, 240–50. For Lady Montague, see *An Elizabethan Recusant House*, ed. Southern, *passim*.

[32] *Execution of Justice*, ed. Kingdon, 12–13.

and with other trayterous enterprises when the Spanish power shall be ready to land'.[33] The avowed loyalty of such a pre-eminent nobleman in the Maritimes might be used to dissuade foreign powers from trusting to such a strategy and to discourage potential fifth columnists within England.

The government, however, was slow to exploit Montague's potential in 1588, no doubt due to anxiety about how far the loyalty of English Catholics might be trusted. Montague was removed from the commission of lieutenancy in Sussex in 1585, 'doubtless as a result of the threat of foreign invasion and the feeling that his continued presence in the commission would hinder a more stringent enforcement of anti-Catholic legislation'.[34] Just such an order from the Council, for example, as that dated January 1587 which ordered the lieutenants of Sussex to look into and restrain all known recusants in the county 'as they shall neither be able to give assistance to the enemie, nor that the enemie should have any reliefe and succour by them'. The 'most obstinate and noted persons' were to be committed to prisons.[35] In the years preceding the Armada of 1588, known recusants had been deprived of their arms, and prevented by the requirement to take the Oath of Supremacy from entering the army.[36]

It may have been the Earl of Montague himself who alerted the government to his propaganda value in 1588. As the Armada approached the English coast in July, those of any significance in the counties were summoned to bring their armed followers either to the camp at Tilbury or to attend directly on Elizabeth's person. On 23 July Lord Montague sent an aggrieved letter to the Council saying that having heard of the firing of the beacon on Portsdown, he was sending a note of the number of his servants in readiness and desired 'to know if he should reserve his forces for the defences of the country, as he had not received letters as others have done for attendance on Her Majesty's person'.[37] Given general government policy towards recusants, it seems improbable that Montague was invited to send his followers, but in October, after the threat of the Armada had receded, Burghley published a pamphlet purporting to be a letter written by a spy in the English camp to the Spanish Ambassador, Don Bernadino Mendoza, but almost certainly written by Burghley himself. In it, Mendoza's supposed informant writes that the first man to appear at Tilbury was the sick and aged Lord Montague, protesting that he now came 'with a full resolution to liue and dye in defence of the Queene, and of his countrie, against all Inuaders, whether it were Pope King or Potentate whatsoeuer, and in that quarrell he would hazard

---

[33] Quoted in *An Humble Supplication by Robert Southwell*, ed. R. C. Bald (Cambridge: Cambridge University Press, 1953), appendix 1, p. 61.

[34] Manning, *Religion and Society*, 223.

[35] *Queen Elizabeth and her Times: A Series of Original Letters*, ed. Thomas Wright, 2 vols. (London: Henry Colburn, 1838), i. 358–9.

[36] Armand J. Gerson, 'The English Recusants and the Spanish Armada', *American Historical Review*, 22 (1917), 589–94.

[37] *CSPD, 1547–1580*, ed. Lemon, 510.

his life his children, his landes and his goods'.[38] Montague, the letter reported, 'came personally him selfe before the Queene, with his Band of horsemen being almost two hundred: the same being led by his owne sonnes, and with them a yong child, very comely seated on horseback, being the heire of his house'.[39] This display of familial loyalty, if it occurred, could not have included one of Lord Montague's brothers, who, it was reported to Walsingham, had been killed aboard a Spanish ship a few days earlier on 3 August.[40]

Montague's position as a loyal Catholic subject—but also as the head of a household which included active supporters of both Jesuits and the Spanish invasion, and as the owner of properties at which missionary priests were thought to have received help and support, particularly on their way to London from the coast—may have inspired both satisfaction and anxiety, in equal measure, in the government.[41] No doubt the arrival of Elizabeth and her court at Cowdray in August 1591, as a threat of invasion from Spain again loomed, was designed not only to remind Montague of the government's scrutiny and of his duty to his sovereign, but also, implicitly, to rebut Spanish or papal hopes of a rising by Catholic gentry to support an invasion by demonstrating Elizabeth's confidence in the loyalty of this leading Catholic subject in the crucial county of Sussex. On this occasion the government did not wait until the invasion was actually under way before calling on Montague as evidence of Elizabeth's favour to, and trust of, her loyal Catholic subjects.

THE ENTERTAINMENT OF 1591

If, as seems the case, the government was happy to manipulate Lord Montague in order to persuade the Catholic world within and without England of his loyalty to the Queen, and thus of the possibility of loyalty from all devout English Catholics, Lord Montague was no slouch at persuasive manipulation in the interests of his own loyal Catholicism. The entertainment he mounted for Elizabeth in August 1591 develops two themes in particular: Montague's own position as a natural leader of the loyal local gentry, and, more daringly, a rebuttal of any association between his Catholicism and treachery, pointing, instead, the finger of accusation at aspects of contemporary Protestant society and morality. Montague's entertainment attempts to appropriate the charged language of loyalty and secrecy to serve his own pro-Catholic purposes.

---

[38] *The Copie of a Letter sent out of England to Don Bernadin Mendoza* (London: I. Vautrollier for Richard Field, 1588), 24.

[39] Ibid. See also Manning, *Religion and Society*, 230.

[40] *State Papers Relating to the Defeat of the Spanish Armada (Anno 1588)*, ed. John Knox Laughton, 2 vols. (London: Navy Records Society, 1894), ii. 29–30.

[41] For Francis Browne, another of Montague's brothers, see Questier, 'Loyal to a Fault', 235, 240.

On Saturday, 14 August, as Elizabeth arrived at Cowdray park, she was greeted by 'a personage in armour' holding a club in one hand and a golden key in the other, an ever vigilant and loyally belligerent porter of the estate, accompanied on each side by wooden porters who have fallen asleep waiting for the foundations to be made 'staid' by 'the fairest and most fortunate of all creatures' (p. 2).[42] The opening manages both to express Montague's awareness of his dependence on royal favour, and to register his extraordinary patience, like the living porter, in remaining dutiful and hopeful throughout many years of uncertainty. The welcome is typical of the way the entertainment gracefully acknowledges and attempts to appropriate the language of hiding and deception commonly applied to Catholics. The porter offers the key to the Queen assuring her she will find nothing hidden, least of all in the host's inner thoughts: 'As for the owner of this house, mine honourable Lord, his tongue is the keie of his heart: and his heart the locke of his soule. Therefore what he speakes you may constantlie beleeue' (p. 3). Montague's very steadfastness in and openness about his Catholic faith becomes a guarantee of his truth.

On Sunday, 15 August Elizabeth and her Council were occupied with deliberations and correspondence concerning her forces in France and disorderly subjects, both Puritan and Catholic, at home. As Breight points out, there would undoubtedly have been Anglican prayers at which Montague and his family would have been present.[43] On Monday, Elizabeth hunted while a song praising her as 'Goddesse and Monarch of this happie Ile' was sung by a 'Nimph' to the accompaniment of 'her Highnesse Musicians' (p. 4), suggesting at least some degree of collaboration between the royal household and those planning the entertainment. More elaborate entertainments continued on Tuesday, when, passing across the park after dinner, the Queen was met by a figure dressed as a pilgrim who complains of being molested by, on the one hand, a 'rough-hewed Ruffian' and, on the other, by a 'Ladie . . . passing frowarde' whose name, paradoxically, is Peace (p. 5). Under Elizabeth's protection, the pilgrim leads the Queen to an oak, hung with the heraldic shields of the local gentry which these two guard. The ruffian turns out to be a wild man, a figure commonly used in heraldry to support coats of arms and embody the fierce spirit of the bearer of the arms.[44] The tree epitomizes the loyal hearts and arms of the gentry of Sussex, which itself forms an epitome of island England: 'All heartes of Oke, then which nothing surer: . . . the wall of this Shire is the sea, strong, but rampired with true hearts, inuincible: where every priuate mans eie is a Beacon

[42] Breight, 'Caressing', 151, notes the similarity between this greeting and that at Kenilworth in 1575.

[43] Ibid. 152. Holmes (*Resistance and Compromise*, 105) cites evidence that Montague had priestly dispensation to attend the Queen to church. For Council business during Elizabeth's stay, see Questier, 'Loyal to a Fault', 230, 232.

[44] John Bloch Friedman, *The Monstrous Races in Medieval Art and Thought* (Cambridge, Mass.: Harvard University Press, 1981), 201.

to discouer: euerie noble mans power a Bulwarke to defende' (p. 6, the wild man is speaking).

The language of the entertainment seems almost directly to answer Burghley's accusation against Catholic priests as 'spial[s] and . . . explorer[s] for the rebel or enemy against his natural prince' who 'wander . . . secretly in his sovereign's camp' to 'measure the depths of ditches or height of bulwarks'.[45] Montague is here displaying his estate, and thus himself, as the natural leader of the loyal and vigilant local gentry, and Sussex as an invincible defensive bulwark of the realm. Cheekily, the pilgrim enlists the Queen's protection against the buffeting of the over-zealous 'Ruffian' who guards the tree and against the waspish words of the Lady Peace, both of whom are unable to distinguish the pilgrim's innocent motives from those of an enemy. Here, Elizabeth's discerning mildness is implicitly distinguished from the misjudging belligerence of her government, its officers, and its anti-Catholic propaganda. Michael Leslie has pointed to the reversals of this encounter, in which the apparent 'ruffian' turns out to be a defender of the loyal oak. The reversals extend to the use of the term 'ruffian'. Burghley had called priests 'roisters and ruffians' in *The Execution of Justice*, and the term was again used in the proclamation against seminary priests and Jesuits, dated 18 October 1591, which, Questier points out, was probably being devised by the Council during the stay at Cowdray.[46] Montague's 'ruffian' turns out to be an over-zealous officer of the state, such a man, perhaps, as Topcliffe himself.

The wild man assures the Queen that the Oak he guards has a 'root so deeplie fastened, that treacherie, though she undermine to the centre, cannot find the windings' (p. 7). The entertainment seems to be appropriating, in order to refute, the language of secret undermining commonly used against Catholics, who, in Burghley's words, pour 'into [the subjects'] hearts malicious and pestilent opinions . . . and [attempt] to search and sound the depths and secrets of all men's inward intentions'. The 1591 Proclamation was similarly to accuse Catholic seminarians of spreading 'by vnderminings of our good Subiects . . . a secret infection of treasons in the bowles of our Realme'.[47] The 'windings' of the root, deep in the soil of a Catholic nobleman's loyal estate, may be hidden, but that is what guarantees the strength and security of the oak.

The theme of hidden treachery is developed through the pilgrim figure who has manoeuvred Elizabeth into bringing him to the tree under her protection. The wild man had refused him access because 'such a disguised worlde it is, that one can scarce know a Pilgrime from a Priest, a tayler from a gentleman, nor a man from a woman. Euerie one seeming to be that which they are not, onelie doe practise what they should not' (p. 8). Given that Elizabeth's Council was aware of at least some of the covert movement of missionary priests through

---

[45] *Execution of Justice*, ed. Kingdon, 36.
[46] Ibid. 34; Questier, 'Loyal to a Fault', 231; for the text of the proclamation, see *An Humble Supplication*, appendix 1, 64.
[47] *Execution of Justice*, ed. Kingdon, 39; *An Humble Supplication*, 63.

Montague's properties in Sussex and London, such a reference to priestly disguise is breathtakingly audacious; Montague must have been very sure of his standing with the Queen to have attempted it.[48] The wild man's suspicions are shown to be groundless; the pilgrim, seeking out the Sussex bulwark, is no more than an innocent traveller who 'desire[s] antiquities' (p. 5). From the loyal Catholic point of view, of course, the wandering, disguised priests were also doing no more than innocently seeking out antiquities, the 'Auncient faithe of the Fathers delivered and received from hand to hande by Contynuall succession'.[49] The pilgrim may be a priest, the entertainment implies, but there is nothing to fear from either.

While the wild man's linking of priests and pilgrims may imply they are actually indistinguishable, his complaint that it is equally difficult to know 'a tayler from a gentleman, nor a man from a woman' repeats familiar conservative gibes against social upstarts and contemporary moral corruption. Social conservatism seems to have been closely allied with religious conservatism in Montague's own sympathies. In his speech to the Lords in 1563, he warned that 'novelties in doctrine and religion' would license those that 'look to wax mighty, and of power . . . by the ruin of noble and ancient men'.[50] The regulation of costume to maintain distinctions of rank or gender was clearly another particular concern of Montague as he was one of a number of noblemen who personally endorsed a royal proclamation of 13 February 1565 against excess in apparel.[51] The view that religious innovation would give rise to more general social and moral ills is one that Montague shared more generally with Catholic polemicists. William Allen described the followers of Protestantism as 'violent and factious men' easily seduced by all the temptations that 'this new religion yieldeth in all fleshly lusts and turpitude'. They were men who were eager to 'break all bonds of obedience, despise domination, make spoil and havoc of all things, and run headlong into all most detestable disorders'.[52] An uproar in London in the latter part of July 1591 must have seemed to Montague and many others confirmation of the dangers inherent in Protestantism. A man called William Hacket, a fanatical Protestant, with two followers, had had himself proclaimed a prophet, preaching the overthrow of the existing ecclesiastical and civil government and the dethroning of the Queen.[53] In the face of such upheavals, the Catholic Montague represents himself and his estate as a bastion of stability and loyalty.

---

[48] For Breight's discussion of the daring nature of the priestly allusions in the exchange of the pilgrim and the wild man, see 'Caressing', 153–4.

[49] I quote from Montague's speech opposing the 1559 legislation, see Timothy J. McCann, 'The Parliamentary Speech of the Viscount Montague against the Act of Supremacy, 1559', *Sussex Archaeological Collections*, 108 (1970), 50–7 (p. 54).

[50] Strype, *Annals of the Reformation*, i.i. 442, 446.   [51] Ibid. i.ii. 540.

[52] Allen in *Execution of Justice*, ed. Kingdon, 140–1.

[53] Curtis Charles Breight discusses this incident in detail in 'Duelling Ceremonies: The Strange Case of William Hacket, Elizabethan Messiah', *Journal of Medieval and Renaissance Studies*, 191 (1989), 35–67.

The themes of contemporary moral corruption and social disorder, along with those of deceit and treachery, were further developed when, on Wednesday, Lord Montague took the opportunity to show off to the Queen his well-stocked fishponds. There she finds an angler, grumbling about the present state of the realm, which he describes as vitiated by exploitation, social innovation, and moral trickery:

I have bin here this two houres and cannot catch an oyster. It may be for lacke of a bait, & that were hard in this nibling world, where euerie man laies bait for another. In the Citie merchants bait their tongues with a lie and an oath, and so make simple men swallow deceitfull wares: and fishing for commoditie is growen so farre, that men are become fishes, for Lande lords put such sweete baits on rackt rents, that as good it were to perch in a pikes belly, as a Tenant in theyr farmes. All our trade is growen to treacherie, for now fish are caught with medicins: which are as vnwholsom as loue procured by witchcraft unfortunate. (p. 9)

As we have seen, it was commonplace for Catholic writers to accuse the Protestant faith of encouraging moral corruption and trickery: 'No promyse or bargayne [is now] kept but onelie for commoditie, & there is no trust to mens wordes any longer', wrote Robert Persons.[54] For Allen, Protestant England was a sink of iniquity: 'Never so much injustice, never so much extortion, never so much theft, never so much pride, ebriety, gluttony, riot, and all other sin and abomination.'[55]

The angler, while complaining of the baits and tricks of others, is apparently willing to practise the same deceptions himself: 'We Anglers make our lines of diuers colours, according to the kindes of waters: so doe men their loues, aiming at the complexion of the faces' (p. 9). Contrasted with the angler is a second fisherman with nets who follows. Where the angler had spoken apparently unaware of the Queen's presence and complains that her glistering beauty spoils his trade, 'Tis best angling in a lowring daie, for here the Sunne so glisters, that the fish see my hooke through my bait' (p. 9), the fisherman draws his nets towards the Queen and addresses her directly. If the angler's trade is one of trickery and deception, the fisherman's is associated with royal virtue and a peaceful state: 'There is no fishing to the sea, nor seruice to the King: but it holdes when the sea is calme & the king vertuous' (p. 10). Where the angler associated himself with criminal deceit, the netter's concern is loyal service to the Queen: 'I come not to tell the art of fishing . . . but with a poor fisher mans wish, that all the hollow hearts to your Maiestie were in my net' (p. 10).

The image of a fisherman casting his nets inevitably recalls the familiar biblical image of Peter, the first Bishop of Rome, as a fisher of men (Matthew 4: 19). In the context of Montague's Catholic entertainment, Elizabeth is thus confronted with a figure, ambiguously both fisherman and priest, who stands before her

---

[54] *An Epistle of the Persecution of Catholickes*, 13.
[55] Allen, quoted in *Execution of Justice*, ed. Kingdon, 221.

offering to rid her kingdom of the true traitors: 'A dish of fish is an vnworthie present for a prince to accept: there be some carpes amongst them, no carpers of states, if there be, I would they might be handled lyke carpes, their tongues pulled out. Some pearches there are I am sure, and if anie pearch higher than in dutie they ought, I would they might sodenly picke ouer the pearch for me' (p. 11). As he displays his many kinds of fish, the netter echoes one of the key biblical sources for the association of fishermen with priests, Ezekiel 47: 10–11: 'And the fishers shall stand: they shall spred out their nets: for their fish shalbe according to their kinds, as the fish of the maine sea, exceeding many. But the myrie places thereof, and the marishes thereof shall not be wholesome: they shalbe made saltpits.'[56] In the language of Montague's entertainment, this becomes the netter's complaint that 'There be some so muddie minded, that they cannot liue in a cleere riuer but a standing poole, as camells will not drinke till they haue troubled the water with their feet: so can they neuer stanch their thirst, till they haue disturbd the state with their trecheries' (p. 10).

The netter's words function not merely to attest the loyalty of Montague and his servants and dissociate them from any treasonous intentions, but, with breathtaking boldness, if the fisherman/priest symbolism is noticed, they assert the loyalty of Catholic priests, the main agents of treason according to the government. The netter offers his service as true patriot ready to protect Elizabeth and her kingdom from the real traitors, the privy carpers, ambitious climbers, and immoral exploiters who operate unchecked within the Protestant state. Opposed to the loyal and virtuous fisherman are the deceptions of the deceitful anglers, who lay bait for the innocent in the English state, including, it is surely implied, innocent Catholics. Only royal watchfulness, and the benign glistering of Elizabeth's personal favour, can protect the anglers' victims from their treacherous deceptions. Countering the common propagandist accusation that Roman Catholic priests use enchantments to bewitch their converts, the fisherman's song, ending the little scene, claims: 'Our habits base, but hearts as true as steele, | sad lookes, deep sighs, flat faith are all our spels.'[57] Whatever tricks others might use, true fishermen use only patience and the baits of a faithful love to catch at hearts.

On Thursday, Elizabeth again dined in Montague's walks at a table 'xlviij yardes long', but even this moment of relaxation was not without its carefully planned messages. After dinner, the country people appeared and danced with a simple tabor and pipe before the Queen 'the Lorde Montague and his Lady among them' (p. 11). Here was no rack-rent landlord, destroying by his selfish exploitation the good old order of England, but an old-fashioned nobleman, following the old

---

[56] I quote the verses in English from the contemporary Geneva Bible. There was no English version of the Old Testament for use by Catholics at this time.

[57] *The Speeches and Honorable Entertainment Giuen to the Queenes Maiestie in Progresse, at Cowdrey in Sussex* (London: Thomas Scarlet for William Wright, 1591) [STC 3907.7], 10. See Carol Z. Wiener, 'The Beleaguered Isle: A Study of Elizabethan and Early Jacobean Anti-Catholicism', *Past & Present*, 51 (1971), 27–62 (esp. pp. 42–3).

traditions, the natural lord of a contented affinity, doing homage to his lawful sovereign.[58] On Friday, the final ceremony of Elizabeth's visit, the knighting of six gentlemen, took place. The selection of beneficiaries seems to have been carefully balanced by the Queen and Council. Three, including George Browne, Montague's son, who had been briefly imprisoned in 1571 in connection with the Ridolfi plot, were known Catholics, and two, Henry Goring and Nicholas Parker, as Breight points out, were shortly to be appointed as commissioners dealing with recusants and seminary priests. Questier's researches, however, have established that neither seems to have pursued their commissions very actively, and that Henry Goring was Montague's brother-in-law.[59] The honours bestowed by Elizabeth nevertheless carefully signal both royal graciousness towards Montague and his Catholic affinities, and a clear indication that there will be no slackening of the penal laws.

TRUTHS AND 'MEERE FICTIONS'[60]

In spite of Montague's attempt to use the occasion to contest the government's definitions of loyalty and treachery, Elizabeth and her Council had reason to be satisfied as they left Cowdray. They had brought the searching presence of royal power into Montague's home and had received a fulsome display of loyalty from one of Elizabeth's leading Catholics that would soon be well publicized through the medium of print. Elizabeth smiled graciously on Montague, but evidently saw no reason to translate his fictions into policy. In the fantasy world of the entertainment, Elizabeth's smiling favour had not only reassured Montague and his household, but had also restrained the mistaken belligerence of ruffian officials who threatened continental travellers as they sought merely to venerate old traditions. She heard about the true causes of social unrest rampant in her kingdom, and her bright favour not only prevented the cruel angling of the catchpoles, but enabled the priest/netter, like the fishermen of Ezekiel, to separate the false from the faithful in order to bring the Queen a harvest of such truly loyal subjects as Montague himself. Royal policy, however, followed a different agenda. Elizabeth's favour to Montague's household lasted only as long as he lived. If Montague's self-justificatory speech to family and local gentry in January 1592 was designed to protect his family from the 'ruffians' of Elizabethan officialdom after his death, it was only partially successful. Questier points out that while neither Goring nor Parker made any arrests of Montague's followers after his death in 1592, the government 'catchpole' Topcliffe pursued members

[58] Breight, 'Caressing', 156, makes this point.
[59] Ibid. 159; Questier, 'Loyal to a Fault', 237-8, (and for Dormer) 250 (n. 106). For George Browne, see Manning, *Religion and Society*, 229.
[60] The phrase is Southwell's, *An Humble Supplication*, 33.

of his household, such as the priests Robert Gray and Francis Rydell, 'all over the country'.[61]

Montague's subtle contesting of terms certainly had little success in persuading the government of the loyalty of Catholics beyond his own household. Two months after her visit, Elizabeth signed a proclamation setting up commissioners to root out priests in the shires, and further criminalizing anyone who supported or concealed them. It expressed the official view in particularly clear terms, defining loyalty in terms of betrayal of Catholic activity and equating Catholic secrecy with 'vnderminings of our good Subiects' and 'treasons in the bowels of our Realme'.[62] A number of Catholic replies to the Proclamation reiterated the prevailing Jesuit position, 'hurling abuse at Elizabeth and inciting rebellion against her'.[63] One pamphlet, however, responded in terms that were thoroughly sympathetic to the loyal Catholic position expressed by Montague in his entertainment.[64]

The terms and strategies of the manuscript pamphlet, *An Humble Supplication*, written in December 1591 by the Jesuit Robert Southwell, are strikingly close to those of the entertainment. English Catholics, it argues, desire royal favour, 'soveraignes favours being the foundation of subiects fortunes and their dislikes the steepest downfall to all vnhappiness', and had proved themselves the most loyal of followers: 'none more forward to do all duties, or liberall to stretch their habilites, then Catholiques were in your Highnes defence'.[65] It is not Catholics who are 'Rufianlike or disordered', but those who prosecute them, 'racking public authority to private purposes' they hide their 'owne dangerous growndes' in 'deluding shrowdes'.[66] Typical of such deceptions was Walsingham's spy Robert Poolie, who drew:

into the nett such greene witts, as (partly fearing the generall oppression, partly angled with golden hookes) might easily be overwrought by Master Secretaries subtill and sifting witt. For *Poolie* masking his secrett Intentions vnder the face of Religion, and abusing with irreligious hypocrasie all Rites and Sacraments, to borrow the false opinion of a

---

[61] Questier, 'Loyal to a Fault', 233 (n. 28), 238, 249–50 (nn. 105, 106).

[62] 'A declaration of great troubles pretended against the Realme by a number of seminarie Priests and Iesuists, sent, and very secretly dispersed in the same, to worke great Treasons vnder a false pretence of Religion, with a prouision very necessary for remedy thereof', in *An Humble Supplication*, appendix 1, p. 63. Although dated 18 Oct. 1591, the Proclamation appears not to have been issued until late November 1591.

[63] Holmes, *Resistance and Compromise*, 170. For a detailed discussion of English Catholic attitudes to rebellion, see ibid. 134–60. For Southwell's position, see ibid. 169–73.

[64] Holmes argues that *An Humble Supplication* does not express Southwell's 'real opinions' (*Resistance and Compromise*, 170–2), but whether this is the case or not, it gives expression to loyal Catholic arguments.

[65] *An Humble Supplication*, 1, 14. This may be a sly reference to Burghley's use of Montague in *The Copie of a Letter* of 1588. For an account of the circumstances in which Southwell wrote the *Supplication*, see Christopher Devlin, *The Life of Robert Southwell: Poet and Martyr* (London: Longmans and Green, 1956), 240–1.

[66] *An Humble Supplication*, 2, 8.

Catholique still fedd the poore gentlemen with his Masters baytes, and he holding the lyne in his hand, suffered them like silly fish to play themselues vpon the hooke, till it were throughly fastened, that then he might strike at his owne pleasure, and be sure to drawe them to a Certaine destruction.[67]

Throughout the pamphlet, Southwell's strategy is to appeal to the 'softnes of [the Queen's] mercifull hand' over the heads of those who persecute Catholics: 'we presume that your Maiestie seldome or never heareth the truth of our persecutions, your lenity and tendernes being knowne to be soe professed an enemy to these Cruelties that you would neuer permitt their Continuance, if they were expressed to your Highnes as they are practised vpon vs'.[68]

  The Cowdray entertainment offered just such a rare opportunity to express to Elizabeth the 'truth of our persecutions' and warn her of the true source of corruption in the state. The author of the entertainment is unknown, although a number of verbal echoes in the text suggest that John Lyly, perhaps through his role as an official of the Revels office, may well have played some part in the writing.[69] If so, then Lyly must have cooperated with, and to a large extent have been directed by, those who shared Montague's loyal Catholic agenda. Southwell's patron was Montague's brother, and Topcliffe thought Southwell himself had been at Cowdray 'the summer before the Queen's Majesty came' there.[70] Topcliffe's evidence is unreliable, but it is an intriguing possibility that the established writer Southwell, who was to use similar arguments and imagery later in the same year, was at least consulted about the important opportunity of Montague's entertainment of the Queen.

<hr/>

  [67] *An Humble Supplication*, 18.   [68] Ibid. 44.
  [69] See the parallels noted by Hotson with both the Mitcham and Chiswick entertainments in *Queen Elizabeth's Entertainment at Mitcham,* ed. Leslie Hotson (New Haven: Yale University Press, 1953), 45, 55, 56, 57.
  [70] For Francis Browne's association with Southwell, see Questier, 'Loyal to a Fault', 240. For Topcliffe's testimony, see Devlin, *The Life of Robert Southwell*, 219.

Note: Michael Questier's authoritative study of the Browne household, *Catholicism and Community in Early Modern England: Politics, Aristocratic Patronage and Religion, c. 1550–1640* (Cambridge: Cambridge University Press, 2006), appeared in print after this essay was at press. References to Questier's 2004 article, cited above, should be supplemented by his book, which provides even more information on Browne's Catholicism.

11

Elizabeth I's Reception at Bisham (1592): Elite Women as Writers and Devisers

Peter Davidson and Jane Stevenson

The woman represented as 'The Lady of the Farm' in the 1592 entertainment of Queen Elizabeth I at Bisham Abbey, in Berkshire, has an interesting history. Elizabeth, Lady Russell, was one of the four daughters of Sir Anthony Cooke, a significant group of highly educated and strong-willed women, roughly contemporary with the Queen, who were the wives and mothers of immensely important men.[1] Elizabeth (1540–1609) had married first Sir Thomas Hoby, scholar, traveller, and translator of Castiglione, and subsequently John, Lord Russell. Her marriage to Sir Thomas, a friend of her father's of long standing, took place in June 1558, a month after he had inherited Bisham from his childless brother, Sir Philip. The couple had interests in common, and the marriage was apparently a happy one that produced a child every other year. In 1566, Hoby took her to Paris where he had been made ambassador, his first major state service, and, as they must both surely have hoped, the opening of a glittering career. But he died there in the same year, leaving his pregnant wife to make her way home with her children and his corpse.[2] Lady Hoby, who retained the wardship of her Hoby children, remained a widow for eight years, looking after the estate at Bisham on behalf of her young son Edward, before marrying John, Lord Russell, heir of the Earl of Bedford, on 23 December 1574. She apparently

---

[1] Stephen J. Barns, 'The Cookes of Gidea Hall', *Essex Review*, 21 [81] (1912), 1–9; Marjorie K. McIntosh, 'Sir Anthony Cooke: Tudor Humanist, Educator and Religious Reformer', *Proceedings of the American Philosophical Society*, 119 (1975), 233–50; Roland H. Bainton, 'The Four Daughters of Anthony Cooke', in *Women of the Reformation, from Spain to Scandinavia* (Minneapolis: Augsburg Publishing House, 1977), 100–15; Mary Ellen Lamb, 'The Cooke Sisters: Attitudes towards Learned Women in the Renaissance', in Margaret P. Hannay (ed.), *Silent but for the Word: Tudor Women as Patrons, Translators and Writers of Religious Works* (Kent, Oh.: Kent State University Press, 1985), 107–25; Jane Stevenson, 'Mildred Cecil, Lady Burleigh: poetry, politics and Protestantism', in Victoria E. Burke and Jonathan Gibson (eds.), *Early Modern Women's Manuscript Writing: Selected Papers of the Trinity/Trent Colloquium* (Aldershot: Ashgate Publishing, 2004), 51–73.

[2] She wrote movingly about this (and also about other personal tragedies) in Latin verse: see *Early Modern Women Poets*, ed. Jane Stevenson and Peter Davidson (Oxford: Oxford University Press, 2001), 44–7.

continued to live between Bisham and Russell House in Blackfriars, which was her home for doing London business for the rest of her life. With Lord Russell, she had another three children, a son who died in infancy, and two daughters, Elizabeth and Anne. Lord Russell himself died in 1584, so her second venture into matrimony, like her first, lasted ten years.

Lady Russell was determined to give her children a good start in life. She moved heaven and earth to match her second son, Thomas Posthumus, with the heiress Margaret Dakins, in which she was eventually successful.[3] She also educated her Russell daughters with care: Henry Lok's sonnet addressed to them refers to their learning.[4] But the daughters were a problem: they were well born, well connected, attractive, and clever, but due to the early deaths of their father and brother, they did not have dowries commensurate with their rank.[5] The only answer was to enhance their personal value. As the court was headed by a Queen, this could most readily be achieved by getting them appointed Maids of Honour, since this would give them power and influence in their own right to enhance the claims for marriageability which they inherited.[6] It is this enterprise that almost certainly lies behind the 1592 Bisham entertainment, in which the parts of Sybilla and Isabella—'two Virgins keeping Sheepe, and sowing in their samplers'—seem to have been played by Elizabeth and Anne Russell, aged 18 and 16, respectively. Inserting the Russell girls into the group of the Queen's ladies was no less of a coup than securing an heiress for Thomas Postumus, and it was not easily achieved. Even with the backing of Lord Burghley, it took not less than five years to achieve, assuming that the Bisham entertainment represents the opening stage of the campaign.

One of the most intriguing questions prompted by the entertainment—the first occasion on which English noblewomen took speaking roles in a quasi-dramatic performance—is who devised and wrote it. Since evidence for Lady Russell's learning and culture is not lacking, it is highly likely that she played a significant part. She published a translation from Latin,[7] and she has left a considerable body of verse, mostly in Latin, with some in Greek and English: almost all funerary. However, the important lesson to be derived from Lady

---

[3] Margaret Dakins married Walter Devereux, younger brother of Robert Devereux, 2nd Earl of Essex, and was a widow at 20 when he was killed at the siege of Rouen. She was immediately sought for remarriage.

[4] Henry Lok, *Ecclesiaste, otherwise called The Preacher* (London: Richard Field, 1597).

[5] Patricia Phillippy, *Women, Death and Literature in Post-Reformation England* (Cambridge: Cambridge University Press, 2002), 194: the Russell girls, unlike the Hobys, were wards of the crown.

[6] On female courtiership, see Barbara J. Harris, 'Women and Politics in Early Tudor England', *Historical Journal*, 33.2 (1990), 259–87, p. 282. See also Pam Wright, 'A Change in Direction: The Ramification of a Female Household, 1558–1603', in David Starkey et al. (eds.), *The English Court: From the Wars of the Roses to the Civil War* (London: Longman, 1987), 147–72 (pp. 158–9).

[7] She translated John Ponet, *A Way of Reconciliation* (published in 1605): see *Protestant Translators: Anne Lock Prowse and Elizabeth Russell*, ed. Elaine V. Beilin (Aldershot: Ashgate, 1998) [unpaginated facsimile reproduction].

Russell's (and indeed her sisters') cultural activities is that she was not merely an epigrapher, but a *deviser*. There is little doubt that she devised the Bisham entertainment, in the same way that she planned the funerary commemoration of all her families (those of her husbands and children, and probably of her parents also). She was perfectly capable of writing the cadenced prose in 'The Lady of the Farm' and the small number of verses therein, but it is her agency, not her authorship, which matters. This essay considers the activities of Lady Russell and other elite women as producers and consumers of a variety of cultural artefacts ranging from tomb sculpture to embroidery to courtly entertainments. In so doing, it not only sheds new light on the 1592 entertainment at Bisham, but also posits the concept of 'devisership' as a new category of early modern women's cultural production.

LADY RUSSELL, WRITER AND DEVISER

Sir Anthony Cooke's tomb at Romford was extensively decorated with verses in English, Latin, and Greek generally attributed to his children. The tomb depicts Sir Anthony, his wife, and two sons (the daughters are not visually represented). But it seems highly likely that since Lady Russell was the most prolific writer of funerary verse of all the siblings, she played a significant part in these compositions. A short poem, 'sir Anthonies farewel to his wife' tilts the balance of probability towards Lady Russell, since it has the same first line ('chara mihi multos conjunx dilecta per annos', 'O wife dear to me for many years') as a poem that Lady Russell later wrote for her nephew Sir Robert Cecil on the death of his wife, dated February 1597.[8]

The English verses on Sir Anthony Cooke's monument, written after 1576, open with a modesty trope that indirectly suggests that it is a daughter who writes:

> You learned men, and such as learning love,
> Vouchsafe to read this rude unlearned verse.
> For stones are doombe, and yet for man's behove
> God lends them tongues sometimes for to rehearse
> Such words of worth as worthiest wights may pierce.
> Yea, stones sometimes when bloud and bones be rot,
> Do blaze the bruit, which else might be forgot.[9]

Fascinatingly, the Latin verses 'under Sir Anthony and his lady' seem to be speaking to an entirely different constituency, as if the semiotics of writing in Latin allow the voicing of a completely different value system. The epitaph opens

---

[8] February 1597: see Hatfield House MSS, Cecil Papers 140, no. 82.
[9] John Strype, *Annals of the Reformation and Establishment of Religion and Other Various Occurrences in the Church of England*, 2nd edn., 4 vols. (London: Thomas Edlin, 1725), iii. 2. p. 606.

conventionally with praise of the wife, but turns after six lines to unstinting praise of the daughters who are not otherwise represented:

> Cur te, Roma, facit Cornelia docta superbam?
> Quam multas tales, et mage, COCUS habet?
> Quinque sciunt natæ conjungere Græca Latinis,
> Insignes claris moribus atque piis.
> [Why does learned Cornelia constitute your pride, O Rome,
> Since Cooke has many of the kind, and more?
> Five daughters know how to put together Greek with Latin
> Famous for their excellent virtue and piety.]

Given that the Cooke brothers, Richard and William, did not leave any reputation for learning, it seems likely that these verses were written either by Lady Russell or by the surviving sisters in committee.

These tomb verses for Sir Anthony Cooke, thus, hint that a Latinate woman might exist simultaneously in two different universes of discourse. The same is true, in a rather different way, of elite widows, who were, on the one hand, mere women, with limited rights within a patriarchal family system, and, on the other, expected to act intelligently in safeguarding their property and their children's interests. Lady Russell and her widowed sister Lady Bacon were remarkable for the strength of their views and the shortness of their tempers. Both were able to finesse their limited legal rights over their husbands' estates into continued enjoyment of their respective marital homes, Bisham and Gorhambury. Lady Russell also took advantage of her long acquaintance with the Queen and her family connection with Lord Burghley to act as an advocate for others: for example, Lady Dorothy Perrott, the Earl of Essex's sister, begged her to intervene with Lord Burghley to prevent her husband's ruin in June of 1592, while Sir Henry Unton acknowledged her good efforts on his behalf to alleviate the Queen's displeasure.[10] Their learning set the Cooke sisters somewhat apart from more conventional women, but it is not learning alone that accounts for their pragmatic assumption of personal power. Elizabeth Shrewsbury, for example, the much-married 'Bess of Hardwick', was not an educated woman, but similarly, she was a brutally effective guardian of the fortunes of herself and her children.[11]

Here we should probably guard against an anachronistically 'feminist' interpretation of Lady Russell's life and actions. Most of the actions of the Cooke sisters can be interpreted within the context of cementing familial networks of the godly for the good of England, and, of course, themselves. Lady Russell's entire career can fruitfully be seen as working for the advancement of her family (a conventionally sanctioned upper-class woman's ambition), while also pushing against social limits on her own behaviour, since she continually claimed the

---

[10] *HMC Hatfield*, IV, pp. 214, 365.
[11] David N. Durant, *Bess of Hardwick: Portrait of an Elizabethan Dynast* (London: Weidenfeld and Nicolson, 1977), 54–7.

maximum status that could be bluffed out of her circumstances. Lady Russell was utterly convinced of her own competence to run her own affairs and those of her children and dependants; but she was not thereby making a point about women. Her advancement of her daughters in terms that might now be read as 'feminist' needs to be considered as part of an overall strategy of welding her children into a mutual benefit association: her ruthless treatment of Margaret Dakins, for example, suggests that she had no respect for any notion of women's individual rights. Rather, Lady Russell was advancing her daughters because they were among the pieces that remained, so to say, on the family chessboard; she was working to see them placed at court, well married, in a position to aid their brothers.

Another example of Lady Russell's attempts to extend her personal power may be seen in her 1600 bid to become keeper, in her own right, of Donnington Castle—even though this was a notionally military position.[12] She failed, but she returned to the attack near the end of her life, when, in May 1606, she brought a suit in Star Chamber seeking to recover the possession of lands of which she considered herself to have been unrightfully deprived. Despite attempts by James VI and I to persuade her to settle her affairs away from the courts, she chose to act for herself. According to the account in Hawarde's reports, the judges decided that she did not have a case, so they 'began to moove the Courte' to adjourn at midday, 'but the Ladye, interruptinge them, desyred to be hearde, & after many denyalls by the Courte, vyolentlye & with greate audacitie beganne a large discourse & woulde not by any meanes be stayed or interrupted, but wente one for the space of halfe an howre or more'.[13] All of which is to say that, as far as Lady Russell is concerned, the ordinary norms limiting women's independent activity applied to her personally only up to a point.

This is reflected in the remarkable tomb complex she created at Bisham towards the end of her life, and which has been extensively discussed by Patricia Phillippy.[14] The first monument, designed in or after 1566, shows Edward and Philip Hoby lying side by side as one would normally expect to find husband and wife, with a handsome verse tribute to both brothers. Lady Russell's original intention, as stated in the Hoby epitaph, was to have been buried modestly in this tomb, where she is not visually represented:

> Et soror et coniunx vobis commune sepulchrum
> Et michi composui, cum mea fata ferent.[15]
> [As sister and wife I have made one tomb for you

---

[12] In *HMC Hatfield*, IX, pp. 51–2, there is a letter from Lady Russell to Sir Robert Cecil, ruefully recalling gifts to Elizabeth worth £500, 'in hope to have Dunnington lease'.

[13] Tim Stretton, *Women Waging Law in Elizabethan England* (Cambridge: Cambridge University Press, 1998), 54–5; John Hawarde, *Les Reportes del Cases in Camera Stellata, 1593 to 1609*, ed. William Baildon (London: privately printed, 1894), 275.

[14] Patricia Phillippy, *Women, Death and Literature in Post-Reformation England* (Cambridge: Cambridge University Press, 2002), 179–210.

[15] Quoted ibid. 187.

And also for myself when my time is come.]

Perhaps it was the social advance represented by her second marriage that caused her evident change of plan. The Russell marriage, as it turned out, put her in a delicate position; the fact that both her Russell son and her second husband let her down by predeceasing their fathers meant that she, and her daughters, might only too easily be written out of Russell history as broken links in the dynastic chain. To identify herself in death with the Hobys would be to concur with that, yet the Russell connection was highly useful to both sets of her children, a reason to defend it.

She was also forced into unconventionality by another oddity of her situation. As Nigel Llewellyn observes, the usual elite pattern in Lady Russell's generation was to place the woman with court connections in the Abbey, and the husband on the family estates.[16] But since Lord Russell did not live to inherit, there was no very good reason to bury him on his family estate of Chenies, in Buckinghamshire, where he had not lived for many years. Nor would it have been appropriate to annex him by burying him in the Hoby family chapel, even though Bisham had been a home to him for a decade. Thus it was the Abbey for Lord Russell, and following on from that, Lady Russell's eventual decision to use her own sepulture to create iconographic readjustment of this complex family history into a personal statement, since it was essentially she and her connections and alliances who determined the status of the survivors, Hoby and Russell alike.

Lord Russell's tomb in St Edmund's Chapel in Westminster Abbey, erected after 1584, therefore speaks eloquently of the most urgent problem which he had left for his wife to deal with: ensuring that Anne and Elizabeth's status as daughters of a future earl was not eroded by their father's death. Unusually, therefore, it includes prominent figures of the two daughters who were later to perform in the Bisham entertainment—not in the accepted position of kneeling ancillary figures at the base or in the background of the monument, but as central elements in the composition. Uncommonly, Anne and Elizabeth had also walked in their father's funeral procession; at the time, women usually only marched in the funeral processions of other women. Further, Elizabeth and Anne are the addressees of Lady Russell's own Latin verses on the tablet above the central coat of arms. This is highly unconventional. Either an address to the deceased, as on the monument to Sir Thomas Hoby, or a speech in the persona of the deceased, like 'sir Anthonies farewel to his wife', would have been more usual. Another very surprising feature of this Russell monument is its inclusion of a verse by Sir Edward Hoby, emphatically declaring his cooperation with his

[16] Nigel Llewellyn, 'Honour in Life, Death and in the Memory: Funeral Monuments in Early Modern England', *Transactions of the Royal Historical Society*, 6th ser. 6 (1996), 184–5.

Figure 11.1. Tomb of Elizabeth, Lady Russell (erected after Lady Hoby's death in 1609, but devised by her in her lifetime), the Hoby Chapel, All Saints' Church, Bisham, Berkshire. Painted alabaster and ironwork. (Illustration by Jane Stevenson)

mother's efforts.[17] It was perfectly within elite social norms for a kinsman by marriage to write verses on the deceased, and for such verses to be affixed to the coffin or to the mourning apparatus at an elite funeral. It is, however, far from usual for them to be actually inscribed on the monument itself, as a permanent record of connectedness and allegiance.[18]

The separate monument that Lady Russell created for herself in the early 1600s is revealing of how she had come to see herself. It is roughly the size

[17] *Reges, reginae, nobiles, et alii in Ecclesia Collegiata B. Petri Westmonasterii sepulti* (London: E. Bullifant, 1606), 44–6, trans. Connie McQuillen, in *Tudor and Stuart Women Writers*, ed. Louise Schleiner (Bloomington: Indiana University Press, 1994), 49.

[18] See Phillippy, *Women, Death, and Literature*, 196–201. Phillippy points out that Hoby originally wrote the verse to adorn the pall (p. 200).

and shape of a four-poster bed: she kneels in front of a lectern in the middle, in the full panoply of aristocratic widowhood. Just in front of her knees lies a sad bolster with tiny protruding feet: the Russell son who died in infancy. Behind her, but within the four columns of the central structure—which thus fences off the dead from the living—kneel her three dead daughters. Outside the structure are the three children who survived her: kneeling facing her, in the place of honour, is Anne Russell, in red velvet and ermine, with her Countess's coronet. Edward Hoby and his brother Thomas Posthumus kneel behind her. Thus, the monument negates any view of Lady Russell as a link in the patriarchal chain that handed Bisham from one generation of Hobys to the next, and elides her failure to form such a link in the chain of Russells. Instead, it foregrounds her motherhood, while arranging the children in order of political importance; significantly, it is her Russell daughter (and son) who are in front of her.

THE 1592 BISHAM ENTERTAINMENT

Bisham Abbey is sited on the Thames, just below Marlow, about thirty miles from Westminster. It was, thus, a very convenient stopping-place for a progress up the Thames towards Oxford, or towards the West Country. The 1592 visit was by no means the first time that entertainment at Bisham had been of political significance. On 8 September 1560, Lady Russell's then husband, Sir Thomas Hoby, gave a party at his house in Bisham, which was the venue of an abortive, but significant, conspiracy. The guests on this occasion included 'The Lord Marques of Northampton, the Erles of Arundell and Hertford, the lord Cobham, the Lord Henry Seimer, Sir Roger Northe, Lady Katerin Grey, Lady Jane Seimer, the Lady Cecill, Mrs Blaunch Appary and Mrs Mansfield'.[19] Of this group, the first three ladies—along with Hoby himself, the Seymours, and Northampton—were leading members of the group that Patrick Collinson has dubbed 'Elizabethan puritans', who were, as Charlotte Merton has observed, very strong among the ladies of Elizabeth's Privy Chamber.[20] Northampton, brother of Queen Katherine Parr, had been Hoby's patron in the 1550s. Lady Cecil (Mildred, wife of Lord Burghley) was by then Hoby's sister-in-law. The process of enquiry into the subsequent marriage between Edward Seymour, Lord Hertford, and Katherine Grey instituted by the enraged Queen revealed that Jane ('lady Jane Seimer') had constituted herself her brother's family, made Hertford's suit to Katherine

[19] *The Travels and Life of Sir Thomas Hoby, Kt, of Bisham Abbey, Written by Himself, 1547–1564*, ed. Edgar Powell, Camden Miscellany, 10 (London: for the Camden Society, 1902), 128.

[20] Charlotte Merton, 'The Women who Served Queen Mary and Queen Elizabeth: Ladies, Gentlewomen and Maids of the Privy Chamber, 1553–1603' (unpublished doctoral thesis, University of Cambridge, 1992), 205.

on his behalf, and made all the arrangements for the wedding.[21] Hertford's final decision had been taken after a day that Edward, Jane, and Katherine had spent at Bisham with Sir Thomas Hoby: presumably, this very occasion, 8 September. Elizabeth Hoby (as she was then) is not mentioned in Hoby's notes on the day, but there is every reason to think that she was also of this party.[22]

It is clear from the inscriptions on Lord Russell's tomb, already discussed, that Sir Edward Hoby and his mother were capable of working harmoniously together, and presenting a united front; and it might seem obvious that, as master of the house, he was responsible for so crucial an entertainment. But one problem has been raised with associating Sir Edward with the entertainment: the perceived ambiguity of his attitude to the theatre. He had a long-standing relationship with a dramatist, Thomas Lodge, who was servitour or scholar under him at Trinity College, Oxford (however, since Lodge was off exploring Brazil and the Straits of Magellan between 1591 and 1593, it is most unlikely that he was called upon to write the Bisham entertainment).[23] But on the other hand, in 1586, Sir Edward had dedicated his translation of Martin Coignet's *Politique Discourses* to his uncle, Lord Burghley, as a New Year's gift. It is a work in which jugglers and stage players are anathematized.[24] However, there is an equally good case for arguing that Lady Russell herself disapproved of the theatre, since it was she who prevented James Burbage from building a theatre on the land he owned at Blackfriars: her name heads the list of petitioners.[25]

In order to account for this, the concept of 'dramatic performance' can usefully be nuanced. In the 1580s, there was a vast gulf between the commercial theatre, the focus of an unremitting hostility from moralists of all stripes which was directed at both the players and the audience, and 'clean' drama, which consisted of the Latin plays performed in the universities, the Children's Company plays—and probably, entertainments presented to the Queen, which resembled university dramas in that they involved aristocratic amateurs. The public stage

[21] The inquisition of Katherine and Edward is held in the British Library: see Harleian MS 6286, and see also *Calendar of State Papers, Foreign, of Elizabeth (1561–62)*, ed. Joseph Stevenson (London: Longman & Co., 1866), 335.

[22] Elizabeth Hoby's absence might perhaps have been explained by the fact that she was actually 'lying in'. She was certainly one of the 'Elizabethan puritans', and the Grey/Seymour marriage, a bid for the succession, was also most certainly aimed at completing the reform of the Church of England along the lines laid down by Edward VI. See Brenda M. Hosington, 'England's First Female-Authored Encomium: The Seymour Sisters' *Hecatodistichon* (1550), to Marguerite de Navarre. Text, Translation, Notes, and Commentary', *Studies in Philology*, 93 (1996), 117–63.

[23] See Alexandra Halasz, 'Lodge, Thomas (1558–1625)', *Oxford Dictionary of National Biography* (Oxford: Oxford University Press, Sept. 2004); online edn. Jan. 2006 (www.oxforddnb.com/view/article/16923, accessed 14 Mar. 2006).

[24] Steven W. May, *Elizabethan Courtier Poets* (Asheville, NC: Pegasus Press, 1999), 346; HMC Hatfield V, p. 487. I. A. Shapiro, 'Richard II or Richard III or . . .?', *Shakespeare Quarterly*, 9 (1958), 240–6.

[25] A. L. Rowse, 'Bisham and the Hobys', in *Times, Persons, Places* (London: Macmillan, 1965), 188–218 (p. 210).

is repeatedly represented as a potential focus for misrule; the courtly stage as an aspect of ruling.

One of the most striking aspects of the Bisham entertainment is that it was the first occasion on which English noblewomen took speaking roles in a quasi-dramatic performance. But the question of whether this is transgressive can be placed in context by Lady Russell's urgent need to showcase her daughters, already witnessed by their participation in their father's funeral, and their unusual prominence on his monument. It is a departure from the norms: however, no contemporary objection to any of Lady Russell's presentations of her female children has come down to us. This absence of dissenting voices may suggest that she possessed a subtly nuanced sense of the limits within which she operated—which were a little wider than those which women ordinarily enjoyed, due to a general, if tacit, elite indulgence towards a well-connected widow working on behalf of herself and her children. Certainly, it is possible to read, as a gesture of sympathy, the permission granted by the Garter King of Arms that she should have the status in death of which she had been narrowly cheated in life, that of a viscountess.[26]

When we examine the entertainment in more detail, we certainly find nothing that Lady Russell could not have devised, however much of the finished text she may have assigned to others, quite possibly including her son. Equally, there is nothing that would preclude her authorship of the whole, especially since it ends with a direct message from herself to the Queen. It is worth noticing that the Russell daughters, as they are presented in the entertainment, are themselves shown as *devisers*, choosing subjects for craftwork that will carry a message just as much as any of the needlework devised by the Countess of Shrewsbury or her unwilling guest, Mary Stuart.[27]

The Bisham progress presented needlework as a quasi-linguistic medium, of a strongly gendered kind:

SYB: Mens tongues, wrought all with double stitch, but one not true.
PAN: What these?
SYB: Roses, Eglentine, harts-ease, wrought with Queenes stitch, and all right. (Aiii[r])[28]

The choice of rose and eglantine as subjects for embroidery is easy to explain: as Roy Strong has established beyond doubt, rose and eglantine were specifically associable with Elizabeth as personal badges. For example, George Peele, in a poem for Elizabeth's birthday in 1595, exhorts the people to:

---

[26] For the Garter's (Sir William Dethick's) allowance (or indulgence) see Phillippy, *Women, Death and Literature*, 206.
[27] Margaret Swain, *The Needlework of Mary Queen of Scots* (Carlton: Bean, 1986, originally published 1973).
[28] All quotations from 'The Lady of the Farm' are taken from Joseph Barnes, *Speeches deliuered to Her Maiestie this last progresse, at the Right Honorable the Lady Rvssels, at Bissam, the Right Honorable the Lorde Chandos at Sudley, at the Right Honorable the Lord Norris, at Ricorte* (Oxford: Joseph Barnes, 1592).

> . . . wear eglantine,
> And wreaths of roses red and white put on
> In honour of that day . . . [29]

Heartsease (wild pansy) was also a flower significant to Elizabeth: she chose heartsease to ornament two embroidered bindings she executed as a child, one for her own translation of *The Mirror or Glasse of the Synneful Soul*, made as a present for her stepmother, Queen Katherine Parr, in 1544, and another for a book of translations made for her father in 1545.[30] Queen stitch, a variation on Hungarian stitch, is a counted-thread embroidery stitch that results in small regular diamonds; it is not very suitable for representing flowers, since it produces a very formal effect—though the choice of it here is, obviously, for the compliment of the name. Similarly, the use of double-stitch to represent men's perfidy is more for the sake of the play on words than of practicalities: 'weomens tongues are made of the same flesh that their harts are, and speake as they thinke: Mens harts of the flesh that their tongues, and both dissemble' (Aiii'). An anonymous poem written within ten years of this entertainment puts together a similar set of symbolic meanings attached to embroidery stitches, tongues, and hearts:

> No false stitch will I make my hart is true,
> Plaine stitche my sampler is for to complaine
> Now men have tongues of hony, harts of rue,
> True tongues and harts are one, Men makes them twain.[31]

Male perfidy was always a popular subject with Elizabeth: she liked to see noble virgins mistrustful of men and apparently committed to singleness, and she detested seeing her Maids of Honour carried off into marriage.[32]

Embroidery, on account both of its social and ethical connotations and its importance for high fashion and conspicuous consumption, was a significant aspect of the formation of networks of sixteenth-century noblewomen, who were both executants and connoisseurs.[33] This is as true of conspicuously learned and literary women as of others. Elizabeth I particularly liked embroidered bindings, her interest and appreciation presumably enhanced by her own mastery of the

---

[29] Quoted in Roy Strong, *The Cult of Elizabeth* (London: Thames & Hudson, 1987), 68–70.

[30] George Wingfield Digby, *Elizabethan Embroidery* (London: Faber and Faber, 1963), 97: the book is Oxford, MS Cherry 36. See Cyril Davenport, *Royal English Bookbindings* (London: Seeley & Co., 1896), 18–19, 25. The strong association of Elizabeth with heartsease was so widely current by the end of the reign that Shakespeare alludes to it in *A Midsummer Night's Dream*, II. i. 166–8 (see *The Arden Shakespeare: Complete Works*, ed. Richard Proudfoot, Ann Thompson, and David Scott Kastan (London: Thomson Learning, 1998; rev. edn. 2001), 896).

[31] *Early Modern Women Poets*, ed. Stevenson and Davidson, 155.

[32] Strong, *The Cult of Elizabeth*, 28.

[33] See Roszika Parker, *The Subversive Stitch: Embroidery and the Making of the Feminine* (London: Women's Press, 1984), and Roy Strong, 'Charles I's Clothes for the Years 1633 to 1635', *Costume*, 14 (1980), 73–89.

skills involved. She bound a favourite copy of the Epistles of Paul printed in 1578—a tiny sextodecimo volume, convenient for carrying about—in black velvet, embroidered with Latin mottoes in silver cord, reflecting her love of black and white, in a style notably different from any professional embroidered bindings of the time.[34] The Countess of Pembroke also was noted for her skill with the needle; John Taylor, in one of six sonnets to women in *The Needles Excellency* (1631), praises her for her patronage, learning, and virtue: 'she wrought so well in Needle-worke, that she, | Nor yet her workes, shall ere forgotten be.'[35] Nearer to home, Margaret Hoby, *née* Dakins, Lady Russell's daughter-in-law, was known for her embroidered hangings, for 'in her younger days, when first a housekeeper, she employed herself and maids much with their needles'.[36] Thus, the Russell girls' needlecraft is an index of their feminine virtue; their choice of subject, a literal inscription of their identification with their Queen. Both are indications of their suitability as Maids of Honour.

But the Bisham entertainment also strikes a more unusual chord. The girls are asked: 'How doe you burne time, & drowne beauty, in pricking of clouts, when you should bee penning of Sonnets?' (Aiiᵛ). The desirability of eloquence and literary ability in young noblewomen is a note seldom sounded directly in late sixteenth-century England, but it is indirectly attested. Although it is far easier to find evidence for the desirability of modest silence in the circles immediately contiguous to the Queen,[37] noblewomen received something of a double message.[38] The overall context for this was probably Italian: that highly influential work, Castiglione's *The Courtier* (1528), translated by Lady Russell's first husband and published in 1561, assumed that eloquence was desirable for women courtiers.[39] Gabriel Harvey also suggested that a court lady should be able to write verse in a 1578 poem:

[34] Oxford, Bodleian Library MS e Mus. 242; illustrated in Cyril Davenport, *English Embroidered Bookbindings* (London: Kegan Paul, Trench, Trübner & Co, 1899), 63.

[35] Margaret P. Hannay, *Philip's Phoenix* (New York: Oxford University Press, 1990), 129–30.

[36] Sir Hugh Cholmley, *Memoirs*, cited in *The Diary of Lady Margaret Hoby*, ed. D. M. Meads (London: Routledge, 1930), 268.

[37] See Stretton, *Women*, 67–8; Pollock, ' "Teach her to live under obedience": The Making of Women in the Upper Ranks of Early Modern England', *Continuity and Change*, 4 (1989), 238–44.

[38] Note, for instance, John Harington's comments on Lady Russell herself, in his translation of Ariosto, *Orlando Furioso in English Heroical Verse* (London: Richard Field, 1591), 314: 'Concerning the great prayse myne author [Ariosto] ascribeth to madame Vittoria [Colonna]

Whose learned pen such priviledge can give
As it can cause those that are dead to live

And for that cause preferreth her before Porcia wife of Brutus and diuers others that dyed voluntarie soone after their husbandes, it was because she wrate some Verses in the manner of an Epitaph, upon her husband after his deceasse. In which kind that honourable Ladie (widow of the late lord Iohn Russell) deserueth no lesse commendation, hauing done as much for two husbands.'

[39] See also Pietro Bembo, *Gli Asolani* (Venice: Aldo Romano, 1505, and subsequent edns.), book II, trans. with introd. by Rudolf B. Gottfried (Bloomington: Indiana University Press, 1954), 122: '[lovers] like sometimes to recite their poems to their ladies, sometimes to hear their ladies do the same'.

Saltet item, pingatque, eadem, comptumque poëma
Pangat, nec Musas nesciat illa meas.[40]
[She should dance, paint, and compose an elegant poem
Lest she be ignorant of my Muses.]

Indeed, court ladies did write verse: apart from Lady Russell herself and her courtier sisters, Mildred Cecil and Ann Bacon, who were Ladies of the Bedchamber, poems survive from Mary Cheke, who served the Queen for her entire reign, and the Maid of Honour Ann Vavasour.[41] Verse exchange, of course, is a kind of writing in which women could engage with some propriety—at least, when they answered rather than initiated the exchange (Lady Mary Cheke's only known poem is an answer). Thus, while the Russell girls' virtue is stressed by their preference for needlework, their implied command of literary skills and their ready wit in answering also makes them appropriate for Elizabeth's consideration as future Maids of Honour.

The symbolism of the Bisham entertainment is, in itself, nothing exceptional, and certainly in no way subversive. It is, however, a little unusual that Lady Russell is the only proprietor who is iconographically visible, and that Sir Edward, notionally master, is neither physically present nor symbolically represented—perhaps because, as Roger Prior has suggested, his father-in-law lay under the Queen's displeasure.[42] The effect is to recreate Bisham as a woman's space like the Queen's own Privy Chamber, where Isabel, Sybil, Ceres, her nymphs, and the Lady of the Farm exist in feminine harmony, effortlessly fending off the encroachments of Pan—and this may be the intention.

The most significant problem that 'The Lady of the Farm' confronts is not generated by the apparently bold innovation of women's speech, but by the dislocations of pastoral and mythological discourse forced upon the deviser(s) by the need to accommodate, within the structure of a pastoral, appropriate tropes of praise for a 59-year-old Virgin Queen. By convention, the praise of fertility has to attend the translation of an English country estate into Arcadia; chaste but productive marriage; a secure transition between past and future. But the Queen, long past childbearing—yet refusing to name her successor—was exceedingly sensitive on just this topic.

Perhaps the most striking feature of the entertainment is that it is not so much unadventurous as positively old-fashioned. The wild man's opening speech, couched in the euphuistic mode of the 1570s and 1580s, is, like himself, the sort of thing that usually welcomed Elizabeth to a great house in the first half of the reign, evoking the Kenilworth entertainment. In traditional style, he is rendered

---

[40] In 'Aulica', a poem of advice to court ladies, *Gabrielis Harveiii Gratulationum Valdinensium, libri quatuor, ad illustrissimam Augustissimam Principem Elizabetam* (London: Henry Binneman, 1578), written for the Queen's visit to Saffron Walden.

[41] *Early Modern Women Poets*, ed. Stevenson and Davidson, 19–23, 25–30, 78–80.

[42] Roger Prior, 'Æmilia Lanyer and Queen Elizabeth at Cookham', *Cahiers élisabéthains*, 63 (Apr. 2003), 17–32.

civil on the instant: 'Thus Vertue tameth fiercenesse, Beauty, madnesse. Your Maiesty on my knees will I follows, bearing this Club, not as a Saluage, but to beate downe those that are' (Aiiᵛ).

The subsequent scene with Pan and the shepherdesses is more problematic: while it steers an effective course through the double messages attending the accomplishments of a noblewoman at court, it leaves one of the daughters making a speech clumsily fitted within the pastoral translation of the household. On the one hand, Elizabeth, chaste, mild, and learned, is a better deity than the adulterous Jupiter or Juno. And, for all her virginal autonomy, she makes England fruitful and peaceful, in contrast to the warring continent ('our Riuers flow with fish, theirs with bloode' (Aiiiᵛ)). On the other hand, however, her intervention in the Netherlands is praised, in a momentary slippage of the tropes of pastoral (this may suggest Lady Russell's direct involvement with the writing, since the 'Elizabethan puritans' lobbied incessantly on behalf of the Protestant cause in Europe).[43] But again, after a learned reference to the myth of Philemon and Baucis, the scene ends with a quick transformation: Pan, like the wild man before him, abandons his essential nature, civilized (or emasculated) by one glance from the Queen's eyes. He breaks his pipe; his wild notes give way to the lyre of Apollo; controlled, court music. By 1592, this imagery of concord must have struck many of the younger spectators as sadly less applicable to the present than to the past.

The point of maximum difficulty for the entertainment as a whole occurs in the third and last scene. 'Ceres with her Nymphes in an haruest Cart' (Aiiijʳ) welcome Elizabeth to the farm; but the praise of fruitfulness and the triumph of Ceres has to be dislocated so that 'in this Ile . . . *Cynthia* shalbe *Ceres* Mistres' (Aiiijᵛ). Cynthia is not the sylvan Diana, but the cold, chaste guardian of peace and civility. Ceres then gives to Elizabeth her own crown of wheatears (secured with a jewel, doubtless the Queen's memento of the occasion). This conclusion leaves the pastoral unnaturally stranded in sterility, against the whole tendency of the genre.

What had been habitual praises of the Elizabeth of the 1570s seem, at this distance in time, forced and troubling as reflections of the post-menopausal Queen of 1592. But they may, for all that, have been highly acceptable to the Queen herself: she was of an age to find the past more comforting than the present. Lady Russell was a contemporary—a person she had known for forty years or so—and a liking for familiar faces was a strong trait in Elizabeth's character. The determinedly backward-looking nature of 'The Lady of the Farm' may have been well calculated to please, precisely because it recalled the entertainments of Elizabeth's heyday, and pretended that the last twenty years could be discounted. Interestingly, the final moments are given over to Lady Russell herself, for Ceres

[43] For a discussion of how different courtly entertainments were used to advocate English military intervention in the Netherlands, see also Elizabeth Goldring's essay in this collection, pp. 163–88.

concludes with her heartfelt delight at receiving the Queen: 'this muche dare we promise for the Lady of the farme, that your presence hath added many daies to her life' (Aiiij^v). The entertainment ends with her prayer that 'your happines haue no end till there be no more daies' (Aiiij^v), a tactful elision of Elizabeth's mortality.

THE MASQUE OF THE MUSES

Lady Russell's direct involvement with the Bisham entertainment is suggested by the fact that she later staged a second entertainment for the Queen, *The Masque of the Muses*, for her daughter Anne's wedding, which also seems to have involved a lady speaking dramatically in public. The text of this, unfortunately, is now lost, and the only accounts that have come down to us stress the general splendour of the occasion rather than precise details of the action and imagery of the entertainment. Thanks to the intervention of Lord Burghley in 1597, Lady Russell was finally able to place her daughters as Maids of Honour to the Queen.[44] And, in 1601, Anne was betrothed to the highly satisfactory Lord Henry Herbert, son and heir to Edward, Earl of Worcester. The Queen, characteristically, then refused to name a day for the wedding, and eventually Lady Russell went to court herself to persuade her.[45] But having finally accepted the marriage, Elizabeth did things in high style. She commanded all the Maids of Honour to accompany the girls, as indeed did all the lords of the court. No fewer than eighteen coaches were needed. The Queen herself arrived by water at Blackfriars stairs, was greeted by the bride and met with a litter provided by Lord Cobham. On it, she was carried by six knights to the wedding at St Martin's, Ludgate. The bride herself was escorted to church by Lord Cobham and Lord Herbert of Cardiff, soon to be the 3rd Earl of Pembroke, and away from it by Roger Manners, 5th Earl of Rutland (within months, to go down with Essex). There was then a dinner at Lady Russell's, where she and Cecil presided over one table, while the new Lady Herbert sat down with another group of guests.

In the evening, the Queen proceeded to Lord Cobham's house, which was handily near, and there the festivities reached their climax in a stately masque. That this was on the cards had been reported two days before the wedding, by Rowland Whyte; who says that 'a memorable masque of eight ladies' had been planned. These were: the bride's sister, Bess Russell, her sister-in-law, Lady Blanche Somerset, Lady Dorothy Hastings, another Maid of Honour, Mary Fitton (soon to be disgraced as Lord Herbert of Cardiff's mistress), and mistresses Cary, Onslow, Southwell, and Derby. Each wore a skirt of cloth of silver and embroidered waistcoats, with a mantle of carnation taffeta looped

---

[44] Strong, *The Cult of Elizabeth*, 26.   [45] Ibid. 28.

under one arm, her hair elaborately dressed but hanging loose to demonstrate virginity. The ladies made their entrance to the music of Apollo after supper, and a speech followed, the drift of which was that they were eight out of the nine muses seeking their lost sister, a plot much to the 'honour and praise' of the Queen. Mary Fitton—perhaps because Bess, Anne's co-actor in the earlier entertainment, was already too ill—led the other masquers, who performed 'a strange dance newly invented'. Afterwards, as was customary, they invited eight ladies from the audience to launch the general dancing. Mary Fitton approached the Queen, and there followed a celebrated interchange: 'Her majesty asked what she was? "*Affection*", she said. "*Affection*", said the Queen, "is false".' Everyone knew that it was the disgraced Earl of Essex that she had in mind.[46]

This entertainment looks forward to the Jacobean masque; but it seems to differ from the later masque in that it was one of the noble dancers who spoke. It is just possible that a professional was involved as Apollo, but another actor is not mentioned in any of the accounts. It may be significant that no singing is mentioned, which would bring the performance more within an amateur compass. In any case, the clearest resolution of the surviving sketchy accounts is that Mary Fitton was the speaker as well as the principal dancer.

THE COUNTESS OF PEMBROKE'S 'THENOT AND PIERS'

It is also useful to compare the Bisham entertainment with another work written by an aristocratic woman near, though not precisely in, the Queen's inner circles, for the occasion of a royal visit to her home. *A Dialogue betweene two shepheards, Thenot and Piers, in praise of ASTREA, made by the excellent Lady, the lady Mary Countess of Pembrook at the Queenes Maiesties being at her house at Anno 15–* was subsequently published,[47] having presumably been written by the Countess of Pembroke for a projected visit of the Queen's to Wilton in the late 1590s that in fact never took place.

'Thenot and Piers', naturally, aims to please and flatter Elizabeth, and addresses the same problem as 'The Lady of the Farm': how to accommodate a representation of the elderly, sterile Queen within pastoral conventions. Although courtiers and politicians (including Edward Hoby and Lord Russell) had been conducting discreet negotiations with the odds-on favourite, James VI of Scotland, since the 1580s, the Countess offers a set of consoling fictions—above all, that the Queen is still all in all, and nobody is thinking about the succession:

---

[46] Whyte to Sidney, 23 June 1600: see *Letters and Memorials of State*, ed. A. Collins (London: T. Osborne, 1746), ii. 203; and *The Letters of John Chamberlain*, ed. N. E. McClure (Philadelphia: for the American Philosophical Society, 1939), i. 98–9, 101–2.

[47] In Francis Davidson, *A Poeticall Rhapsody containing, Diverse . . . Poesies* (London: V. S. for John Baily, 1602), sigs. B5ʳ–6ʳ.

THEN.: ASTREA is our chiefest joy,
        Our chiefest guard against annoy,
            Our chiefest wealth, our treasure.
PIERS: Where chiefest are, there others bee,
        To us none else but only shee;
        When wilt thow speake in measure? (sig. B5ᵛ)

The dialogue form has a strong association with pastoral, due to Virgil's *Eclogues*; but the Countess adapts the mode to create a structure of argument that is essentially theological. It draws on the tradition of describing God in negatives, since no positives can be superlative enough.

What 'Thenot and Piers' has in common with 'The Lady of the Farm' is that they are both entertainments offered by women from inner court circles. Though the Countess of Pembroke, unlike Lady Russell, was seldom at court, her mother, Lady Sidney, had been so significant among the Queen's ladies that it was she who had had the momentous task of nursing Elizabeth through smallpox. Like Lady Russell, the Countess of Pembroke was, therefore, a part of the world in which the Queen had grown up, and grown old.[48] It is thus interesting that, like Lady Russell, the Countess's approach is not so much conventional, as archaizing; she tropes back to the praise literature of the 1570s:

THEN.: ASTREA may be justly sayd,
        A field in flowry Roabe arrayd,
        In season freshly springing. (sig. B5ᵛ)

In 1600, the old Queen's resemblance to the Goddess of Spring will not have been marked, but this is not maladroitness. Another verse associates her with evergreens, palm, and bay, 'her verdure never dying' (sig. B6ʳ). The Countess and Lady Russell are conniving in a fantasy—which they perhaps shared; they themselves were, after all, ageing women reluctant to let go of power. These entertainments, devised and probably written by two women profoundly inward with the Queen's background and personality, have some light to shed on the last, bitter years of Elizabeth's reign.

CONCLUSIONS: WOMEN AS DEVISERS, ALTERNATIVE PATTERNS OF CULTURAL PRODUCTION

Perhaps it is timely to introduce the notion of a 'deviser' to the study of early modern women's cultural production. There is certainly a very considerable range of activity in all the arts that is not at all accurately expressed by the notion of 'patron'. In addition, there is a case for expanding our ideas of what constitutes a cultural intervention to consider works that communicate a woman's intentions

---

[48] Hannay, *Philip's Phoenix*, 17.

without necessarily being created by her own hand. The systems of representation in place in the sixteenth century allowed for sophisticated encodings in media other than words. Poets might make play with rue and heartsease or the conventions of knighthood. So, too, might embroideresses, and women undertaking the design of funerary monuments.

'The Lady of the Farm' raises the subject of embroidery as an important aspect of elite women's cultural activity, a clue that modern scholars have been reluctant to address. Discussion of needlework has focused on craft and techniques of execution to the neglect of the intellectual content, imagery, and overall meaning of the works thus produced—which is sometimes as meaningful as any literary work. The Countess of Shrewsbury, for example, though not a 'poet' or 'writer', was nonetheless a deviser of houses and gardens, as well as a needleworker. The large-scale works known as the 'Hardwick Black Tapestries' are considerably more than mere decoration.[49] Female personifications of the arts and virtuous women of antiquity stared down on her cherished granddaughter, Arbella Stuart, whom she hoped to see as Elizabeth's successor. The Countess's unwilling guest, Mary Stuart, though also a poet, created other kinds of statements, too: her embroideries, which again are iconographically coded, and also her final, and carefully literary, self-fashioning as a martyr. The Scottish Queen's choice of clothes and her behaviour on the scaffold were consciously devised to turn an execution into a passion play.[50] The category of 'deviser' would also fit the *oeuvre* of the slightly younger Helena Wyntour, whose sets of stupendously designed and iconographically sophisticated vestments, now in the Stonyhurst College museum, may yet prove to be the most important work in the visual arts of any early modern Englishwoman.[51]

A number of aristocratic women engaged in some combination of monument creation and other activities in order to make their points,[52] but the person above all whose life and work becomes more comprehensible if she is identified primarily as a deviser is Lady Anne Clifford, a niece by marriage of Lady Russell's. Her personal agenda is eloquently declared by a whole set of artefacts, none of which is from her own hand: the 'Great Picture' that she commissioned; the buildings

[49] Santina M. Levey, *An Elizabethan Inheritance: The Hardwick Hall Textiles* (London: National Trust Enterprises, 1988), 21, 34, 67–8. See also Margaret Ellis, 'The Hardwick Wall Hangings: An Unusual Collaboration in English Sixteenth-Century Embroidery', *Renaissance Studies*, 16 (1996), 280–300.

[50] Dr Anne Dillon of the University of Cambridge has made the inspired suggestion that Mary modelled her self-fashioning as martyr, especially in the letter to the King of France written the night before her execution, on the already-established iconography and imagery attending the proto-martyr of the English schism, St Thomas More (personal communication).

[51] Discussed by Sophie Holroyd in a forthcoming article, in Arthur Marotti, Frances Dolan, and Ron Corthell (eds.), *Catholic Culture in Early Modern England* (Notre Dame, Ind.: Notre Dame University Press, forthcoming).

[52] An interesting example is Elizabeth Richardson: as Sylvia Brown shows, she created a series of family monuments as well as writing *A Ladies Legacie to her Daughters* (London: Thomas Harper, 1645): see *Women's Writing in Stuart England* (Stroud: Sutton, 1999), 146–7.

she created or repaired; and, not least, the highly elaborate tombs of herself and her mother, and the very markedly plainer tomb of the father who had been estranged from her mother and who had tried to divert her inheritance to male relatives. Lady Clifford's father's tomb at Skipton is a decent, but not enthusiastic, commemoration of her father erected almost half a century after his death. The Earl of Cumberland is buried with his father and grandfather and is given the allowance due to him, no less but certainly no more; a tomb chest, with heraldry, but no effigy, commissioned from a local stonecutter. The choice of location also places him at a considerable distance from the central narrative of Lady Clifford herself and her mother, which is located at Appleby in Westmoreland.[53]

The monuments at Appleby, however, represent the most that custom and status allow, in a mode highly reminiscent of Lady Russell's monument to herself. The form of the monument to Countess Margaret (erected, in stark contrast to the memorialization of Lady Clifford's father, a year after her death, in 1617) is a tomb chest with a very competent full-length portrait statue and verses, perhaps Lady Clifford's own, perhaps commissioned. It is closely modelled on Maximilian Colt's monument for Elizabeth I and therefore represents an act of deliberate positioning in time: Colt's monument to Elizabeth evoked the monumental style, and therefore the glory days, of the 1580s. It was decidedly old-fashioned by 1617. Lady Anne's own monument is magnificent and as unremittingly heraldic as the pennants of the railings round Elizabeth Russell's tomb at Bisham. It was erected in her lifetime, for, like Lady Russell, she left nothing to chance.

A final, still later, example of a widow as a deviser and maker of a family narrative through funerary monuments is the only example of the phenomenon that could be sensibly described as transgressive. Though Lady Clifford and Lady Russell alike constructed elaborate family narratives and fought for their own positions, ultimately they were preserving the family assets for (male) heirs, and their religious positioning was wholly conformist. By contrast, the recusant Catholic Isabella Shireburn of Stonyhurst erected a little-known and extraordinary series of tombs in the 1690s at Mitton on the Yorkshire–Lancashire border. Though the church of All Hallows was an Anglican church, the Catholic Shireburns seem to have maintained an absolute control over their family chapel within it. It contains three monuments devised by Isabella Shireburn, for Richard Shireburn (d. 1667), Richard and Isabel Shireburn (d. 1689 and 1693), and a third Richard Shireburn (d. 1690). It is the form of the tombs that makes an extraordinary and (for once actually) subversive statement, together with the highly legible encoding of their English-language inscriptions; a litany of recusant alliances, with a markedly absolute silence about the public careers of the men commemorated, since, as recusants, they did not have them. The

[53] Nikolaus Pevsner, *The Buildings of England, Cumberland and Westmorland* (Harmondsworth: Penguin, 1967), 217.

Figure 11.2. The Shireburn tombs (1690s), carved by William Stanton, Church of All Hallows, Great Mitton, Lancashire (formerly in Yorkshire). (Photograph by Jane Stevenson)

design of the monuments—high tomb chests with recumbent effigies, harking back to medieval tombs—makes a very clear statement about continuity and the entitlement of the Shireburns to the place denied them (at least theoretically) in the elite. Their relationship to the past is clarified by the three older recumbent effigies in this chapel, an abraded medieval original and a tomb chest with effigies of (the possibly church papist) Sir Richard (d. 1694) and his wife, which is patently an antiquarian copy of the older effigy, down to minor details.

The 1690s recumbent effigies are extremely elegant sculptures, with dressing gowns and lace cravats replacing the armour of a hundred years before, but they speak eloquently of a family looking firmly to the past as precedent and authority. Pevsner is certain that these are the last recumbent effigies on tomb chests in England until the nineteenth-century Gothic revival. In essence, the statement that these sculptures make is about continuity, antiquity, and armigery, affirming that the Shireburns' allegiance to the faith of the first medieval Shireburn commemorated had not changed any more than their real status had changed, and suggesting that their public eclipse was part of the aberrant innovations of the Elizabethan settlement—those very innovations that Elizabeth Russell and her kinsfolk had struggled to introduce and maintain.

12

Elizabethan Entertainments in Manuscript: The Harefield Festivities (1602) and the Dynamics of Exchange

Gabriel Heaton

What can the material texts of Elizabethan entertainments tell us about how those entertainments were produced, how they were circulated to a wider readership, and how they were valued by the culture that produced them? These written accounts were the only point of access to royal entertainments for many contemporaries and they are also our main source of information about them.[1] Although the printed pamphlet is perhaps the most familiar of the many forms taken by pageant texts, entertainments also circulated frequently as manuscript separates: individually circulated short manuscripts produced as discrete bibliographical units, the text written onto no more than three or four sheets of paper folded into bifolia, the final page usually left blank.[2] The resulting manuscript could then be folded up into a small packet, with the final blank on the outside used as an address panel or for endorsement. These texts were produced for exchange, and this essay is predicated on the assumption that texts have social lives and we should pay attention to the company they keep.

An earlier version of this work was presented at the John Nichols Project's 'Elizabethan Progresses Conference', held at the Shakespeare Centre in Stratford-upon-Avon in April 2004; I am very grateful for the feedback received on that occasion. I would also like to thank Dr H. Neville Davies for discussing the Elvetham entertainment with me, and I am particularly indebted to my former colleagues at the University of Warwick with whom I worked on the Nichols Project.

[1] Texts describing pageantry do not provide unmediated access to the pageants themselves, and many critics have drawn attention to their partial and interpretative nature, revealing the inherent discontinuity between pageant texts and the events they describe. See, for example, Paula Johnson, 'Jacobean Ephemera and the Immortal Word', *Renaissance Drama*, NS 8 (1977), 151–71; Wendy Wall, *The Imprint of Gender: Authorship and Publication in the English Renaissance* (London: Cornell University Press, 1993), 111–67; and Helen Watanabe-O'Kelly, 'The Early Modern Festival Book: Function and Form', in J. R Mulryne et al. (eds.), *Europa Triumphans: Court and Civic Festivals in Early Modern Europe*, 2 vols. (Aldershot: Ashgate, 2004), i. 3–18.

[2] For a bibliographical definition and discussion of the separate, see Harold Love, *Scribal Publication in Seventeenth Century England* (Oxford: Clarendon Press, 1993), 13–19.

As is now widely recognized, manuscript was an entirely viable medium for the dissemination of texts; it was not necessarily a precursor to print and it was common for texts that circulated in manuscript not to be printed for many years (if at all). This essay begins with an overview of the production and dissemination of entertainment texts, and then turns to consider the 1602 Harefield entertainment in detail, since this is a case in which the unusual wealth of surviving textual evidence means that the processes of production, dissemination, and reception can be reconstructed in some detail.

Reproducing and circulating a text entails collaboration, and the text's meaning is inflected by the community that produces it—in this case, by those who made copies and gave or received manuscript separates.[3] As this essay will demonstrate, the demands and interests of readers played a significant part in the construction of individual texts, with readerly interests falling into two broad categories: court news and elite coterie literature. Both are central to understanding the reception of entertainments, but the focus in each case is different. Reading a text as news placed the emphasis on its original occasion and performance, while reading it as literature placed greater emphasis on its content and authorship.

I

Entertainment texts have often been understood by scholars as propaganda originating in and promulgated by a single body—the crown or sometimes the host—but this interpretation provides a narrow and impoverished basis for understanding these complex texts. An entertainment was never under the control of a single agent: from inception to reception, it was an intensely collaborative form. Host, hired poet, musicians, actors, the Queen, and the watching court: all played a part in constructing entertainments as events. The views the host wished to promote had to be balanced against what would be acceptable to the Queen, and both Queen and host knew that their interaction was being watched and judged by the courtly audience. Whoever then produced the written texts imposed his own interpretation on the entertainment, and the dissemination of texts, which can be glimpsed most clearly in manuscript form, depended on various individuals with distinct agendas—authors, hosts, scribes, letter writers, and other intermediary figures.

The patron of the entertainment and host of the Queen had a privileged position among these intersecting interests. When a dramatic figure addressed the Queen at an aristocratic estate, he or she was usually speaking words written by a hired poet, but was unequivocally speaking for the aristocratic host: 'Vnder my person', said the Poet greeting Elizabeth at Elvetham in September 1591,

---

[3] The most influential formulation of this argument is D. F. McKenzie, *Bibliography and the Sociology of Texts* (London: The British Library, 1986).

'*Semer* [Edward Seymour, Earl of Hertford] hides himselfe.'[4] The hired poet was asked to perform an act of ventriloquism, to understand and express, often with considerable nuance and delicacy, the agenda of the host. The initial unification of host and poet in a single voice required close collaboration. The poet's job would often have been to develop the host's initial idea—at the very least, the poet's text would have been subject to final approval from the host.

Direct evidence for collaboration between host and hired poet can be found in one of the rare surviving working manuscripts of an Elizabethan entertainment: two leaves, originally a bifolium, containing the 'Hermit's Welcome' that was spoken, perhaps by Robert Cecil, at Theobalds in May 1591.[5] The 'Welcome' went through two stages of revision: the first set of revisions is apparently authorial, being in the same hand that initially wrote out the verses, but the second is in a different hand. The reviser, who had a focused interest on Burghley's wish to retire and leave his place to Robert Cecil, was probably Cecil himself: the sample is admittedly small (seventeen words) and written to fit into a limited space, but the writing has a strong resemblance to Cecil's distinctive rapid italic.[6] The first passage altered by the reviser dealt with recent deaths in the family that had led to Lord Burghley's increasing wish to retire from the court: a passage deleted in the first stage of revision was reinstated but with 'many funeralles' changed to 'bitter accidents'. Both this and the other intervention by the reviser, by which the death of his wife 'broght' rather than 'inforst' Burghley to a 'solitary aboad', softened the way in which Burghley's retirement was described.

---

[4] *The honorable Entertainement gieuen to the Queenes Maiestie in Progresse, at Eluetham in Hampshire, by the right Honorable the Earle of Hertford* (London: John Wolfe, 1591), sig. B3ʳ.

[5] BL, Egerton MS 2623, fos. 15–16. This manuscript once belonged to John Payne Collier; he claimed the manuscript was subscribed 'George Peele', but the portion of manuscript on which this subscription was supposedly found has since been mutilated. The entire manuscript was denounced as a forgery in Marion Colthorpe, 'The Theobalds Entertainment for Queen Elizabeth I in 1591, with a Transcription of the Gardener's Speech', *REED Newsletter*, 12.1 (1987), 2–9. This claim was refuted on the basis of internal evidence by Curtis C. Breight, 'Entertainments of Elizabeth at Theobalds in the Early 1590's', *REED Newsletter*, 12.2 (1987), 1–9. Codicological evidence also shows that the manuscript is genuine. The paper is of approximately the correct date, with a crossbow watermark of a type found in the 1590s (C. M. Briquet, *Les Filigranes*, 4 vols. (Geneva: Jullien, 1907), nos. 728–37, and especially www.gravell.org, CRSBW.004.1); the hands do not have graphs similar to those picked out by Anthony G. Petti as indicative of Collier forgeries in *English Literary Hands from Chaucer to Dryden* (London: Edward Arnold, 1977), 89; and Collier's own transcription in *The History of English Dramatic Poetry to the Time of Shakespeare*, 3 vols. (London: Murray, 1831), i. 283–7, contains a number of errors.

[6] Similar features include: the relative lack of ligatures; the presence of hooks on many letters (including 'w', 'y', 'd', 'h', and 't'); the formation of 'b' by a single pen-stroke; the open bowled terminal 'd'; the 'ht' and 'ts' ligatures; the secretary-influenced 'h', the back of which does not always fully descend to the base-line; and the use of both long and short initial 's'. The documents that formed the basis of this comparison are a 1592 letter (Hatfield House, Cecil Papers 21/33); letters from 1593–5 (BL, Stowe MS 166, fos. 72, 210, 218); and his interlineated revisions to a later letter (Hatfield House, Cecil Papers 195/30–32). Dr Marie-Louise Coolahan agrees that the reviser was probably Cecil. See her edition of materials relating to Theobalds in Jayne Archer et al. (eds.), *Court and Culture in the Reign of Queen Elizabeth I: A New Edition of John Nichols's 'Progresses of Queen Elizabeth'* (Oxford: Oxford University Press, forthcoming).

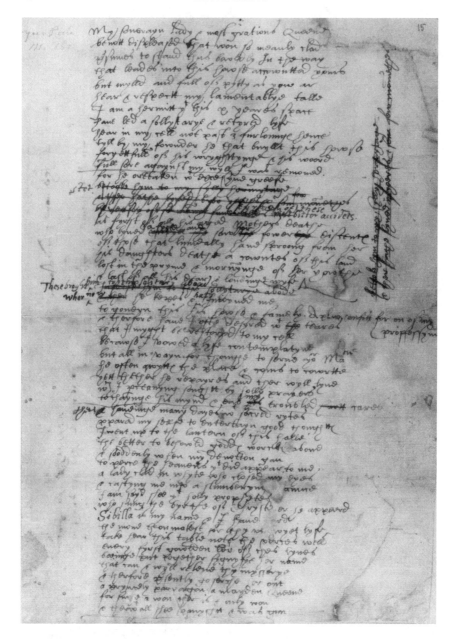

Figure 12.1. The first page of the 'Hermit's Welcome' to Queen Elizabeth I, spoken at Lord Burghley's residence of Theobalds on 10 May 1591. On this page can be seen both the authorial hand and the revising hand; the latter is probably that of Cecil. (By permission of the British Library, London, Egerton MS 2623, fo. 15ʳ)

Entertainments such as the 'Hermit's Welcome' dwelt on major personal and political issues, so it is not surprising to find that hosts kept a careful eye on what was to be spoken in their name. The terms upon which the crucial relationship between poet and patron was based can be glimpsed in two letters by John Davies, the most popular author of entertainments in Elizabeth's last years, accompanying texts Davies was sending to patrons.[7] Davies unambiguously situated final ownership of the text with the commissioning patron, inviting comment and stating his willingness to make any changes the patron might demand. One of these letters, written to Sir Robert Cecil and apparently referring to a speech for Barriers to be performed at the Inns of Court, provides a number of details about the process of commission:

about 6 of clock this euening, my lord of Cumbreland signified your honours pleasure vnto me; that I should instantly conceaue a speach for introduction of the barriers . . . .This speech doth nothing satisfie me, & thefore much lesse will it seem passable in your honours Iudgment . . . I humbly beseech your honour to lett your eie passe a little over it; & to lett me know what your Iudgment mislikes, & I shall quickly correct it. The gentleman that is to speake it must not know that it comes from me, for then he will never learne it. I am not ambitios to be reputed the autor of a speach, but am zealous to have things donne according to your honours pleasure.

Davies figures the text as a manifestation of his service. He claims that what gives the text significance to him is not his work itself but that it demonstrates commitment to his patron and, implicitly, his desire for further service. Davies recognized that the author's job was to provide a text over which the patron could assume control and ownership. On some occasions, control over the author was probably nominal, but many patrons were actively involved in the production of entertainments presented in their name.[8]

Control over the performance text was one thing, but any subsequent wider circulation of a text lessened the control of the patron-host. Entertainment texts, whether in manuscript or print, were not produced by or for a monolithic central authority. There is occasional indirect evidence that suggests some texts were suppressed or censored, just as there is some evidence that the Queen ensured some performances never took place.[9] However, in contrast to the festival books

[7] BL, Lansdowne MS 88, fo. 4 (to Sir Michael Hickes, 22 Jan. 1600 [1601]); Hatfield House, Cecil Papers 90/69 (to Sir Robert Cecil, 1601?). The letters are printed in *The Poems of Sir John Davies*, ed. Robert Krueger (Oxford: Clarendon Press, 1975), 415–16 and p. xxviii.

[8] Robert Cecil remained closely involved in entertainments throughout his life, and Robert Devereux, 2nd Earl of Essex, also took a close interest in entertainments. See James Knowles, ' "To raise a house of better frame": Jonson's Cecilian Entertainments', in Pauline Croft (ed.), *Patronage, Culture and Power: The Early Cecils* (New Haven: Yale University Press/The Paul Mellon Centre for Studies in British Art, 2002), 181–95; Paul E. J. Hammer, 'Upstaging the Queen: The Earl of Essex, Francis Bacon, and the Accession Day Celebrations of 1595', in David Bevington and Peter Holbrook (eds.), *The Politics of the Stuart Court Masque* (Cambridge: Cambridge University Press, 1998), 41–66.

[9] David Scott, 'William Patten and the Authorship of "Robert Laneham's *Letter*" (1575)', *English Literary Renaissance*, 7 (1977), 297–306 (p. 301), prints a letter from William Patten to

published in many European countries, the English crown did not finance the publication of entertainments—even when they had the political significance of, for example, the 1559 pre-coronation entry into London.[10] To suggest that entertainments spoke for the crown, that they were propaganda, is to elide the complexity of who, exactly, was speaking in an entertainment.

Entertainment texts mostly appeared in one of two related forms: manuscript separates and pamphlets. Both were short, quickly produced, and ephemeral. Separates were well suited to the pattern of demand for entertainments, which was strongest in the short period immediately after the performance. Multiple manuscript copies could be produced more rapidly than a pamphlet could be printed and separates were regularly produced in sizeable numbers, if not the hundreds turned out by the printing press. Separates were typically produced on an individual basis with a specific recipient in mind; they could be individuated in any number of ways and were usually transmitted, not by sale, but as enclosures within personal letters. They were therefore enmeshed within specific interpersonal relationships to a greater degree than printed texts. The fact that they tended not to be exchanged commercially, together with their restriction to relatively elite social groups, made separates a particularly appropriate mode of dissemination for royal entertainments—the entertainment being a form accessible only to an elite few and to which gift-giving was a basic gesture.[11]

It would be misleading to think of printed pamphlets as the normative textual moder for entertainments. Ten pamphlets of entertainments for Queen Elizabeth survive (including the coronation entry and one poem describing a tiltyard entertainment); at least three more are known to have been printed; and it may well be that others have disappeared without trace (several pamphlets survive in only one or two copies).[12] But, as detailed in Appendix 12.1, at least

Lord Burghley that suggests an attempt was made to suppress *A letter at Killingvvoorth Castl*. Pressure was probably applied to change the text of the Elvetham entertainment and its claims about the Queen's response to the entertainment (e.g. the suggestion that Hertford 'should finde the rewarde [for the entertainment] in her especiall fauour' was removed). The most contentious performances usually revolved around the Queen's marriage (Susan Doran, 'Juno vs Diana: The Treatment of Elizabeth I's Marriage in Plays and Entertainments, 1561–1581', *Historical Journal*, 38.2 (1995), 257–74). For a discussion of two performances scheduled for the 1575 Kenilworth festivities, but apparently aborted at the eleventh hour, see Elizabeth Goldring's essay in this volume, pp. 163–88.

[10] For publications in other European countries, see Watanabe-O'Kelly, 'The Early Modern Festival Book', 6–15. For the 1559 entry into London, see Hester Lees-Jeffries's essay in this volume, pp. 65–85.

[11] For manuscripts and gift exchange, see Natalie Z. Davis, 'Beyond the Market: Books as Gifts in Sixteenth Century France', *Transactions of the Royal Historical Society*, 5th ser. 33 (1983), 69–88; Jason Scott-Warren, *Sir John Harrington and the Book as Gift* (Oxford: Oxford University Press, 2001); Gabriel Heaton, 'Performing Gifts: The Manuscript Circulation of Elizabethan and Early Stuart Royal Entertainments' (unpublished doctoral thesis, University of Cambridge, 2003). For gift-giving on progress, see Felicity Heal's essay in this volume, pp. 46–61.

[12] The poem mentioned is George Peele, *Polyhymnia* (1590). The only known copy of *The Princely Pleasures at Kenilworth* (London: Richard Jones, 1576) was destroyed by fire in 1879. Thomas Churchyard's list of his printed works in *Churchyardes Challenge* (1593), sigs. *–**

twenty-two entertainments circulated in manuscript, of which nine survive as separates. Given the fragile nature of the manuscript separate, the original number was probably much greater. Furthermore, closer analysis of the pattern of these texts' appearance suggests that the separate usurped the place of the printed pamphlet in the 1590s as the preferred medium for royal entertainments. Pamphlet publications clustered around two relatively short periods: the latter half of the 1570s (four publications) and 1590–2 (four publications).[13] After 1592, no further pamphlets are known to have been printed; by contrast, two-thirds of those entertainments known to have circulated as separates were written in the final decade of Queen Elizabeth's reign (see Appendix 12.1).

One reason for this apparent shift from print to manuscript may have been a change in the pattern of the progresses themselves: the 1570s and early 1590s saw Elizabeth's most ambitious progresses,[14] but in the last decade of the reign, although dramatic entertainments and increasingly costly displays of hospitality were still regular occurrences, progresses became shorter and therefore less public events, less likely to command the interest of a wide public.[15] Wider cultural issues also seem to have been at play in this shift to manuscript. As has been noted, entertainments fed the distinct readerly desires for coterie literature and court news, and there was an increasingly hungry demand for both in the 1590s that was largely fed by manuscript separates. This was a period of great activity among sophisticated communities reading and writing poetry at the Inns of Court and elsewhere (with prominent figures including John Donne and John Davies). It was also a time when networks of newsmongers and intelligencers like Rowland Whyte and John Chamberlain were becoming increasingly widespread. Many of these same figures were involved in circulating royal entertainments.

The circulation of these manuscripts depended on a range of people, starting with the Queen herself since—though there is no evidence that she encouraged their production—circulation usually depended on a successful performance.

included two lost entertainment pamphlets: 'The deuises of warre and a play at Awsterley, her highnes being at sir Thomas Greshams', and 'The deuises and speeches that men and boyes shewed within many prograces'.

[13] The years 1575–8 saw the publication of: *A letter at Killingwoorth Castl*; a now-lost pamphlet on the 1575 progress, *The Pastime of the Progresse*; Thomas Churchyard, *A Discourse of the Queenes Maiesties entertainement in Suffolk and Norffolk* (London: Henry Bynneman, 1578); and Bernard Garter, *The ioyfull receyuing of the Queenes most excellent Maiestie into hir Highnesse Citie of Norwich* (London: Henry Bynneman, 1578). In 1590–2 were published: Peele's *Polyhymnia*; *The honorable Entertainement . . . at Eluetham*; *The honorable entertainment giuen to the Queenes Maiestie in progresse, at Cowdrey in Sussex, by the Right Honorable the Lord Montecute* (London: Thomas Scarlet, 1591); *Speeches delivered to Her Maiestie this last progresse, at the Right Honorable the Lady Russels, at Bissam, the Right Honorable, the Lorde Chandos, at Sudley, at the Right Honorable, the Lord Norris, at Ricorte* (Oxford: Joseph Barnes, 1592).

[14] Mary Hill Cole, *The Portable Queen: Elizabeth I and the Politics of Ceremony* (Amherst: University of Massachusetts Press, 1999), provides a synopsis of the pattern of progresses (pp. 33–4) and a detailed chronology of royal visits (pp. 180–202).

[15] For the inflation in the expense of entertaining the Queen towards the end of the reign, see Lawrence Stone, *The Crisis of the Aristocracy, 1558–1641* (Oxford: Clarendon Press, 1965), 452–4.

Just as the observing courtiers were integral to the dynamic engagement between different parts of the social and political elite of Elizabethan society that was at the heart of the entertainment, those same courtiers and court watchers were also a primary readership for entertainment texts, and the Queen's response was likely to influence their own. At Worcester in 1575, for example, the Queen 'gaue wytnes' to her appreciation of the Deputy Recorder's welcoming oration (she may not have known he was a recusant), and after this favourable response, 'dyuers honorable afterward willed to haue copies therof, which was doone accordynglie'.[16]

Royal response and readerly interest were beyond the control of aristocratic hosts who could but hope that their expenditure and planning paid off; but since the aristocratic patron stood to gain from widening the audience of an entertainment, we would expect to find that the hand of the patron was sometimes guiding that of the scribe. This was almost certainly the case with some copies of the entertainment staged at Harefield in late July and early August 1602.[17] However, the desire of aristocrats to promulgate a particular self-image was only one factor behind the circulation of entertainment texts, which must be seen alongside the response of the Queen, the agendas of authors and others with access to texts, the ability of intermediary figures to supply texts, and the varied interests of individual readers.

II

It is possible to trace in some detail the interlocking agencies and interests behind the dissemination of one particular entertainment text performed during Queen Elizabeth's last summer progress. The entertainment at Harefield, which was written by John Davies and performed at the house of the Lord Keeper Sir Thomas Egerton and his wife Alice, Dowager Countess of Derby, survives in thirteen early sources and is referred to in seven contemporary letters.[18] No other Elizabethan entertainment survives in so many manuscript copies; indeed, few pamphlets survive in such numbers (the largest number of surviving copies recorded is thirteen for Garter's *Ioyfull Receyuing into Norwich* and seventeen and one fragment for the Kenilworth *Letter*).

The 1602 progress was brief: though there had been plans to travel as far as Bristol, in the event Elizabeth travelled for only two weeks and barely passed outside the area covered by modern London. This short progress nevertheless included several visits to local landowners, and her reception was recorded in a

---

[16] Worcester County Record Office, *Chamber Order Book 1539–1601*, fo. 124ʳ.

[17] Another potential example is provided by the Earl of Essex's 1595 tiltyard device, which may have been promulgated by Essex's own secretariat (see Hammer, 'Upstaging the Queen'), 44–5.

[18] For a full list of these sources, see my edition of the Harefield entertainment in Archer et al. (eds.), *Court and Culture*.

number of contemporary newsletters. John Chamberlain reported a synopsis of the progress to his friend Dudley Carleton on 2 October:

The Q. progress went not far, first to Cheswicke to Sir William Russells, then to Ambrose coppingers who because he had ben a master of art intertained her himself with a Latin oration, then to Harvill [i.e. Harefield] to the L. Kepers. So to Sir William Clarkes by Burnham, who so behaued himself that he pleased nobody, but gaue occasion to haue his miserie and vanitie spread far and wide. Then to Otelands, where she continues to the seuenth of this moneth that she comes to Richmond. the causes that withheld her from the erle of Hartfords and the L. cheife Iustice were the fowle weather, and a generall infection of the small pocks spred ouer all the countrie.[19]

Chamberlain's comment on Sir William Clarke's reception of the Queen exposes the importance of entertainments to their hosts' reputations, and also the part played by letters in establishing reputations; it was, of course, letters like Chamberlain's that ensured Clarke's inhospitality was 'spread far and wide'. Chamberlain, who had not accompanied the court himself, was not the only writer to comment on Clarke. When the Earl of Northumberland provided Lord Cobham with a report on the state of the court on 6 August, he began with a complaint:

wee are at Sir Willam Clerkes and shall be here till monday, whoe nether giues mete nor monny to any of the progressers; the house her ma: hathe at commandement, and his grasse the gards horses eate, he shafes, and this is all[.][20]

Entertaining the Queen brought a great deal of attention to the host, so—even apart from an unwillingness to anger the Queen—few hosts were willing to make a public display of inhospitality.[21] The correlative motive was the prestige successful entertainment could bring: Lord Keeper Egerton paid out over £2,000 for food, drink, and preparations to the house for the Queen's visit to Harefield, and we can be sure that he hoped to have his hospitality and expenditure widely reported.[22] The production and dissemination of manuscript texts was closely entangled with this business of reputation building, since those same letter writers crucial to the formation of public reputations were also the main conduits for the circulation of manuscript separates.

The hosts at Harefield had particular reasons for demonstrating their noble hospitality. Sir Thomas Egerton may have been Lord Keeper, but he was an illegitimate son from a minor Cheshire family. In contrast, his wife Alice was the daughter of Sir John Spencer of Althorp, one of the wealthiest untitled men in England. She was, moreover, the widow of Ferdinando Stanley (d. 1594),

---

[19] National Archives, SP 12/285/23 (fo. 47ᵛ).   [20] National Archives, SP 12/284/97.
[21] Clarke was not the only host willing to snub the Queen, especially in the last years of her reign, but these moments of overt disharmony were relatively infrequent. See Cole, *Portable Queen*, 85–96.
[22] Egerton's expenditure is preserved in a series of accounts which are now in the Huntington Library, MS EL 122 and 124–7 (EL 123 is a forgery by John Payne Collier), printed in *The Egerton Papers*, ed. John Payne Collier (London: Camden Society, 1840), 340–57.

Earl of Derby, a great-great-grandson of Henry VII. This disparity of status
was especially important to the Dowager Countess, as she had three daughters
from her first marriage: girls with the blood royal running through their veins
who had lost the earldom that sustained their status, and whose inheritance was
being contested by their uncle William Stanley, the current Earl of Derby.[23]
Lavish hospitality publicly displayed that Egerton was capable of maintaining
the magnificent lifestyle appropriate to his wife's noble status and her daughters'
royal lineage.

When the Queen entered the grounds of the estate on 31 July, she was met
by a dairymaid and a bailiff, who gave a comic dialogue in which they pretended
not to know the identity of the visitor, but ended their welcome with the gift
of two jewels shaped as a rake and a fork.[24] A second welcome followed at the
entrance to the house, where the personification of the Place, 'in a partie-colored
roabe, lyke the brickes of the howse', discussed with Time (who has stopped for
the Queen) the honour of the royal visit. This dialogue also culminated with
a gift, a jewel in the shape of a heart. Over the next days, two further devices
were presented: a petition, accompanied with a gift of a 'gown of rainbows',
that supposedly came from St Swithin, in which he explained that he was not
responsible for the poor weather; and a lottery in which the Queen and her
ladies drew gifts with attached verses from a box of booty in the possession of a
mariner. At Elizabeth's departure, Place once again appeared, now in mourning,
to lament her going and to present yet another jewel (an anchor).

Egerton and his wife could manage events at Harefield so it appeared that the
whole of society—even Place and Time—wished to perform their duty to the
Queen, and only the English weather remained beyond her command. The hosts
could ensure that every device culminated in an expensive gift to the Queen,
but they could not control the responses of letter writers and gossips, which
determined how the display would shape their public reputation. While the major
expenditure and witty dialogues ensured that the Harefield entertainment was
seen as one of the more comment-worthy events of the summer, the individuality
of responses could not be stifled.

Sir George Savile sent a copy of the farewell speech to his patron, the
Earl of Shrewsbury. In the accompanying letter, Savile provided a particularly
enthusiastic report of the entertainment: '[t]he Iewell my lord keper presented
was held Richly worth 1000[li.] as I was credibly told. Another Iewell said worth vi
C.[li.] And the Gowne of Raynbows very Riche embradrid', while the richness of
the feast was 'much talked of in London'.[25] But Savile makes clear that his main
reason for providing the text was 'my desire to do your lordship some service', so

---

[23] Barry Coward, *The Stanleys, Lords Stanley and Earls of Derby, 1385–1672* (Manchester:
Manchester University Press, 1983), 41–55.

[24] Quotations from the Harefield entertainment are taken from the forthcoming edition in
Archer et al. (eds.), *Court and Culture*.

[25] Nottingham Archives, DD/SR 1/D/14.

it was in his interest to emphasize the significance of the text as a worthy gift for the Earl. The letter also shows the importance of speedy production, since Savile hoped that the text would be sufficiently new to please his patron, reminding Shrewsbury that acquiring such a text was 'hard for me to doe, for your lordship hath so many frendes of bitter Intelligence'.

The amount of money spent by Egerton impressed Savile, but not all writers were inclined to interpret massive expenditure as the bountiful largesse of a happy and wealthy court. An intelligencer writing under the name 'Anthony Rivers' wrote to Robert Persons, the Superior of the Jesuit Mission to England in Rome, that the Queen had been 'most royally entertained and feasted at the Lord Keepers his charge in that behalf, amounting to about 4,000 li'.[26] He, however, interpreted the expenditure as waste and the progress as exposing disharmony. While Chamberlain had blamed the weather and smallpox for the brevity of the progress, Rivers claimed that local discontent had influenced the decision, and explained to Persons that the Queen was primarily motivated by 'a covetous humour (as most of her late progresses have been), to receive rich presents and jewels'. Rivers also revealed how Elizabeth had responded to her entertainment:

[The Queen] being at the Lord Keeper's, in her merriest vein, the Countess of Derby (his wife) moved that it would please her to accept of the Lady Strange [Anne Stanley] and her sister [Frances Stanley] to wait on her in her privy chamber, and to bestow them in marriage where she thought fit, or at least to give her leave to bestow them; at which motion the Queen was exceedingly passionate and commanded silence on that behalf. The younger, as is supposed, is contracted to the Keeper's son, and the parents hoped the Queen would have approved it, and made him knight. Now they are at a nonplus, and know not how to proceed[.]

Rivers thus reverses the role of the Queen: although she is represented in the entertainment itself as the source of bounty and harmony, Rivers figures her as a source of disharmony and ingratitude. 'Anthony Rivers' was certainly partisan, but he was well informed (he may have been William Sterrell, confidential secretary to a Privy Counsellor, Edward Somerset, Earl of Worcester).[27] The match between Frances Stanley and John Egerton had been agreed when the Dowager Countess married Thomas Egerton, but they had not been able to gain the Queen's consent, and it is entirely plausible that tension over this subject resurfaced at Harefield.[28] Indeed, it may have been this tension that

[26] *Records of the English Province of the Society of Jesus*, ed. Henry Foley SJ, 7 vols. (London: Burns and Oates, 1877–83), i. 46.

[27] Patrick Martin and John Finnis, 'The Identity of "Antony Rivers"', *Recusant History*, 26 (2002), 39–74. Although this article provides considerable and detailed evidence, the initial link between Sterrell (under the alias 'Peter Halyns') and Rivers is a reference to an order for gloves (p. 45); Martin and Finnis also admit that Rivers's handwriting does not correspond to Sterrell's, so suggest that the handwriting was deliberately disguised (p. 57).

[28] The couple married in secret before the Queen's death (see *The Letters of John Chamberlain*, ed. Norman Egbert McClure, 2 vols. (Philadelphia: American Philosophical Society, 1939), i. 188–91)

Thomas Edmondes, diplomat and Clerk of the Privy Council, referred to when he reported to the Earl of Shrewsbury that 'Her Highness hath been very honourably entertained at my Lord Keeper's house, and many times richly presented; yet all men are not confident that the same will procure an abolition of former unkindness.'[29]

These differing interpretations of events at Harefield were written in the days and weeks immediately following the Queen's visit. The Queen left Harefield on 2 August and the earliest surviving report of the entertainment (by Thomas Edmondes in the letter quoted above) was written just one day later. The earliest record of a text of the Harefield entertainment is found in a letter to Sir Robert Sidney, governor of Flushing, from his deputy Sir William Browne dated 12 August, shortly after the court returned to the royal palace of Oatlands. This letter reported in detail Browne's recent audience with the Queen in Sir William Clarke's garden at Hitcham, and in a postscript mentions, 'I send you with this letter all the Queenes enterteinment at Cheswick and att my Lord keepers I haue gotten them coppyed out for you.'[30] Savile sent his copy of the text to Shrewsbury two days later. Several other copies, though they cannot be dated so precisely, probably also date from August 1602.

The text quickly spread throughout England and beyond, mostly among courtly insiders then absent from the centre of power—though the August report to the exiled Jesuit Robert Persons shows that no one could control to whom it was reported. Other early recipients of reports or texts included Gilbert Talbot, Earl of Shrewsbury and member of the Privy Council; Dudley Carleton, secretary to the English Ambassador in Paris; Matthew Hutton, Archbishop of York; Sir Robert Sidney, Governor of Flushing; Sir Edward Conway, Lieutenant Governor of Brill (Flushing and Brill were among the English Cautionary Towns in the Low Countries); and a member of the wealthy Warwickshire Newdigate family.

These early manuscripts of the Harefield entertainment were produced over a short period and circulated within a relatively coherent social group, but the texts are notably heterogeneous. No copy contains all of the devices and although some of the copies derive from the same (lost) exemplars, no two copies are written in the same hand or on the same paper. So they were probably not the result of a coordinated campaign of manuscript publication. Sir William Browne's letter also suggests that there was no deliberate campaign of circulation, since Browne specifies that he had the text copied (as opposed to having been given it or having purchased a copy). Two of the surviving copies do have characteristics

and already may have been married when the Queen came to Harefield: the entries on both Frances Stanley and John Egerton in the *Oxford DNB* suggest their marriage took place in 1601.

[29] Edmund Lodge, *Illustrations of British History*, 2nd edn., 3 vols. (London: Chidley, 1838), ii. 562–3.

[30] Centre for Kentish Studies, U1475 [De L'Isle MSS] C8/135 [misdated 1601], quoted by kind permission of Viscount De L'Isle from his private archive deposited at CKS for safekeeping. The copies of the Harefield and Chiswick entertainments are not known to survive.

that associate them with the household at Harefield, but the household was only one of the sources from which texts were acquired.

One of the copies associated with the Harefield household was sent to Matthew Hutton, Archbishop of York, who on 30 August wrote enthusiastically to the President of the Council of the North, Lord Sheffield, that 'As for hir Maiestes entertainment at my Lord Keepers house, I am glad to heare it was to hir good likinge & best contentment.'[31] Hutton's letter goes on to give an elaborate and good-humoured description of 'Place and Time', commenting that they were exceedingly lively given their advanced age (which he calculates at 5,564 years). The text that belonged to Matthew Hutton was written on two sheets of paper folded into bifolia, in a rapid but clear secretary hand. This text is unique in showing awareness of all the different devices that took place at Harefield.[32] It also provides more detail about the various gifts and their costs than any other source; it is this text, for example, that tells us that the 'gown of rainbows' given to the Queen by St Swithin cost £340, was made of cloth of silver, and was accompanied by sleeves embroidered with rubies and pearls. It is the presence of such details that suggests the origin of this text was the household of the Lord Keeper and Dowager Countess, who are throughout referred to as 'My Lord' and 'My Lady'.

The second copy that probably came directly from the Harefield household is found in the papers of the Newdigate family of Arbury Hall in Warwickshire.[33] The Newdigates had been the owners of Harefield House until 1586 and their interest in the Queen's entertainment at their ancient family home is easily explained. Even after the sale of Harefield, the family retained property in the area and developed a number of links to the household of Egerton and the Dowager Countess.[34] The Newdigate copy is closely related to Hutton's: it also consists of two sheets of paper folded into bifolia. Although written in a different hand, it was probably copied from the same exemplar; and descriptive passages are phrased in a manner that suggests the scribe was present at the performance. For example, the dialogue of 'Place and Time' is said to have begun, 'When her Maiestie was alighted from her horse, and ascended 3 steeps neare to the entering into the house, a carpet and chaire there sett for her.'[35]

Both of these texts catered to the desire of the hosts at Harefield to broadcast their hospitality, but the Newdigate manuscript also seems to have been produced with the sensitivities of the Newdigate family in mind. Their copy lacks the

[31] Hutton's copy of the entertainment is North Yorkshire County Record Office (Northallerton branch), ZAZ 1286/8282–89. The letter is ZAZ 1286/8290.

[32] This copy does not include the text of the initial dialogue between the bailiff and the dairymaid, but notes that it took place.

[33] Warwickshire County Record Office, CR 136/B2455.

[34] Vivienne Larminie, *Wealth, Kinship and Culture: The Seventeenth-Century Newdigates of Arbury and their World* (Woodbridge: Boydell, 1995), 21–35.

[35] WCRO, CR 136/B2455, fo. 1ʳ. Although a common source is postulated here, the textual relationship between the Hutton and Newdigate copies is complex; see Archer et al. (eds.), *Court and Culture*.

'Lottery', a celebration of the female centre of the Elizabethan court, in which gifts were given to the Queen, her Maids of Honour, Ladies of the Privy Chamber, and other attendant women. Given the close connections between this manuscript, the Hutton manuscript, and the household at Harefield, the scribe probably had access to the 'Lottery', which in turn suggests that the section was deliberately omitted from the Newdigate manuscript. A likely explanation for this omission is found in the family of the mistress at Arbury Hall, Anne Newdigate, *née* Fitton. Her sister was Mary Fitton, who had been a Maid of Honour until 1601, when she became pregnant by the Earl of Pembroke: he had 'utterly renounceth all marriage' and Mary had retreated to Arbury Hall in disgrace.[36] A decision could well have been made that the Newdigates would not appreciate a celebration of the privileged group from which one of their number had been irrevocably expelled, in which, for example, the Maids' obedience and chastity were extolled when their chaperone was presented with a scarf: 'Take you this skarfe binde Cupid hand & foote | Soe loue must aske yow leaue before hee shoote.'

The Newdigate manuscript was not the only copy tailored to its individual recipient. Some copies were heavily abbreviated, notably those sent in letters by Sir George Savile and John Chamberlain. In their accompanying letters, both men said they were sending the full entertainment, but both texts consisted only of the farewell speech of Place. This abbreviated text easily fitted onto a single page and so was particularly suitable for passage within the letter writer's flow of news and gossip. Collation reveals that these two copies contain almost identical texts and almost certainly shared a common exemplar. Savile seems to have acquired his text while the court was at Oatlands in August, but Chamberlain was not able to send a text to Carleton until 19 November, six weeks after his first letter describing the summer progress, but just a few days after the court's return to London.[37] Since both men acquired their copies when in proximity to the royal court, it is likely that Browne and Chamberlain got their texts from the same source, and that this shared source was a courtier.

A more complex case is the text sent to Sir Edward Conway in Brill. The source and date of Conway's copy are unknown, but his position meant that he was in frequent correspondence with the court in England and, as mentioned, Conway's colleague Sir Robert Sidney had been sent a copy of the entertainment (now lost) by Sir William Browne on 12 August. Although when Conway became Principal Secretary in the 1620s King James joked that he had an illiterate secretary, Conway collected a great many verse manuscript separates including a number of royal entertainments.[38] Conway's text of Harefield is another separate written in

[36] Lady Newdigate-Newdegate, *Gossip from a Muniment Room* (London: David Nutt, 1897), 38.

[37] The Queen returned to Whitehall on 15 November in time for the Accession Day celebrations two days later. E. K. Chambers, *The Elizabethan Stage*, 4 vols. (Oxford: Clarendon Press, 1923), iv. 115.

[38] For Conway as a collector, see James Knowles, 'Jonson's *Entertainment at Britain's Burse*', in Martin Butler (ed.), *Re-Presenting Ben Jonson* (Basingstoke: Macmillan, 1999), 114–51 (pp. 123–5).

a neat secretary hand.[39] This copy includes the verse parts of the entertainment but none of the prose speeches, a pattern of omissions that suggests the text was constructed to reflect Conway's personal interest, which (as his surviving collection attests) was for manuscript poetry. Conway's text is less closely tied to the original performance or the household at Harefield: the occasion of the performance is given but the copy provides little more circumstantial detail about the performance. The contrast between this copy and those belonging to Newdigate and Hutton brings us back to the two alternative ways of reading an entertainment discussed near the beginning of this essay, as court news or coterie literature. While some other copies were clearly produced for readers who were expected to be interested in the entertainment as an occasion and as a reflection on the hosts, it was literary form (i.e. prose/verse) that determined what was included in Conway's copy.

The Harefield entertainment was initially disseminated to a relatively coherent elite social group that was absent from but oriented towards and in regular contact with the royal court. Other copies, most of which are textually corrupt and were probably produced at a slightly later date, show that the circulation of the entertainment soon passed outside this group. One copy of the 'Lottery' survives in the 'diary' of the Middle Temple student John Manningham, which reveals that the text of Harefield was circulating around the Inns of Court by February 1603.[40] Given the number of errors in Manningham's copy, it seems certain that it was a second-generation copy or later. Scribal literature flourished at the Inns of Court and there are many routes by which copies could have reached Manningham: through its circulation within London, from the Egerton family's close links with Lincoln's Inn, from a member of another well-connected family with a member at the Inns, or from the entertainment's author John Davies. For all the social connections and access to elite circles provided by membership in the Inns of Court, the Harefield entertainment's circulation there made it accessible to a significantly less exclusive readership, of which John Manningham, the adoptive heir of a prosperous London mercer, is a good example.

Two other miscellanies not known to have belonged to anyone close to the entertainment contain derivative texts produced in about 1605, reinforcing the link between the quality of a text and the social connections of the original owner.[41] The full pattern of circulation, however, was more complicated. There

---

Conway owned texts including Jonson's *The Entertainment at Theobalds* (1607), *The Entertainment at Britain's Burse* (1608), and *The Gipsies Metamorphosed* (1621), Middleton's 1622 *Barkham Entertainment*, and the anonymous *Running Masque* (1620).

[39] Folger Shakespeare Library, MS X.d.172.

[40] BL, Harleian MS 5353, fo. 95[v]. See *The Diary of John Manningham of the Middle Temple*, ed. Robert Parker Sorlein (Hanover, NH: University Press of New England, 1976). The Harefield text is between entries dated 4 and 6 Feb. 1603.

[41] Yale University, Beinecke Library, Osborn MS fb 9; Folger MS Z.e.28.

are surviving copies of the 'Mariner's Song' with musical settings that are likely
to have come from musicians involved in the entertainment.[42] Another poetical
miscellany includes a version of the 'Lottery' with a number of individual lots not
found in any other copy.[43] This manuscript preserves the earliest known version
of the lottery but is found alongside texts of a slightly later date and was produced
sometime shortly after the Queen's death. Although the unidentified compiler
of this miscellany had close connections at court, his source on this occasion
seems to have been John Davies's own drafts.[44] Its compiler clearly found the
text worth copying, but he did not show much interest in the circumstances of
the entertainment's production: it is not dated, the place is not specified, Egerton
is not named, and he is given the imprecise title of Lord Chief Justice.

In 1608, the 'Lottery' was printed in the second edition of *A Poetical Rapsodie*,
which was edited by Francis Davison, the son of Elizabeth's disgraced former
secretary William Davison.[45] The inclusion of the entertainment in a poetical
miscellany clearly treats it as a literary text rather than as court news. In its
appearance in the *Poetical Rapsodie*, the Harefield entertainment thus was no
longer keyed to the reputation of Egerton and his wife—to be understood
alongside feasts, gifts, and hospitality—but rather was re-contextualized with
sonnets and epigrams. By 1608, with the old Queen long dead, the entertainment
was no longer news nor was it relevant as a manifestation of the hosts' status. By
this time, Ben Jonson had published two masque quartos that included prefatory
comments strongly defending the masque's artistic validity, and this may well have
had an effect on how other royal entertainments were read.[46] One consequence
of the shift towards the literary merits of the Harefield entertainment was that its
authorship took on a new significance, especially given that Sir John Davies (as
he was by 1608) was a well-known poet. None of the manuscript texts, or even
any of the letters, had noted Davies's authorship of the entertainment: *A Poetical
Rapsodie* is the only early text to provide any record of authorship. Despite this
reorientation, Harefield's prestigious origin remained significant in the *Poetical
Rapsodie*. Davison was careful to note the fact of its performance before Queen
Elizabeth, and this was presumably one reason for the entertainment's prominent
position as the second item in the collection. Nonetheless, by 1608, the details
of that performance were becoming hazy, for the *Poetical Rapsodie* placed the
entertainment at 'The Lord Chancellor's house' in 1601.

---

[42] BL, Add. MS 24665, fos. 19^v–20^r; Robert Jones, *Ultimum Vale* (London: n.p., 1608).

[43] BL, Add. MS 22601, fos. 49–51^r. The miscellany includes a number of works by Davies,
including a similarly distinctive copy of *A Contention betwen a Wife, a Widowe and a Maide*.

[44] The best evidence of a link to the court is the sequence of poems by King James (fos. 24–5,
32–6) otherwise known only from a manuscript belonging to the royal household (BL, Add. MS
24195). For the text of the 'Lottery', see *Poems of Davies*, ed. Krueger, 409–10.

[45] *A Poetical Rapsodie* (London: Nicholas Okes for Roger Jackson, 1608), sigs. B2^v–B4^v.

[46] Jonson had published: *Hymenaei* (London: V. Sims for T. Thorp, 1606); *The Characters of
Two Royall Masques. The One of Blacknesse, the Other of Beautie* (London: G. Eld, 1608).

Although this analysis of manuscript circulation has returned, in the end, to print publication, it should be emphasized that the Harefield entertainment was printed as a result of its earlier circulation in manuscript. Fragmentary surviving lists of Francis Davison's manuscripts reveal that the *Poetical Rapsodie* was largely produced from his extensive personal collection of manuscript verse.[47] Early in the reign of James I, Davison wrote out a list of 'manuscripts to get' which included 'sports masks & Entertaynments to the Late Queen The King. &.c.'.[48]

It is a heterogeneous list: entertainments are placed alongside political items like the letters of Essex, as well as translations of the Psalms, satires, and the poems of Jonson. What connected these disparate entities was readerly interest. Davison had himself written *The Masque of Proteus* for the Gray's Inn Revels of 1594 so could be expected to have a particular interest in entertainments, but he had more than an amateur interest in acquiring manuscript texts.[49] Davison acted as a nodal point in the exchange of manuscripts: his list of manuscripts 'to get' was not a personal wish list, but rather a list of genres in which there was a strong interest. This confirms what the example of Harefield has already demonstrated: there was a widespread interest in entertainment texts that was catered for through the medium of manuscript.

APPENDIX 12.1: ELIZABETHAN ENTERTAINMENTS THAT CIRCULATED IN MANUSCRIPT

This list includes entertainments for which there is evidence for circulation in manuscript; it excludes texts that survive only in copies that belonged to the author or host of the entertainment. These texts did not all circulate as separates. Those that survive as separates (or are known to have circulated as such) are marked with an asterisk (*), though the true number that once existed in that form is certainly higher.

1566 The Oration before the Queen at Coventry*
1566 Masque at the Marriage of Frances Radcliffe and Thomas Mildmay
1572 The Oration before the Queen at Warwick
1575 The Oration before the Queen at Worcester*
1575 Sir Henry Lee's Entertainment at Woodstock
1577? Tiltyard Entertainment by Philip (later Sir Philip) Sidney
1578? The Earl of Leicester's Entertainment at Wanstead
1581 Tiltyard Speech for the Earl of Arundel
1584? Thomas Heneage's Entertainment at Heneage House
1580s? The Queen's Welcome to Greenwich
1590 Song from Sir Henry Lee's tiltyard entertainment

---

[47] BL, Harleian MS 280, fos. 102–5.   [48] BL, Harleian MS 298, fo. 159ᵛ.
[49] The masque is included in *A Poetical Rapsodie* from its first edition (1602), and a manuscript copy of the masque in Davison's own hand is in BL, Harleian MS 541, fos. 138–45.

1591 Lord Burghley and Sir Robert Cecil's Entertainment at Theobalds*
1592 Sir Henry Lee's Entertainment at Ditchley
1594 Lord Burghley and Sir Robert Cecil's Entertainment at Theobalds
1595 Tiltyard device for the Earl of Essex*
1596 Tiltyard speech for the Earl of Sussex
1599 Thomas Cecil, Lord Burghley's Entertainment at Wimbledon
1600 Tiltyard speech for the Earl of Cumberland*
1600? Tiltyard speech for Lord Compton*
1602 Sir William Russell's Entertainment at Chiswick*
1602 Sir Thomas Egerton and the Dowager Countess of Derby's Entertainment at Harefield*
1602 Sir Robert Cecil's Entertainment at Cecil House*

PART IV

AFTERLIFE

Caroline and Antiquarian
Perspectives

13

'In the purest times of peerless Queen Elizabeth': Nostalgia, Politics, and Jonson's use of the 1575 Kenilworth Entertainments

James Knowles

Writing his *Declaration for his Resolution of Marching into Yorkeshire* (1642), William Cavendish, Earl of Newcastle—staunch royalist and general of Charles I's forces north of the River Trent—summoned up the memory of Elizabeth I to protect himself against accusations of organizing a papist army against his countrymen:

> To conclude, I wish from my heart there were Recusants of no kinde in this Kingdome; I am Resolved, as I have lived, so to dye in the profession of the true Reformed Religion, as it now standeth established by the Lawes of the Land, as it was professed, and practised in the purest times of peerlesse Queene *Elizabeth* . . . [1]

Later, in his *Advice to Charles II* (*circa* 1660), Cavendish frequently invoked Elizabeth's rule—'the beste presedent for Englands Governmente'—as a model of policy and national unity.[2] Cavendish's use of the Elizabethan image reiterates the importance of nostalgia as a political discourse in the later Jacobean and Caroline periods. Martin Butler has described the 'quite extraordinary cult of the memory of Elizabeth', which not only overshadowed James and Charles as monarchs, but also fuelled 'an emotional concern for values . . . which cast suspicion on the whole tendency of Stuart government'.[3] These values of

---

[1] *Declaration for his Resolution of Marching into Yorkeshire* (York: Stephen Bulkley, 1642 [Wing, N879]), sig. A5ʳ.

[2] *Ideology and Politics on the Eve of the Restoration: Newcastle's Advice to Charles II*, ed. Thomas P. Slaughter (Philadelphia: American Philosophical Society, 1984), 45. Unless otherwise stated all references are to this edition and abbreviated as Cavendish, *Advice*. Later, Margaret Cavendish noted his view of the importance of nobility and gentry retaining local judicial office: see *The Life of William Cavendish Duke of Newcastle*, ed. C. H. Firth (London: Routledge, 1906), 128.

[3] Martin Butler, *Theatre and Crisis 1632–1642* (Cambridge: Cambridge University Press, 1984), 198.

opposition to Spain and Catholicism, anti-popery, foreign intervention in support
of beleaguered Protestant allies, and a unified national Church governed by a
godly prince, were fuelled by the republication of myriad images of Elizabeth's
reign, memorializations of her achievements, and panegyrics of Elizabethan naval
and military heroes, and often have been seen as politically charged signs of
opposition to the Stuarts.

Cavendish's appeal to the 'purest times' of Elizabeth I illustrates how 'enthusiastic retro-Elizabethanism' (as one recent study terms this nostalgia), and,
particularly, the ideals of national and religious unity, could be deployed by
supporters of the Stuart regime as much as by its critics.[4] Discourses, like Elizabethanism, and the struggles over their meanings and the political and cultural
concepts that those debates articulate, have recently attracted much attention
from historians, and the discursive turn in history has dominated new interpretations of the 1620s and the 1640s.[5] Most recently, these approaches have begun
to be applied to the apparently stable and harmonious languages and ideas of
the 1630s. Post-revisionist accounts of this decade now stress its continuities
with the more fissiparous political culture of the 1620s, and have emphasized
how the Caroline cult of peace of the 1630s not only obscures Charles I's earlier
bellicosity, but also underestimates how that peace was 'contested, controversial
and fragile'.[6]

This revised sense of the 1630s places in a new, more complex light the
appropriation by Cavendish and Ben Jonson of aspects of the 1575 Kenilworth
festivities for the *Entertainment at Welbeck* staged for Charles I at Welbeck
Abbey on 21 May 1633. Like the 1575 'princely pleasures', the entertainments
at Welbeck, situated on the Nottinghamshire–Derbyshire border, punctuated
a royal progress—in this case, Charles I's journey north for his much-delayed
Scots coronation in 1633. This occasion used the celebrated Kenilworth revels
as a receptacle for a series of loosely interconnected Caroline issues and values,
including the role of popular culture, the importance of chivalric values and
military training, monarchical governance, attitudes towards the populace and
their political and religious views, the role of aristocratic magnates, and the
functions of magnificence.[7] Two encompassing concerns, monarchical style

[4] M. Dobson and N. J. Watson, *England's Elizabeth: An Afterlife in Fame and Fantasy* (Oxford: Oxford University Press, 2002), 49.

[5] See 'Politics of Discourse: Introduction', in K. Sharpe and S. Zwicker (eds.), *Politics of Discourse: The Literature and History of Seventeenth-Century England* (Berkeley and Los Angeles: University of California Press, 1987), 3–7; K. Sharpe, *Remapping Early Modern England: The Culture of Seventeenth-Century Politics* (Cambridge: Cambridge University Press, 2000), 86, 119–20; and 'Introduction: after Revisionism', in R. Cust and A. Hughes (eds.), *Conflict in Early Stuart England: Studies in Religion and Politics 1603–1642* (Harlow: Longman, 1989), 19–21.

[6] Julie Sanders and Ian Atherton, 'Introducing the 1630s: Questions of Parliament, Peace and Pressure Points', in *The 1630s: Interdisciplinary Perspectives* (Manchester: Manchester University Press, 2006), 3.

[7] Cedric Brown, 'Courtesies of Place and Arts of Diplomacy in Ben Jonson's Last Two Entertainments for Royalty', in T. Raylor (ed.), *Special Issue: The Cavendish Circle*, in *Seventeenth*

and the role of the regions and regional culture, give shape to this nexus of ideas and beliefs. As an outstanding exemplar of aristocratic hospitality, the 1575 Kenilworth entertainments showed how aristocracy and monarchy might interact, and how monarchy might present itself to the populace in 'the theatre of reciprocity' enacted during a royal progress.[8] The image afforded by Kenilworth of national unity under a populist monarch has particular resonances for a regime that has often been regarded by both contemporary commentators—Cavendish among them—and modern historians as failing to 'project an effective public image'.[9] Indeed, this inability of the Caroline regime to communicate remains, even after revisionism and post-revisionism, one of the key explanations for the British civil wars.

Equally, the location of Kenilworth—in north-central Warwickshire—and its function in presenting Robert Dudley, Earl of Leicester as a Midlands magnate, provided a different interpretation of the role of regional culture in national politics. Several critics, like Cedric Brown, have attended to the 'courtesies of place' offered in entertainments like that at Welbeck in 1633 that were staged away from London and the court.[10] Leah Marcus, through her exploration of the political role of rural sports in Jacobean and Caroline England, has heightened our awareness of the significance of the country, its recreations and values, in political discourse.[11] The intertextual relations between the Kenilworth and Welbeck entertainments complicate our understanding of these cultural contexts, and suggest that the emphasis upon 'courtly negotiations in the country', or the royal agenda which appropriates rural customs while offering a 'tribute to the superior culture of the court', underestimates the significance of Cavendish's critical distance from the Caroline court.[12]

This essay argues, then, that the appropriation of elements from the 1575 Kenilworth entertainments belongs to Cavendish's almost 'feudal' view of aristocratic culture and the role of the aristocrat in society, and that these appropriated elements are combined to articulate a critique of Caroline court culture. Moreover if, as Leah Marcus has argued, the Caroline emphasis upon regional

Century, 4 (1994), 147–71 (p. 153) has also noted the parallels with Kenilworth in 1633, and describing the reception of Charles and Henrietta Maria at Welbeck in 1634 Tim Raylor notes the 'pungently Elizabethan flavour' of that occasion: see Raylor, 'A Manuscript Poem on the Royal Progress of 1634: An Edition of John Westwood's "Carmen Basileuporion" ', in *The Cavendish Circle*, 173–95 (p. 174). Jonson's borrowings were first noticed in C. R. Baskervill, 'The Sources of Jonson's *Masque at Christmas* and *Love's Welcome at Welbeck*', *Modern Philology*, 6 (1908–9), 257–69.

  [8] J. M. Richards, 'The English Accession of James VI: "National" Identity, Gender and the Personal Monarchy of England', *English Historical Review*, 117 (2002), 513–35 (p. 534).
  [9] Malcolm Smuts, 'Public Ceremony and Royal Charisma: The English Royal Entry in London, 1485–1642', in A. L. Beier et al. (eds.), *The First Modern Society: Essays in English History in Honour of Lawrence Stone* (Cambridge: Cambridge University Press, 1989), 65–93 (p. 91).
  [10] Brown, 'Courtesies of Place', *passim*.
  [11] Leah S. Marcus, *The Politics of Mirth* (Chicago: University of Chicago Press, 1986), 129.
  [12] Brown, 'Courtesies of Place', 147, and Marcus, *Politics of Mirth*, 129.

culture and the encouragement of rural pastimes contributed to an attempt to strengthen the social basis of the sacramentalized view of kingship, then in *The Entertainment at Welbeck*, the language of the regions responds to that programme by validating cultures beyond the court.[13] In this context, nostalgic Elizabethanism becomes the means of signalling a commitment to a vision of national and theological unity, but also of insisting on a critical and more truly national definition of that cultural unity, one which includes the Midlands and the north.

'WHEN MEN OF HONOUR FLOURISHED': CAVENDISH AND THE EARL OF LEICESTER

William Cavendish was one of the most significant—and still neglected—patrons of Caroline England. He both supported and practised a series of interconnected intellectual and cultural activities, ranging across the visual arts and architecture, equestrianism, scientific experiment, and literary production (in a variety of forms). As an important Midlands landlord, he also engaged with local government, acting as Lord Lieutenant of two shires (Nottinghamshire in 1626 and Derbyshire in 1628), and becoming Governor to Prince Charles in 1638. Although Cavendish was a grandson of Bess of Hardwick and had been one of Prince Henry's companions, his position as the son of a youngest son seems to have spurred him to a conscious consideration of his family, the meaning and function of aristocracy, and a careful cultivation of his landholdings and his political power. Whether it was the influence of Hobbes, the impact of sceptical scientific enquiry, or even contact with writers like Jonson and painters like Van Dyck, Cavendish, although deeply rooted in a deferential aristocratic culture, was also capable of sustained meditation on the workings of aristocratic and political culture, including a critical stance towards the Caroline court.[14] This political philosophizing has its fullest expression in the *Advice for Charles II*, but much of Cavendish's literary and cultural output debates the function and meaning of aristocratic culture.

Cavendish's career is shaped by a series of cultural and political models, such as Prince Henry, although in his discussions of aristocratic honour, manliness, and lineage he frequently harked back to 'quasi-feudal paternalism'.[15] Among

[13] Marcus, *Politics of Mirth*, 5, also pp. 128–33.

[14] His position is close to what Richard McCoy aptly terms 'aristocratic constitutionalism': see R. McCoy, 'Old English Honour in an Evil Time: Aristocratic Principle in the 1620s', in R. Malcolm Smuts (ed.), *The Stuart Court and Europe*, (Cambridge: Cambridge University Press, 1996), 133–56 (p. 138).

[15] This phrase is used by Thomas Cogswell of the earls of Huntingdon: see Cogswell, *Home Divisions: Aristocracy, the State and Provincial Conflict* (Manchester: Manchester University Press, 1998), 5–7. The differences in the uses of this paternalism are instructive: the Hastings family

the recurrent themes in Cavendish's works are frequent invocations of Queen Elizabeth's ideal rule, and the enhanced role of the magnates during her reign.[16] In particular, he praised George Talbot, 6th Earl of Shrewsbury, for his use of aristocratic ceremonial during installations to the Order of the Garter. He also singled out Robert Dudley, Earl of Leicester, as one of his models, even though Leicester's support for the reformed religion caused him some anxiety.[17] Cavendish regarded Leicester as a symbol of bygone manliness and of the proper position of the magnate as counsellor to the monarch—as a loyal vice-regent in the provinces.

This choice of Leicester rather than Robert Devereux, 2nd Earl of Essex, as the exemplar of ancient virtue distinguishes Cavendish from the more oppositional use of Essex in retro-Elizabethan discourse.[18] Although Leicester benefited from the Caroline tendency to glorify all things Elizabethan, his reputation remained tainted by the historical accounts of Elizabeth's reign published in the 1630s, and by the libels about him that still circulated. Camden's *Annales* (1625) depicted Leicester as an 'upstart', 'raised from the dust' by the Queen, and blackened his name as a self-serving temporizer, although Camden also praised him as a 'compleat courtier, magnificent, liberall'.[19] Camden's account chimes with other histories written in the 1630s—such as Naunton's *Fragmenta Regalia*, unpublished until 1641, but probably completed *circa* 1633-4—and with the numerous anti-Leicestrian satirical tracts such as the very widely circulated *A Copy of a Letter* (Paris, 1584), otherwise known as *Leycester's Commonwealth*, '*Leicester's Ghost*' (MS, *circa* 1605), and 'Newes from Heaven and Hell'.[20] The 1575 entertainments at Kenilworth are absent from the Caroline discussions of Leicester's career, although his equestrian portrait was engraved sometime in the 1620s.[21] Furthermore, Cavendish may also have accessed more personal information both from his father who had been a beneficiary of Leicester's patronage,[22] and through Lettice,

required it to stave off a declining financial position; the Cavendishes used it to embed a rising social and financial situation.

[16] Cavendish, *Advice*, 45.   [17] Ibid. 47.

[18] McCoy, 'Old English Honour in an Evil Time', 135–6, 138, 142–3; see also J. S. A. Adamson, 'Chivalry and Political Culture in Caroline England', in Kevin Sharpe and Peter Lake (eds.), *Culture and Politics in Early Stuart England* (Basingstoke: Macmillan, 1994), 161–97 (p. 167).

[19] William Camden, *Annales* (London: printed [by George Purslowe, Humphrey Lownes, and Miles Flesher] for Beniamin Fisher, 1625), 288.

[20] *Leicester's Commonwealth . . . and Related Documents*, ed. D. C. Peck (Athens: Ohio University Press, 1985), 224–6; Henry Woudhuysen, *Sir Philip Sidney and the Circulation of Manuscripts, 1558–1640* (Oxford: Clarendon Press, 1996), 148, describes the 'mass circulation' of this text and adds four more MSS to Peck's list. See also T. Rogers, *Leicester's Ghost*, ed. F. B. Williams (Chicago: University of Chicago Press, 1972), and D. C. Peck, ' "Newes from heaven and hell": A Defamatory Narrative of the Earl of Leicester', *English Literary Renaissance*, 8 (1978), 141–58.

[21] A. M. Hind, *Engraving in England*, 3 vols. (Cambridge: Cambridge University Press, 1955–64), iii (1964), 57, and plate 31. This portrait occurs in *Baziliωlogia* (1618, 1628, and 1630): see Hind, *Engraving*, ii. 115–44.

[22] Elizabeth Talbot, Countess of Shrewsbury, to Robert Dudley, Earl of Leicester, 23 May ?1578, in *HMC Calendar of the Manuscripts of the Marquis of Bath Preserved at Longleat, Wiltshire*, 5 vols. (London: HMSO, 1904–80), v (1980), ed. G. Dynfallt Owen, 196–7.

Dowager Countess of Leicester, who only died in 1634.[23] Her grandson Gervase Clifton, who wrote her epitaph and other occasional poetry associated with her household, was one of Cavendish's closest associates in county governance.[24]

Many aspects of Leicester's aristocratic self-presentation are echoed in Cavendish's patronage, including the political use of a substantial art collection, architecture and gardening, and a fascination with genealogy, heraldry, and local culture. But the central point of contact between the two careers lies in horses and horsemanship. Most crucially, Leicester had transformed the position of Master of the Horse into a politically significant office (due to the frequency and proximity of access to the sovereign), showing how such a post could become the foundation of court power.[25] Leicester's activities in extending the royal stud were well known; he imported the Italian riding master Claudio Corte to England (a fact mentioned by Cavendish in *La Nouvelle Methode*); and he was the dedicatee of several horsemanship manuals, such as Blundeville's *Four Chiefest Offices Belonging Horsemanship* (1575), widely used by early modern riders.[26] Horse-breeding and *manége* were central to Cavendish's sense of his aristocratic position, and in the 1630s he was developing his reputation as an expert horseman. In his 'Epigram. To William Earl of Newcastle', Jonson depicted Cavendish as embodying both the 'ancient art of Thrace', and as the chivalric Sir Bevis from the medieval romance tradition.[27] In 1633, the Venetian Ambassador reported the rumour that Cavendish was about to be appointed Master of the Horse, and although nothing came of this, his position as Governor required him to instruct Prince Charles in horse-riding.[28]

As is well known, Cavendish's most extended response to Leicester occurs in his play *The Varietyie* (performed *circa* 1641), in which proper English masculinity is embodied in Manly, who dresses in Elizabethan costume like the Earl of Leicester:

I am bold to present a suit to you—I confess it was not made by a French tailor. I can make a leg and kiss my hand, too, after the fashion of my clothes. This served

---

[23] Kenilworth is absent from John Stow's *Annales* (London: John Beale, Bernard Alsop, Thomas Fawcett, and Augustine Mathewes, 1632) although both Stow (sig. 3O4ʳ) and Raphael Holinshed's *The Third Volume of Chronicles* (London: Henry Denham, 1586), 1421–2, provide lavish descriptions of Leicester's gubernatorial feast at Utrecht in 1586.

[24] See P. R. Seddon, 'Sir Gervase Clifton and the Government of Nottinghamshire, 1609–1640', *Transactions of the Thoroton Society*, 97 (1993), 88–97.

[25] P. E. J. Hammer, *The Polarization of Elizabethan Politics: The Political Career of Robert Devereaux, 2nd Earl of Essex, 1585–97* (Cambridge: Cambridge University Press, 1999), 60–1, and n. 108; M. M. Reese, *The Royal Office of the Master of the Horse* (London: Threshold Books, 1976), 154–64; C. M. Prior, *The Royal Studs of the Sixteenth and Seventeenth Centuries* (London: Horse and Hound Publications, 1935), 4–7.

[26] *Methode et inuention nouuelle de dresser les cheuaux* (Antwerp: Van Meurs, 1658), sig. A1ᵛ.

[27] Ben Jonson, 'An Epigram. To William Earle of Newcastle', in *The Underwood* (1640), in *Ben Jonson*, ed. C. H. Herford et al., 11 vols. (Oxford: Clarendon Press, 1925–52), viii (1947), 232–3.

[28] *Calendar of State Papers Venetian*, xxiii: *1632–1636*, ed. A. B. Hind (London: HMSO, 1921), 87, and Prior, *Royal Studs*, 62.

in those honest days when knights were gentlemen and proper men took the wall of dwarves... These things were worn when men of honour flourished, that tamed the wealth of Spain, set up the States, helped the French king, and brought rebellion to reason and government.[29]

For Manly, these times were typified by the proper and full Garter procession on St George's Day, and 'the best knight of the country with the ragged staff on their sleeves' (*The Varietie*, 41)—the Dudley emblem having been the bear and ragged staff. Against Manly stands the figure of the foppish French dancing master Galliard, who claims that dancing to the French fiddle, following the precepts of Montagut (the Duke of Buckingham's French dancing master), forms the basis of good governance, as 'they are so bissy to learn a de dance, dey vill never tink of de rebellion' (*The Varietie*, 36). Later, in his *Advice to Charles II*, while insisting on the importance of giving major nobles offices close to the King, Cavendish dismissed Charles I's court:

There was a pretty way they had att Courte, that meane people were aboute the king, & the Queen, would Jeere the Greatest Noble man in England, Iff hee did not make the Laste months Reverance, a La mode, that came with the Laste Dancer, from Paris, packt upp in his fiddle Case, & no matter of Regarde of the Nobilety at All ... [30]

This passage probably refers to Cavendish's experience in the late 1630s, but it also suggests Cavendish's distance from the Caroline court, despite his pursuit of office, and, in particular, the importance of his sense of an English aristocratic identity.[31]

This sense of critical distance from the court and the establishment of an aristocratic style rooted in local political networks and the exercise of royal offices was emerging as a major dimension to Cavendish's activities in the 1630s. Indeed, at the time of the *Entertainment at Welbeck*, Cavendish was developing his position as regional magnate both through the acquisition of lands around his Nottinghamshire estate at Welbeck, and through his accretion of local offices, such as the lords lieutenancy of both Nottinghamshire and Derbyshire. Contemporary commentary on his self-presentation notes a deliberate, almost archaic, use of chivalric ideas. 'On Bolsover Castle' alludes equally to the military function of the original Castle—built in Derbyshire during the 'Barons' Wars',

---

[29] William Cavendish, *The Varietie*, in *The Country Captaine and The Varietie, Two Comedies* (London: Humphrey Robinson and Humphrey Moseley, 1649), 39.

[30] Cavendish, *Advice*, 48.

[31] 'I find a great deal of venom against me', see Cavendish to Elizabeth Countess of Newcastle, 8 Apr. 1636, in *HMC Report on the Manuscripts of the Duke of Portland Preserved at Welbeck Abbey*, 10 vols. (London: HMSO, 1891–1931), ii (1893), ed. R. Ward, 127. Contemporary reports, indeed, even suggest that he may have been regarded as a figure of fun: 'I hear my Lord of Newcastle doth not grow much in their Majesties' estimation for he did lately complain to the King that the Queen had laughed at him, and upon this complaint, I think, they did both bestow that favour on him ... [Cavendish is] more ridiculous than it is possible he should be' (*HMC Report on the Manuscripts of the Right Honourable Viscount De L'Isle and Dudley*, ed. G. Dyfnallt Owen, 6 vols. (London: HMSO, 1925–66), vi (1966), 157.

when 'Just liberties were got with unjust jars'—and to its more recent use, as a bridge between court and country ('Loved by the King, feared by the clowns').[32]

His building projects manifest similar tendencies. Bolsover Castle has attracted much attention for its 'chivalric' antecedents and for the resemblances between its neo-Gothic style and the fantasy architecture of Prince Henry's masques. Recently, it has been argued that the fusion of styles found in the Castle is the deliberate creation of a 'new paradigm', derived in part from the Unionist politics and imagery of those entertainments.[33] Welbeck Abbey, in contrast, was associated with use rather than pleasure, and functioned as administrative centre for the estates, and as the repository of family documentary history, although it too exuded a deliberate archaism.[34] Described as 'Your best of ancient and of modern mixed', the house was highly eclectic, combining the remains of the original abbey, the south-west (state) wing built by Robert Smythson (*circa* 1608), and the 'Gothic', castellated porch which typifies what Mark Girouard calls 'Cavendish-Smythson medievalism'.[35] The choice of a hybrid architectural style that eschewed the classicism of the new courtier houses, and instead embodied the hospitality and spirituality of the former abbey, may have been deliberate. Richard Andrewes, in his poem on the Cavendish houses, evokes the past and present functions of these buildings, depicting them as surpassed by Rufford Abbey for alms-giving, in a nostalgic vision that once more recalls the feudal and family past as Rufford had been a Talbot (Shrewsbury) property.[36]

From the evidence of the household post-Restoration, it also seems that Cavendish utilized spaces such as the Great Hall to recreate old-fashioned dining styles in line with his praise of the Earl of Shrewsbury's inclusion of his country neighbours. Designed to manifest his local power, the Great Hall was probably hung with a series of horse portraits interspersed by pictures of the twelve Caesars, and was used for Cavendish's expansive hospitality, to announce his status as county magnate, and also to present his own brand of neo-chivalric aristocratic

[32] George Aglionby, 'On Bolsover Castle', ll. 58 and 67, in *The Country House Poem: A Cabinet of Seventeenth-Century Estate Poems and Related Items*, ed. Almastair Fowler (Edinburgh: Edinburgh University Press, 1994), 170. The Barons' Wars are the civil wars of 1264–6.

[33] Lucy Worsley, 'The Architectural Patronage of William Cavendish', in Lynn Hulse and James Knowles (eds.), *Prince of the Northern Quarter: The Patronage, Culture, and Politics of William Cavendish, 1st Duke of Newcastle* (forthcoming). On Henry's hybrid architecture, see John Peacock, 'Jonson and Jones Collaborate on *Prince Henry's Barriers*', *Word and Image*, 3 (1987), 172–94 (p. 186).

[34] Lucy Worsley, ' "An habitation not so magnificent as useful": Life at Welbeck Abbey in the 17th Century', *Transactions of the Thoroton Society*, 107 (2003), 123–43.

[35] M. Girouard, *Robert Smythson and the Elizabethan Country House* (New Haven: Yale University Press, 1983), 256.

[36] See *The Country House Poem*, ed. Fowler, 159–65. See also S. Adams, ' "Because I am of that countrye and mynde to plant myself there": Robert Dudley, Earl of Leicester and the West Midlands', *Midland History*, 20 (1995), 21–74 (p. 28).

courtesy and honour.[37] This choice of pictures and even their hanging illustrates Cavendish's combination of 'modern' and 'ancient' ideals in that this specific combination of equestrian and imperial portraits echoed the gallery at St James's Palace, which had initially been devised for the highly chivalric Prince Henry, and which King Charles had completed in 1633 with the addition of the massive equestrian portrait of himself accompanied by Monsieur de Saint Antoine painted by Van Dyck.[38] This use of the Great Hall and Cavendish's allusion to royal decorative schemes signals a clear sense of Cavendish's position in the locality, and in this way the internal spaces and furnishing of Welbeck, as well as its external architectural style, embody a distinctive aesthetic and political position, complimenting the King while also recalling his martial brother.[39] This deployment of mixed social space also locates Cavendish as an inheritor of the feudal traditions of magnates and their hospitality in contravention of the Caroline trend towards aristocratic dining in smaller, socially exclusive spaces, and harks back to older 'feudal' models. At Welbeck, the architecture, the use of social space, and even the decorative schema all recall an older chivalric and feudal culture that is of a piece with Cavendish's interest in his own genealogy. Cavendish was especially proud of his matrilineal title, the barony of Ogle, which could be traced back to the Norman Conquest, and this genealogical interest bears comparison with Leicester's earlier concerns with his own lineage and the Saxon origins of Kenilworth.[40]

The nostalgic view of aristocratic honour and chivalric culture is perhaps summed up best by Leicester's political heir the Earl of Essex who, even when Elizabeth still reigned, eulogized an England 'most mighty when the nobility led and commanded in war and were great housekeepers at home'.[41] The combination of martial values and domestic magnificence might equally describe Cavendish's regional patronage, although his practice placed particular emphasis on chivalric values in the fullest sense. Of course, such concern with the cultivation of these values and manliness was not solely the preserve of provincial magnates, and, as John Adamson has shown, Charles himself reformed the Order of the Garter and used a refined and translated form of chivalric imagery as part of his sacralized and centralized monarchy.[42] Adamson argues that even though Cavendish and others emphasized different strands

[37] L. Worsley, 'A Set of Seventeenth-Century "Caesars" from Bolsover Castle', *English Heritage Collections Review*, 2 (1999), 61–4. See also Raylor, 'A Manuscript Poem on the Royal Progress of 1634', 192, which evokes the impact of the house and its furnishings.

[38] T. Wilks, ' "Paying Special Attention to the Adorning of a Most Beautiful Gallery": The Pictures in St. James's Palace, 1609–49', *Court Historian*, 10 (2005), 149–72 (pp. 157–69).

[39] It is tempting to speculate whether this regional use of pictures by a would-be magnate recalls Leicester's collections and especially his use of them as part of royal entertainments: see E. Goldring, 'Portraits of Queen Elizabeth I and the Earl of Leicester for Kenilworth Castle', *Burlington Magazine*, 147 (2005), 654–60, and also Goldring's essay in this volume, pp. 163–88.

[40] Worsley, ' "An Habitation" ', 140. On genealogy, see F. Heal and C. Holmes, *The Gentry in England and Wales, 1500–1700* (Basingstoke: Macmillan, 1994), 36.

[41] Cited in McCoy, 'Old English Honour in an Evil Time', 138.

[42] Adamson, 'Chivalry and Political Culture', 174.

within a broad chivalric tradition perhaps even to 'encode hostility towards the prevailing ethos of the court', such differences cannot easily be translated into opposition to the crown in the later 1630s.[43] Nonetheless, the position adopted by Cavendish criticizes the court—or, at least, provides an alternative policy—stressing the practicality of martial exercise for all rather than a spiritualized chivalric cult embodied by the new Caroline Garter.[44] This re-inflection of the chivalric language deployed by the court suggests that chivalric discourse can not only become a point of contact between court and provincial culture, but also provides a shared language through which matters of state can be articulated.

From his own letters it is clear that while Cavendish actively pursued court office during the 1630s, he was often a marginalized figure. His letters to Strafford also reveal that he was by no means uncritical of Caroline policy, commenting that they both have had 'but little thankes above neither', although 'we have taken a great deal of paynes in vayne'.[45] This critical distance reminds us that although in the *Entertainment at Welbeck* the rural is reformed (another key Caroline term), this occurs through the agency of the local magnate, echoing Cavendish's own actions in refurbishing the militia and reinvigorating forest governance, so that the text does not simply invoke obedience to court-centred policy. This position re-inflects Caroline policy, or at least uses the Caroline extension of local governance powers and functions to insist on the position of the local magnates as key parts of the government whose views need to be respected and accommodated.

Cavendish's presentation of the importance of local culture and governance effectively speaks back to the centre in its own language (country sports and exact militia), but also adapts the discourse of Elizabethanism, with its images of national community and undegenerate English manliness. In effect, Cavendish uses his position as local magnate—Prince of the Northern Quarter, as he was later called—to mediate between different views of culture and politics.[46] This response, through a discourse often used by those opposed to crown policies, espousing the idea of rural sports under proper gentry supervision which was used by the crown itself, ultimately represents a different model of understanding the relation of monarch to people, court to provinces. As we shall see, *The Entertainment at Welbeck* encapsulates all these ideas but, again, uses the image of Leicester—and, specifically, the 1575 Kenilworth entertainments—as a vehicle for a critique of royal governance.

---

[43] Adamson, 'Chivalry and Political Culture', 181.

[44] 'I would not have you too studious, for too much contemplation spoils action, and virtue consists in that', Cavendish to Prince Charles, in *Life of William Cavendish*, appendix II, p. 184.

[45] Strafford Papers 12/151, 219, cited in Heal and Holmes, *The Gentry in England and Wales*, 194.

[46] L. Hutchinson, *Memoirs of the Life of Colonel Hutchinson*, ed. N. H. Keeble (London: Dent, 1995), 85.

'THIS SERVED IN THOSE HONEST DAYS': KENILWORTH RECREATED

Charles I's much delayed journey north for his Scots coronation was an important moment in the redefinition of the relationship between crown, court, and country. The 1633 visit was also the first major royal journey to Scotland since 1617, and court officials took much trouble to investigate the mechanics of the previous occasion, seeking to bring the progress in line with Charles's preferred formality and ceremoniousness.[47] Royal progresses offered an opportunity to display the magnificence and majesty of the monarchy, and both Elizabeth I and (to a lesser extent) James VI and I recognized the 'essentially reciprocal nature of such journeyings', using them to enact the relationship between monarch and nation, as loyal acclamation was rewarded with justice, charity, and patronage.[48] Whereas earlier sovereigns had used progresses to cement the bonds between monarch and nation, Charles, despite his frequent journeys around the south of England, seems to have converted the summer progresses into hunting trips, and in 1633 the Venetian Ambassador reported the King's desire for speed, hunting, and privacy as he travelled to Scotland.[49] Indeed, Charles travelled by carriage rather than on horseback, and his 'privatized' mode of transport seemed to some to defeat the purpose of royal ceremony.[50] In contrast, writing to Prince Charles in 1638, William Cavendish noted 'what preserves you Kings more than ceremony . . . for in all triumphs whatsoever or public showing yourself, you cannot put upon you too much king', and later he advised the Prince 'to shew your Selfe Gloryously, to your People; like a God'.[51]

Cavendish's *Entertainment at Welbeck*, the most elaborate of the 1633 events—and a demonstration of his views on glorious display—borrowed elements from the 1575 Kenilworth festivities, the zenith of Elizabethan aristocratic progress entertainments.[52] Current critical accounts of the 1575 Kenilworth

[47] Marcus, *Politics of Mirth*, 128; Judith Richards, '"His Nowe Majestie" and the English Monarchy: The Kingship of Charles I before 1640', *Past and Present*, 113 (1986), 70–96 (p. 78).

[48] Richards, '"His Nowe Majestie"', 83; Smuts, 'Public Ceremony and Royal Charisma', 67, 78.

[49] Kevin Sharpe, *The Personal Rule of Charles I* (London: Yale University Press, 1992), 630–1; *Calendar of State Papers . . . Existing in the Archives and Collections of Venice, and in Other Libraries of Northern Italy*, ed. Allen B. Hind et al., 37 vols. (London: HMSO, 1864–1947), xxiii (1921), 107, 110, 117, 125, 131.

[50] Mark Brayshay, 'Long-Distance Royal Journeys: Anne of Denmark's Journey from Stirling to Windsor in 1603', *Journal of Transport History*, 25 (2004), 1–21 (p. 17).

[51] Cavendish to Prince Charles, in *Life of William Cavendish*, appendix II, p. 186; *Advice*, 45.

[52] The Caroline accounts of Leicester's career omit mention of Kenilworth, but two main textual sources were available: *The Princely Pleasures*, an account of the courtly entertainments, first printed in pamphlet form by Richard Jones in 1576 and subsequently included in editions of George Gascoigne's *Works*; and Robert Laneham's *Letter*, a description of the non-courtly shows, the printing history of which is uncertain (though the survival of seventeen copies and one fragment

festivities stress the competition between the Queen and Dudley for control over the agenda, especially around the sensitive issue of the Queen's marriage.[53] The significance of these topics, even if recalled by the Dowager Countess of Leicester, had diminished by the 1630s—though the entertainment's notable militarism, and its espousal of interventionist Protestantism, still resonated in a county in a high state of martial preparedness. Although it remains difficult to be certain what appealed to Cavendish and Jonson, much of the influence of the Elizabethan occasion resides not in direct borrowings, but in less tangible elements such as the presentation of 'a social world permeated by chivalric forms at all levels', and in the vision of national unity through military activity that the *Entertainment at Welbeck* recreates.[54]

Nostalgia for the heroic past as much as chivalry characterized the Kenilworth entertainments which had alluded to Saxon and Danish history, Arthurian legend, and to the mythic origins of Kenilworth to glorify the Earl of Leicester's lineage and martial mien. Much of the occasion had been constructed around a series of chivalric and quasi-chivalric engagements that stressed aristocratic agency. Indeed, Kenilworth was suffused with the idea of returning England to an ideal Arthurian age when 'men of stature' ruled.[55] These topics can be related to other interconnected elements in the 1575 entertainments which also retained their force for Cavendish: the creation of a dynastic estate, the promulgation of the ancientness of his line, and the importance of local allegiances. Simon Adams has shown how the Kenilworth festivities demonstrated Dudley's Warwickshire connections and celebrated the re-edification of Kenilworth Castle as the centrepiece of his 'estate of inheritance', a symbol of his Beauchamp

---

of this work, in two editions, suggests that it enjoyed a wide circulation). Jonson certainly knew the *Letter*, as he had alluded to it in his *Masque of Owls*, staged at Kenilworth for Prince Charles in 1624; he may well have consulted other sources, such as Camden, on that occasion; and there may have been personal information (see above, pp. 251–2). I have continued to refer to 'Laneham's *Letter*', even though there are at least two spellings of his name (Laneham/Langham), and even though William Patten has been identified as a possible author: see Robert Langham, *A Letter*, ed. R. J. P. Kuin (Leiden: Brill, 1983), and Kuin, 'The Purloined *Letter*: Evidence and Probability Regarding Robert Langham's Authorship', *The Library*, 6th ser, 7 (1985), 115-25. I have used Kuin's edition for ease of reference.

[53] Susan Frye, *Elizabeth I: The Competition for Representation*, (Oxford: Oxford University Press, 1993; repr. 1996) 78–86, and Matthew Woodcock, *Fairy in 'The Faerie Queene': Renaissance Elf-Fashioning and Elizabethan Myth-Making* (Aldershot: Ashgate, 2004), 44. In the new *Oxford Dictionary of National Biography*, Simon Adams suggests the occasion was designed to get the Queen to signal his freedom from his pursuit of her so that he might marry elsewhere: see Simon Adams, 'Dudley, Robert, Earl of Leicester (1532/3–1588)', *Oxford Dictionary of National Biography* (Oxford: Oxford University Press, 2004) (www.oxforddnb.com/view/article/8160, accessed 26 Feb. 2006).

[54] *The Progresses and Public Processions of Queen Elizabeth*, ed. John Nichols, 2nd edn., 3 vols. (London: John Nichols, 1823), i. 68–9; Alex Davis, *Chivalry and Romance in the English Renaissance* (Cambridge: Brewer, 2003), 82. Davis (pp. 75–98) presents an important study of the complexities of this occasion, and of Laneham's report. Direct borrowings are noted in Baskervill: see n. 7 above.

[55] *Progresses* ed. Nichols, 2nd edn., i. 59, 62.

ancestry.[56] The implications of these local and baronial emphases were clear in the Kenilworth entertainments, and Leicester even daringly saluted the Queen's resolution to 'abide in this country' and follow 'the direction and advice of these peers and counsellors'.[57]

The elements chosen from the Kenilworth pageants, then, emphasize chivalry, but with the participation of both nobles and plebeians, and highlight the role of local magnates in unifying the nation, supporting a form of military training that appeals across the classes. Alex Davis has traced this use of chivalry that is 'simultaneously both cross-cultural, and socially exclusive' in Laneham's *Letter*, and this complex combination of aristocratic differentiation and cultural unity may have appealed to Cavendish and Jonson in the 1630s as it coincides with the agenda they were pursuing.[58] Certainly, Laneham's *Letter* presents an image of cultural unity that chimed with the depictions of the Elizabethan period favoured in much Caroline Elizabethanism. Indeed, Laneham's *Letter* stresses royal laughter ('her Majesty laught well', l. 729), dancing, and hunting, to create an image of a monarchy in touch with its local cultures, and a nation anxious to contact its monarch, notably in the throng of townsfolk that gathered to invite Elizabeth to visit them. Such interpretations of the Kenilworth occasion seem to have begun shortly after the original event as one contemporaneous (Elizabethan) translation of the Latin title-page verses to the *Letter* noted:

> While that oour neighbours Reamz (alas) uprore dooth rend asunder,
> In mirth amoong the subiectes that her Maiesty ar vnder,
> She (thankes too God) leads pleazaunt daiz: let spite & mallis wunder.[59]

Although we do not know which edition of Laneham's *Letter* Jonson used, let alone which copy, these verses added to two exemplars, despite some of the tonal ambivalences found elsewhere in Laneham's text, foster the presentation of a 'vision of England as a community one might participate in', and even foreshadow the Caroline royal propaganda of England's 'halcyon days'.[60]

Both the 1575 Kenilworth entertainments and *Welbeck* were also designed, through the variety offered under the rubric of 'entertainment', to provide an adroit mix of sophistication, diversion, pleasure, and wonder as manifestations of the patron's political and cultural magnificence. The range of entertainments at Kenilworth—masques and speeches, chivalric tilts, elaborate symbolic visual effects, complex emblematic gardens, and Italian tumblers, alongside more local sports, notably hunting, and the Coventry-based entertainments—and the combination and even hybridization of forms, were both a manifestation

---

[56] Adams, ' "Because I am of that countrye and mynde to plant myself there" ', 38.

[57] *The Princely Pleasures*, in *Progresses*, ed. Nichols, 2nd edn., i. 80 (farewell speech by Sylvanus).

[58] Davis, *Chivalry and Romance*, 97.   [59] Langham, *A Letter*, 35.

[60] The two copies to which this handwritten translation has been added are now in the Huntington Library, California, and at the University of Illinois at Urbana-Champaign. For cultural unity in Laneham, see Davis, *Chivalry and Romance*, 98.

of Leicester's syncretic cultural power, and a demonstration of how he could promote national and cultural unity.

The King's Entertainment echoes the heterogeneity of the Kenilworth festivities, providing a variety of diversions for the monarch.[61] Events began with a musical dialogue between the Passions (Doubt and Love), and a Chorus of Affections (Joy, Delight, and Jollity), which may have been set to music by the court composer William Lawes, and which celebrates Charles's arrival as 'the heart, that quickens ev'rything' (l. 32), bringing new life to the already verdant '*Sherewood's* head' (l. 20) of Welbeck.[62] The main 'after dinner' section, staged in the 'outer court', frames the comic brideale of Pem the Derby ale-wife and Stub the Sherwood yeoman, with a comic debate between Accidence, the schoolmaster of Mansfield, and Fitzale, Pem's father and 'Herald of *Darbie*' (l. 88), wearing a fantastic tabard of fragments of old documents and branches from the forest. The bridegroom and his supporters, dressed in 'hoods' (ll. 175–86) designed to echo Robin and his Sherwood band, ride at the quintain, before the bride arrives accompanied by her maids, the bride-squires, Cake-Bearer, Cup-Bearer, bagpipe dances, hornpipes, and jolly drinking songs. These rustic festivities are then interrupted by 'an Officer or servant of the *Lord Lieutenants*', who chastises and banishes the unsuitable rustics (ll. 288–9). The entertainment closes with a substantial speech emphasizing the paternal and sacral nature of kingship (his 'office' as both 'parent' and 'pastor' (ll 296–7)), the national unity embodied by Charles, and the hope presented for the future by his son.[63]

Whereas at Kenilworth the quintain was presented by the citizens of Coventry from outside Dudley's household as a tribute to his regional power, the *Entertainment at Welbeck* uses the fictional figures of Accidence and Fitzale as presenters, and also connects their appearance explicitly to the issue of militia reform. Initially, the 'yeomen' who perform the quintain embody English manliness:

FITZALE: Next Blue Hood is, and in hue
                Doth vaunt a heart as pure, and true

---

[61] The 'gestes' of the progress describe Cavendish's entertainment as consisting of a magnificent feast and 'a standinge banquet after dinner amountinge to the value of seuen hundred pound' followed by 'in the outer court . . . a speech made to the Kinge, then a marriadg betweene an exceedinge tall wench and a very lowe dwarfe with Quintance and daunceinge': see Bodleian Library, Oxford, MS Rawlinson D. 39, fo. 1ᵛ. Although the details given differ slightly from both the manuscript text—found in BL, Harleian MS 4955 (the Newcastle MS)—and the printed text of F2 (see n. 69, below), the key elements of *The King's Entertainment at Welbeck* are clear enough, showing that what Cavendish offered was a condensed form of a multi-sectional Elizabethan progress entertainment.

[62] *Ben Jonson*, ed. Herford et al., vii (1941). All references are to this edition unless otherwise stated.

[63] Charles II had been born 29 May 1630; the lines may hint at Cavendish's early manoeuvring for the governorship of the Prince (achieved in March 1638). See Lynn Hulse, 'Cavendish, William, First Duke of Newcastle upon Tyne (*bap.* 1593, *d.* 1676)', *Oxford Dictionary of National Biography* (Oxford: Oxford University Press, 2004) (www.oxforddnb.com/view/article/4946, accessed 26 Feb. 2006).

ACCIDENCE:
As is the sky . . .
Of old England the yeoman blue. (ll. 178–82)

The values of 'old England' are associated with the surrounding region: Stub, the leading 'bachelor', is descended from the 'Forrest-blood | Of old *Sherewood*' (ll. 139–40), and they are all 'bold', 'doughtie', and 'brave' (ll. 146, 151, 222). The audience is asked, as Fitzale says, to 'Gi' the old *England* Yeoman his due' (l. 219), but these rustics are also associated with the royal space of the forest, with the policy of the government, and, crucially, with the actions of the lord lieutenants who were responsible for the militia.

These issues are explicit in Accidence's commentary on the quintain, where Stub and his followers are described as:

> Bold Batchelors they are, and large,
> And come in at the Countrey charge;
> Horse, Bridles, Saddles, Stirrups, Girts,
> All reckoned o'the *Countie* skirts!
> And all their Courses, misse or hit,
> Intended are, for the *Sheere*-wit,
> And so to be receiv'd. Their game
> Is Countrey sport . . . (ll. 187–94)

The financial pun ('reckoned'), and the allusion to the 'country charge' links the yeoman to the Caroline militia policy which was designed to strengthen the forces available to the government, especially during the first years of the reign, when an active foreign policy was being pursued.[64] Early in his reign, Charles I proclaimed the need for a 'perfect' or 'exact militia', and Cavendish was one of the most assiduous of the lords lieutenant, regularly mustering the militia, providing training and arms, and reporting back to Whitehall that the Nottinghamshire forces were 'completely furnished every way after the modern fashion'.[65] Significantly, Cavendish was also willing to assert his independence from the Privy Council's demands, especially when dealing with 'his' county. In contrast with his neighbour the Earl of Huntingdon in Leicestershire, another assiduous county lieutenant, Cavendish was prepared to resist unreasonable royal pressure to raise additional men, and as early as 1626

[64] See H. Langelüddecke, ' "The chiefest strength and glory of this kingdom": Arming and Training the "Perfect Militia" in the 1630s', *English Historical Review*, 118 (2003), 1264–303. Langelüddecke notes (p. 1269) the responsibility of the community rather than individual landowners for training the militia: this fits well with the unificatory rhetoric of the *Entertainment at Welbeck* and its emphasis upon the shire.

[65] Cavendish's reports are in: *Calendar of State Papers, Domestic Series, of the Reign of Charles 1, 1627–8*, ed. John Bruce (London: Longman, 1858), 284; *CSPD, 1628–29*, ed. John Bruce (1859), 333 and 362; *CSPD, 1629–31*, ed. John Bruce (1860), 61, 346, and 414; and *CSPD, 1631–33*, ed. John Bruce (1862), 163 and 431.

had warned that Nottinghamshire was already 'deeply charged' for its militia commitments.[66]

Although it is tempting to regard the somewhat incompetent 'bold bachelors' at quintain and the chivalric language of the text (Stub is a 'champion' and a 'doughty elf') as parodic, the laughter is more inclusive, more communally festive than directly satiric and discriminatory. Crucially, too, five of the seven hoods successfully demonstrate their manly skills, while only Motley Hood (a lawyer) and the final Russet Hood fail at the exercise. This differentiated response, which does not preclude laughter at the rustics, but which still registers the significance of the national manliness they embody, has its parallels in the 1575 Kenilworth entertainments, and particularly Laneham's *Letter*, which is filled with an unstable combination of high and low styles which contribute to the mixture of comic and serious material. The Elizabethan material, with its vision of a festive and unified nation, also allows the Welbeck entertainments to develop an important implication of the Caroline rural festivity. The 'Directive' added to the *Declaration of Sports* (reissued in October 1633, shortly after this entertainment) explicitly included 'manlike and lawfull Exercises' among the country sports to be encouraged.[67] The *Entertainment at Welbeck* links the Caroline promotion of rustic sports, festive culture, military training, and the militia reforms, suggesting that among the local cultures that need to be protected by the crown, in concert with the local magnates, are the martial sports and rituals that provide such good military training. The implication of the 'Directive' is that this will improve the raw material of the locality so that they become—again echoing the 1575 Kenilworth festivities—specimens of old English manliness.

Equally, although rustic sports play a central role in the entertainment, alongside issues of governance and civility, it is too simple to subsume this text within Caroline festive culture. Leah Marcus noted that the *Entertainment at Welbeck* actually presents a 'much more severe' rejection of rustic sports than that associated with monarchical policy, and even differentiates the King and his policy (he acts to 'foster merriment', while 'he himself is too exacting, too severe' to allow it to obtrude on his duty).[68] Marcus's interpretation at this point relies heavily on the printed version as given in the *Works* (1640)

---

[66] The National Archives, London, SP 16/38/62, Cavendish to the Privy Council, 27 Oct. 1627; see Cogswell, *Home Divisions*, 122–6, 137–47. Cavendish actually borrowed the money for the militia improvements on his own credit to facilitate the payment of the 1626 benevolence, but in 1627, although he used his authority to ensure payment of the loan, he also sought reassurances on the legality and repayment of the loan: see Seddon, 'Sir Gervase Clifton', 94–5.

[67] *A Declaration of Sports* (1617, 1618) included in the list of licit recreations not only 'May-Games, Whitson Ales, and Morris-dances', but 'Archerie for men, leaping, vaulting': see *The Minor Prose Works of James VI and I*, ed. J. Craigie and A. Law (Edinburgh: Scottish Text Society, 1982), 107, 239.

[68] Marcus, *Politics of Mirth*, 131.

which Jonson extensively altered from the earlier version given in the Newcastle manuscript.[69] The printed version states: 'Sports should not be obtruded on great Monarchs, | But wait when they will call for them as servants' (ll. 305–6). Cavendish's manuscript version insists that the rustics *'must* not be obtruded' (my italics).[70] This even severer dismissal in the manuscript version may have been softened by 1640 to register the tenser climate between King and country, but it also marks a key change in agency in the text.

In both the manuscript and printed versions, the rustics are reproved by 'an Officer, or servant of the *Lord Lieutenants*, whose face had put on, with his Cloathes, an equall authoritie for the businesse' (ll. 288–90). The appearance of this figure raises the fascinating issue of who might have spoken these lines, and, also, the possibility that Jonson had daringly broken the fictive frame of the entertainment, bringing a real 'gentleman' from Cavendish's household on stage. Whether or not the lines were spoken by an actor or an actual member of the household, the choice of a gentleman from within the Cavendish household, possibly dressed in his livery, differentiates the gentry and the court, placing the authorization of pastimes not simply in the hands of the court but of the local nobility. The severer control of pastimes belongs not to the King, but to his appointed deputy, the Lord Lieutenant.

Indeed, throughout, the *Entertainment at Welbeck* accentuates the connections between festive culture and military preparedness, but it does so in the context of local traditions and independence. The text carefully distances itself from the court, insisting on the significance of the local wonders of the Peak, giving weight to local culture and traditions, and even arguing that the 'Mine-mens farce' equals French dancing (ll. 97–8). The depiction of the quintain as '*Sheere*-wit' has important resonances, for although the dominant sense is that of 'country sport' (as at l. 192), the term can also imply 'sheer wit', that is, downright or absolute wit. This punning between 'shire-wit' and 'sheer-wit', part of an extended series of phonic plays on 'shire', 'sheer', and 'Sherwood' throughout *Welbeck*, recalls the double-edged oppositions Jonson established in his contemporaneous play *A Tale of a Tub*.[71] There, the 'Prologue' purports to 'bring you now, to show what different things | The cotes of clowns are from the courts of kings'.[72] These lines can be read to suggest the exact opposite of what they apparently say, combining similarity (in the aural proximity cote/court), and also marking just 'how far from the reality of provincial life' Charles I's government

---

[69] *The Entertainment at Welbeck* was extensively rewritten for *Workes* (London: Richard Bishop, 1640), usually referred to as F2, and appears as *Love's Welcome at Welbeck* in 'The Underwood' (sigs. 2N4ᵛ–2O4ᵛ, pp. 272–80), rather than with the other masques and entertainments.

[70] BL, Harleian MS 4955, fo. 198ʳ.

[71] Jonson may adopt a household pronunciation (and possibly pun) at this point as George Aglionby's poem 'On Bolsover Castle' (in BL, Harleian MS 4955) describes Derbyshire as the 'subject sheer' (line 50): see *The Country House Poem*, ed. Fowler, 170.

[72] *A Tale of a Tub*, 'Prologue', ll. 11–12, in *Ben Jonson*, ed. Herford et al., iii (1927).

had become.[73] At Welbeck 'shire-wit', suitable rustic comedy to entertain the court, which might suggest the distance of court from provincial life, becomes 'sheer-wit', encompassing the absolute wisdom and knowledge of the older, more communal methods of governance represented in royal forests, such as Sherwood.

Equally, although the gentleman's final speech echoes the earlier *Irish Masque at Court*, the nuances differ. In 1613, when Erse rudeness was replaced by Anglo-Irish civility, the focus was crucially upon royal power, and on James as the guarantor of the bardic prophecies of peace ('This is the man thou promis'd should redeeme' (l. 161)).[74] Indigenous culture is reformed by the 'ciuill gentleman of the nation' (l. 143), while the bardic culture is validated by and subordinated to royal power, so that the masquers 'come forth new-borne creatures all' (l. 182).

The structural echo in *The Entertainment at Welbeck* of an earlier banishment of colonial incivility and its reformation through royal power highlights the connections between central government power, regional culture, and the practical implementation of government policy. In contrast to the colonial spaces of Ireland, where royal control is absolute, the English Midland space of Cavendish's power embodies the possibility of a unified and public, negotiated, national space. It has often been noted that the Cavendish entertainments, like Leicester's at Kenilworth, were markedly expensive; Clarendon commented that 'both King and Court were received and entertained . . . in such an excess of feasting, as had never been known in England'.[75] Although Cavendish's feasts have been characterized as instances of aristocratic extravagance, it can be argued that they belonged to his attempts to demonstrate his policies of aristocratic display and monarchical publicity. The fragmentary surviving evidence about *The Entertainment at Bolsover* (1634), *Welbeck*'s companion piece, suggests that many from the surrounding county attended, and the 1633 royal journey is likely to have attracted an even larger audience. Thus, the choice of the meal as the occasion for display may have been a very public attempt to mediate between the King's preference for formal, public dining, and Cavendish's own use of socially mixed spaces such as the Great Hall to display his baronial style.[76] This insistence on public display may also explain the location for the quintain and brideale in the less exclusive 'outer court' of the house. This space differed from the 'great court'—which was shut away from the road and from public display—and may

---

[73] I owe this point to Julie Sanders, ' "The Collective Contract Is a Fragile Structure": Local Government and Personal Rule in Jonson's *A Tale of a Tub*', *English Literary Renaissance*, 27.3 (1997), 443–67, (p. 443).

[74] *The Irish Masque at Court*, in *Ben Jonson*, ed. Herford et al., vii (1941). All references are to this edition unless otherwise stated.

[75] Edward Hyde, Earl of Clarendon, *The History of the Rebellion and Civil Wars in England*, ed. William Dunn Macray, 6 vols. (Oxford: Clarendon Press, 1888; repr. 1992), i. 104.

[76] Worsley, 'An Habitation', 130.

have allowed a larger audience to see the King, as the area was fenced with a balustrade which would permit visibility whilst maintaining suitable distance. Although this use of the outer court may, in part, have had a practical dimension, the choice of this open space for an entertainment that uses elements of chivalric and popular culture may also have embedded a further deliberate echo of the 1575 Kenilworth festivities, where the imported local entertainments had taken place in the great court, itself a symbolic, socially mixed space of display.[77] In Cavendish's house at least—in the subtlest but also the most meaningful re-creation of the Kenilworth festivities—monarch, county society, and nation might mingle again.

CONCLUSION: REMAKING COURTLY STYLE

The final speech of the *Entertainment at Welbeck* alludes to Jonson's *Panegyre*, presented to James VI and I as part of the volume that contained *The King's Entertainment* and *A Particular Entertainment to Althorp*, and which marked the first Jacobean parliament.[78] The 1604 quarto represented the manifesto of the recently arrived Stuart dynasty and presented their new, highly public, and festive style to the nation. These resonances cannot have been lost in the context of a reverse journey to Scotland for coronation and parliament. The final speech of the *Entertainment at Welbeck*—although addressed to the rustics in describing the seriousness of royal labour, and even while locating their activities firmly under royal control—still stresses the duties of kingship not solely to the rustics but to the listening monarch.

The Entertainment at Welbeck must be placed in the context of Cavendish's understanding of royal ceremonial. In the *Advice to Charles I*, he devotes almost equal weight to the importance of military power ('he that has the sovereign power is always *generalissimo*') and ceremony ('nothing in itself, and yet doth everything'), and he articulates a policy that recognizes the national political function of royal 'Devertisementes'.[79] Among the many forms of royal amusement Cavendish praises, he never loses sight of the practical, political importance of these expensive 'Toyes' (to use Francis Bacon's term), and he recommends that masques, in particular, should be staged at least three times, with different sections of the political nation invited—the aristocracy, the inns of court, and civic dignitaries—to the correct performance.[80] Although Cavendish's views may have been sharpened by the civil wars, these passages also suggest that

---

[77] Ibid. 127–9; Langham, *A Letter*, l. 500.
[78] *The Entertainment at Welbeck*, ll. 320–2 recall *Panegyre*, 125–7.
[79] *Advice*, pp. xviii, 44, 60.
[80] Francis Bacon, 'Of Masques and Triumphs', in Bacon's *The Essayes or Counsells, Civill and Morall* (London: John Haviland, 1629), 223; Cavendish, *Advice*, 60.

the decision to recreate Kenilworth was a carefully executed strategy. Rather than being 'softened and nostalgic' in its use of material from Kenilworth, the choice of subject matter, the form of the entertainment, its style, and even the location of the performance, all on the occasion of Charles's first major state journey, suggest that Cavendish was as much presenting an argument to the King—or rather a demonstration—of how ceremonial and local politics could and should work. Such a royal journey, with the opportunities for interaction with different sections of the populace along the route, presented an ideal arena in which the King could display both authority and accessibility.

If nostalgia for Cavendish was about an intervention in current politics and engagement with a debate about the nature of monarchic representation, for Jonson the Cavendish commission offered the opportunity to argue for a different kind of masque. It has often been noticed that the *King and Queen's Entertainment at Bolsover* (1634) continues Jonson's personal attacks on Inigo Jones, but it also proposes an important mediatory function for verbal rather than visual culture. A year earlier, the rewriting of an Elizabethan progress entertainment articulated a similar critique by staging an entertainment based in local, popular culture, and in spoken comedy rather than visual forms. *The King's Entertainment at Welbeck* also illuminates Jonson's ambivalent attitudes to relations with the court in the 1630s, and suggests his reinvigorated engagement with politics and political and intellectual groups often at considerable variance with Caroline political culture. Jonsonian nostalgia is neither an example of his 'dotages', nor an abdication from politics, but rather marks a significant engagement with—sometimes a negotiation with, and containment of—the oppositional and awkward voices and ideas that had haunted his earlier career, and which continued, albeit in different circumstances, in the 1630s. This entertainment, staged geographically away from court, marks a further distancing of Jonson from the Caroline court, but also illustrates a fascinating process of self-rewriting that Jonson undertook in the 1630s, revisiting and reshaping earlier texts, such as the *Panegyre*, the *Irish Masque at Court* (1613), *The Challenge at Tilt* (1613), and even *Gypsies Metamorphosed* (1621) for new purposes.

The image of these rural communities—and the deliberate use of an imagined, archaic tradition of chivalric culture—politically and formally registers a distance from Charles and his court. Although *Welbeck* stresses Charles's self-depiction as a Scoto-Britannic monarch and his insistence on an imperial British monarchy, Jonson and Cavendish imply that the correlative of such an emphasis lies in the recognition of regional and provincial voices within the kingdom, and their proper placing rather than a simple subordination to a central government agenda. The medievalism of the text, too, carries political import, as later Caroline masques pointedly preferred mystical images of a distant Druidic British past to the politically contentious era of the Anglo-Saxons, the Norman yoke, and the medieval inheritance of common laws and rights. To recall, in the allusions to the 'Panegyre', the foundational moment of the Stuart dynasty as English monarchs, and to recapitulate the role of his work in the creation of that monarchy, implicitly restating his view of the true function of royal ceremonial as education through praise, allows Jonson to suggest the distance between James's regime and the Caroline court. At Welbeck, the reworking of Elizabethan and Jacobean materials pointedly locates the proper models for monarchy not in the mystic past, but in the reigns of Charles's two predecessors, and highlights the importance of the mutuality of duties, and the significance of other, critical voices, in the creation of a properly governed kingdom.

14

A Pioneer of Renaissance Scholarship: John Nichols and *The Progresses and Public Processions of Queen Elizabeth*

Julian Pooley

Scholars owe John Nichols (1745–1826) an immense debt for collecting over 250 state, borough, church, and family manuscripts, and over 850 early printed books, for his editions of *The Progresses and Public Processions of Queen Elizabeth*. It has taken an international team of scholars using research libraries and Internet catalogues to reassemble his materials. This essay will explore Nichols's career as a printer, literary scholar, and antiquary and, using the *Gentleman's Magazine* and the enormous archive that he accumulated, will show how the *Progresses* was just one of many antiquarian, biographical, and literary projects that he undertook during a career of over sixty years.

The Progresses and Public Processions of Queen Elizabeth, first published between 1788 and 1821, and extensively revised in 1823, was arguably the greatest of Nichols's intellectual achievements. It grew from the vast archive he collected and the many scholarly contacts he made as editor of the *Gentleman's Magazine*. Its development over nearly four decades was, like many of Nichols's publications, an ongoing act of collection, selection, and refinement. Whereas in the first volumes Nichols presented his readers with texts that, often separately paginated, could be arranged and bound into any order, in the second edition of 1823 he assumed command of his burgeoning materials, setting them in chronological order and cementing them in place with a bridging narrative based on the extensive assistance he had received from the antiquarian community. The new edition provided Nichols's readers with a historical narrative of the Queen's progresses and the entertainments prepared for her; but even that was not the

This essay is based on a paper given to the Renaissance Society of America in New York, April 2004. I would like to thank the British Academy for awarding me an Overseas Conference Grant to attend this conference. I am greatly indebted to the private owners of Nichols papers for allowing me to consult the papers in their care. I am also grateful to Robin Myers, Mike Page, and Rosemary Sweet for commenting upon earlier drafts of this essay.

Figure 14.1. *John Nichols*, by Gerard van der Puyl, 1787. Oil on canvas. (Private collection. Reproduced by permission of the owner. Photograph by Julian Pooley)

end of the process. As we shall see, the discovery of Nichols's own copy of this edition, heavily annotated and enlarged by inserted letters and new texts, shows that, even in his late seventies, he continued to refine his work and collect materials for a third edition.

Nichols's interest in the cultural life of Elizabethan England was not unique. Gerald Newman has observed that the late eighteenth century witnessed 'unprecedented activity in the collection, study and promotion of everything to do with the national cultural heritage'.[1] This growing cultural nationalism, which stressed the importance of native language and literary tradition, was evident in Thomas Percy's *Reliques of Ancient Poetry* (1765), Thomas Warton's *History of English Poetry* (1774), and Samuel Johnson's *Lives of the Poets* (1779–81). Late eighteenth-century scholars saw the reign of Elizabeth as a 'Golden Age' of English government, learning, and artistic achievement, and Nichols's *Progresses* should be set in the context of their endeavours to uncover and celebrate the flowering of the English language in the later sixteenth century.[2] As a printer at

---

[1] Gerald Newman, *The Rise of English Nationalism: A Cultural History, 1740–1830* (New York: St Martin's, 1997), 112–15.

[2] Jack Lynch, *The Age of Elizabeth in the Age of Johnson* (Cambridge: Cambridge University Press, 2003), 5–7.

Figure 14.2. *John Nichols*, by John Jackson, 1811. Oil on canvas. (Private collection. Reproduced by permission of the owner. Photograph by Julian Pooley)

the heart of the antiquarian network, Nichols united the energies of literary scholars and local historians in a work that appealed as much to his contemporaries as it does to students of sixteenth-century culture today.

THE GENESIS OF THE IDEA OF THE *PROGRESSES*

Nichols's works are representative of those of a host of like-minded scholars whose interests in the past were intrinsic to eighteenth-century culture.[3] Antiquarian study was a key part of an eighteenth-century gentleman's education, but it was also a science in which coins, sculpture, and rare literary fragments were collected, identified, and tested against each other to exacting standards of accuracy.[4] The insistence of antiquaries such as Richard Gough (1735–1809) and Samuel Pegge (1704–96) on the need to rediscover England's past in order to understand the present underlies the success of Nichols's *Progresses* just as it underlies the plethora of late eighteenth-century county histories.

[3] Rosemary Sweet, *Antiquaries: The Discovery of the Past in Eighteenth Century Britain* (London: Hambledon and London, 2004).
[4] Rosemary Sweet, 'Antiquaries and Antiquities in Eighteenth Century England', *Eighteenth-Century Studies*, 34 (2001), 181–206.

Nichols met Gough and Pegge while apprenticed to the London printer William Bowyer the Younger (1699–1777). As well as teaching Nichols a trade, Bowyer set him Latin exercises and introduced him to his scholarly clients. Bowyer's influence on the career and interests of John Nichols cannot be overestimated. He had spent time at St John's College, Cambridge, and regarded printing as a form of historical scholarship. From Bowyer, Nichols acquired the taste for literary and antiquarian research that shaped his career. In 1762, aged 17, he helped Bowyer to edit *The Works of Jonathan Swift*.[5] Bowyer was one of England's most learned printers, working for erudite societies and private scholars. His customers included Pope, Swift, and Johnson as well as theologians and antiquaries. When Nichols succeeded to the business on Bowyer's death, he inherited one of London's largest printing houses with contracts to parliament, the Royal Society, the Society of Antiquaries, and a national network of learned customers.[6] Almost immediately, he began to gather materials for a biography of Bowyer that would include anecdotes of his learned friends. Like so many of Nichols's works, this monumental achievement grew by accretion, from a fifty-two-page pamphlet in 1778 into the seventeen volumes of the *Literary Anecdotes of the Eighteenth Century* and *Illustrations of the Literary History of the Eighteenth Century* (1812–58). They are indispensable for biographers and historians of the book trade, and they are a key source for the history of the *Progresses*.

Nichols's association with Gough enabled him to bring the discipline of antiquarian research to the wider field of literary and biographical scholarship. While draughtsmen preserved artefacts through engravings, Nichols used his press to copy records of English culture.[7] The success of Percy's *Reliques* showed that there was a market for such studies and Nichols ensured that his press catered for the demand.[8] There was, however, a shift in the nature of this demand between 1788 and 1823. While the first edition of the *Progresses* had included texts in Latin, Greek, and even Hebrew, the second omitted many of them in favour of English texts uncovered by Nichols in the intervening years. The two editions reflect the changing priorities of antiquarian and literary scholarship between the late eighteenth and early nineteenth centuries. There had always been a debate among antiquaries as to whether to present the reader

---

[5] *The Bowyer Ledgers*, ed. Keith Maslen and John Lancaster (London: The Bibliographical Society, 1991), 383.

[6] Keith Maslen, 'Printing for the Author: From the Bowyer Printing Ledgers, 1710–1775', *The Library*, 5.27 (1972), 302–9.

[7] Sam Smiles, *Eye Witness: Artists and Visual Documentation in Britain 1770–1830* (Aldershot: Ashgate, 2000), 28, 44; Sweet, *Antiquaries*, 278–307.

[8] Harriet Kirkley, 'John Nichols, Johnson's *Prefaces* and the History of Letters', *Review of English Studies*, NS 49.195 (1998), 281–305; Harriet Kirkley, *A Biographer at Work: Samuel Johnson's Notes for the 'Life of Pope'* (Lewisburg, Pa: Bucknell University Press, 2002). See also Julian Pooley, ' "And a Fig for Mr Nichols!" Samuel Johnson, John Nichols and their Circle', *New Rambler*, E VII (2003/4), 30–45.

with a text in the original Latin or to translate it into English. In 1788, the preference was still for Latin, so Nichols included nearly 130 pages of verses composed by the English universities on the death of Queen Elizabeth;[9] thirty years later, however, the market had changed. Though the reading public for English historical texts had expanded, fewer readers had the requisite Latin to plough through pages of original texts. Nichols's audience in 1823 was more interested in texts that brought to life the personalities and culture of Elizabeth's reign and, with space at a premium, he jettisoned the longer Latin texts for more recent, English discoveries.

Many of these discoveries were made with the help of the readers of the *Gentleman's Magazine*. Nichols's acquisition of the printing of the *Gentleman's Magazine* in 1778 proved crucial to the growth of the *Progresses*. Founded by Edward Cave in 1731, it was the first periodical of its kind and the most successful. Cave and his successors disguised their editorship behind the pseudonym of 'Sylvanus Urban', thereby appealing to both provincial and city readers. By encouraging readers to submit historical and biographical articles, Nichols gathered materials for his own projects and forged links with those able to research locally on his behalf. Both Nichols and his readers used the *Gentleman's Magazine* in the same way that many scholars use Internet listserves today: an enquiry posted in the correspondence pages prompted replies from around the country, some of which produced further correspondence 'off-list' through which Nichols could draw from his correspondents' local knowledge.[10] Between 1784 and 1826, Nichols submitted over sixty pseudonymous queries about the *Progresses* to the magazine to promote his research. They allow us to chart the history of the *Progresses* and understand its protracted publication. Mindful of the length of his publications, the magazine often became an overflow tank for materials discovered too late for inclusion in Nichols's books or which would have swelled them to unmanageable proportions. It was an extension of his published works and should be read in parallel with them.

Nichols was not the first to study the peregrinations of Elizabeth's court. The prefaces of both editions of the *Progresses* show that they had already fascinated Thomas Percy, Samuel Henley, and Michael Tyson. Percy was diverted from this undertaking by his appointment as Bishop of Dromore in 1782, while Henley was sidetracked by his translation from French into English of William Beckford's *Vathek* (1786). Michael Tyson's letters to Gough suggest that he had

[9] *Academiae Oxoniensis pietas erga serenissimum et potentissimum Iacobum Angliae Scotiae Franciae & Hiberniae Regem, fidei defensorem, beatissimae Elisabethae nuper Reginae legitimè & auspicatissimè succedentem* (Oxford: Joseph Barnes, 1603); *Threno-thriambeuticon Academiae Cantabrigiensis ob damnum lucrosum, & infoelicitatem foelicissimam, luctuosus triumphus* (Cambridge: John Legat, 1603).
[10] For Nichols's use of the *Gentleman's Magazine* to elicit materials relating to Samuel Johnson, see Edward L. Hart, 'The Contribution of John Nichols to Boswell's *Life of Johnson*', *PMLA* 68.4 (June 1952), 391–410, and 'An Ingenious Editor: John Nichols and the *Gentleman's Magazine*', *Bucknell Review* (Mar. 1962), 232–42.

planned to complete their work, but he died in 1780.[11] Though Gough was orchestrating the project, anonymously encouraging readers of the *Gentleman's Magazine* to search for materials, he could not proceed alone.[12] Nichols, with whom he had already collaborated on the *Collection of Royal and Noble Wills* (1780), was the ideal candidate to continue the work and accordingly, in 1784, Nichols announced his involvement in the *Gentleman's Magazine*:

> Having collected, occasionally, such tracts as fell in my way, descriptive of the ELIZABETHAN Progresses, with the pageants and Devices exhibited before the Queen at the mansions of the Nobility, I am persuaded that, if they were uniformly republished, with illustrations, they would be favourably received by the public. Such a volume is now actually in the press; but, as I could wish to make it as complete as possible, I take this mode of requesting your valuable correspondents to communicate such 'Progresses' or 'Pageants' of that reign as they may happen to possess; which shall be thankfully acknowledged, and returned with care; or, if more agreeable, shall be purchased.[13]

With Gough's topographical collections at his disposal and the assistance of George Steevens, 'whose intimacy with the writings of the Elizabethan age was unbounded',[14] Nichols published the first two volumes of the *Progresses* in 1788. However, the promised third volume did not appear for another seventeen years, because Nichols was now preoccupied with another great project, his *History and Antiquities of Leicestershire*, published between 1795 and 1812. The intermittent printing is reflected in the different papers and fonts used in this third volume. The review of it in the *Gentleman's Magazine* in 1806 shows that Nichols had continued to gather materials for the *Progresses* closer to home, seeking wills of eminent citizens among the records of the Corporation of London and references to rare tracts among the records of the Stationers' Company and Sion College library.[15]

Completion of volume four was dogged by disaster. In 1807, Nichols broke his thigh in a fall at work and, in 1808, a fire that destroyed his printing house consumed nearly £30,000 of stock, including back issues of the *Gentleman's Magazine* from 1783 and numerous works passing through his press.[16] Worse still was Gough's death in 1809, which left a desolate Nichols facing the

---

[11] John Nichols, *Literary Anecdotes of the Eighteenth Century*, 9 vols. (London: Nichols, Son, and Bentley, 1812–16), viii. 567–672 (esp. pp. 627–30). The original letters are Bodleian Library, Oxford, MSS Gough gen. Top. 44.

[12] Gough submitted 'The Honourable Entertainment giuen to the Queene's Majestie in Progresse, at Elvetham in Hampshire, by the right Honourable the Earle of Hertford. 1591' to the *Gentleman's Magazine* in 1779, under the pseudonym of 'A Constant Reader'.

[13] *Gentleman's Magazine*, 54.2 (1784), 728–9.

[14] *The Progresses and Public Processions of Queen Elizabeth*, ed. John Nichols, 2nd edn., 3 vols. (London: John Nichols, 1823), i, p. v.

[15] *Gentleman's Magazine*, 76.2 (1806), 837–42.

[16] James M. Kuist, *The Nichols File of the Gentleman's Magazine* (London: University of Wisconsin Press, 1982), 6–10, and Alan Broadfield, 'John Nichols as Historian and Friend: Suum Cuique' (unpublished manuscript (1974–83), New College Library, Oxford), 276, 708–16.

unenviable task of sorting and transferring his colossal topographical collections
to the Bodleian Library. In 1810, Nichols was so overwhelmed by the *Progresses*
that he looked for a co-editor. Thomas Park, antiquary, bibliographer, and
engraver, who had completed Walpole's *Royal and Noble Authors* in 1806,
seemed ideal: 'You have my full license, privilege & authority', Nichols wrote,
'to reprint the Progresses of Queen Elizabeth in any manner you think either in
whole or in part . . . You shall have any assistance I can give, & shall see the few
notes made in my copy.'[17]

   This was an astonishing proposal from Nichols; he did not usually offer his
projects to other people. However, though Park arranged for another printer
and bookseller to join him, the idea came to nothing.[18] In 1814, with the
History of Leicestershire and first seven volumes of the *Literary Anecdotes* safely
published, Nichols announced his return to the *Progresses* by describing a
bill of Hugh Morgan, the Queen's apothecary, in the *Gentleman's Magazine*,
which he hoped to include in a further volume.[19] In October 1820, writing
as 'Caradoc', he requested details of Ambrose Cottinger of Hillingdon and in
December he answered himself as 'Antiquarius', asking if any entertainments
existed in the Russell family papers at Woburn Abbey.[20] Finally, in 1821, having
published volume four on 14 February, his seventy-sixth birthday, Nichols
announced a 'new and regularly arranged Edition' of the *Progresses*, asking his
readers to communicate 'any material Corrections which may have occurred to
them . . . and more especially transcripts . . . of Entertainments . . . which have
escaped my former tolerably diligent investigation'.[21] He then asked whether
there were references to the Queen's 1564 visit to Huntingdon in the parish
records and sought the location of Churchyard's publication of the 1578
entertainment at Osterley Park. How many of the magazine's readers knew
that 'J.N.' and the editor, 'Sylvanus Urban', were one and the same? Did
they know that 'Caradoc', 'Antiquarius', 'Hinckliensis', 'Eugenio', 'An Old
Subscriber', 'Biographicus', and 'M Green' (his second wife's maiden name)
were really all John Nichols? Sometimes he teased them. In 1822, he puffed
the appearance of the new edition of Elizabeth by announcing, this time
as 'FSA':

It is with much satisfaction that I see a new Edition announced of a Work that I have
long wished to possess, but the price of which, in consequence of its rarity, has been out
of the reach of my finances; and it is to be hoped, and expected, that the very appropriate
appeal made by the industrious and patriarchal Editor for literary assistance will not be
made in vain.[22]

   [17] Broadfield, 'John Nichols as Historian and Friend', 753, and Park to Nichols, 17 Aug. 1810
(Bodleian, MS Eng. lett. c. 361, fo. 99). See also Nichols to Park, 17 Aug. 1810 (Bodleian, MS
Eng. lett. c. 361, fo. 100).
   [18] Bodleian, MS Eng. lett. c. 361, fo. 101.   [19] *Gentleman's Magazine*, 84.2 (1814), 3.
   [20] Ibid. 90.2 (1820), 290, 487.   [21] Ibid. 91.2 (1821), 390–1.
   [22] Ibid. 92.1 (1822), 6–7.

METHODS OF COMPILATION

Beyond the *Gentleman's Magazine*, Nichols used his business and personal friendships to gain access to manuscripts throughout the country. Although clues to these sources are strewn throughout the *Progresses*, the enormous archive that Nichols accumulated, now scattered among over eighty repositories and private collections, allows us to reconstruct the influences on his research and the ways in which he acquired materials.[23] Initially, his interests were literary. As a friend of Johnson, Malone, Reed, and Steevens, he was at the heart of the eighteenth-century enterprise to discover the sources of Shakespeare's plays and study the panorama of the Elizabethan and Jacobean stage. Johnson's edition of Shakespeare and *Lives of the Poets* established his authority as a champion of Elizabethan literature, and Thomas Warton proclaimed that, 'In reading the works of a poet who lived in a remote age, it is necessary that we should look back upon the customs and manners which prevailed in that age.'[24] Nichols agreed. His modest claim, as printer of Johnson's *Lives*, to have 'conciliated his esteem by several little services', conceals his considerable biographical and editorial contribution to the work.[25] He shared Johnson's enthusiasm for historical research to support literary scholarship and, after revising George Steevens's *Six Old Plays* in 1779, published the edition of *The Plays of William Shakespeare* by Malone in 1786.[26] These literary excavations were part of a wider antiquarian endeavour to discover and preserve sixteenth-century culture. Nichols opened the pages of the *Gentleman's Magazine* to these Shakespearian scholars and his printing shop became a focus for the principal characters in this literary circle.

In the same way, Nichols's antiquarian interests increased his enthusiasm for preserving historical sources. As the historian of Leicestershire, he corresponded with antiquaries throughout the country. His letters identify his collaborators and highlight his strengths and weaknesses as an editor. Some correspondents, notably Ralph Churton of Brasenose College, Oxford, assisted him over many years. Although in 1823 Nichols thanked Churton in his preface for supplying the 'Queen's Entertainment by the Countess of Derby at Harefield', their letters show that Churton had been providing Elizabethan transcripts to Gough and

---

[23] Julian Pooley, 'The Papers of the Nichols Family and Business: New Discoveries and the Work of the Nichols Archive Project', *The Library*, 7th ser. 2 (Mar. 2001), 10–52. For details of the Nichols Archive Project, see www.le.ac.uk/elh/staff/jpa.html.

[24] Thomas Warton, *Observations on the Fairy Queen of Spencer*, 2 vols. (London, 1762); quoted by Lynch, *The Age of Elizabeth in the Age of Johnson*, 41.

[25] Nichols, *Literary Anecdotes*, ii (1812), 550.

[26] *Six Old Plays on which Shakespeare founded his Measure for Measure, Comedy of Errors, Taming of the Shrew, King John, King Henry IV and King Henry V, King Lear*, ed. John Nichols, 2 vols. (London: John Nichols, 1779).

Nichols since at least 1784, when he sent Nichols the 'Hermit's Oration at
Theobalds' and 'Babington's letter from prison to the Queen'.[27] 'The copy I
hope is sufficiently legible,' he wrote, 'but it is not as fair as I could wish,
the gentleman who wrote it not having attended to the spelling, and having
other business on my hands, I thought it less trouble to correct the mistakes
than to transcribe the whole.' This raises important questions concerning the
reliability of Nichols's texts. As we shall see, he often printed first and asked
questions later. If the materials he printed were flawed or if no one asked the right
questions, then his texts are unlikely to bear modern critical scrutiny. Moreover,
Nichols's bridging narrative was frequently drawn from the covering letters of
his contributors.[28] In 1787, Churton put Nichols in touch with the owner of
letters between Elizabeth and Essex,[29] and in 1820 he sent him:

an account of Queen Elizabeth's Entertainment at Harefield, copied from a manuscript
which Mr Newdigate . . . accidentally discovered after many a fruitless search . . . The
MS itself is still in some place of intended security, not of concealment, where it may
remain undiscovered . . . I shall be glad to see this very correct copy of it . . . preserved
from perishing and made publici juris from your Press.[30]

The Nichols papers illustrate the extent of the help he received from other
antiquaries. Although Nichols credits William Bray, the historian of Surrey, for
'several particulars'[31] in the preface to the *Progresses*, privately owned Nichols
records show that Bray was sending references to royal visits to Surrey to Nichols
from the More Molyneux papers stored at Loseley, near Guildford.[32] Throughout
his projects, Nichols's local correspondents checked facts, improved his narrative,
and uncovered further materials. In 1823, he thanked George Ormerod, historian
of Cheshire, for a:

kind Communication which I shall proudly adopt as one of the brightest Gems in the
Collection and which shall be used without alteration in any way as I should have used
a scarce old printed tract had I found such a one on this subject . . . I will take care that
you shall have a Proof of your own very acceptable Communication.[33]

The relationships were often reciprocal. William Hamper, a Birmingham brass-
founder and magistrate, used his influence with the Mayor of Warwick to consult
the corporation's records on Nichols's behalf. In return he hoped Nichols could

[27] Bodleian, MS Eng. Lett. c. 354, fo. 122 [NAD4922]. Churton used Bodleian, MS Rawlinson
D 692, where the 'Hermit's Oration' is transcribed on fos. 106r–109r. My thanks to Dr Marie-
Louise Coolahan for this reference. Documents on the Nichols Archive Database have two references:
a unique number, prefixed NAD; and a reference number used by the public repository holding the
original document or devised to preserve the order of the documents in the private collections.
[28] Churton to Nichols, 16 Oct. 1820, Bodleian, MS Eng. lett. c. 354, fos. 225–6 [NAD4935].
[29] Churton to Nichols, 8 Oct. 1787, Bodleian, MS Eng. lett. c. 354, fo. 125 [NAD4924].
[30] Churton to Nichols, 4 Oct. 1820, Bodleian, MS Eng. lett. c. 354, fos. 223–4 [NAD4934].
[31] *Progresses*, ed. Nichols, 2nd edn., i, p. xlvii.
[32] Nichols to Bray, 22 Jan. 1821, and 3 Feb. 1821, PC2/4/f5/1–2 [NAD4019–20].
[33] Nichols to Ormerod, 2 Feb. 1823, PC2/4/f179 [NAD4474].

spare some deeds, as 'they are to me as precious as new Stars to an Astronomer, or new Plants to a Botanist; & my Collection begins to assume a very respectable appearance'.[34]

George Ashby hoped that Nichols's collections of New Year gift rolls might identify a prayer book supposedly made for the Queen by Lady Elizabeth Tyrwhitt.[35] He also sought to draw Nichols into his dispute with John Whitaker concerning letters allegedly forged by Elizabeth to incriminate Mary Queen of Scots; but Nichols's sole aim was to print a chronological arrangement of texts illustrating the Queen's progresses, leaving others to argue over their interpretation. Like his alter ego Sylvanus Urban, he avoided *ad hominem* criticism and debate, though his works are infused with the robust political and religious sentiments of his day. For Nichols, the reign of Elizabeth marked the dawn of a 'brilliant Sun to cheer the Nation' after the horrors of the Catholic state. He regarded the materials he had gathered as:

marking a period to which men were emerging from the barbarity and ignorance wherein they had long been held both by the Church and State. . . . What they obtained was still disfigured and interrupted by the jargon, the quidlibets, and absurdities of the Schools, which, under a parade of learning and instruction, readily promoted ignorance. . . The principles of liberty also, and of religious reformation, which began to take place, were as yet but imperfectly understood. . . The Queen herself. . . retained a love to some kind of Popish pomp and ceremony, together with high notions of the sacred rights of Royalty.[36]

The contrast with contemporary political and religious decay was obvious:

We who live in an age when religion and morality are equally neglected, and that greatest blessing of Protestantism, Religious Liberty, is so shamefully abused, cannot conceive the effect of such a glorious change. . . If any of our affairs can be compared with that at Elizabeth's accession, it is that which took place at the Revolution, when the former triumphs of Truth over Superstition and of Peace over Persecution, were fresher in every man's mind.[37]

Many of Nichols's prefaces to the *Gentleman's Magazine* were written in the same spirit and yet, behind the printed page, Nichols's friendships were surprisingly diverse.[38] Unlike some antiquaries, he happily collaborated with dissenters noted for their learning or good character.[39] While railing in print against the abuse of religious liberty, Nichols was on intimate terms with prominent nonconformists such as John Coakley Lettsom, Theophilus Lindsey, and John Calder. Though divided by religion, they were united through scholarship.

---

[34] Hamper to Nichols, 22 June 1813, Bodleian, MS Eng. lett. c. 357, fos. 49–50 [NAD5159].
[35] Ashby to Nichols, 12 Apr. 1788: *Illustrations of the Literary History of the Eighteenth Century*, ed. John Nichols, 8 vols. (London: Nichols & Bentley, 1817–58), viii (1858), 422–3.
[36] *Progresses*, ed. Nichols, 2nd edn., i, pp. vi, xi.   [37] Ibid., p. xi.
[38] Broadfield, 'John Nichols as Historian and Friend', 767.
[39] Ibid. 536. I am grateful to Dr Grayson Ditchfield for help with Nichols's religious views.

Calder was Nichols's 'worthy old friend' supplying trees for Nichols's garden and explanations of Hadrian's coins for the *History of Leicestershire*.[40] The *Progresses* owed as much to Nichols's zeal to be of service to those he esteemed as to his own historical interests and the commercial demands of his press. He was also keen to associate his editorship of the *Gentleman's Magazine* and Elizabethan research with the monarchy of his own day, confessing, in his preface to the 1823 edition of the *Progresses*:

> some complacency in the idea that when the Progresses of King GEORGE THE THIRD shall become the subject of Antiquarian curiosity, . . . [the] diaries preserved in another Repository [the *Gentleman's Magazine*] will furnish some future Collector of Progresses with ample and authentic materials; and enable him to inform posterity, that in popularity that amiable MONARCH at least equalled the renowned ELIZABETH and that his Visits were not less gratifying to his admiring subjects.[41]

Nichols's genial personality and political acumen opened doors to many official archives. As printer of the votes of the House of Lords, senior liveryman of the Stationers' Company, and Common Councilman of the City of London, he was on familiar terms with many custodians of official records. He was also able to draw on a wide network of librarians, archivists, and clerks who searched records in their care on his behalf and arranged for transcripts to be made. In Oxford, John Price at the Bodleian Library and John Gutch, historian of the University, arranged for records to be copied for Nichols. Other helpers included Samuel Ayscough, librarian and index maker, and Thomas Astle, one of the keepers of the State Paper Office. The *Progresses* may not have been on the same scale as the *Rotuli parliamentorum* (1777) or Sir Joseph Ayloffe's *Calendar of the Ancient Charters* (1774), but they were part of the wider enterprise to preserve in print national and local records.[42] On a personal level, Astle's help to Nichols was enhanced by his own remarkable collection of manuscripts. He had inherited the library of his father-in-law Philip Morant, historian of Essex, and readily made it available to fellow antiquaries. Lists of New Year gifts between 1571 and 1574, domestic accounts of Hatfield House, inventories of the Queen's jewels, and transcripts of her translation of Boethius all found their way into Nichols's *Progresses* from Astle's rich library.[43]

Nichols recycled his sources among his publications and those who helped him with one book were frequently involved with the next. This is witnessed by Nichols's correspondence with the Herrick family of Beaumanor, Leicestershire. John Herrick first contacted Nichols in 1791 when he invited him to see a chest of papers that his family had accumulated since Sir William Heyricke the goldsmith

[40] Calder to Nichols, n.d., Bodleian, MS Eng. MS c. 132, fo. 10, and Broadfield, 'John Nichols as Historian and Friend', 765–6.
[41] *Progresses*, ed. Nichols, 2nd edn., i. l.   [42] Sweet, *Antiquaries*, 282–3.
[43] I am grateful to Dr Jayne Archer for these references.

and banker had purchased Beaumanor in 1595.[44] Nichols subsequently visited Beaumanor whenever he toured Leicestershire and Herrick revised countless proof sheets of the county history.[45] The Herrick archive included New Year gifts rolls for 1557 and 1600. Nichols used them in the first edition of the *Progresses* in 1788 and again in his *Illustrations of the Manners and Expenses of Antient Times* in 1797. The gift rolls feature in his county history and he returned to them when preparing the second edition of the *Progresses* in 1823.

Nichols was also a prodigious collector of manuscripts and rare books. He was literary executor to Samuel Pegge, Richard Gough, and the literary critic George Hardinge, and their papers 'formed materials for many of his future literary labours'.[46] He also bought heavily in salerooms, driven by a desire to use the research collections of his friends. Jayne Archer's analysis of Nichols's footnotes and remarks throughout the *Progresses* shows how he collated manuscripts in his collection with copies held elsewhere. The 'Commentarii Hexameri Rerum', relating to entertainments for the Queen's visit to Cambridge in 1564, for example, was purchased by Nichols at the sale of Dr Askew's library in 1786, then collated with a transcript by Thomas Baker in the British Museum.[47] Similarly, though Nichols was unable to obtain a copy of 'The Supplication of John Lesley, Bishop of Ross 1573' that was printed in Paris in 1574, he tells us that a transcript of it, from a manuscript in the library of Trinity College, Cambridge, had fallen into his hands among some papers of the late Dr Mason.[48] In 1790, he bought the New Year gift roll for 1579 at Gustavus Brander's library sale.[49] Nichols also owned New Year gift rolls for 1559[50] and perhaps 1594,[51] as well as 'The Masque of Mountebankes', performed at Gray's Inn, 1618.[52]

[44] On Nichols and the Herrick family, see Broadfield, 'John Nichols as Historian and Friend', 424–33.

[45] Many of these letters are now held by Yale University Library: Osborne Collection, Nichols Family Correspondence [hereafter Yale Nichols Correspondence]. I am grateful to Leicestershire Archaeological and Historical Society for enabling me to purchase copies of these letters.

[46] Annotation by John Bowyer Nichols, 25 May 1846, in Family Records, viii, PC4/1/fo. 82 [NAD2169].

[47] The Baker manuscript is British Library, London, Harleian MS 7037, but the 'Commentarii' used by Nichols came from the 'Triumphs of the Muses' (1564) that he had bought at Askew's sale and which is now Society of Antiquaries, MS 30.

[48] *Progresses*, ed. Nichols, 1st edn., 4 vols. (1788–1821), iii (1805), 61–76.

[49] Jayne Archer, unpublished report on 'New Year's Gifts'; *Progresses*, ed. Nichols, 2nd edn., ii. 249–75. It was lot 2767 in John Gough Nichols's library sale in 1874.

[50] Archer, 'New Year's Gifts', notes that Nichols probably owned this in 1804. He used it in the *History and Antiquities of the Town and County of Leicester*, ed. John Nichols, 4 vols. (London: Nichols, Son, and Bentley, 1795–1811), iii. ii. 674. It was lot 2766 in John Gough Nichols's library sale of 1874. It is now in the John Rylands Library, University of Manchester.

[51] *Progresses*, ed. Nichols, 2nd edn., iii. 252. It was lot 2772 in John Gough Nichols's library sale of 1874. Its present location is unknown.

[52] Ibid. 320–48, where Nichols explains that 'The Second Part was first published in the former Edition of these Progresses from a MS then in the Editor's possession, and afterwards given to Mr. Gough.'

Catalogues of Nichols's libraries contain further clues to materials in Nichols's hands. Although Sotheby's sold John Nichols's own library with that of 'another gentleman' in 1828, a catalogue of his books and papers that I have found in a private collection sheds new light on the sources he used. Tantalizing references to 'Princely Pleasures of Kenilworth'[53] or 'Speeches to Queen Elizabeth 1 vol'[54] hint at the contents of his huge reference library of nearly 1,500 titles. The family retained many items, notably Nichols's own copy of the 1823 edition of the *Progresses* that passed to his eldest daughter, Sarah. It still bears her bookplate and contains numerous annotations and inserted papers showing how Nichols used his personal copy to file letters and memoranda as they came to hand in preparation for a further edition. In 1825, for example, Edmund Henry Barker forwarded a letter to Nichols that he had received from J. Burrell Faux of Thetford:

Dear Sir
    I shall be obliged by your presenting the enclosed to Mr Nichols with my compliments—I should have been very glad, to have sent him the full entries, but I can find no one able to decipher them—if Mr Nichols is of opinion they are worth sending any person down to examine—the Books shall be forthcoming.[55]

Letters and memoranda are pasted to the endpapers of the volumes. An anonymous suggestion for an illustration, reading 'For your Elizabethan progresses—an Engraving of Smallbridge Hall, which is hastening rapidly to decay' is fixed inside volume two,[56] and the following letter from Joseph Haslewood to John Bowyer Nichols is fixed to the end of volume three:

Certain devices and Shewes presented to her majestie by the gentlemen of Grayes Inne at her Highnesse Court in Grenewich. At London printed by R Robinson, 1587
    Dear Sir,
    There is a MS Copy with the above title (which of course appears to have been printed) in Malone's collection at Bodleian lib: Has your father any knowledge of it, as it is easy to obtain a copy I should suppose thro' Dr Bliss
    Yours truly
    J Haslewood[57]

Nichols's daughters, who regularly served as his amanuenses, annotated the volumes. Volume three includes Anne Nichols's transcript of Sir Walter Ralegh's letter to Sir Robert Cecil dated July 1592.[58] In *circa* 1827 Isabella Nichols asked

    [53] John Nichols's Library Catalogue, 1826, PC1/26/1, fo. 27ᵛ, item 763.
    [54] Ibid. fo. 11ᵛ, item 295.
    [55] J. Burrell Faux to E. H. Barker, 30 Nov. 1825, in Nichols's copy of *Progresses*, 2nd edn., PC1/69/1/5.
    [56] Anonymous note in Nichols's copy of *Progresses*, 2nd edn., PC1/69/2/9.
    [57] Haslewood to J. B. Nichols [before 1826], in Nichols's copy of *Progresses*, 2nd edn., PC1/69/3/11.
    [58] Private collection, PC1/69/3/4.

her brother to help them complete their two sets of *The Progresses of King James I* (1828). Although they had 'the clean sheets also as far as were worked off in November last' she asked him to give them the remainder, 'as in no work of my dear Fathers were we ever so much interested, & concerned; & when we have our sets complete we wish both copies bound up according to his directions'.[59] Many of John Nichols's books remained with his family and are identifiable in subsequent Nichols library sales. That of John Bowyer Nichols's library in 1864 included books by Samuel Pegge containing annotations and letters by Pegge, Gough, and John Nichols.[60] Ten years later, the sale of the library of John Gough Nichols included thirty-six letters of Robert, 1st Earl of Salisbury and his son William, Lord Cranborne (written 1602–10).[61]

PRINTING THE *PROGRESSES*

Nichols has been justly criticized for the maddening arrangement of his works: indeed, the first edition of the *Progresses*, produced intermittently over more than three decades and bedevilled by countless changes of pagination, is a prime example of the way in which his methods might seem to obscure his achievements. But the steady accretion of his works ensured their lasting value. As a printer, Nichols the historian could print materials as he discovered them, refining them through a robust framework of peer review. To be a correspondent of John Nichols, or even of the *Gentleman's Magazine*, was also to be a corrector of his press and collaborator in his research. People found that a letter to the magazine triggered a succession of proof sheets as he eagerly engaged them in his projects. It was a trick he had learned when printing Camden's *Britannia* for Richard Gough, who had insisted that proofs of the work be 'forwarded to those who were likely to be most actively useful'.[62] Nichols ran off as many proofs as he needed and sent them to everyone who might help. It was a luxury that only a historian who was his own printer could afford.[63] Those drawn into this frenetic activity were often exasperated but usually impressed. George Ashby commented on the 'uncommon and great advantage he hath as a Printer, to be

---

[59] Isabella Nichols to J. B. Nichols [*circa* 1827], Bodleian, MS Eng. c. 6165, fo. 51.

[60] *The First Portion of the . . . Library of the Late John Bowyer Nichols*, 24 May 1864, and *The Concluding Portion of the Library of the Late John Bowyer Nichols*, 19 Dec. 1864: lot 1107, Samuel Pegge, *Forme of Cury* (1780), annotated by Pegge, Gough, and Nichols; lot 1212, Samuel Pegge, *Curialia*, interleaved with many manuscript notes and ALSS of Pegge, 1782–1806; lot 1215, Samuel Pegge, *Antiquarian Tracts*, comprising 45 articles including ALSS. Lot 1235 was the *Processionale ad usum insignis ecclesiæ Sarisburiensis with musical notes, 1555 and Queen Elizabeth's prayer Book, 1590*.

[61] *The Extensive and Valuable Library of the Late John Gough Nichols*, 4 Dec. 1874, lot 725.

[62] Nichols, *Literary Anecdotes*, vi. 273, and Broadfield, 'John Nichols as Historian and Friend', 703.

[63] Broadfield, 'John Nichols as Historian and Friend', 700.

able to throw off a few copies . . . in order to give the *Cognoscenti* an opportunity of communicating their thoughts . . . The being able to set up so many sheets at once and keep them un-worked off, and send them about for correction, is what, I believe, never happened before; and must contribute wonderfully to the perfection.'[64] Although no proof sheets of the *Progresses* are known to survive, sufficient examples of cancelled sheets of other works by Nichols do exist which testify to the constant refinement of his texts.[65]

It is hard to measure how far the accuracy of Nichols's texts was lost amidst the whirlwind of his research. He was at the mercy of his contributors, some of whom provided faithful transcripts that pass modern critical scrutiny, while others omitted whole lines and adapted the text to suit their own interpretations. Modern scholarship is only beginning to disentangle these conflicting voices. Nichols could also be compromised by the wishes of the owners of manuscripts. He relied on their goodwill and, ever the pragmatist, would omit sensitive material to ensure the inclusion of the rest of the archive in the finished work. Though John Herrick of Beaumanor was happy to entrust him with manuscripts from his family's archive, he was keen to retain editorial control. In 1797, while printing Herrick muniments in his *History of Leicestershire*, Nichols assured him that he had 'endeavoured to select what is curious without being offensive' and would readily omit any other lines Herrick cared to indicate.[66] At the same time he often asked Herrick to check his transcriptions against the original letters: 'In old Mary's letter (if you can find it) pray see if poundegarnyte and read heayringe are spelt right. I wish to be accurate in that letter.'[67]

Why that particular letter? Was Nichols happy to ignore inaccuracies in texts he did not regard as crucially important? Although capable of silently 'correcting' archaic spelling in many documents, he could be meticulous with others. On 1 March 1797 he asked Herrick for an accurate copy of the will of Nicholas Herrick containing directions for his funeral because he wished 'to use exactly his own words',[68] as 'There is a solemnity in giving the very exact words and form of such a deed, much preferable to the substance.'[69] Such editorial foibles were compounded by the fact that Nichols did not always acknowledge his sources. After printing a text he had only seen at second hand, he often made matters worse by incorporating comments supplied by his unacknowledged contributor within his bridging narrative. The fact that an editorial preface is written in the

[64] Ashby to W. Stevenson, 14 May 1791, in Nichols, *Literary Anecdotes*, xi. 684–5.
[65] See especially the proof sheets for the West Goscote hundred of the *History of Leicestershire* in which Nichols was assisted by Samuel Pipe Wolferstan, Leicestershire Record Office, DE6308, and the heavily reworked proof sheets of Owen Manning and William Bray's *History and Antiquities of Surrey*, Surrey History Centre, G120/36/33, which show how Nichols, Bray, and Richard Gough all revised the text and arrangement of the work as it was printed.
[66] Nichols to Herrick, 24 Mar. 1797, Yale Nichols Correspondence, Box 14 [NAD4650].
[67] Nichols to Herrick, 22 Mar. 1797, Yale Nichols Correspondence, Box 14 [NAD4648].
[68] Nichols to Herrick, 1 Mar. 1797, Yale Nichols Correspondence, Box 14 [NAD4646].
[69] Nichols to Herrick, 7 Mar. 1797, Yale Nichols Correspondence, Box 14 [NAD4697].

first person does not necessarily indicate that Nichols wrote it. Indeed, Nichols later admitted that the preface to the first volume of the *Progresses* was actually written by Richard Gough.[70] He was equally happy to rewrite work supplied by a contributor and yet still attribute it to them. At times, as Alan Broadfield has observed, it seems easier to 'harmonise the Gospels' than tease apart the layers of authorship in a text printed by Nichols.[71]

Nichols printed his own works during 'down-time' at his printing house. This kept his compositors employed but pressurized those correcting the sheets to return them promptly. With only a finite stock of printing types Nichols could ill afford to hold his presses against the demands of parliamentary printing and the monthly production of the *Gentleman's Magazine*. His collaborators found they had to work at his speed; and he worked fast. Alexander Chalmers remarked that from his youth Nichols was quick at everything: 'he read with rapidity . . . he spoke quickly, and that whether in the reciprocity of conversation or . . . in a set speech'. He also wrote 'with great rapidity; but this, he used jocularly to allow . . . did not tend to improve his hand'.[72] Nichols's handwriting was (and still is) infamous, largely because he rarely bothered to raise his pen from the paper until he had reached its edge. In 1776 William Cuming of Dorset lamented 'what a pity 'tis that you write so small, so close, & upon such shabby scraps of paper, you that wallow in that commodity',[73] and by 1820 Nichols's hand had degenerated so much that Ralph Churton, acknowledging forty pages of proofs of the *Progresses*, could barely read the covering letter.[74] Nichols rarely supplied his compositors with copy he had written himself. Instead, he numbered and annotated the transcripts and corrected proof sheets, leaving his pressmen to compose them. Any errors easily passed unnoticed into the final text. A sheet could be worked off in an afternoon, corrected, and reprinted the same evening.[75] This facility to print and revise so rapidly is the key to his enormous output, but was clearly not without its risks.

RECEPTION OF THE *PROGRESSES*

In his review of the first two volumes in 1788, Richard Gough praised Nichols for completing Tyson's work but lamented the disorder and the desperate need for an index.[76] In 1823, Thomas Fosbroke hailed the work as a 'great literary curiosity of high Archaeological and Historical Value'.[77] He drew parallels with Lodge's

[70] Nichols, *Literary Anecdotes*, vi (1812), 323.
[71] Broadfield, 'John Nichols as Historian and Friend', 815–16.
[72] *Gentleman's Magazine*, 96.2 (1826), 489–504.
[73] Cuming to Nichols, 14 Feb. 1776, Bodleian, MS Top. Gen. C. 8, fo. 392.
[74] Churton to Nichols, 21 Dec. 1820, Bodleian, MS Eng. lett. c. 354, fos. 227–8 [NAD4936].
[75] Broadfield, 'John Nichols as Historian and Friend', 706.
[76] *Gentleman's Magazine*, 58.1 (1788), 425.   [77] Ibid. 93.1 (1823), 531–5.

Illustrations, the Paston papers, and Evelyn's *Diary*, remarking that, while they were the produce of a single muniment room, Nichols had presented his readers with a 'complete body of Court History' assembled from all attainable sources: 'These are the result of an Octogenarian life of attentive research; without them the Work had lost more than half its interest, and so copious and various are they, that no person but the Editor . . . could have produced an equal store of satisfactory information.'[78]

Fosbroke's use of the word 'Archaeological' captures the spirit behind Nichols's achievement. The *Progresses* had grown from the wider antiquarian enterprise to study and preserve the materials of the past. By collecting letters, orations, narratives, and literary entertainments of Elizabeth's reign he had brought to life the inventories of New Year gifts and had displayed in authentic detail the manners and entertainments of Tudor England. His achievement was framed within the discipline of antiquarian scholarship and helped to establish the idea that such records belonged to the general public, rather than just their official or private custodians. By 1823, helped by the success of Joseph Strutt's *Sports and Pastimes of the People of England* (1801), popular imagination had been seized by the romance of England 'in the Olden Time'. Nichols's *Progresses* appealed to this new audience as much as it had to the more rarefied scholars of the eighteenth century. C. R. Leslie's romantic evocation of Tudor England in his painting of 'May Day Revels in the Time of Elizabeth' (1821), and the proclamation of the *Saturday Magazine* at its launch in 1832 that it aimed to reissue the great books of the past in a more portable and digestible form, owed as much to Nichols's Elizabethan enterprise as they did to the success of Sir Walter Scott's historical novels.[79] Both the *Saturday Magazine* (January–September 1838) and the *Penny Magazine* (January–December 1843) ran successful series on Queen Elizabeth's *Progresses*, and in 1847, a popular illustrated magazine hailed the Elizabethan era as the most important in English literary history.[80] At the same time, Nichols's work encouraged scholars to publish accurate editions of Elizabethan and Jacobean literary manuscripts. The formation of specialist record publishing societies, such as the Camden Society in 1837, was rooted in the enthusiasm of Nichols and his contemporaries to make historical sources more widely available. His legacy is exemplified in the work of his grandson John Gough Nichols (1806–73), whose learned editions included *London Pageants: Accounts of Sixty Royal Processions and Entertainments in the City of London* (1831), *The Unton Inventories, 1596–1620* (1841), *The Fishmongers' Pageant*

---

[78] *Gentleman's Magazine*, 95.2 (1825), 521–3.

[79] Peter Mandler, ' "In the Olden Time": Romantic History and English National Identity, 1820–50', in Laurence Brockliss and David Eastwood (eds.), *A Union of Multiple Identities: The British Isles, c.1750–c.1850*, (Manchester: Manchester University Press, 1997), 78–92, and Philip Connell, 'Bibliomania: Book Collecting, Cultural Politics and the Rise of Literary Heritage in Romantic Britain', *Representations*, 71 (Summer 2000), 24–47.

[80] *Sharpe's London Magazine*, 4 (1847), 247–48, cited by Mandler, ' "In the Olden Time" ', 86, 87, 91.

With anger foaming and of vengeance full,
Why belloweth John Nichols like a bull?

Figure 14.3. Thomas Rowlandson, engraving of John Nichols at work on the *Progresses* (1788), in Peter Pindar [i.e. John Wolcott], *A Benevolent Epistle to Sylvanus Urban, alias...J. Nichols* (1790). (By permission of the British Library, London, shelfmark 840.k.14(1))

on Lord Mayor's Day, 1616 and *Chrysanaleia* by Anthony Munday (1844), *The Diary of Henry Machyn. 1550–1563* (1848), *The Chronicle of Queen Jane and of Two Years of Queen Mary* (1852), and the *Literary Remains of Edward VI* (1857–8).

Not everyone, however, was convinced. Though Nichols had many friends, he also made a few enemies, notably John Wolcot, a popular satirist writing as 'Peter Pindar', who never forgave him for a scathing review of his work in the *Gentleman's Magazine*.[81] Wolcot published several 'Benevolent Epistles' satirizing Nichols's achievements, of which the 'Ode to Mr J Nichols on his History of the Progresses of Queen Elizabeth' is significant because it testifies to the wide appeal of his work: if the *Progresses* had only been read by a small circle of specialists there would have been little point in poking such scurrilous fun at its author:

> John, though it asks no subtilty of brain
> To write Queen Bess' Progress through the land
> Excuse the freedom, if I dare maintain
> The theme too high for *thee* to take in hand.
>
> On Vanity's damned rock what thousands split!
> Thou should'st have laboured on some humbler matter—
> On somewhat on a level with thy wit—
> For instance—when her majesty made water.[82]

Thomas Rowlandson accompanied Wolcot's verses with a crazy engraving of Nichols, fists clenched over a copy of the *Progresses*, with stray letters and doggerel poetry littering the floor around him. Two centuries later, the editors of the new edition of Nichols's *Progresses* may be forgiven for cursing him as they have wrestled with the knotted provenance of his sources, but they would agree that, without his energy and zeal to hunt down myriad materials for the life of the Elizabethan court and his genial ability to engage people across the country in his research, our understanding of the political and cultural life of her reign would be very much the poorer. The *Progresses* is the achievement of an outstanding bibliographer and of a learned printer at the heart of the late eighteenth-century antiquarian network. It confirms John Nichols as a pioneer of Renaissance scholarship and continues to influence modern historiographies of the reign of Queen Elizabeth I.

---

[81] *Gentleman's Magazine*, 58.2 (1788), 816, 1102.
[82] *The Works of Peter Pindar* (London: Jones & Co., 1824), 178. The *Epistle* was written in response to volumes i and ii of the first edition of *The Progresses and Processions of Queen Elizabeth*, published in 1788.

Select Bibliography of Secondary Criticism

ADAMS, SIMON, *Leicester and the Court: Essays on Elizabethan Politics* (Manchester: Manchester University Press, 2002).

ADAMSON, J. S. A., 'Chivalry and Political Culture in Caroline England', in Kevin Sharpe and Peter Lake (eds.), *Culture and Politics in Early Stuart England* (Basingstoke: Macmillan, 1994), 161–97.

ALFORD, STEPHEN, *The Early Elizabethan Polity: William Cecil and the British Succession Crisis, 1558–1569* (Cambridge: Cambridge University Press, 1998).

ANGLO, SYDNEY, *Spectacle, Pageantry, and Early Tudor Policy* (Oxford: Clarendon Press, 1969; repr. 1997).

ARCHER, JAYNE ELISABETH, CLARKE, ELIZABETH, and GOLDRING, ELIZABETH, (eds.), *Court and Culture in the Reign of Queen Elizabeth I: A New Edition of John Nichols's 'Progresses of Queen Elizabeth'* (Oxford: Oxford University Press, forthcoming).

ARNOLD, JANET, *Queen Elizabeth's Wardrobe Unlock'd* (London: Maney, 1988).

ASTINGTON, JOHN, *English Court Theatre, 1558–1642* (Cambridge: Cambridge University Press, 1999).

ATTREED, LORRAINE, 'The Politics of Welcome: Ceremonies and Constitutional Development in Later Medieval English Towns', in Barbara A. Hanawalt and Kathryn Reyerson (eds.), *City and Spectacle in Medieval Europe* (Minneapolis: University of Minnesota Press, 1994), 208–31.

AXTON, MARIE, 'Robert Dudley and the Inner Temple Revels', *Historical Journal*, 13.3 (1970), 365–78.

_____ *The Queen's Two Bodies: Drama and the Elizabethan Succession* (London: Royal Historical Society, 1977).

BASKERVILL, C. R., 'The Sources of Jonson's *Masque at Christmas* and *Love's Welcome at Welbeck'*, *Modern Philology*, 6 (1908–9), 257–69.

BERGERON, DAVID M., *English Civic Pageantry 1558–1642* (London: Edward Arnold, 1971; rev. ed. Tempe: Arizona State Medieval and Renaissance Studies, 2003).

_____ 'The Bible in English Renaissance Civic Pageantry', *Comparative Drama*, 20 (1986), 160–70.

_____ 'Stuart Civic Pageants and Textual Performance', *Renaissance Quarterly*, 51 (1998), 163–83.

_____ *Textual Patronage in English Drama, 1570–1640* (Aldershot: Ashgate, 2006).

BERLIN, MICHAEL, 'Civic Ceremony in Early Modern London', *Urban History Yearbook*, 13 (1986), 15–27.

BERRY, PHILIPPA, *Of Chastity and Power: Elizabethan Literature and the Unmarried Queen* (London: Routledge, 1989).

_____ and ARCHER, JAYNE ELISABETH, 'Reinventing the Matter of Britain: Undermining the State in Jacobean Masques', in David J. Baker and Willy Maley (eds.), *British Identities and English Renaissance Literature* (Cambridge: Cambridge University Press, 2002), 119–32.

BLAKELEY, ERIK, 'Tournament Garniture of Robert Dudley, Earl of Leicester', *Royal Armouries Yearbook*, 2 (1997), 55–63.

BOYLE, ANDREW, 'Henry Fitzalan, 12th Earl of Arundel, Politics and Culture in the Tudor Nobility' (unpublished doctoral thesis, University of Oxford, 2002).

BOYLE, H. H., 'Elizabeth's Entertainment at Elvetham: War Policy in Pageantry', *Studies in Philology*, 68 (1971), 146–66.

BRAYSHAY, MARK, 'Long-Distance Royal Journeys: Anne of Denmark's Journey from Stirling to Windsor in 1603', *Journal of Transport History*, 25 (2004), 1–21.

BREIGHT, CURTIS C., 'Entertainments of Elizabeth at Theobalds in the Early 1590s', *REED Newsletter*, 12.2 (1987), 1–9.

____ 'Caressing the Great: Viscount Montague's Entertainment of Elizabeth at Cowdray, 1591', *Sussex Archaeological Collections*, 127 (1989), 147–66.

____ 'Duelling Ceremonies: The Strange Case of William Hacket, Elizabethan Messiah', *Journal of Medieval and Renaissance Studies*, 191 (1989), 35–67.

____ 'Realpolitik and Elizabethan Ceremony: The Earl of Hertford's Entertainment of Elizabeth at Elvetham, 1591', *Renaissance Quarterly*, 45 (1992), 20–48.

BUTLER, MARTIN, *Theatre and Crisis 1632–1642* (Cambridge: Cambridge University Press, 1984).

BUTTERWORTH, PHILIP, 'Royal Firework Theater: The Fort Holding, Part I', *Research Opportunities in Renaissance Drama*, 34 (1995), 145–66.

____ 'Part II', *RORD*, 35 (1996), 17–31.

____ 'Part III', *RORD*, 37 (1998), 99–110.

COLE, MARY HILL, 'Ceremonial Dialogue Between Elizabeth I and Her Civic Hosts', in Douglas F. Rutledge (ed.), *Ceremony and Text in the Renaissance* (Newark: University of Delaware Press, 1996), 84–100.

____ *The Portable Queen: Elizabeth I and the Politics of Ceremony* (Amherst: University of Massachusetts Press, 1999).

COLTHORPE, MARION, 'An Entertainment for Queen Elizabeth I at Wimbledon in 1599', *REED Newsletter*, 10.1 (1985), 1–2.

____ 'Entertainments for Elizabeth at Theobalds in the Early 1590s', *REED Newsletter*, 12.2 (1987), 1–9.

____ 'The Theobalds Entertainment for Queen Elizabeth I in 1591, with a Transcript of the Gardener's Speech', *REED Newsletter*, 12.1 (1987), 2–9.

____ 'The Disputed Date of the Theobalds Entertainment, 1591', *REED Newsletter*, 19.2 (1994), 19.

COOPER, HELEN, 'Location and Meaning in Masque, Morality and Royal Entertainment', in David Lindley (ed.), *The Court Masque* (Manchester: Manchester University Press, 1984), 135–48.

CRANE, MARY THOMAS, ' "Video et Taceo": Elizabeth I and the Rhetoric of Counsel', *Studies in English Literature, 1500–1900*, 28.1 (Winter 1988), 1–15.

CROFT, PAULINE (ed.), *Patronage, Culture and Power: The Early Cecils* (New Haven: Yale University Press/The Paul Mellon Centre for Studies in British Art, 2002).

CUNLIFFE, J. W., 'The Queenes Majesties Entertainment at Woodstocke', *PMLA*, 26 (1911), 92–141.

DAVIS, ALEX, *Chivalry and Romance in the English Renaissance* (Cambridge: Brewer, 2003).

DORAN, SUSAN, 'Juno versus Diana: The Treatment of Elizabeth I's Marriage in Plays and Entertainments, 1561–1581', *Historical Journal*, 38.2 (1995), 257–74.

_____ *Monarchy and Matrimony: The Courtships of Elizabeth I* (London: Routledge, 1996).

_____ *England and Europe in the Sixteenth Century* (New York: St Martin's, 1999).

_____ 'Virginity, Divinity and Power: The Portraits of Elizabeth I', in Susan Doran and Thomas Freeman (eds.), *The Myth of Elizabeth* (Basingstoke: Palgrave Macmillan, 2003), 171–99.

DORMAN, THOMAS, 'Visits of Two Queens to Sandwich', *Archaeologia Cantiana: Transactions of the Bristol and Gloucestershire Archaeological Society*, 15 (1980), 1–44.

DOVEY, ZILLAH, *An Elizabethan Progress: The Queen's Journey into East Anglia, 1578* (Stroud: Allan Sutton; Madison, NJ: Farleigh Dickinson University Press, 1996).

DUNLOP, IAN, *Palaces & Progresses of Elizabeth I* (London: Jonathan Cape, 1962).

ELLIOTT Jr., JOHN, 'Queen Elizabeth at Oxford: New Light on the Royal Plays of 1566', *English Literary Renaissance*, 18 (1988), 218–29.

_____ 'Drama', in Nicholas Tyacke (ed.), *The History of the University of Oxford*, iv: *Seventeenth-Century Oxford* (Oxford: Clarendon Press, 1997), 641–58.

FRYE, SUSAN, *Elizabeth I: The Competition for Representation* (Oxford: Oxford University Press, 1993; repr. 1996).

_____ 'Entertainments at Court', in Susan Doran (ed.), *Elizabeth: The Exhibition at the National Maritime Museum* (London: Chatto & Windus, 2003), 73–80.

GOLDRING, ELIZABETH, 'The Funeral of Sir Philip Sidney and the Politics of Elizabethan Festival', in J. R. Mulryne and Elizabeth Goldring (eds.), *Court Festivals of the European Renaissance: Art, Politics and Performance* (Aldershot: Ashgate, 2002), 199–224.

_____ 'Portraits of Queen Elizabeth I and the Earl of Leicester for Kenilworth Castle', *Burlington Magazine*, 147 (2005), 654–60.

_____ ' "So lively a portraiture of his miseries": Melancholy, Mourning and the Elizabethan Malady', *British Art Journal*, 6.2 (2005), 12–22.

GUY, JOHN (ed.), *The Reign of Elizabeth I: Court and Culture in the Last Decade* (Cambridge: Cambridge University Press, 1995).

HACKETT, HELEN, *Virgin Mother, Maiden Queen: Elizabeth I and the Cult of the Virgin Mary* (London: Macmillan, 1995).

HADFIELD, ANDREW, 'Spenser, Drayton, and the Question of Britain', *Review of English Studies*, 51 (2004), 592–9.

HAMMER, PAUL E. J., 'Upstaging The Queen: The Earl of Essex, Francis Bacon, and the Accession Day Celebrations of 1595', in David Bevington and Peter Holbrook (eds.), *The Politics of the Stuart Court Masque* (Cambridge: Cambridge University Press, 1998), 41–66.

HARDIN, WILLIAM, ' "Pipe-Pilgrimages" and "Fruitfull Rivers": Thomas Middleton's Civic Entertainments and the Water Supply of Early Stuart London', *Renaissance Papers* (1993), 63–73.

HARDING, VANESSA, 'Reformation and Culture 1540–1700', in Peter Clark et al. (eds.), *The Cambridge Urban History of Britain*, 3 vols. (Cambridge: Cambridge University Press, 2000), ii. 263–88.

HEAL, FELICITY, *Hospitality in Early Modern England* (Oxford: Clarendon Press, 1990).

HEATON, GABRIEL, 'Performing Gifts: The Manuscript Circulation of Elizabethan and Early Stuart Royal Entertainments' (unpublished doctoral thesis, University of Cambridge, 2003).

HELGERSON, RICHARD, *Forms of Nationhood: The Elizabethan Writing of England* (Chicago: University of Chicago Press, 1992).

HENDERSON, PAULA, *The Tudor House and Garden: Architecture and Landscape in the Sixteenth and Seventeenth Centuries* (New Haven: Yale University Press/The Paul Mellon Centre for Studies in British Art, 2005).

HOTSON, LESLIE, (ed.), *Queen Elizabeth's Entertainment at Mitcham* (New Haven: Yale University Press, 1953).

HOWARD, PATRICIA, 'Time in Entertainments for Queen Elizabeth I: 1590-1602', *University of Toronto Quarterly*, 65.3 (Summer 1996), 467–81.

INGRAM, R. W., '1579 and the Decline of Civic Religious Drama in Coventry', *Elizabethan Theatre*, 8 (1979), 114–28.

JAMES, MERVYN, *Society, Politics and Culture: Studies in Early Modern England* (Cambridge: Cambridge University Press, 1986).

JOHNSON, PAULA, 'Jacobean Ephemera and the Immortal Word', *Renaissance Drama*, NS 8 (1977), 151–71.

KANTOROWICZ, ERNST, *The King's Two Bodies: A Study in Mediæval Political Theology* (Princeton: Princeton University Press, 1957; repr. 1981).

KING, JOHN N., *Tudor Royal Iconography: Literature and Art in an Age of Religious Crisis* (Princeton: Princeton University Press, 1989).

—— 'Queen Elizabeth I: Representations of the Virgin Queen', *Renaissance Quarterly*, 43 (1990), 30–74.

KING, ROS (ed.), *The Works of Richard Edwards: Politics, Poetry and Performance in Sixteenth-Century England* (Manchester: Manchester University Press, 2001).

KIPLING, GORDON, '"He That Saw It Would Not Believe It": Anne Boleyn's Royal Entry into London', in Alexandra F. Johnston and Wim Hüsken (eds.), *Civic Ritual and Drama* (Amsterdam: Rodopi, 1997), 39–76.

—— 'Wonderfull Spectacles: Theater and Civic Culture', in John D. Cox and David Scott Kastan (eds.), *A New History of Early English Drama* (New York: Columbia University Press, 1997), 153–71.

KISBY, FIONA, 'Kingship and the Royal Itinerary: A Study of the Peripatetic Household of the Early Tudor Kings, 1485–1547', *Court Historian*, 4.1 (1999), 29–39.

KLEIN, L. M., '"Your humble handmaid": Elizabethan Gifts of Needlework', *Renaissance Quarterly*, 50 (1997), 463–71.

KNOWLES, JAMES, 'Jonson's *Entertainment at Britain's Burse*', in Martin Butler (ed.), *Re-Presenting Ben Jonson* (Basingstoke: Macmillan, 1999), 114–51.

—— '"To raise a house of better frame": Jonson's Cecilian Entertainments', in Croft (ed.), *Patronage, Culture and Power*, 181–95.

KUIN, R. J. P., 'Robert Langham and his "Letter"', *Notes and Queries*, NS 25 (1978), 426–7.

—— 'The Purloined *Letter*: Evidence and Probability Regarding Robert Langham's Authorship', *The Library*, 6th ser. 7 (1985), 115–25.

LEAHY, WILLIAM, *Elizabethan Triumphal Processions* (Aldershot: Ashgate, 2004).

LEES-JEFFRIES, HESTER, 'Fountains in Renaissance Literature' (unpublished doctoral thesis, University of Cambridge, 2002).

LESLIE, MICHAEL, 'Spenser, Sidney, and the Renaissance Garden', *English Literary Renaissance*, 22 (1992), 3–36.

—— 'The *Hypnerotomachia Poliphili* and the Elizabethan Landscape Entertainments', *Word and Image*, 14 (1998), 130–44.

_____ '"Something nasty in the wilderness": Entertaining Queen Elizabeth on her Progresses', *Medieval and Renaissance Drama in England*, 10 (1998), 47–72.

LEVIN, CAROLE, *The Reign of Elizabeth I* (Basingstoke: Palgrave, 2002).

_____ CARNEY, JO ELDRIDGE, and BARRETT-GRAVES, DEBRA (eds.), *Elizabeth I: Always her Own Free Woman* (Aldershot: Ashgate, 2003).

LINDLEY, DAVID (ed.), *The Court Masque* (Manchester: Manchester University Press, 1984).

LYNCH, JACK, *The Age of Elizabeth in the Age of Johnson* (Cambridge: Cambridge University Press, 2003).

McCONICA, JAMES (ed.), *The History of the University of Oxford*, 5 vols. (Oxford: Clarendon Press, 1984–92), iii: *The Collegiate University* (1986).

McCOY, RICHARD C., *The Rites of Knighthood: The Literature and Politics of Elizabethan Chivalry* (Berkeley and Los Angeles: University of California Press, 1989).

_____ 'Old English Honour in an Evil Time: Aristocratic Principle in the 1620s', in R. Malcolm Smuts (ed.), *The Stuart Court and Europe* (Cambridge: Cambridge University Press, 1996), 133–56.

McGEE, C. E., 'Politics and Platitudes: Sources of Civic Pageantry, 1486', *Renaissance Studies*, 3.1 (1989), 29–34.

_____ '"The Visit of the Nine Goddesses": A Masque at Sir John Crofts' House', *English Literary Renaissance*, 21 (1991), 371–84.

_____ 'Fireworks for Elizabeth', *Malone Society Collections XV* (1993), 85–8.

McLAREN, A. N., *Political Culture in the Reign of Elizabeth I: Queen and Commonwealth 1558–1585* (Cambridge: Cambridge University Press, 1999).

MANLEY, LAWRENCE, *Literature and Culture in Early Modern London* (Cambridge: Cambridge University Press, 1995).

MARCHITELLO, HOWARD, 'Political Maps: The Production of Cartography and Chorography in Early Modern England', in Margaret J. M. Ezell and Katherine O'Brien O'Keeffe (eds.), *Cultural Artifacts and the Production of Meaning: The Page, the Image, and the Body* (Ann Arbor: University of Michigan Press, 1994), 13–40.

MARCUS, LEAH S., *The Politics of Mirth: Jonson, Herrick, Milton, Marvell, and the Defense of Old Holiday Pastimes* (Chicago: University of Chicago Press, 1986).

MASSEY, DAWN, '*Veritas Filia Temporis*: Apocalyptic Polemics in the Drama of the English Reformation', *Comparative Drama*, 32 (1998–9), 146–75.

MEAGHER, JOHN C., 'The First Progress of Henry VII', *Renaissance Drama*, NS 1 (1968), 45–73.

MENDELSON, SARA, 'Popular Perceptions of Elizabeth', in Levin et al. (eds.), *Elizabeth I*, 192–213.

MERTON, CHARLOTTE, 'The Women who Served Queen Mary and Queen Elizabeth: Ladies, Gentlewomen and Maids of the Privy Chamber, 1553–1603' (unpublished doctoral thesis, University of Cambridge, 1992).

MONTROSE, LOUIS A., 'Gifts and Reasons: The Contexts of Peele's *Araygnement of Paris*', *English Literary History*, 47 (1980), 433–61.

_____ '"Eliza, Queene of shepheardes", and the Pastoral of Power', *English Literary Renaissance*, 10 (1980), 153–82.

_____ *The Theatrical City: Culture, Theatre and Politics in London, 1576–1649* (Cambridge: Cambridge University Press, 1995).

MORGAN, VICTOR, *A History of the University of Cambridge*, 4 vols. (Cambridge: Cambridge University Press, 2004).

MULLANEY, STEVEN, 'Mourning and Misogyny: *Hamlet* and the Final Progress of Elizabeth I', *Shakespeare Quarterly*, 5.2 (1994), 139–58.

MUNBY, JULIAN, 'Queen Elizabeth's Coaches: The Wardrobe on Wheels', *Antiquaries Journal*, 83 (2003), 311–67.

NEALE, J. E., *Queen Elizabeth I* (London: Jonathan Cape, 1934; repr. 1957).

NELSON, ALAN H., *Early Cambridge Theatres: College, University and Town Stages, 1464–1720* (Cambridge: Cambridge University Press, 1994).

ORGEL, STEPHEN, *The Jonsonian Masque* (Cambridge, Mass.: Harvard University Press, 1967; repr. New York: Columbia University Press, 1981).

PALMER, DARYL W., *Hospitable Performances: Dramatic Genre and Cultural Practices in Early Modern England* (West Lafayette, Ind.: Purdue University Press, 1992).

PARRY, GRAHAM, *The Triumphs of Time: English Antiquaries of the Seventeenth Century* (Oxford: Oxford University Press, 1995).

PEACOCK, JOHN, 'Jonson and Jones Collaborate on *Prince Henry's Barriers*', *Word and Image*, 3 (1987), 172–94.

PECK, LINDA LEVY, ' "For a King not to be bountiful were a fault": Perspectives on Court Patronage in Early Stuart England', *Journal of British Studies*, 25 (1986), 31–61.

PRIOR, ROGER, 'Æmilia Lanyer and Queen Elizabeth at Cookham', *Cahiers Élisabéthains*, 63 (Apr. 2003), 17–32.

RAVELHOFER, BARBARA, 'Dancing at the Court of Queen Elizabeth', in Christa Jansohn (ed.), *Queen Elizabeth I: Past and Present* (Munster: Lit, 2004), 101–15.

RAYLOR, TIMOTHY, 'A Manuscript Poem on the Royal Progress of 1634: An Edition of John Westwood's "Carmen Basileuporion" ', in Timothy Raylor (ed.), *The Cavendish Circle* (*Seventeenth Century*, 9.2 (Special Issue) (Autumn 1994), 173–95.

RICE, GEORGE P., *The Public Speaking of Queen Elizabeth* (New York: Columbia University Press, 1951).

ROSENBERG, ELEANOR, *Leicester: Patron of Letters* (New York: Columbia University Press, 1955).

SACKS, DAVID HARRIS, 'Celebrating Authority in Bristol, 1475–1640', in Susan Zimmerman and Ronald F. E. Weissman (eds.), *Urban Life in the Renaissance* (Newark: University of Delaware Press, 1989), 187–223.

SAMMAN, NEIL, 'The Progresses of Henry VIII, 1509–1529', in Diarmaid MacCulloch (ed.), *The Reign of Henry VIII: Politics, Policy, and Piety* (London: Macmillan, 1995), 59–73.

SARGENT, RALPH M., *At the Court of Elizabeth: The Life and Lyrics of Sir Edward Dyer* (Oxford: Oxford University Press, 1935).

SCOTT, DAVID, 'William Patten and the Authorship of "Robert Laneham's *Letter*" (1575)', *English Literary Renaissance*, 7 (1977), 297–306.

SHENK, LINDA, 'Turning Learned Authority into Royal Supremacy', in Levin et al. (eds.), *Elizabeth I*, 78–96.

SHERMAN, WILLIAM S., *John Dee and the Politics of Reading and Writing in the English Renaissance* (Amherst: University of Massachusetts Press, 1995).

SMUTS, MALCOLM, 'Public Ceremony and Royal Charisma: The English Royal Entry in London, 1485–1642', in A. L. Beier et al. (eds.), *The First Modern Society: Essays in English History in Honour of Lawrence Stone* (Cambridge: Cambridge University Press, 1989), 65–93.

_____ 'Progresses and Court Entertainments', in Arthur F. Kinney (ed.), *A Companion to Renaissance Drama* (Oxford: Blackwell, 2004), 281–93.

STALLYBRASS, PETER, 'Patriarchal Territories: The Body Enclosed', in Margaret Ferguson, Maureen Quilligan, and Nancy Vickers (eds.), *Rewriting the Renaissance: The Discourse of Sexual Difference in Early Modern Europe* (Chicago: University of Chicago Press, 1986), 123–42.

STERN, VIRGINIA F., *Gabriel Harvey: His Life, Marginalia and Library* (Oxford: Clarendon Press, 1980).

STRONG, ROY, *The Cult of Elizabeth: Elizabethan Portraiture and Pageantry* (London: Thames and Hudson, 1977).

_____ *Gloriana: The Portraits of Queen Elizabeth I* (London: Thames and Hudson, 1987; repr. London: Pimlico, 2003).

SUTTON, JAMES M., 'The Retiring Patron: William Cecil and the Cultivation of Retirement, 1590–98', in Croft (ed.), *Patronage, Culture and Power*, 159–80.

_____ *Materializing Space at an Early Modern Prodigy House: The Cecils at Theobalds, 1564–1607* (Aldershot: Ashgate, 2004).

THURLEY, SIMON, *The Royal Palaces of Tudor England* (New Haven: Yale University Press, 1993).

TITTLER, ROBERT, *The Reformation and the Towns of England: Politics and Political Culture, c.1540–1640* (Oxford: Clarendon Press, 1998).

TRIBBLE, EVELYN B., ' "We Will Do No Harm With Our Swords": Royal Representation, Civic Pageantry, and the Displacement of Popular Protest in Thomas Deloney's *Jacke of Newberie*', in Alvin Vos (ed.), *Place and Displacement in the Renaissance*, Medieval and Renaissance Texts and Studies (Binghamton: State University of New York, 1995), 147–57.

WALKER, JULIA (ed.), *Dissing Elizabeth: Negative Representations of Gloriana* (Durham, NC: Duke University Press, 1998).

WALL, WENDY, *The Imprint of Gender: Authorship and Publication in the English Renaissance* (London: Cornell University Press, 1993).

WATANABE-O'KELLY, HELEN, 'The Early Modern Festival Book: Function and Form', in J. R. Mulryne et al. (eds.), *Europa Triumphans: Court and Civic Festivals in Early Modern Europe*, 2 vols. (Aldershot: Ashgate/MHRA, 2004), i. 19–31.

WEIR, ALISON, *Elizabeth the Queen* (London: Jonathan Cape, 1998).

WERNHAM, R. B., *After the Armada: Elizabethan England and the Struggle for Western Europe 1588–1595* (Oxford: Clarendon Press, 1984).

WILSON, JEAN, *Entertainments for Elizabeth I* (Woodbridge: Brewer, 1980).

_____ 'The Harefield Entertainment and the Cult of Elizabeth I', *Antiquaries Journal*, 66 (1986), 315–29.

WOODCOCK, MATTHEW, *Fairy in 'The Faerie Queene': Renaissance Elf-Fashioning and Elizabethan Myth-Making* (Aldershot: Ashgate, 2004).

WOODWORTH, A., 'Purveyance for the Royal Household in the Reign of Queen Elizabeth', *Transactions of the American Philosophical Society*, 35 (1945), 1–89.

YATES, FRANCES A., *Astraea: The Imperial Theme in the Sixteenth Century* (London: Routledge & Kegan Paul, 1975).

YOUNG, ALAN, *Tudor and Jacobean Tournaments* (London: George Philip, 1987).

Index

Index compiled by Lawrence Green.